Dr Greg Clydesdale lectures in in New Zealand. His expertise span economic growth and human welfare. His previous books include *Entrepreneurial Opportunity: The right place at the right time* and *Human Nature: A guide to managing workplace relations*.

WAVES OF PROSPERITY

INDIA, CHINA AND THE WEST: HOW GLOBAL TRADE TRANSFORMED THE WORLD

Greg Clydesdale

ROBINSON

ROBINSON

First published in Great Britain in 2016 by Robinson

A CIP catalogue record for this book
is available from the British Library.

ISBN 978-1-47213-900-9 (paperback)

Typeset by Ellipsis Digital Limited, Glasgow
Printed and bound in Great Britain by CPI Group (UK) Ltd, Croydon CR0 4YY

Papers used by Robinson are from well-managed forests and
other responsible sources

MIX
Paper from
responsible sources
FSC
www.fsc.org FSC® C104740

Robinson
is an imprint of
Little, Brown Book Group
Carmelite House
50 Victoria Embankment
London EC4Y 0DZ

An Hachette UK Company
www.hachette.co.uk

www.littlebrown.co.uk

CONTENTS

LIST OF MAPS

ACKNOWLEDGEMENTS

I would like to acknowledge the support of Peter Earl,
Amal Sanyal, Tony Berggren and Freda Clydesdale,
whose support made this book possible.

WAVES OF PROSPERITY

When Marco Polo visited China at the end of the thirteenth century, he was visiting the wealthiest nation in the world. China possessed the world's most productive agricultural system, its industries created the most technologically advanced products, while the nation's vast market generated an unprecedented level of economic activity. China could be described as the world's leader technologically, industrially and in terms of quality of life. Yet in the centuries that followed, China fell from grace. Such was the extent of the decline that by the middle of the twentieth century it had become one of the world's poorest countries. With China's economic decline also came a reduction in its cultural, political and military influence, its position taken by other nations, in particular Britain and the United States who, in their time of eminence, also had the strongest commercial sectors.

In the first quarter of the twenty-first century, the East is once again on the rise and we are forced to confront the age-old question: why do countries become rich or poor? Could the West wake up one day and find that it has lost what it previously had taken for granted? The implications of such a shift are immense, for not only does economic prosperity impact on our quality of life, but it is also the basis of military and political power. The changing nature of business and industry is of importance, not just in its own right but for the implications that flow from it.

1

Many books have attempted to explain the wealth of nations, but most have suffered from a Eurocentric focus. Books such as North and Thomas's *The Rise of the Western World* and *How the West Grew Rich* by Nathan Rosenberg and L. E. Birdcell Jr have explicitly focused on the West as, for the last 300 years, Western nations have been the most successful at generating wealth. However, in limiting their study to the period of Western predominance, these books have failed to understand some of the most important aspects of change. Even David Landes, the esteemed economic historian from Harvard University, has fallen into this trap. In his book, *The Wealth and Poverty of Nations*, he focuses on the cultural and institutional advantages of the West that culminated in the Industrial Revolution. But this ignores the fact that China and India had prosperous industries long before Europe. Landes admits that Indian merchants became rich, but his explanation dramatically understates their commercial ability:

> How then did some Indian traders, bankers and lenders manage to get rich? The answer is they laid golden eggs. They paid and bribed, hoarded and shared; and when they died, the family hid as much wealth as they could.[1]

Landes treats the Chinese with more respect, admitting that they had a sophisticated economy. Yet, in reference to China's twentieth-century decline, he says the 'mystery is in China's failure to reach its potential'.[2] The irony is, if we went back in time to the year 1500, China was so much ahead of Europe, the mystery would be why the West had not achieved its potential. compared with the great markets of Asia, Europe had little to impress. Vasco da Gama discovered this on his first visit to the East. When he arrived in India, in state of the art European ships, the locals laughed at the products he offered to trade. They suggested he offer them gold instead. In fact, Europeans would be dependent on bullion to pay for imports with Asia for centuries, up until the Industrial Revolution.

This book attempts to present a more global picture of the changing face of global fortune. It begins in the days when the 'riches of the East' were the envy of every European merchant and, in the centuries that follow, we see economic leadership change hands from nation to nation. Throughout this process, the oceans of the world are mastered, providing the first links in what will become a global economy. Each new leader introduces technologies and knowledge that make the world a smaller place.

As the oceans of the world were brought together, each nation rode its own individual economic wave, following pathways that sometimes led to wealth and other times to poverty. If we do not want to relive the experiences of nations that have gone before us we must understand these changing patterns.

This book explains how global trade has changed over time and shaped the world in which we live. It should not be interpreted as an unadulterated celebration of materialism. Economic growth is never smooth or even, and many people in developed countries do not enjoy the affluence of others. At times, businesses have caused irreversible negative effects on the environment and, recently, climate change has been linked by many scientists to the output of industry. These negative effects are well documented and so need not be repeated in this book, which has different goals. This book explores how business has changed the world over the last 800 years, tying the globe into networks of trade and exchange that have improved the livelihoods of those involved.

Waves of Prosperity reveals the rise and fall of the richest nations in history, from Sung China to modern-day Japan and the United States, nations that at different times have found new ways of creating wealth and developed successful economic cultures. We see a number of industries at work, including ceramics, textiles and automobiles.

However, to identify some of the recurring features clearly, it is necessary to follow the fortunes of one industry closely. For this, the shipping industry has been chosen.

There are several reasons why shipping has been selected. First, it is a very old industry so there is considerable historical data available. Second, shipping has an international nature that enables us to compare commercial leadership between nations. Finally, shipping is the industry that carries cargoes, thereby illuminating the commercial activity around it. The shipping industry is observed in a number of environments, time contexts and cultures, revealing the forces that have acted on its success and decline.

In the following chapters, we move from China in the days of Marco Polo, to the great East India Companies, to Astor, Vanderbilt, the Toyoda family in Japan and Andrew Grove of Intel. In so doing, this book illustrates how commerce has changed over time and created a path to globalization. The result is a global view of economic evolution and the changing lives of the people on our planet.

In searching for an explanation of the wealth of nations, it is common to start with Adam Smith, the father of modern economics who taught at the University of Glasgow in the mid-eighteenth century. But even starting with Smith may provide a Eurocentric bias, for 400 years before Smith wrote, an Islamic scholar by the name of Ibn Khaldun made many of the observations that Smith later made famous. Ibn Khaldun was born in Tunis in 1332. Highly educated, he began a political career at the age of twenty which lasted until 1375 when he started to write his history of the world. The first volume, entitled *Muqaddimah*, contains many observations on economics which Adam Smith would later pronounce.[3]

For Ibn Khaldun the main driver of production and prosperity was human labour: 'Everything comes from God. But human labour is necessary for [man's livelihood].' To maximize the product of human labour, people need to specialize and cooperate:

> What is obtained through the co-operation of a group of human beings satisfies the need of a number many times greater than themselves. For instance, no one, by himself, can obtain the share of the wheat he needs for food. But when six or ten persons, including a smith and a carpenter to make the tools, and others who are in charge of the oxen, the ploughing of the soil, the harvesting of the ripe grain, and all other agricultural activities, undertake to obtain their food and work toward the purpose either separately or collectively and thus obtain through their labour a certain amount of food, that amount will be food for a number of people many times their own.[4]

Prosperity increases when people specialize. If they focus on one job, such as ploughing or making tools, they become better at it and more productive. But specialization requires people to cooperate with each other, and this means the state must play an important role providing a strong infrastructure and political stability. Without political stability and order, the producers have no incentive to produce. Ibn Khaldun stressed the idea that productivity improvements based on specialization are determined by the size of the market (or civilization); 'With regard to the amount of prosperity and business activity in them, cities and towns differ in accordance with the different size of their civilization.' A person cannot specialize in something like tool-making unless there are sufficient customers for the tools, hence Khaldun stressed that production is determined by population: the larger the population, the greater the production. Thus we can expect greater prosperity in cities than the countryside.

Through specialization and social cooperation, people can produce output far beyond that necessary to satisfy their personal needs, and this surplus can be traded with other regions. The returns from trade enable people to purchase imported goods and services, which in those days meant products of luxury. For Ibn Khaldun, it was the 'conditions and customs of luxury' that laid the basis of trade. It is no coincidence that Ibn Khaldun made these observations four centuries before Adam Smith. Islamic market activity was far more active and prosperous than anything in Europe at the time. Adam Smith's observations only addressed themselves to Europe, where he could observe the same phenomenon on a significant scale in his own environment.

If there is a problem with Ibn Khaldun's writing, it is that he focuses too strongly on labour as the source of prosperity and denies the importance of resources. The earliest empires can all trace their initial prosperity to favourable resource endowments. For example, China and India benefited from river systems that provided the water and minerals for agriculture, which in turn could support a large population. Hence, the earliest centres of population and civilization around the world are all on fertile river systems. This can explain why places like China and India have such large populations: they are areas of high fertility and dynamic river systems. Even today, China has 2.5 per cent of the world's land mass but 20 per cent of the world's people.

Chinese thought on international trade was born out of the political debate over whether China should trade with foreign nations who they perceived as barbarians. While the Confucian doctrine was traditionally against merchants, progressive officials, such as T'ang Shu and Chang Han who wrote in the mid-sixteenth century, suggested China would benefit from international commerce. They advocated freeing trade because of the 'mutual benefits' for all involved. These mutual benefits recognize that different regions have different goods in different levels of abundance, and people could benefit from 'exchanging what you have for what you do not have'. Another Chinese official arguing for trade was Lan Ting Yuan (1680–1733) who stressed that countries should also trade if there were cost differentials between them. He noted that ships and rice could be produced much more cheaply in South-East Asia than in China, so it made sense to import from them. By contrast, China was a low-cost producer of many manufactured goods. Therefore trade would allow both peoples to benefit from the absolute cost advantages.[5]

In the West, it was not until the eighteenth century that Adam Smith announced the concept of 'absolute advantage' in which a nation should export if it is the world's low-cost producer. Adam Smith's book *The Wealth of Nations* was to inspire another young Briton, David Ricardo, into the field of economics. In 1817 Ricardo introduced the idea of 'comparative advantage' where a nation might forgo its low-cost advantage in one industry if it is more competitive in producing other goods. The advantages of specialization are so great that all nations will benefit if they focus on what they do best, even if another country does it more cheaply. The concept of comparative advantage became the bedrock of Western classical thought on international trade.

Our understanding of trade and wealth has grown dramatically since the nineteenth century. A large population is no longer necessary for wealth as countries can gain access to markets through exporting. In fact countries with the highest populations often rank among the poorest. It is not necessary to go through all the theories of international trade, but one economist worth mentioning is Michael Posner who worked at the University of Cambridge. In 1961 Posner suggested that trade is generated by differences in the rate and nature of innovation between nations. Comparative advantage in industries is determined by the rate of technical change in an industry which is a result of differences in investment. Since then much of the work done by economists and business analysts has focused on the importance of innovation.

Trade and wealth are driven by innovation: new product, new processes, new markets. China during the late T'ang (AD 618–907) and Sung (AD 960–1279) dynasties produced many new products and processes that propelled its economy forward, as did the Netherlands in the late sixteenth and early seventeenth centuries. Britain's period of leadership was also born from a period of innovation. From railways to factories, porcelain to steamships, it was an age of innovation and improvements. Historian John H. Plumb goes as far as saying 'improvement' was the most overused word of the eighteenth century in Britain followed closely by 'new method' and 'latest fashion'. In the late twentieth century, it was the Japanese who made *kaizen* (continuous improvement) a corporate philosophy, which propelled them into global leadership.

History shows us that the wealthiest nations are those that have gone through a period of innovation. Ironically, many nations began their periods of innovation by imitating other nations that previously had a superior record. For example, in the early seventeenth century, as European nations were beginning to carve out their maritime empires, Francis Bacon claimed that the three greatest inventions that the world had known were the compass, printing and gunpowder. These inventions, which allowed Europe to rise to global supremacy, were all created in China. This is not an isolated phenomenon. At the end of the nineteenth century, the United States imitated technologies that had been developed in Europe and took them to a higher level. In the second half of the twentieth century, many American inventions fell into the master hands of the Japanese, who were criticized as being only capable of imitating.

They soon shook off this criticism.

The worrying thing is that once prosperous nations can go through periods of stagnation and decline. From a preliminary view, it appears that industrial leadership is a process of imitation, innovation, supremacy and decline. If there is such a process at work, economists require a closer understanding of the forces involved in order to understand industrial development and competition.

Not all innovations lead to growth. Among the earliest companies listed on the English Stock Exchange was one that proposed to make square cannon-balls, and another to extract butter from beech trees. To succeed, innovations must be faithful to the basic premise of business; that is 'the creation and exchange of value'. Cargoes that cross the distant oceans do so because someone, somewhere values them. With this in mind, we can say that innovations that lead to growth do at least one of four things. They involve either developing resources into forms that people value, adding value to existing products and services, developing markets or reducing costs so that more people can obtain those goods.

The history of the world that follows is a history of value creation and exchange. Our story begins with 'The Riches of the East', when a young Venetian named Marco Polo arrived in China to find a dynamic, flexible economy where every town and city appeared to 'live by trade and industry'. China had built a large market economy on its large population and agricultural base. On top of this, transportation and communication networks were built by which goods were carried from region to region. Marco Polo observed huge Chinese junks that mastered the oceans of the East, taking manufactured goods such as silks and ceramics to other countries in the region.

In the Indian Ocean from the fifteenth to the eighteenth centuries,

Gujarat also developed a strong market economy in a region of high fertility. This was an economy of the highest order: a system of highly specialized craftsmen, weavers, dyers, brokers, merchants and seamen all reliant on each other for their prosperity. Ships from Gujarat sailed to the pulse of the monsoon winds, carrying textiles, spices and high-quality crafts to the major civilizations of the Indian Ocean. The ocean networks were the paths on which many merchants made their fortunes.

Europe took more time to develop its trading potential, but, once it had, it created the links that made the world an integrated whole. With a crusader's zeal, the Spanish and Portuguese capitalized on the trade routes carved by Columbus and Magellan to create the world's first truly global trade network. They conquered the Atlantic and Pacific, creating new markets and developing newly found resources. Lubricated by gold and silver from South America, Iberians traded from Macao in the east to Brazil in the west, while the famed Manila Galleon provided the first established link between Asia and North America. It is common in the West to see this network as evidence of European trading supremacy, but the Chinese and Gujaratis still dominated the oceans of the East. Europeans might travel farther, but the cargoes of the Asians had greater value and volume.

While the Iberian nations conducted research in geography and discovered new trading routes, northern Europeans invested in new industrial techniques and organizational forms. The Dutch built an economic system in which trade and industry propelled each other forward on a mutually reinforcing growth. Imported ingredients like sugar, spices and tobacco came from places like Brazil and Indonesia to the Netherlands where industries powered by peat and wind created new products and new patterns of consumption. Windmills became the symbol of industrial supremacy, particularly in the Zaan industrial belt outside Amsterdam. On the oceans, the

Dutch East India Company became a multinational corporation coordinating activities that spanned the world signalling a new age of globalization.

The English were long jealous of Dutch success and set out to imitate their achievements. The English government erected trade barriers to protect industries trying to acquire Dutch technologies. Before long the British had stopped imitating and were producing their own innovations, exploiting their coal resources to become an even more effective industrial power. Machines in coal-powered factories now provided the cargoes that travelled the world. Those same technologies placed in ships freed trade from the tyrannies of wind and wave. Steamships were not dependent on the wind and could carry cargoes when and where they wanted. For the first time, Asians started to lose primacy in their own waters.

The British brought North America into the global economy, opening the resources of a new continent for people like Vanderbilt, Astor and Ford to exploit later. The demands of a mass market led to innovations in organization and new levels of cooperation. American business method was based on mass production, economies of scale, scientific management and the age of the corporation. Americans also brought the Japanese into the global economy, and the Land of the Rising Sun soon established its own variants of the modern corporation. The Japanese also introduced innovations in production like 'just in time' and 'quality circles' that further increased customers' value for money.

The process of specialization and coordination that Ibn Khaldun saw in Islamic cities 700 years ago now spans the world. With internationalization of production a product may contain components from many countries. The global economy links countries that might otherwise be at war in the peaceful pursuit of prosperity. But, in an age of machines, Ibn Khaldun's focus on humans as the drivers of productivity no longer seems appropriate. However, human knowledge is still the driver of innovation. It is the norm for companies to call upon advances of science in their pursuit of value creation. In fact, companies are often the drivers of scientific advance.

Although each of the countries in this book have their own peculiarities, they share common patterns of development. No nation can excel unless it creates goods and services that people want to buy. Hence, the first stage of growth is one in which the country acquires new productive capabilities. This often involves the use of trade barriers to protect the infant industry, as England used at the beginning of its commercial rise. The most successful nations then go through a period of innovation in which they create new or better products, new markets or reduce costs. To exploit the new products and production techniques, new relationships, new ways of thinking and new skills are required. Once adopted, these methods become so successful that industries become defined by them, and find it hard to change when the world moves on. Unfortunately, this leads to the last stage in which a country becomes trapped by its past and enters a period of decline.

Although the focus in this book is on shipping, we should not ignore other industries, for shipping can only thrive if cargoes exist to be carried, and cargoes are the products of other industries. It is no coincidence, for example, that the Chinese were the most advanced shipping nation at the same time that they excelled in many other industries. With shipping, we gain an insight into the underlying commercial activity of each nation and the business environment at the time. Shipping reflects the nature of changing business and the changing world. After all, it was the ships of Columbus, Magellan and Tasman that first linked Asia, America and Australia in an integrated world. And the changes that occurred on board ships reflect the changing patterns of production that have occurred over time, from wind, to steam, to automation.

This story is also about people – the traders, bankers, factory-owners who all played a specialized role in their country's growth. This book presents an international array of innovators, entrepreneurs and administrators, including Zheng He, Howqua, Josiah Child, Jan Pietersz Coen, Virji Vora, Abdul Ghafur and Josiah Wedgwood. Unfortunately, we lack the tales of ordinary sailors or weavers simply because history has not given their words and deeds as much attention. The result appears, at first, like a 'Great Men of History', but this is not the intention. Men like Marco Polo and Magellan were products of their environment and could only achieve what they did because of the technological opportunities they inherited. Magellan's discoveries only came at the end of centuries of ship evolution which resulted in a ship that enabled him to sail the globe. Others with similar potential may have lived earlier, but were denied the opportunity because shipping technology had not reached a stage that would enable long distant voyages. Seen in this light, Magellan owes his success to the lesser-known people whose efforts led to the evolution in ship design that he inherited

This is a history of humanity. After all, it is humans who buy, produce and consume. Today we take it for granted that our coffee comes from Brazil or Kenya, our cars from Japan, or the Internet technology from the United States; but without those products our lives would be decidedly poorer. Our lives are a smorgasbord of cargoes that have come from across the oceans. And that smorgasbord is about to get more complicated as the giants in the East are once more on the rise. India and China are going through a process of imitation, acquiring the capabilities to produce the goods that we will consume. This book explains the process by which we got to our current position. It reveals the underlying dynamics of industrial competitiveness and the changing nature of global commerce. With this knowledge, we may better understand and prepare for our future.

A brief note is necessary regarding the use of place names. Given the nature of the book, historical names are used for Indian cities. So for example, Bombay is used for Mumbai, and Madras is used for Chennai.

1

THE RICHES OF THE EAST

At the end of five days' journey lies the splendid city of Zaiton, at which is the port for all the ships that arrive from India laden with costly wares and precious stones of great price and big pearls of fine quality. It is also a port for the merchants of Manzi, that is, of the surrounding territory, so that the amount of traffic in gems and other merchandise entering and leaving this port is a marvel to behold. From this city and its port goods are exported to the whole province of Manzi. And I assure you that for one ship that goes to Alexandra to pick up pepper for export to Christendom, Zaiton is visited by a hundred.

Marco Polo

The most widely read book in Europe during the Middle Ages was *The Travels of Marco Polo*. These were the tales that inspired Christopher Columbus to cross the Atlantic in search of the riches of the East. The book spoke of the wealth of China, a land of thriving trade and industry, where merchants were 'so many and so rich and handle such quantities of merchandise that no one could give a true account of the matter'.

Despite coming from Europe's wealthiest city, Marco Polo was overwhelmed by the prosperity he witnessed. The Chinese economy was arguably the most successful in world history. For 800 years it kept more people at a higher level of prosperity than any other country in the world. This wave of prosperity had its origins in

China's early history and culminated in an economic revolution during the T'ang and Sung dynasties (AD 618–1279). At this time China became one of the first nations in the world to abandon the confines of feudalism. It was one of the earliest and largest market economies in the world, supported by a sophisticated government bureaucracy.

That China built a market economy so early can be attributed both to geographic and to political reasons. As early as the first dynasty, the Chinese recognized that a feudal system was not in the nation's best interests. Under the old system, feudal lords had regional power bases that they could draw on to wage war and destabilize the nation. So a systematic effort was made to get rid of them.[1] Throughout the following centuries, feudal lords disappeared and were replaced by the world's first government bureaucracy, the mandarins.

To train this corp of government officials, an academy was established where fledgling mandarins were given an education based on Confucian principles. Confucianism was an ideal philosophy as it stressed social harmony and expected the highest moral principles from its devotees. According to Confucius, people should act with respect, humility, obedience and submission, values that would help the government gain compliance from the peasantry. In return, the state had an obligation to provide 'harmonious government'.

Under Confucian belief, the emperor only maintained his 'mandate from heaven' while he ruled effectively and fairly. If the emperor failed, he became vulnerable and liable to be overthrown. Consequently, the government was preoccupied with maintaining economic and social order. The mandarins were an important part of this. To attain harmony the scholar-officials managed the nation's resources and performed key tasks in the economy. This included managing the public granaries for use in times of famine and other natural disasters. Another key task was controlling the nation's waterways. Agriculture,

16

which was the foundation stone of the economy, was dependent on the ebbs and flows of the Yellow and Yangtze rivers. Controlling them was fundamental to maximizing the nation's economic potential and the mandarins introduced many innovations in hydraulic engineering. Other government activities included preparation of the calendar by which agricultural operations were conducted, maintenance and construction of all public works and organization of the nation's defence. In performing these key economic tasks, the scholar-officials gained a position of omnipotence in society, even though they were small in number.[2]

Other factors that contributed to this economic shift included the many improvements in transport and agricultural production. Innovations in production techniques and equipment were adopted across the nation. Farmers learned the benefits of preparing their soil with manure, lime and river mud for fertilizer. Tools were improved and new ones developed. New seeds were introduced, the most common being Champa rice from Vietnam in about AD1012, which could produce two to three crops per year.[3]

The status of people in the Confucian society reflected their economic roles. Scholar-officials were placed at the top of society, followed by farmers and artisans. The respect given to farmers reflected the fact that the basis of the Confucian economy lay in the productivity of agriculture. Merchants, who produced nothing and made money from buying and selling other people's output, were given a low position on the Chinese social ladder.

Despite the low ranking given to merchants, the Confucian paradigm actually contributed to the development of a market economy. In China people produced goods to trade. This stands in contrast to Europe which was still a feudal economy where people produced for their lord and their own needs. The shift to a market economy was not a planned innovation, but it represented a huge advance.

The government also played a key role in raising productivity. Officials opened and operated large polders, the low-lying land used for rice production. They taught hydraulic techniques and introduced pumping equipment in areas unfamiliar with them. To encourage farmers to take up the new rice crops they provided tax relief and credit systems. The spread of rice cultivation resulted in agriculture productivity significantly higher than we would find in the West. China's output could support a population twice the size of Europe's.

Increased productivity led to surplus. If farmers could transport their stock to a market, they could trade. To do this, the country needed to upgrade its transport and communications systems and many improvements occurred during this period.[4] These innovations included hauling, poling, canals, locks and the development of specialized craft. It soon became possible to transport large quantities of goods across the nation. Marco Polo spoke of how people in the city of Ho-kien-fu (Cacianfu) modified their waterways to allow trade with Peking.

> Through the midst of the city flows a great river, by which quantities of merchandise are transported to Khan-balik (Peking); for they make it flow thither through many different channels and artificial waterways.

These improvements opened up distant markets to farmers who soon realized they could earn more growing produce for those markets instead of trying to be self-sufficient. They began to devote their energies to those crops that grew best in their local climate and soils. In making use of the market, the peasantry changed from subsistence farmers to adaptable, profit-orientated, petty entrepreneurs.

Agriculture was not the only area where new skills and techniques appeared. Market expansion gave birth to new occupations and industries, including ceramics. Ceramic pots were initially made by farming families when they were not working in the field. The growing market made it possible for some producers to live purely by ceramic production and, by Sung times, some families had given up farming altogether. With all their time concentrated on making ceramics, they gained experience by which they learned to make better quality products faster.

The advantages of specialization could also be seen in the silk industry. China had a long history of silk production and, by the T'ang dynasty (AD 618–907), it had become the mainstay of the provincial economies of Zhejiang and Jiangsu. The process of making silk involved the rearing of silkworms, cultivation of mulberry trees, reeling of silk, dyeing and weaving. By the Sung dynasty, dyers and weavers became increasingly separated from those involved in sericulture. Weaving and dyeing became prominent economic activities in urban areas where growing pools of artisans lived. Many of the towns that Marco Polo visited were based on the silk industry. For example at Suzhou he noted that the people 'live by trade and industry, have silk in great quantity and make much silken cloth for their clothing. There are merchants here of great wealth and consequence.' By the fifteenth and sixteenth centuries large factories with more than twenty looms were operating in cities such as Hangzhou, Jiaxing and Suzhou. At the same time, a number of technological innovations and improvements in looms and dyeing techniques appeared. The result of this growth in production and marketing power was a tremendous variety of silk products.[5]

During the Sung dynasty (AD 960–1279), a change in government policy accelerated the central role of the market. Under threat of invasion in the country's north, the government needed to increase its resources and lifted restrictions on market activity. Taxation policies were changed so that the government only took a fixed share of a farmer's output, after which the farmer could keep or sell anything else produced. This served as an incentive to raise output and promote market activity.[6] Markets were established as alliances between local clan chiefs, merchants and the local government officers. Merchants needed official approval to operate markets, and mandarins were generally prepared to approve them in return for financial consideration.[7] In this way, a symbiotic relationship between state and commerce developed.

A national market the size of China's provided a diverse range of products. Markets developed for oils, vegetables, fruit, sugar, timber, cattle and fish, and paper of every sort, including toilet paper. The rich wore the finest silk and ate off porcelain dishes. In the restaurants of the capital, gourmets could choose between northern, southern and Szechwan cuisines. The Chinese became the best-fed population in the world with the highest standards of living.[8]

Villages developed markets and grew into small or medium sized towns, each with their share of merchants and artisans. By the time Marco Polo arrived, people were living by trade and industry in every town he visited. The southern Sung capital of Hangzhou, with 6,000,000 inhabitants became the world's largest city. In comparison, Venice, Europe's largest city, had only 160,000.[9]

Marco Polo was impressed by Hangzhou. The name he uses to refer to it, Kinsai, means 'City of Heaven'. He claimed it merited that description, 'because it is without doubt the finest and most splendid city in the world'. The city had ten principal market places and innumerable local ones. The principal markets were linked by a canal:

On the nearer bank of this are constructed large stone buildings, in which all the merchants who come from India and elsewhere store their wares and merchandise, so that they may be near and handy to the market squares. And in each of these squares, three days in the week, there is a gathering of forty to fifty thousand people, who come to market bringing everything that could be desired to sustain life. There is always abundance of victuals, both wild game, such as roebucks, stags, harts, hares and rabbits, and of fowls, such as partridges, pheasants, francolins, quails, hens, capons, and as many ducks and geese as can be told.

Surrounding the market squares were high buildings in which 'every sort of craft is practised and every sort of luxury is on sale'. But it was in streets away from the market squares that Marco Polo made his most memorable purchases, from the women of the town:

These ladies are highly proficient and accomplished in the uses of endearments and caresses, with words suited and adapted to every sort of person, so that foreigners who have once enjoyed them remain utterly besides themselves and so captivated by their sweetness and charm that they can never forget them. So it comes about that, when they return home, they say they have been in Kinsai, that is to say in the city of Heaven, and can scarcely wait for the time when they may go back there.

Another popular activity involved hiring a barge and taking a cruise on the lake in the southern part of the city. Ringed by palaces and mansions, a cruise provided scenery and other enjoyments that Marco Polo clearly relished:

Anyone who likes to enjoy himself with female society or with his boon companions hires one of these barges, which are kept continually furnished with fine seats and tables and all the other requisites for a party . . . On the lake itself is the endless procession of barges thronged with pleasure-seekers. For the people of this city think of nothing else, once they have done their work of their craft or trade, but to spend a part of the day with their womenfolk or hired women in enjoying themselves either in these barges or in riding about the city in carriages.

The extent to which entrepreneurship could flourish in this environment can be gauged by the size of the workforce of the enterprises. Records, from the earlier T'ang period, speak of a businessman named Ming-yuan who operated 500 looms weaving silk damask, as a result of which he became very rich. During the Sung dynasty, Wang Ko ran an iron smelter with a workforce numbering several thousand. Such employment levels in the iron industry would not be surpassed until the creation of the Urals iron industry in Russia in the eighteenth century.[10] Marco Polo came across very wealthy merchants who, he claimed, lived 'a life of refinement as if they were kings. And their wives too are most refined and angelic creatures, and so adorned with silks and jewellery that the value of their finery is past compute.' Given the Confucian attitude to profit-making, the commercialization of Chinese society was not always well received. For example, in the eleventh century Feng Shan made it clear that 'Heaven and earth bring things forth in constant [quantity], and the piling up of wealth is not a policy to be approved of.'[11] However, others, such as Ts'ai Hsiang, approved of the pursuit of wealth:'It is human nature for everyone to desire riches. Even peasants, artisans and merchants all scheme away night and day in search of profit.'[12]

Economic wealth also generated advances in science and technology. As the economy grew, more people could take up non-agricultural-based jobs, including the priesthood.[13] Buddhist and Taoist monks were an active source of innovation. During the T'ang dynasty, Buddhist monks invented wood-block printing for the purpose of religious propaganda. By the Sung dynasty, huge libraries of books on astronomy, medicine, mathematics, botany and political and economic theory had built up. The country achieved the highest rates of literacy in the world, and printing became the foundation of scientific discussion across the nation.

The structure of business organization increased in complexity and innovations were introduced that improved efficiency. To help perform calculations, the abacus became a favoured tool of businessmen. To make it easier to transfer money, an early form of bill of exchange was invented by merchants who found carrying large amounts of cash cumbersome and perilous. With this new 'flying money', merchants could deposit cash at one provincial office and receive a written receipt guaranteeing reimbursement in another.

Commercial brokers became a powerful force in the economy. They played a pivotal role in market transactions, mediating between buyers and sellers, and drawing up deeds of sale. In so doing, they helped to reduce transaction costs and raise efficiency in the market. Brokers were generally better educated and more resourceful than ordinary people. It was said of the broker Wang Keng:

> He was deeply versed in the ways of the world and gifted at contriving plans. Whenever the people of his community desired anything, they would go to him and be told what means they should use. The rural population round-about placed great confidence in him.[14]

Given that T'ang and Sung law gave only minimal commercial protection, the government promoted the use of brokers to ensure fairness in business transactions. Brokers could also report transactions and collect tax on behalf of the government. The collection of brokerage tax was part of an overall trend by the government to move away from taxing agriculture to taxing trade.

This, in turn, reflected a change in the way government perceived commerce. The traditional Confucian paradigm coexisted with a market-merchant mentality but, in all cases, the state was in control. A high degree of state–business cooperation existed in a number of industries, such as the iron and salt trades. In these trades, the government held a state monopoly but granted licences to private merchants to operate the monopolies on behalf of the government. This 'government supervision merchant operation' became a long-lived organizational structure in the economy and a major source of income for the government.[15] It reflected the successful partnership being built between merchants and the state.

During the Sung dynasty, improvements in the education system led to a huge leap in government efficiency. In particular, a new form of examination was introduced as a requirement for entering the civil service. Previously, positions in government were granted on the basis of family connections, but with the new 'eight-legged' examination, candidates were chosen on merit. This ensured that the Chinese bureaucracy absorbed the most able minds in the country. In state-sponsored colleges, students received a Confucian-based education in law, art, poetry, mathematics and engineering. These provided the future elite with a skill base and wisdom far advanced of any other nation in the world.

This system where government officials were appointed on the basis of their ability had one important drawback. Under a system of merit, an appointee could not hand down his position to his children. The scholar-officials therefore realized they had to strike while the iron was hot and this led to all sorts of corruption and short-term thinking. On being placed in the bureaucracy, a young official established relations with protectors, and proceeded to enhance his financial position by extracting from the people he administered. The Confucian doctrine, which stressed the importance of family over outside forces, actually encouraged this racket of protectionism and nepotism.[16] Consequently, milking and corruption became a feature of the economic system.

Businessmen were frequently milked by the bureaucrats and often suffered at their hands. However, there are differences in opinion as to how far this affected business. Some researchers[17] believe the state had a tendency to clamp down on any form of private enterprise, killing initiative and the slightest attempt at innovation. This situation was made worse by a secret police atmosphere and the arbitrary character of Chinese justice. However, more recent research[18] suggests that there was a genuine concern among state officials not to ruin or seriously impede merchants' activities, even in the relatively conservative Ming and Ching dynasties. To do otherwise would destroy a source of income. Nevertheless, merchant behaviour was affected by the pervasive mandarins. Merchants never dared to push against the state in order to gain the laws and liberties that merchants in Europe had. This created a commercial culture in which businessmen preferred to compromise rather than fight, to imitate safe precedents and to invest money safely in preference to undertaking risky industrial enterprises. On obtaining wealth, a merchant's goal was to finance his children's or grandchildren's education so that they could become elite scholar-officials themselves.

Commercial success came to depend, to a large degree, on a merchant's bureaucratic connections.[19] Apart from stocking the right goods and maximizing sales, a merchant also had to devote significant resources and energy to cultivating connections with his local officials. In this way, Confucianism defined the goals of businessmen and shaped what was considered rational business behaviour.

★　★　★

The combination of high output, large national market and Confucian bureaucracy made China the wealthiest nation in the world. However, the mandarins remained suspicious of international trade and shipping. In the early days, government policy was driven by Confucian thought which placed a low value on trade and merchants, so trade and shipping received little government support or approval. Consequently, China had little in the way of an international merchant marine. Long-distance shipping was considered too full of risk from storms and unfavourable oceanic conditions.

During the T'ang dynasty (AD 618–907), Chinese shippers travelled to Korea and Japan but not the southern seas, where trade was in the hands of South-East Asian, Persian and Arab ships from the Indian Ocean. The development of any industry is a consequence of business opportunities and constraints, and the transformation of the Chinese economy during the T'ang and Sung dynasties created a healthy environment for shipping entrepreneurs. Government policy became more conducive to foreign trade and shipping, as commercial and state goals becoming more closely aligned. The rise in manufactured goods provided export cargoes for ships, while an increase in domestic wealth created a demand for imported foreign cargoes. The rise in Chinese wealth also increased the amount of capital available to finance shipping ventures. Finally, with economic growth came an increase in education and technology, with applications to shipping.

If the Chinese were to develop their productive capabilities in the shipping industry, it made sense to adopt some of the achievements of those nations that were successfully sailing the seas. Navigation and geographic achievements of the Arabs and the Hindus were studied by Chinese scholars who eventually created their own star and sea charts, studies of tides and currents and navigational manuals.[20] From the Indonesians, they adopted the canted square sail which they then evolved into the more effective balanced lug sail.[21]

26

These innovations resulted in the sea-going junk which appeared in the tenth and eleventh centuries. With the development of the junk, the Chinese had a safe ship with which they could conduct transoceanic trade.[22] The Chinese introduced a number of innovations that made the junk a safe, strong ship. These included watertight bulkheads, buoyancy chambers and bamboo fenders to protect the ship from sinking. The junks were built with iron nails and possessed a strength superior to competitors' boats, and, in the oil of the t'ung tree, the Chinese had a superb natural preservative for waterproofing. A significant advance was made in steering where the placement of the rudder at the stern dramatically increased control of the ship. Marco Polo was impressed to find ships with up to four masts in Ch'uan-chou:

> They have one deck: and above the deck, in most ships, are at least sixty cabins, each of which can comfortably accommodate one merchant. They have one steering oar and four masts. Often they add another two masts, which are hoisted and lowered at pleasure.

The masts were staggered so, not being placed directly behind each other, no sail would becalm the others. Chinese sails resembled a Venetian blind or fan. They were comprised of narrow sections of canvas or matting stretched between transverse batons of bamboo. Although less efficient than the Arabian or Western sail, they had the advantage of being easier to control when close-hauled or damaged.

Taoist monks were a valuable source of knowledge that proved of assistance to Chinese shippers. Taoists sought to understand the harmony of the cosmos and included among their pursuits the search for immortality. One of their medicinal mixtures (a mixture of sulphur, saltpetre and charcoal), which was originally used to treat skin diseases and as a fumigant against insects, was eventually discovered to have other properties important for the defence of ships – as gunpowder. Another Taoist innovation was the magnetic compass that they originally developed for feng shui (the art of siting graves and buildings in harmony with supposed terrestrial forces). Before the arrival of the compass, seamen navigated by studying the stars. However, this was only possible when skies were clear enough to see the stars. Safety and speed could not be assured on cloudy days. The compass was eventually introduced to shipping and is first mentioned in a nautical context in 1119. The compass revolutionized navigation, making voyages possible in all but the worst weather. Ships could now be more economically utilized, carrying cargoes on cloudy days that previously would have kept them confined to port.

The most consistent contributor to technological advance in the industry came from the official education system. Official science was primarily devoted to those areas that would help maintain order in society. This included the reading of stars to foresee future events.[23] Maritime navigation in China had a strong advantage, given that astronomy was a subject given great attention by the officials. As early as the Zhou dynasty (1111–25 BC), astronomical observation had become a profession.[24] Before long Chinese astronomers had records showing that a star's height above the horizon varied depending on how far north or south you were taking your record. This meant that Chinese could find their latitude by observing the height of a star above the horizon. Although this research was performed on land, sailors eventually began to use it to find their locations at sea and, by the T'ang dynasty a 'star-measuring ruler' and 'handy ruler' had been invented which made astronomical navigation possible. With increased knowledge of sea routes and astronomical knowledge, it became possible to create navigation charts. The earliest of these include *A Chart to Overseas Countries* which was presented to the throne in AD 1003 and the *Comprehensive Charts of Islands on the way to Korea*, produced in AD 1123 by Xu Jing.

With these innovations Chinese navigators were building up experience and reaping the economies of specialization. As they developed their navigation skills and gained experience of the wind systems, they greatly reduced the length of time they needed to make their voyages. Whereas a trip to Singapore in Han times (202 BC–AD 220) took some 150 days, by the Sung–Yuan period (AD 960–1368), a similar trip to Sumatra took only forty days.[25]

During the Southern Sung dynasty, a change in government policy led to a rapid expansion in foreign trade. The cause of the policy change was an external military threat. At that time the country was under constant attack from invaders in the north who eventually succeeded in capturing the Sung capital of Kaifeng in 1127. The government fled south, creating a new capital at Hangzhou, just south of the Yangtze River. The invasion meant that the government now had only half the agricultural land to tax. To compensate for the loss of income, trade was liberalized. A Maritime Trade Commission was established and seven more ports were opened to foreign trade along the Guangdong and Fujien coasts.

The change of policy did not reflect the Confucian value system, so a process of legitimization was required. Given that being a merchant was traditionally seen as a lowly occupation in China, there was need for a new attitude towards trade and profit. The Emperor Gao Zong (1127–62) exclaimed: 'Profits from maritime commerce are very great. If properly managed, they can amount to millions of strings of coins. Is this not better than taxing people?'[26]

The policy change reflected a new alignment in merchant and government goals. Official rank was given to any merchant whose annual overseas trade exceeded 50,000 strings of cash and any government official supervising commercial activity greater than 1,000,000 strings of cash would be promoted one grade. While the new policy allowed merchants to increase their wealth and status beyond that normally approved of, it also brought the desired returns to government. Revenue from overseas trade jumped from half a million strings of coins at the end of the eleventh century to 1,000,000 in the early twelfth century and 2,000,000 by the middle of the twelfth century.[27] The contribution of foreign trade to total government revenues grew from 0.82 per cent in 1098 to 20 per cent in 1131.[28]

To help raise the competitiveness of the Chinese merchant fleet, the government targeted the shipping industry with a number of forms of assistance, including financial aid.[29] Government funds were allocated to improve harbours, widen canals to accommodate ocean-going junks, build warehouses for merchants, and construct a costly system of navigation beacons along the coast. The Chinese experience showed that a policy of direct targeting could be conducive to the development of an innovation-driven industry.

Many advances in the merchant marine originally came from government investment in naval technology. The navy was an important source of research and development, with the Emperor offering cash rewards to spur innovation in ship design. The age was one of continual innovation and inventions, included ships steered by paddle wheels invented by the engineer Kao Hsuan, and iron-plated armour designed by Chin Shih-Fu.[30] With the best boats, the Chinese captured the bulk of the sea trade from their competitors[31] and Ch'uan-chou became the greatest mercantile city in East Asia.[32] A pan-Asiatic trade ring developed in which Chinese traded with Koreans, Japanese, Vietnamese, Siamese, South-East Asians, Bengalis, Persians and Arabs. Two forms of trade existed between China and its Asian neighbours: trade conducted by private operators and tribute trade conducted by the government. Tributary trade was an arm of diplomacy in which surrounding nations sent gifts to China as a sign of respect. The tribute system provided China with supplies of foreign luxuries while cementing its superiority over the subordinate kingdoms. In return, the Chinese exported products as a kind of gift or reward for paying respect to the Imperial order of China.[33] To give an idea of the quantities of tribute trade, in 1394, Zenla (Cambodia) sent 60,000 jin of incense to China as tribute (35.8 metric tons) and in 1475 Japanese envoys sent as many as 38,610 swords to China, enough to equip all Ming commanding officers down to the company level.[34]

However, the bulk of international trade was in private hands where profit was the prime motive. The earliest organization of shipping was one in which a merchant would arrange transport of goods in his own ships. The small family business held the pivotal place in the shipping industry, particularly on inland and coastal routes. The extended family firm was usually headed by a mature male who shared decision-making with older members of the family. The family firm was an efficient form of organization. Its small decentralized structure gave the firm flexibility in responding to changes in the marketplace. Families also solved problems of controlling and monitoring workers. Commercial relationships built on family linkages had an underlying trust that instilled loyalty. In addition, the Confucian value system placed a high importance on family, so officialdom approved of the structure.

A major problem with the family firm was that its growth was limited by the size of the family and its resource base. These were serious constraints, given the high cost of ships, the high risk and the length of a voyage that tied up capital for long periods of time. Over time, new forms of organization came into being which made it easier to raise capital for larger-scale shipping ventures. Frequently, small businesses would form commercial networks and partnerships with others in the same business. Many partnerships were for only one voyage and profits were shared at the end of the venture. Others were more permanent.

Hsu Meng-hsin wrote in 1137 in his *Collected Materials on Relations with the Northern Tribes* that investment in shipping and commerce became commonplace:

> There are numerous commercial transactions at the capital conducted by merchants from every part of the country, and the city is therefore reputed for its wealth and population. Most of those who possess capital engage in stockpiling or storage . . . pawnbroking . . . or trading in ships. How could they permit their accumulated wealth to lie idle, or buy gold for hoarding at home?[35]

Pao Hui, another commentator writing during the Southern Sung dynasty, spoke of the willingness of even relatively poor people to invest in the sea-going ventures of others: 'They invest from 10 to 100 strings of cash and regularly make profits of several hundred percent.'[36]

With official support, wealthy families in port towns invested in ocean-going ships and cargo. Their success had a demonstrative effect on lesser trading families, skilled artisans and the merchant classes in smaller ports who also began investing in ships for the overseas trade. By the Sung dynasty, owners of ships had grown to include members of the imperial household, civil and military officials, Buddhist and Taoist monasteries and temples, owners of manors, powerful families, peasants and fishermen. A geographical spread in investment created a chain of minor ports along the coast, eventually growing into major trading centres. [37]

Ships left Chinese ports for foreign harbours where merchants frequently established offshore agencies. Small Chinese merchant communities grew in places as distant as Champa (Vietnam), Cambodia, Sumatra and Java. Agents in foreign ports performed a key economic role. When a ship arrived in port, it created a huge increase in demand for local goods and pushed up prices. It might also find an insufficient supply to fill the hull. An organization that used agents overcame these problems. An agent could buy stock over a longer period of time at lower prices and ensure that the ship on arrival would have a cargo. Similarly, if a ship arrived and unloaded a warehouse-full of cargo into the market at one time it dramatically decreased the prices for the goods it sold. An agent overcame this problem by storing goods in a warehouse and releasing stock gradually over time, thereby maintaining a higher price.

Agents played a key role developing foreign markets. They provided information on market conditions in foreign ports and indicated what types of goods should be brought to the port and what sort of prices they could expect. Consequently, with the use of agents, Chinese merchants were moving from free markets to organized markets, and improved their profit in the process.

Chinese exports were principally manufactured goods, while imports were dominated by raw materials.[38] Confidence in their products made it easier for Chinese traders to venture offshore in search of foreign markets eager for their goods. These included silk, ceramics, t'ung oil, bamboo baskets, wooden combs, straw mats, paper, refined sugar, woods and books.

Shipping and the manufacturing industries created a complementary relationship in which success in one industry helped the other. The high quality manufacturing industries provided key cargoes for shippers. In return, shipping expanded the range of markets for Chinese manufacturers. A flow of information between the two ensured that cargoes were prepared to maximize competitiveness in the foreign market.

The rising export trade, in particular, stimulated development in the ceramics industry. Chinese manufacturers learnt to make specific products and shapes for export to take account of the ritual and cultural requirements in their target market.[39] Different kilns worked for different markets. Inside the kilns, efficiency was improved through increased division of labour. Different workers would design, throw and finish the product. Dividing work up in this way dramatically improved the quality. By 1712, when the Jesuit missionary Père d'Entrecolles visited the kilns at Ching-te Chen, the industry had achieved an exceptionally high division of labour:

> One workman does nothing but draw the first colour line beneath the rims of the pieces; another traces flowers, while a third one paints . . . The men who sketch outlines learn sketching, but not painting; those who paint (that is, apply the colour) study only painting, but not sketching.[40]

The demands on output created by the growing export market put pressure on the industry to obtain a level of industrialization unheard of in the West. In the late thirteenth and early fourteenth centuries, family-owned kilns gave way to large-scale industrial complexes controlled by commercial syndicates.[41] As demands on the industry increased, more and more craftsmen gave in to the increased security of a well organized industry.

The transformation to a mass-production industry was made possible by the large demand and advances in the technology of production. As the Chinese developed their productive capabilities, they built an extensive knowledge of clays, fluxes and glaze chemistry, controllable high temperatures and industrial production methods.

With a high division of labour and large-scale dragon kilns that could produce as many as 35,000 pieces at a time, the Chinese created the first industry based on mass production, reaping the benefits of economies of scale and specialization. By the time of Père d'Entrecolles's visit, the industrial city of Ching-te Chen housed 1,000,000 people, and had 3,000 furnaces.

No path of growth is smooth or even. Changing crop conditions and political regimes are just two of the factors that can shape the future, and China was not immune to these forces. In 1279 the Sung dynasty was overthrown by the Mongol leader Khubilai Khan, who established the Yuan dynasty. Khubilai Khan was well aware of the importance of business to the economy, and industry and commerce probably received their biggest state support during his reign. Being a Mongol, Khubilai was not influenced by Confucian attitudes to merchants[42] and actively supported merchant communities. He placed them on a higher social scale, much to the resentment of the Confucian elite.

The new regime continued to provide targeted government assistance to the shipping industry. A joint-venture system was introduced called Government-Invested Ships in which the government provided ships to merchants with expertise to undertake maritime trade. Profits from ventures were split in a seven to three ratio. In 1285, the government allocated 100,000 ding (about 19 tons) of silver, to build ships for the scheme. Merchants were also given the opportunity to acquire finance at interest rates of 3–4 per cent per month.[43]

Khubilai Khan also supported the ceramics industry in recognition of the export revenue that it earned. A Porcelain Bureau was established which issued regulations on the capacity and production of kilns. The regulations accelerated the movement from crafts to industrial operations. The government also played an important role in the industry as a sophisticated consumer. Imperial kilns were created to serve the court. Representatives of the imperial court would visit the kilns and select the products they liked. The high standard of demand helped to raise the technical standards of the kilns.

In addition, under Khubilai China was just one part of the large Mongol Empire that stretched from China to the Caspian Sea. Khubilai utilized the full range of abilities in the empire and promoted skilled foreigners to high positions in the Chinese civil service, despite the fact they had not completed the civil service examinations. This led to an anti-foreigner mentality among the mandarins who found their status in decline. Of all merchant activity, mandarins were particularly keen to suppress foreign trade as its offshore component made it very hard to control. Nor did mandarins approve of private merchants profiting at the expense of official trade missions.

In 1368, the Mongols were overthrown by the Ming dynasty. The new dynasty brought with it a return to traditional attitudes to trade and the government banned all private trade and overseas travel. Foreign maritime trade was restricted to official tributary trade from nations acknowledging Chinese suzerainty. Fortunately, the Confucian-trained civil servants were not the only stakeholders at the Chinese court. Much power rested in the hands of eunuchs who were strongly involved in foreign trade. The mandarins might restrict private trade, but the eunuchs were going to increase the scale of tributary trade. The eunuchs had enough clout to gain support for the great voyages of Admiral Zheng He who was himself a eunuch. Zheng He was born in 1371, in the south-western province of Yunnan. His family had held high positions in the county government under the Mongols, but when the Ming forces invaded in 1382 his father was killed, and the eleven-year-old Zheng He was taken prisoner. A common practice at the time involved castrating captured prisoners and Zheng He endured this fate, to be taken as a slave into the court of the future emperor. With a tremendous personality and exceptional intelligence, he rose rapidly in the court and as a military strategist played a key role in cementing the new emperor on the Chinese throne. It was in recognition of his loyalty and achievement that the emperor gave him the name Zheng He, 'the Eunuch of the Three Gems'.

In 1405 Zheng He was sent on the first of seven great maritime expeditions into the Indian Ocean. The Chinese had previously travelled this far on a number of occasions. In fact, Marco Polo had returned to Europe taking such a journey on a diplomatic mission for China in 1298. However, the fifteenth-century missions reached a new scale of maritime activity. The voyages of Zheng He illustrated that Chinese shipping could move more tonnage more kilometres than any other nation could dream of. The fleet of the fourth voyage (1413–15) consisted of sixty-three large vessels and a crew of 22,670 men, while the fifth fleet sailed as far as East Africa.[44] The fleets were composed of trading ships, warships and support vessels. The treasure ships represented a peak in naval engineering and were the biggest vessels afloat. There has been some uncertainty over their size but even conservative estimates of 1,500 tons show they were at least five times the size of the ships used by Vasco da Gama at the end of the century.[45]

The treasure fleets were the most powerful example of the tribute system, encouraging trade and impressing upon other nations that China was the leading cultural and political power. With their powerful armies, these fleets sailed as far away as Ceylon and Zanzibar, where they used their power to force the rulers of these lands to acknowledge the supremacy of China and the Chinese emperor. In Africa, they reached the Swahili towns of Mogadishu and Mombasa. In Jidda and Dhufar, they exchanged their silks and porcelains for aloe, myrrh and other medicinal drugs.

The prestige of Zheng He's voyages irritated the Confucian

bureaucrats who would have loved to put an end to the voyaging. In a battle between opposing stakeholders, external threats could play an important role in determining outcomes. During the first half of the fifteenth century circumstances changed in a way that strengthened the conservative forces at the court. An increased threat of invasion by the Mongols meant the government's limited military resources had to be drawn away from the coasts to guard the trouble spots in the north.[46] This included building the Great Wall of China. The nation could no longer afford expensive luxuries like voyages.

Another factor that contributed to a change in policy was the government's concern with attacks on the Chinese coast by Japanese pirates.[47] Many Chinese had joined the pirates so the government restricted navigation as much as possible. Inflation also contributed to a change in policy. In the tribute trade, paper money was used, but severe inflation reduced the value of the money to 1 per cent of its face value. The Ming dynasty's favourable exchange rate with foreign countries evaporated, due in part to the loss of prestige following the emperor's capture by the Mongols and the hoarding of goods for private trade. Foreign countries were no longer prepared to accept paper currency and the Ming government was forced to pay market value for the goods. This undermined the profitability and rationale of tribute trade.[48]

As a result of these changing circumstances, the Confucians gained the upper hand in the court, and imperial edicts banning overseas trade and travel were issued in 1433, 1449 and 1452. Any merchant caught engaging in foreign trade was defined as a pirate and executed. The contribution of foreign trade to government revenue plummeted from 20 per cent during the Southern Sung dynasty to 0.77 per cent in the Ming.[49]

A ban on foreign trade would have a devastating effect on the economy of maritime provinces like Fukien. Given its importance to the livelihoods of so many people, an illegal trade continued to operate on a large scale. The illegal trade had the support of local officials, many of whom were complicit. For example, the family of Lin Xiyuan (c. 1480–1560), a high court judge from Fukien, owned a large commercial fleet with a business network spreading to South-East Asia. Such was the influence of the traders that Zhu Wan, the commanding officer responsible for suppressing shipping, was put in jail because of pressure from the smugglers and their official lobbyists in the imperial court. Zhu had made the mistake of starting a crusade to enforce the anti-maritime legislation. He was dismissed from his position and placed in prison where he eventually committed suicide.[50]

Eventually, in 1567, the government repealed the maritime prohibition. Although merchants were now free to trade, they received no government support, previously a key source of competitive advantage. Nevertheless, Chinese private traders continued to dominate the pan-Asian trade, given the technologically superior products they carried. However, they took far shorter journeys, restricting themselves to the China Sea. The junk trade followed the rhythms of the monsoons in the South China Sea, trading northwards in June or July, southwards from China in January or February and southward from Japan a little earlier.[51] Along the way, speculative calls might be made at minor ports in the hope of striking some business. Communities of Chinese traders spread themselves out around the key trading centres in East Asia, forming networks which coordinated the flow of goods and information.

Chinese sailors no longer sailed to the Indian Ocean, preferring to meet Indian traders at midway points. There was much economic logic in this decision. First, the wind conditions of the Indian Ocean were very different from those in the China Sea. Chinese junks were specifically designed for the wind conditions of East Asia. Second,

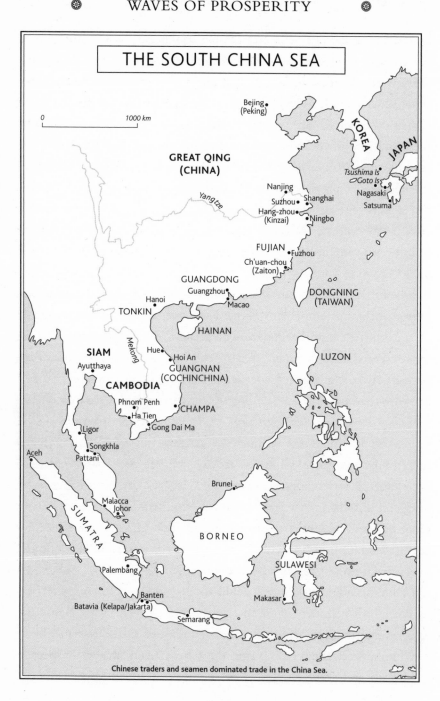

THE SOUTH CHINA SEA

0   1000 km

Bejing (Peking)

KOREA

JAPAN

GREAT QING (CHINA)

Yangtze

Nanjing

Suzhou
Hang-zhou (Kinzai)

Shanghai
Ningbo

Tsushima Is
Goto Is
Nagasaki
Satsuma

FUJIAN

Fuzhou

Ch'uan-chou (Zaiton)

GUANGDONG

Guangzhou
Macao

DONGNING (TAIWAN)

Hanoi

TONKIN

HAINAN

SIAM

Mekong

Hue
Hoi An

LUZON

Ayutthaya

GUANGNAN (COCHINCHINA)

CAMBODIA

Phnom Penh
Ha Tien

CHAMPA

Gong Dai Ma

Ligor

Songkhla
Pattani

Aceh

Brunei

SUMATRA

Malacca
Johor

BORNEO

SULAWESI

Palembang

Banten
Batavia (Kelapa/Jakarta)
Semarang

Makasar

Chinese traders and seamen dominated trade in the China Sea.

by restricting their travel to East Asian waters, Chinese seamen could concentrate their navigational skills and energies on the routes and wind systems with which they had the most experience. At the same time, Indians could travel in boats more specifically designed for the Indian Ocean and develop expertise in these waters that increased the efficiency of their operations. Experience no doubt led to faster trips and reduced losses. A further factor that would have influenced the decision of private shippers to restrict their activities to the China Sea was the rise of Malacca.

Malacca was established by Parameswara, a prince fleeing from Palembang around 1400. At that time Malacca was nothing more than a fishing village, but Parameswara's intention was to create the best port in the region. He persuaded some ship-owners and traders to use the port and built excellent warehouses and accommodation for seamen waiting for favourable winds. Within three years, Malacca's population had grown to over 2,000 and it was eventually regarded as being the best port and emporium in all South-East Asia.[52]

The success of Malacca was further ensured in 1405 when Parameswara visited the Chinese court. Swearing his allegiance to the Ming emperor, Zhu Di, he gained Chinese protection at a time when the fledgling city-state was in fear of its neighbours in Java, Sumatra and Siam. An edict was sent by the Chinese emperor to the King of Siam warning him not to attack Malacca. It serves as a useful illustration of how the Chinese tribute trade could be exploited by contributing states for their own ends. The edict also illustrates the Chinese world view and unashamedly speaks of its superiority.

I reverently took on the mandate of Heaven and I rule the Chinese and the yi . . . You king have been able to respect Heaven and serve the superior, and have fulfilled your tribute obligations. I have been greatly pleased by this for a long time. Recently Iskandar Shah, the King of the Country of Melaka, inherited the throne. He has been able to carry out his father's will and has personally brought his wife and children to the court to offer tribute. This loyalty in serving the superior is no different from yours. However, I have learned that without reason you have intended to send troops against him . . . You must not rashly send troops on this account.[53]

Chinese support became a visible reality when Zheng He called at Malacca on his great voyages. Ma Huan, who travelled on Zheng He's ships describes how, when they arrived at port, they took over the town:

> Whenever the treasure ships of the Central Country arrive there, they at once erected a line of stockading, like a city wall, and set up towers for the watch-drums at four gates; at night they had patrols of police carrying bells; inside again, they erected a second stockade, like a small city wall, [within which] they constructed warehouses and granaries; [and] all the money and provisions were stored in them. The ships which had gone to various countries returned to this place and assembled; they marshalled the foreign goods and loaded them in ships.[54]

With Chinese protection and the business from the fleets, the period 1403–30 was one of expansion. However, the change in Chinese government policy against foreign trade and the end of the great fleets caused a minor recession in Malacca. From this point on no one nation dominated the trade as China had. Malacca entered a period of more balanced growth, attracting merchants from a number of nations.

Malacca's success was based on its location. On the Malaysian

Peninsula, it was a point where the monsoons of the Indian Ocean met the trade winds of the China Sea, a natural rest and transhipment point for sailing ships. Chinese traders who wished to trade with the Indian Ocean preferred to rest at Malacca where they met and exchanged goods with hundreds of merchants from Arabia, Persia, India and the Malay–Indonesian region.[55] By the time the first Europeans visited the port at the beginning of the sixteenth century, Malacca was a cosmopolitan melting pot where the humblest Malayan fisherman lived with merchants from around the globe. As the Portuguese traveller Tome Pires described:

> No trading port as large as Malacca is known, nor any where they deal in such fine and highly prized merchandise. Goods from all over the East are found here; goods from all over the West are sold here. It is at the end of the monsoons, where you find what you want, and sometimes more than you are looking for.[56]

Malacca's growth provided ample opportunity for social mobility. Merchants who rode this wave of rising trade became very rich and powerful. In those days, a rich merchant was someone who could buy the valuable cargoes of three or four ships, and then load his ships with goods from his private stock of merchandise. The richest merchants owned town and country houses, some of which were veritable pleasure gardens with orchards and ornamental lakes, and had many slaves to serve them.

With the rise of Malacca as a transhipment point, Chinese shipping grew, exploiting its competitiveness in East Asian conditions. It also contributed to growth in Indian Ocean shipping where a number of other nations enjoyed the benefits of the growing trade, but none more so than Gujarat.

2

TEXTILES AND SPICES

The Kingdom of Guzarette is very great and possesses many towns and cities both along the coast and inland and many seaports with much sea trade, wherein dwell great merchants both Moors and Heathen who trade here in great abundance of goods.[1]

Duarte Barbosa

The Indian Ocean in the fifteenth century was a thriving merchant arena. Ships driven by monsoon winds linked the major civilizations of the region in an expanding network of trade routes and ports. This new economic wave gave birth to a highly developed and flexible merchant capitalist system. However, growth was not stable or even. It fluctuated with the ebbs and flows of political and economic activities on land, including the rise and fall of states, contraction and expansion of economies, and periods of famine and plenty. These activities all affected the direction of trade and placed demands on merchants to be highly flexible. The result was a merchant capitalist system in which flexible merchants responded to changing conditions through their buying and selling decisions.

The nation that most exploited and contributed to this growth path was Gujarat in north-west India. In the fourteenth century Gujarat had been part of the Delhi sultanate that ruled northern India. In 1398, the sultanate was shattered by Turkish warriors who invaded India and left the empire in pieces. Gujarat emerged as an independent kingdom and entered upon a period of economic development that would make it one of the richest nations in the world.

The ruler most strongly linked to the kingdom's growth is Sultan Mahmud Begada (1459–1511).[2] Early in his reign Mahmud made the decision to devote all of the state's revenue to the army, which he used to expand the kingdom's borders. There were several motives behind his expansion, not least his desire to spread Islam. His wars were a jihad, military campaigns to defeat the Hindus for whom he had little tolerance. But many of his campaigns also had commercial goals. For example, his conquests of Barur and Soorath were partly inspired by the need to control piracy, to which end Mahmud built and maintained a large fleet.[3]

Mahmud's success in expanding the borders secured him a reputation as a great leader. He is regarded as a shrewd statesman, soldier and diplomat, while his judgements in domestic policy reveal a generous leader committed to justice and the law of Islam. An imposing figure in life and history, Mahmud's life became the stuff of legends. His moustache was so long that he would tie it over his head, while his beard flowed down to his waist. His love of food was legendary. It was said that at breakfast he would eat a cup of honey and 150 bananas, clearly an exaggeration but no doubt reflecting a grand appetite. His chronicler noted that if God 'had not raised Mahmud to the throne of Gujarat who would have satisfied his hunger?'[4] His sexual desire was no smaller than his appetite for food and it is said that his women numbered between 3,000 and 4,000 and the women with whom he spent the night were always found dead in the morning. Clearly, this was not so, as sons were born to him from women who must have survived the encounter.

Mahmud's reign was a golden age for the arts and humanities. Muslim painters received state sponsorship while Hindu painters explored their own religious subjects. Towns were decorated with beautiful gardens, and colleges and mosques were built to encourage education. Sometimes the mosques were created from renovated Hindu temples, creating an interesting combination of Islamic and Hindu architecture. Architects from around the kingdom were put to work on palaces, tombs and mosques. Such was the creativity that it is said that there is not a fragment of architecture in Gujarat which is not associated with Mahmud's name.

Mahmud was very aware that the region's prosperity relied on trade and industry. He introduced what would equate to a medieval infant industry policy in which the state actively encouraged domestic craft production. An early Gujarati historian records that:

> Most of the elegant handicrafts and ingenious arts now prac-tised in Gujarat were introduced under Mahmud. Clever men from various distant cities were settled there; and people of Gujarat were thus, by the Sultan's exertions, instructed in knowledge and practice of the conveniences and elegancies of civilised life.[5]

The policies were successful in developing the nation's productive capabilities and before long a lively industrial base had been built. Crafts flourished under an atmosphere of state care and patronage, and by the end of Mahmud's reign, the city had a wide array of craftsmen with a strong reputation. This included stone- and gold-smiths, and craftsmen producing ivory bracelets, handles for swords, chess pieces and chess boards. In the leading city of Cambay, the Portuguese explorer Barbosa claimed 'the best workmen in every kind of work are found'.[6]

The region also produced a rich range of agricultural products. Gujarat was blessed with four rivers that irrigated the region which an English trader would later describe as the 'Garden of the World'. The region produced indigo, shellac, opium, honey, wax, wheat, barley, millet, rice, sesame oil, meat, butter, soap, raw-hide and manufactured leather goods, along with some variety of medicines.[7] However, the product with which Gujarat's trade was most identified was cotton textiles. The river valleys flowing through Gujarat were endowed with a black soil well suited to the requirements of cotton growing.[8] Cotton textiles were probably the most important manufactured item in the world at the time and India was the greatest producer.[9]

Having marketable products gave the incentive for local merchants to buy ships and look for markets across the ocean and, before long, Gujarat textiles were sold in every major market in the Indian Ocean. A Portuguese explorer observed that 'every one from the Cape of Good Hope to China, man and woman, is clothed from head to foot with cotton stuffs made in Gujarat'.

Nature handed the sultanate one last bounty to help the development of its maritime trade: a strategic position in the Indian Ocean. Gujarat had a central situation on the major trade routes between Aden and Malacca. On the seaboard of northern India, Gujarat served as the natural gateway to the sea for north-west India.[10] Easy communication to the hinterland gave business a firm basis on which to grow and, as trade expanded, the area served grew to include the Gangetic plains to the north-east and the Indus valley in the north-west.[11]

The port and manufacturing town of Cambay was the initial centre of Gujarat's maritime trade; however, silting in the upper reaches of the Gulf of Cambay made it dangerous for large ships, so trade shifted to Surat. Together these two ports held an ascendancy

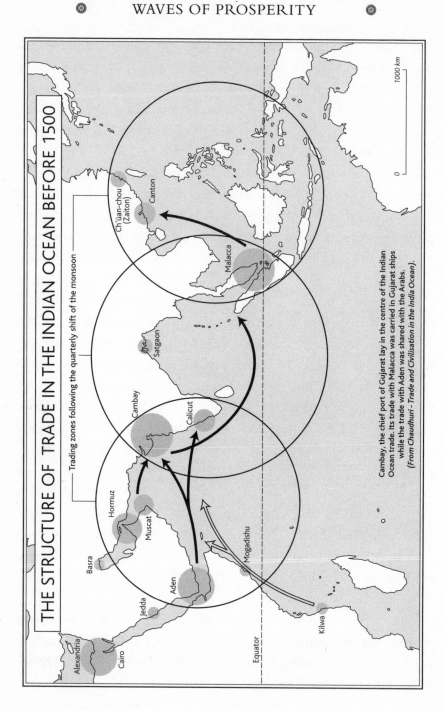

THE STRUCTURE OF TRADE IN THE INDIAN OCEAN BEFORE 1500

Trading zones following the quarterly shift of the monsoon

Cambay, the chief port of Gujarat lay in the centre of the Indian Ocean trade. Its trade with Malacca was carried in Gujarat ships while the trade with Aden was shared with the Arabs.
(From Chaudhuri - Trade and Civilisation in the India Ocean).

48

over India's overseas trade for about four centuries. From these two cities, the products of northern India were taken all over the Indian Ocean. In the eastern Indian Ocean, Gujarati ships sailed to the Maldive Islands, Pegu in Burma, Siam, the Malay Peninsula, the Indonesian archipelago and Ceylon, from where elephants and cinnamon were imported.

However, the most important trade was that to Malacca. This was the linchpin of the nation's fortune and shipping on this route was almost monopolized by Gujarati ships.[12] Some of the first Europeans to observe this trade were Portuguese who arrived in the Indian Ocean at the beginning of the sixteenth century. One of these, Tome Pires, wrote that 'Cambay merchants make Malacca their chief trading centre . . . Malacca cannot live without Cambay, nor Cambay without Malacca, if they are to be very rich and prosperous.'[13]

Gujarat's ships also sailed to a number of destinations in the western Indian Ocean. The main port in the west was Aden on the Arabian Peninsula, which performed a similar role to Malacca in the east, although the trade was not at the same level. Here Gujarati ships were met by traders from nearby ports like Jidda, Zeila and Berbera, and others from as far as Cairo and the Mediterranean world. They supplied Gujarati merchants with opium, copper, mercury, vermilion, gold, woollen textiles, rose water and madder[14] which they carried back to India. Other destinations in the western Indian Ocean included the east coast of Africa, where cotton cloths were exchanged for gold and ivory. At Hormuz in the Persian Gulf, Indian products were transhipped to Persia and Iraq, then carried overland to central Asia, western Asia and Europe.

These centres provided Gujarat with markets for its produce and products for the return trip. With Gujarat in the centre, these trading ports became the hubs on which shipping in the Indian Ocean reached new heights. Tome Pires wrote:

Cambay chiefly stretches out two hands, with her right arm she reaches out to Aden and with the other towards Malacca as the most important places to sail to and the other places are held to be of less importance.[15]

Ships travelled to and from Gujarat, whose ports began to earn a reputation as major entrepôts for the redistribution of products from all corners of the Indian Ocean. Before long, Gujarat had established a reputation that helped it to attract even more business. It also benefited from economies of scale; that is, as the scale of business grows, it becomes more efficient and costs come down, making it an attractive place to do business. Merchants from around the world came to Gujarat as they knew they could obtain reliable supplies and shipping services there. Success fed on success and Gujarat became the keystone of Indian Ocean commerce.

Today, we tend to think of economic growth in terms of technological advance but this was not the case in Gujarat. The region rose on the back of the technologies that had been widely available in the Indian Ocean for centuries. There were no significant changes in the major maritime routes or products exchanged, nor the skills used by ship captains in the Indian Ocean.[16]

The ships used by the Gujaratis evolved from the Arabo-Indian maritime tradition. This was the broad class of vessels commonly referred to as the dhow. The typical ocean-going dhow was a two-masted vessel of about 125 tons with triangular lateen sails. It seems that the Gujaratis developed a regional variation on the dhow. Their ships were larger, averaging 300–600 tons, and could go as high as 800 tons. And, unlike the traditional V-shaped hulls, Gujarati dhows had rounded hulls which no doubt provided greater carrying capacity. The technologies used by Gujarati pilots were also based on an earlier tradition and were no different from those used by others in the region. They used the compass and maritime charts and, by the late fifteenth century, elaborate sailing directions were available for most of the Indian Ocean and Indonesian area. They utilized celestial navigation in which the Southern Cross or South Polar Star were used as points of reference.

Although production methods were not new, the Gujarati business environment was so favourable that it encouraged people to develop productive capabilities that they might not develop in other regions. Strategic location and marketable products gave local merchants better opportunities to invest in shipping than other regions. Gujarati seamen were well placed to gain experience in the requirements of shipping and navigation in the Indian Ocean. Any merchant wanting to transport goods safely across the ocean would naturally prefer to use a reputable, experienced operator rather than risk a new entrant or develop his own services. And here the Gujaratis excelled, as Tome Pires noted: 'The Gujaratees were better seamen and did more navigating than the other people of these parts, and so they have larger ships and more men to man them. They have great pilots and do a great deal of navigation.'[17]

Such success invariably attracted fortune-seekers. All the major trading communities of western Asia were found in Gujarat's ports. Hindus, Jains, Arabs, Turks, Persians and native Gujarati Muslims all conducted trade and accumulated large capital. Some of the foreign fortune-hunters rose to high positions in the local nobility. For example, Khwaja Safar had been a soldier in the Italian wars before coming to India to seek his fortune. He was one of the most successful merchants in the sixteenth century, eventually becoming a noble and the Governor of Surat.[18]

In the great city of Cambay, wealthy merchants vied with one another in building fine houses and wonderful mosques, turning the city into one of the most beautiful of the day. Here, the numerous merchants and skilled craftsmen lived a luxurious life of pleasure and vice. They were well accustomed to good food and clothing, 'washed and anointed their bodies with sweet smelling unguents and decorated their hair with jasmine and other flowers.'[19] However, wealth was not evenly spread. Many of the poorer classes had their economic opportunities restricted by caste rules and earned very low incomes. Nevertheless, by the standards of the day, Gujarat was fabulously wealthy.

European observers marvelled at the wealth and trade of the country. An Italian in the 1560s noted: 'In fine, the kingdom of Cambaia is a place of great trade, and hath much dooing in the traffique with all men.' The country's customs revenue alone in the early 1570s was nearly three times the total revenue of the whole Portuguese empire in Asia at its height in 1586–7. As a Portuguese visitor claimed: 'if in any land it can be said that gold and silver flow, it is Cambay.'[20]

From the beginning of the fifteenth century, Gujarat rode a wave of economic prosperity until a number of wars with bordering nations created barriers to overland trade.[21] The constraints continued until 1573 when Gujarat was conquered by the Mughals, an Islamic people coming from what is modern day Afghanistan.

Defeat in war, though unwelcome, at least removed many of the obstacles to trade with the hinterland as Gujarat became part of the Mughal empire and there were no longer political barriers or conflicts to limit the movement of merchants trading with northern India. A dramatic fall in organized violence stimulated a rise in commercial activity. As with China, the political stability created by a unified empire accelerated the development of a market economy.

With peace, stability and freedom to trade, a great flow of resources was unleashed. Goods and materials could travel freely from all over the empire, aided by supportive government policies. The Mughal Emperor Akbar introduced a number of policies that contributed to the region's prosperity. These included a road-building programme that improved transport and communication across the empire. The taxation system was rationalized with the establishment of a uniform customs duty of 2.5 per cent for goods moving within the empire and, in 1590–91, Akbar abolished a number of duties completely. Again, as in China, changes in taxation policy accelerated the move towards a market economy, in particular Akbar's decision to accept land tax payments in cash instead of crops. This caused people to engage in market activity to raise cash.[22] In rural districts growers who previously shared their productive activity between their own food and cotton requirements began to concentrate on cash crops. Agriculture's focus shifted from producing for one's own use to market-oriented production.

With market expansion came increased specialization. Francisco Pelsaert, who travelled to India with the Dutch East India Company, noted 'a job which one man would do in Holland here passes through four men's hands before it is finished'.[23] Such specialized expertise must have contributed to the high quality of output being produced.

The Emperor Akbar created a centralized bureaucracy to administer the empire.[24] Below the emperor, four ministries were created with responsibilities for finance and revenue, army and intelligence, judiciary and religious patronage, and the royal household. Another layer of government included the amirs (nobles) and highly ranking mensabdars who created a warrior-aristocracy class across the nation. Under the mensabdar system, noblemen were assigned their respective personal ranks (zat) and an area of land from which they collected revenue (jagir). They were expected to use the jagir to maintain a required number of troops. Consequently, they performed twin roles of tax collectors and military commanders, contributing greatly to the security of the region. Strict rules issued by the financial ministry determined the methods and levels of taxation, thereby preventing the mensabdars from abusing the system.

Government policy also contributed to the growth of the textile industry. Mughal emperors introduced a variety of measures to assist the industry, including the granting of concessions to cultivators of cotton crops.[25] The government also conducted activities that increased the confidence of those using the market. For example, cloth, once produced, appears to have been brought to a market where state officers stamped their seals on each piece and collected a duty from the cloth dealers on each transaction. The stamping of goods by state officers acted as a security that prevented merchants from cheating weavers. Merchants were also required to sign a bond pledging that they would report all business deals. The merchants then either gave the cloth further finishing or retailed the goods as they were to the wholesale dealers who distributed them to local dealers, peddlers and foreign merchants. Complying with these procedures might increase the costs for merchants, but these compliance costs were more than offset by the reduced chance a business partner had to defraud another. The attention placed on textiles by the Mughals was an indication of how important the industry had become. The cotton textiles industry was now universal: 'No city, town, paraganah, casbah or village seems to have been devoid of this industry.'[26] In fact, the impact it had on the region's economy was so strong that movements in urban population levels have been linked to movements in textile output.

Nobles frequently invested in facilities to develop local markets.[27] Their motive was both selfish and public-spirited. An emporium helped the local people, thereby earning the noble religious merit. It also increased tax revenues, while the produce of the emporium could meet the needs of the nobleman's own entourage. Some less scrupulous nobles ignored imperial regulations and imposed their power on the local markets, buying goods at low prices and setting themselves up as monopolists. More entrepreneurial nobles might invest in long-distance trade, even buying ocean-going ships. However, nobleman were reluctant to earn the odium of being a mere *baniya* (village trader). If aristocrats did invest in trade (which the royal family itself did) they would normally distance themselves from the activity and hand it to a merchant to manage.[28]

The wealth and power of the nobles made them highly public figures and gossip of their scandals and sexual intrigues filled the bazaars and coffee-houses of urban India.[29] Their personalities and habits were the topics of endless rumour and speculation. News of royal favour, marriages and illnesses spread across the empire. Cruel and capricious nobles were widely condemned while humane and responsible nobles were praised.

As in China, the Mughal value system was intrinsically linked with land. Land was the crucial resource, for control over land gave control over men. A wealthy man with status was a man with a large well-populated land area under his control and a large contingent of cavalry. This is reflected in the fact that Gujarat maintained a large army but virtually no navy. Glory was not won at sea. The prevailing belief was: 'Wars by sea are merchants' affairs, and of no concern to the prestige of kings.'[30]

This land-based ethos and the vast agricultural territories available to tax meant the state took little interest in sea trade. The government seldom interfered in the affairs of merchants and this was particularly so for ocean-going commerce. As long as trade operated smoothly and contributed to the state revenues, the Muslim

rulers of Gujarat were content to provide merchants with protection but otherwise, left them alone.[31] The lack of government
interest in trade meant merchants operated with a great deal of
freedom. Locals and foreigners were all granted freedom of access
to maritime trade and no attempt was made to regulate their coastal
movements. The unwritten law (*qanun*) of Indian society was that
every individual was entitled to work at the post to which he had
been born and was entitled to the profits he had earned.[32]

This individualism could be seen in the organizational structure
of business. The basic business unit was the individual merchant and
his family firm, with an occasional trading partner from the same
social group. These small adaptable enterprises were highly competitive and placed a premium on autonomy. They were very flexible
to changing market conditions, deciding what they produced, with
what materials, on the basis of market forces. The family firm was
also the source by which businessmen acquired their commercial
skills. The French traveller Jean-Baptiste Tavernier who visited India
six times in the middle of the seventeenth century explains how
business education worked:

> They accustom their children of an early age to shun sloth-
> fulness, and instead of letting them go into the streets, teach
> them arithmetic which they learn perfectly, using for it neither
> pens nor counters, but the memory alone, so that in a moment
> they will do a sum no matter how difficult it may be. They are
> always with their fathers who instruct them in trade, and do
> nothing without at the same time explaining it to them.[33]

Commercial expertise was of the highest standard that the world at
that time could provide, and was greatly admired by the Europeans
who witnessed it. The Portuguese traveller, Tome Pires[34] compared

Hindus with the Italians, who were the top European merchants of the day. He praised their bookkeeping and commercial tactics and advised young Portuguese who wished to become clerks to apprentice themselves to the Hindu merchants of Gujarat. The Dutchman Jan van Linschoten claimed that the vanias of Gujarat:

> are the subtilist and politiquest Marchauntes of all India . . .
> They are most subtil and expert in casting accounts and writing,
> so that they do not only surpasse and goe beyond all other Indi-
> ans and other nations thereabouts, but also the Portingales:
> and in this respect they have much advantage, for [that] they
> are very perfect in the trade of merchandise and very ready to
> deceive men.[35]

Family firms operated under a culture of individualism, described as 'a merciless world of almost unrestrained competition which often degenerated into feuding'.[36] This could lead to conflict and herein lay one of the weaknesses of Gujarat's free market. Although the government generally gave merchants freedom to engage in economic activity without interference, the other side of this coin meant the state gave them little support. The state did not pass legislation that made business safer.

If a merchant wished to enforce a contract or recover a debt he could not hire a lawyer as none existed. The merchant would have to appear in front of the authorities and plead his case in person. He would have been well aware that, even if his case was solid, it would need to be supported by bribery or a statement of some influential person speaking on his behalf. If the merchant was able to out-bribe or out-influence his opponent, legal decisions could be achieved quickly. Without prior knowledge of his opponent's influence or budget, a merchant would have to judge if it was worthwhile setting the wheels of justice in motion. Given the arbitrary nature of justice, merchants cultivated access to political power, and frequently employed a *vakil* (one who pleads, or represents a case, on behalf of others) and retainers in the courts of emperors and princes to represent them should they have a grievance.[37]

Given the weakness of official justice, merchants preferred to restrict their business activity to members of the same social group (Hindus, Jains, Muslims). This was particularly so for international trade where distance and problems of communication made it difficult to control activities in foreign ports. Members of the same social group had similar values and a stronger sense of community, so were less likely to have disputes. Solving disputes through custom and tradition was much cheaper than expensive court costs and saved interference from government officials. This also helped businessmen to retain a degree of autonomy from the government.

Independence and autonomy from the state were further provided by trade guilds. Indian trade guilds (*mahajan*) were similar to those that existed in Europe in the Middle Ages. They looked after all the economic interests of the city, ruled the city traders, and organized the economic life of the merchants. Their authority included the power to fix prices and productivity, thereby avoiding any unhealthy competition.[38]

Religious differences, however, impacted on the structure of trade. In Islamic society the occupation of merchant was open to all, whereas other social groups such as Hindus had caste restrictions placed on them at birth.[39] At Surat, Muslims dominated shipping. The Prophet Mohammed had himself been a merchant, so trade and shipping were fully complementary with Islamic values. However, Islamic doctrine prohibited usury and this stopped Muslims entering areas of finance. Consequently, the business of providing loans and other financial services fell to non-Muslims.

Hindus were especially active as suppliers of financial and brokering services, but they were reluctant to become involved in shipping. They would not embark on Muslim ships for fear of coming into contact with unclean persons.[40] However, at Diu and other ports along the coast, Hindus were involved in shipping. Clearly, the opportunities of merchant capitalism were strong enough to overcome even religious proscriptions not to cross the sea. However, while travelling, Hindus would try their best to avoid offending their faith, for example by not eating contaminated food at sea or compensating for any bad karma by living devout lives on shore. An interesting description showing how religious beliefs affected Indian business operation is provided by Jan van Linschoten, who observed Konkan Hindus:

> When they will make a voyage to Sea, they use at least fourteene days before they enter into their ships, to make so great a noyse with sounding of Trumpets, and to beat pots, that it may be heard and seene both by day and night, the ships being hanged about with flagges, wherewith (they say) they feast their Pagode, that they may have a good Voyage.[41]

Religious beliefs also affected commercial practices on shore. Money-lending and banking practices of Jains and Hindus were reinforced by a lifestyle of commercial devotionalism. 'The tools of their trade, account books, pens and ink, came to symbolise deities in the expansive Hindu/Jain pantheon.'[42] Jains were very pious and would not kill any bird, animal or living being and dedicated a large portion of their wealth towards charity. It has been suggested this is the reason they became merchants and not warriors.[43] Some Muslims found a novel way to exploit these religious divisions. They frequently played upon the soft nature of the Jains by threatening to kill animals like rats and snakes in front of them. The Jains, out of sympathy, would offer money for not killing the animals.

Gujarat's location as the gateway to the Mughal empire was a strategic asset that other budding shipping regions could not replicate. It placed Gujarat oceanic transportation in the centre of a broader transport and economic system that buttressed their competitive strength. With Gujarat in the centre, Indian Ocean trade formed a flexible system, the arteries of which were the ships and road transport that linked the main producing areas and the commercial emporia. From the ports of Gujarat, camels, horses, donkeys, oxen and wheeled vehicles linked the hinterland with the sea, where ships would await their cargoes. The result was a long chain of producers and distributors each playing a key role.

A vital link in the chain were the textile producers who provided the export products. The process of manufacturing cotton textiles began with the collection of cotton from the fields after which it was cleaned and spun into yarn. The yarn was then woven into a cloth that was bleached and dyed. The cloth could be used to produce quilts, mattresses, pillows, cotton sheets and bed covers, draperies, cushions, carpets, tents and, most important, clothing.

The textile sector became more efficient during this time, a result of an increased market orientation, a rise in specialization and increasing division of labour among producers. Many agricultural peasants gave up the land to become full-time weavers and spinners. As the volume of production increased a division of labour became more apparent: spinning, weaving, bleaching and dyeing became specialist professions. An accompanying result of the increased scale of production was the development of a market for the sale and purchase of weavers' tools.[44]

Textiles and other products of the hinterland were carried overland to the ports. The chief link in the chain were the general brokers who brought the goods and supplied the ship-owner merchants. They obtained and distributed goods through a network of middle men and sub-brokers in the region's small towns. They also provided warehousing facilities and reduced commercial risks by testing and weighing products. In the ports their goods were purchased by merchants and seamen who carried them to distant ports.

The *sarrafs* (or *shroffs*) of the mint formed another link in the economic system. They were the money merchants of the empire, changing foreign currency into Mughal rupees. They also bought and sold bills of exchange, supplied marine insurance (for goods, not ships) and loans. They also developed an early form of deposit banking and were an important factor in the efficient flow and utilization of financial capital.

Another important link in the chain existed in the foreign ports where Gujaratis sold their goods. At these ports, merchants would frequently place family members they could trust to act as agents. If their level of business activity was not very high, they would use an agent of the same social group based in that port. The agent was paid a commission and the merchant would not have to endure the permanent expense of paying wages when no commercial activity was happening. Merchants maintained regular correspondence with their offshore agents, interchanging commercial intelligence on the state of the markets, what products were in demand or in fear of being oversupplied.

At major foreign ports such as Malacca, the Gujaratis appointed one of their number to be a *shahbander*. The shahbander would look after the interests of the traders, managing the markets and ware-houses, ensuring standards and measurements were observed and adjudicating on disputes within the expatriate community. He also represented Gujaratis when dealing with the Sultan of Malacca. A similar arrangement occurred at other major ports where the Gujaratis traded, such as Mombas and Malindi.[45]

As this description illustrates, a ship-owning merchant was just one part of a long chain of highly specialized individuals. Even the richest merchants were dependent on the links down the chain and had little control over the processes that brought the product to port. The idea of investing further down the chain would not have been attractive to a merchant, given the uncertainty of the markets abroad.[46] In a rapidly changing market, it would be folly to make permanent arrangements with weavers and other producers downstream.

The career of Abdul Ghafur usefully illustrates some of the characteristics of trade at the time.[47] His success turned him into the wealthiest merchant in Surat by the end of the seventeenth century. It is believed Abdul Ghafur came to Surat in the late 1660s from the northern town of Patan where he had been a teacher at a mosque. He was very poor on arrival but his background suggests he was educated and literate, therefore giving him some skills needed to succeed in commerce. He soon made a fortune, most probably on the Red Sea trade. The Red Sea was the destination of many Indian Muslims going on pilgrimage to Mecca and an active trade grew around the shipping that serviced this route.

Experience on the route was of great competitive value as the first ship to the market (and first to return) found a pent up demand and received the highest prices. The earliest ships to return were also the first in transmitting valuable commercial intelligence on market conditions that was very useful when planning what to order. Ghafur knew there was also some virtue in being the last ship and picking up the late freight. The size of his fleet allowed him to cover an array of strategies.

In the hinterland of Gujarat, Ghafur depended on brokers and sub-brokers who dealt with the headmen of the weavers in long tortuous chains that kept him some distance from the production process. With little interest or control over production, he would not be likely to have had any interest in investing downstream, given the uncertainty of offshore markets.

Abdul Ghafur was inclined to be thrifty. By the middle of the 1680s he was among the richest ship-owner merchants of Surat, and by 1700 he was fabulously wealthy. However, his meteoric rise in fortune had not happened without making many enemies on the way. If Ghafur saw an advantage, he would make his own rules and crush smaller competitors. He once attempted to obtain a monopoly on the Red Sea run, ruining several small fry in the process, but the market was too open to limit new competitors. Consequently, he was disliked in the city by other merchants who welcomed any sign that he had lost money.

Even when he appeared to be cooperating with other merchants, he would exploit the situation for his own benefit. This could be seen at a time when European ships arrived in the Indian Ocean and started harassing Gujarati shipping. Ghafur had the most ships and the most to lose from the European attacks so was keen to see them come to an end. He convinced the other local shippers to stop sailing until the Europeans compensated them for their losses, but, before doing so, made sure his warehouse in Mocha was full. The Gujaratis agreed to stop sailing, and with no supplies coming into the Red Sea, Ghafur could sell the products at his warehouse at very high prices. The other seamen saw what was happening and their joint action came to an end.

Ghafur relied on shroffs to coin the bullion he brought into the country. Of course, Ghafur's money man was a Hindu, as too was his broker, Gangaram. His broker's name is recorded as he and Ghafur had a dispute in the second decade of the eighteenth century. We do not know the details of the dispute but it caused a sensation in the city and was talked about for years to come.

The scale of Ghafur's operations was without parallel. Of the city's fleet of 112 ships, at the end of the seventeenth century, he owned seventeen. By contrast, his nearest rivals, the Turkish Chellabie family, had only five ships. Ghafur used his ships on the full range of Asian trade routes from Manila to Mocha. In 1701, he provided eight of the nineteen ships that made the Red Sea run to Mocha where he owned warehouses and one of the largest mansions in town. His *nakhudas* (or captains) would stay in the house during their stopover and sometimes around the year to supervise the sale of merchandise. The *nakhudas* in command of each venture were either his relatives or important businessmen in the city with whom he had connections. Decision-making was centralized around Ghafur himself, with strict instructions given to each *nakhuda*. With the total tonnage of his fleet at 5,000 deadweight tonnes, his operations were comparable to the European companies operating in Asia at the time. However, he never received the social and political support that a company like the Dutch East India Company received from its state.

Abdul Ghafur, like other successful entrepreneurs in Gujarat, rode a wave of prosperity provided by the healthy economic environment which produced its own business structures and ways of thinking. The dhow was the most efficient form of shipping in Indian Ocean conditions, but, being a light ship, it could not carry much in the way of armaments so it was to the merchant's advantage to trade peacefully. This attitude also reflected the religious outlook of some of the traders.

Other rational business practices included placing an agent in a foreign port, trying to anticipate market demand, and buying the products that he thought he would be in demand. These products were shipped when the monsoon winds were favourable. A merchant with large resources might even try to corner the market in a particular commodity, but at the risk of attracting an aggressive response. In adhering to these ways of thinking, a merchant was conforming to what the culture considered rational economic behaviour.

There are clearly strong similarities between the rise of Chinese and Gujarat shipping. Both provided an environment that supported shipping entrepreneurs and the acquisition of maritime capabilities. In particular, political stability and unity gave businessmen in these countries access to large markets and productive bases. Shippers in both nations were buttressed by supporting industries that exhibited the best productive technologies of the day and prosperous local demand conditions. These advantages eventually led them to gain experience and skills that attracted custom from other nations. Clearly, being a gateway to a mighty empire was a strategic asset of value to the industry.

Organizational structures were very similar, with the family being the basis of all shipping organizations (excepting the Chinese tribute trade). In the supporting industries, there was more organizational variation. Chinese ceramics evolved into a more concentrated mass production industry while Indian textiles remained fragmented and widely dispersed. Nevertheless, both achieved a high degree of specialization. The reason for the variances in structure possibly relates to the geographic diffusion of raw materials and also the production technology. With the technologies of the day, it was easier to build a large dragon kiln than mechanized textile machinery.

One noticeable weakness in the Gujarat economy is the lack of any body involved in advancing knowledge. This would go a long way in explaining why Gujarat's success was based on the diffusion of existing technologies, not innovation. While China's monks and official scholarship contributed a range of innovations, Gujarat does not illustrate the same process, even though its economy could support a number of monks and scholars. In earlier centuries, the Islamic–Hindu world had produced a number of innovations and technological prowess far above Europe's, but by the time Gujarat rose to eminence innovation seems to have stopped. This can be partly explained by the nature of their scholarship. compared with the Chinese, who were very worldly and materialistically minded, the great majority of Hindus were engrossed in their struggle to free themselves from physical existence and saw the visible world as an illusion. The effect of this might not be so strong on the day to day life of the average peasant but it certainly affected the most educated members of the Hindu community from which we might expect innovations to come.

The Islamic community was not bound by these issues so, given that Gujarat contained important centres of Islamic learning, we might expect a higher level of innovation. However, Islamic learning seems to have incurred its own process of institutionalization by this time. Scholarly debate had lost the urgency of early years and had been transformed to scholarly tradition. It was no longer exciting and innovative and had become a closed world of strictly bookish scholarship. Nevertheless, at this stage, scientific stagnation did not affect the competitiveness of Gujarat trade. The competitiveness of the Gujarat shipping industry was a function of features of the domestic environment, such as supporting industries, knowledge resources and domestic demand.

To understand how effective Gujarat and Chinese shipping was, it is worth looking at South-East Asia, which had a strong maritime heritage. Up until the end of the fifteenth century, Java possessed trading fleets of ocean-going vessels (the *jong*) that sailed in both the Indian Ocean and the China Sea. However, as the Gujaratis and Chinese increased their activities, Javanese shippers had trouble competing.

In the face of this competition, we might expect the Javanese to imitate their superior competition in order to survive and adapt their technologies and ways of doing business. Some modification seems to have occurred, especially during the Ming bans on shipping which forced Chinese merchants to build their ships offshore.[48] This gave the Javanese an opportunity to improve their shipping technology. However, the hybrid ships they built did not have the same range of technical features of their Chinese counterparts, which reflected a technological supremacy in ship design and construction.[49] Technology was only one part of the northerners' success. The success of Chinese and Gujarat shippers was also built on a domestic economic system that buttressed their competitiveness. This would be far harder to replicate.

Although South-East Asian trade underwent a considerable boom in the sixteenth century, Javanese shipping did not share in this boom. Long-distance shipping changed hands, with Gujaratis taking the market to their west and the Chinese in the east. In the sixteenth century, the competitive strength of the Gujaratis and Chinese was just too strong. The Javanese were reduced to operating on regional networks, and their great ocean-going jong fleets disappeared.[50]

3

GOD, GOLD AND GLORY

William Shakespeare's 1598 play *The Merchant of Venice* is based on two fourteenth-century Italian stories and captures many of the themes of medieval European commerce. Set in a leading commercial city, the main character is a Jew, a man from a people to whom much of early European trade fell. In the play, Shylock the Jew lends money to Bassanio, who is pursuing a beautiful heiress. Bassanio's friend Antonio offers to act as guarantor for the loan, despite ill-feeling between Antonio and Shylock. Antonio has made a habit of berating Shylock, going as far as spitting on him. Nevertheless a loan is agreed but with a twist – if it is not repaid, Shylock can take a 'pound of flesh' from Antonio.

The play reveals important aspects of the medieval economy, in particular a culture in which 'all that glisters is not gold'. While economists see this era as one of 'bullionism', when gold and silver ruled, Shakespeare's play reveals one overwhelming incentive and value that economists frequently overlook: the combination of Christian values with economic activity.

Christian values and institutions strongly shaped the economic development of the day. God, gold and glory were the motives that led the European explorers to carve out the early trade routes. It was the age of the *reconquista* paradigm when Spanish and Portuguese sailors ruled the waves. Seamen like Columbus and Magellan opened a new development path in an epoch when sailors from the Iberian Peninsula strode the globe like none before.

For centuries Europe was the economic runt of the Eurasian continent. After the fall of Rome, the south fragmented into disjointed states. Divided by geographical barriers, Europe was a political patchwork of kingdoms and principalities lacking the strength, stability and economic vitality of its eastern neighbours. The governments of Europe were small and uneducated, while trade was practically non-existent. This was a feudal economy of peasants, priests, warriors and artisans. Europe did not provide a favourable environment for entrepreneurs. There were few industries with the productive capabilities found in the East. This poor manufacturing base provided few products to trade, a situation not helped by low levels of education. The poverty of the region meant there was little demand capable of supporting trade, while few merchants, if any, had the capital to finance international trading ventures. This environment would need to change before any international trade or shipping industry would be viable. During the Middle Ages the European economy underwent a process of agricultural, commercial and technological change. The process was long and gradual and involved both indigenous developments and imitation of Eastern technology and commercial methods. In the process, Europeans developed the capabilities to produce new products and services. In agriculture there was a steady increase in land reclamation, as drainage, irrigation and land clearance increased the amount of land available for agriculture. Production increases supported population growth and provided surpluses that could be traded (or taxed). More people could be employed in non-agricultural pursuits with a rise in the number of people involved in government, religion and crafts. As in China and the Islamic nations, markets became a more common method for allocating resources, at first through temporary fairs that eventually grew into more permanent market towns.

The dominant institution at the time was the Church, and Christian values were not totally conducive to a merchant-based economy. Christians gave merchants low social status, seeing them as gold-hungry and non-productive. Usury, the practice of lending money and charging interest, was considered unethical. Jews were not constrained by these values so filled the vacuum and became successful traders and bankers. Many Jews spread out across the important ports and cities of Europe either to escape persecution or in search of trade. Jews were particularly important in providing a neutral trade link between Catholic Europe and the more advanced countries of the Islamic world.[1]

It is in this role as money-lender that Shakespeare cast Shylock in his play the *Merchant of Venice*. For all the importance that Jews played in the European economy, this conflict of values made them ripe targets for discrimination and Shakespeare used this conflict to create one of the most eloquent speeches in English drama:

Hath not a Jew eyes? Hath not a Jew hands, organs, dimensions, senses, affections, passions? fed with the same food, hurt with the same weapons, subject to the same disease, healed by the same means, Warm'd and cool'd by the same winter and summer, as a Christian is? If you prick us do we not bleed? If you tickle us, do we not laugh? If you poison us do we not die? and if you wrong us, shall we not revenge? If we are like you in the rest, we shall resemble you in that. If a Jew wrong a Christian, what is his humility? Revenge. If a Christian wrong a Jew, what should his sufferance be by Christian example? Why, revenge.

The relationship between the medieval church and business was close, complex and uneasy.[2] In the twelfth century the clergy opposed the establishment of schools that sought to provide basic merchant education as they felt the Church monopoly on education would be threatened. In Italy, a company's books normally opened with a prayer for the success of the business, and the health and safety of the personnel. In the north, the Flemish introduced their financial statements 'to the Glory of God'. Of particular relevance to daily business activity was the concept of the 'just price' sanctioned by the Church. Prices should not be exploitative but should be based on an underlying fairness that recognized demand as well as costs.

The productive capabilities of Europeans were greatly improved as they adopted foreign techniques of production. Islamic nations were an important source of new technologies. Europeans adopted techniques of linen production from Islamic peoples who also introduced cotton production to Spain. The spinning wheel first arrived in Europe from the East in the thirteenth century. Venice acquired its famous capabilities in glass-making from Syria, while sugar production was learnt by the crusaders who brought it back to Europe. Islamic influence was also felt in mining, a subject on which the only publications available until the mid-fifteenth century were Arabic translations.[3]

During the twelfth century, the imitation process took a huge leap when the crusades increased interaction with the Islamic world. It opened up a vast pool of technological wealth. This included the rediscovery of ancient Greek classics and more recent Islamic scientific texts that became available to Europeans in increasing numbers. They included Al-Khwarismi's texts on mathematics, medical works of Galen and Hippocrates, and Ptolemy's *Geography*, which strongly influenced European shippers and explorers. Universities were established, based on the Islamic style of learning. First was Bologna, in about 1100, followed by the University of Paris in about 1150. The

Islamic system of *madrassas* became the model, where the emphasis was on debate and exploring the issue from both sides, in contrast to the memory-based examinations of China.

The imitative nature of early European commerce can be traced in the language we use today. The word cheque is derived from the Arabic word *sakk*. The word ream comes from *rismah*, meaning bundle of paper. The word fund comes from the Arabic *funduq*, while risk comes from the Arabic *rizq*.

It was in the sea ports of the Mediterranean that the process of imitation was the strongest, in particular the Italian cities of Venice and Genoa. These towns benefited from the crusades that had introduced Europeans to exotic products from the Middle East. Galleys from the Italian cities regularly visited Islamic trading ports bringing back products and technologies from the East. The Italians were the first Europeans to introduce the compass and borrowed other innovations such as lateen sails and navigational charts. They most probably adopted the *commenda* form of business organization from their Islamic trading partners, a vital ingredient in the rapid growth of European maritime trade.[4] The commenda model provided limited liability to on-shore investors. Although the partner travelling with the cargoes was fully exposed, the protection to those on-shore helped to encourage investment in maritime trade.

The introduction of double-entry bookkeeping, probably from Hindus, helped merchants to keep track of their operations and the activities of their partners and agents. It also gave them a record by which they could learn from the past how to plan for the future. Bills of exchange came into common use and, by the late fourteenth century, Italians had derived formulas for marine insurance contracts. All these factors reduced the cost of using the market, which became an increasingly effective method of allocating resources.[5]

One key difference between Europe and the East came in the area of dispute resolution. Initially traders relied on custom to deal with disputes in the same way that Indians did. However, as literacy spread, the customs associated with business became codified, Italy developing the first written law to enforce trade agreements. At first, there was not a lot of difference between custom and written law, but, as governments acted to enforce these laws, it gave traders greater confidence to conduct business. Secure in the knowledge that their agreements would be upheld by the law, merchant activity expanded. Italian city-governments were particularly keen to support merchants. These Italian cities had a narrow agricultural base so became dependent on ocean trade. Consequently, the interests of merchants became so important that the state took charge of their protection and merchants became very active in municipal government.[6]

It was from the Italians that other Europeans came to realize the value of maritime trade. Although the Italian ports were not great by world standards, the wealth they created set a benchmark for Europe and was the envy of other European states. Such wealth could finance navies and armies and Europe developed a strong awareness of the economic and strategic value of sea power. As Sir Walter Raleigh would later state:'Whosoever commands the sea commands trade, whosoever commands the trade of the world commands the riches of the world, and consequently the world itself.'[7]

Italian success served as a model for other European states to imitate. Governments recognized that if they supported merchants, they could expand their tax base. To assist business, they passed laws to enforce contracts and protect private property, the Italians once again providing the template.[8] Monopolies might be granted to traders, and letters of introduction given to help merchants establish themselves in foreign courts. They might be given the status of ambassador for similar reasons.

The level of government support that merchants received was

much greater than Chinese or Indian merchants received from their governments. This high-level state support was a consequence of Europe's fragmented political landscape. The smaller nations in Europe meant rulers had less agricultural land to tax than China and the Mughal empire, so were more likely to support merchants in an attempt to raise income.[9] Small size also meant rulers were closer to merchants and the other people under their rule. Consequently, they were more in tune with their needs. There are similarities here with modern business organizations in which decentralized business structures allow decisions to be made closer to where problems occur. This would contribute to increased economic efficiency in Europe compared with the giants in the East.

Decentralization also meant one other vital factor – competition. The states of Europe were constantly fighting among themselves, and a competitive arms race needed to be financed. European rulers became dependent on their merchants as a source of income. Consequently, despite China and Europe sharing a low view of merchants, it was in the interests of European states to support their merchants.

The nature of Europe's political map provided other advantages for economic advance. The existence of many divided kingdoms meant there was no central power to suppress commercial activity or original thought. If a European government tried to stop trade, as happened in Ming China, the merchants could move to another state. There was always a lord or a prince somewhere who would tolerate merchants and, if they were being oppressed, they moved on. Europe certainly had its share of incompetent rulers but they could only restrict business or scientific advance in their limited region. For example, though the Pope did suppress the discoveries of Galileo, Galileo's discoveries could be taken up by Protestant thinkers in Holland, England or Geneva.

The competitive and decentralized environment in Europe affected the way that technology progressed and many of the Eastern technologies imitated by the Europeans underwent further development in their new environment. For example, the blast furnace had been introduced from China and made it possible to cast iron at higher temperatures. Church bells had provided an early demand for the blast furnace technology, but it was in conjunction with another Chinese invention, gunpowder, that the political competitive environment of Europe encouraged innovation. Blast furnaces were first used in Europe for casting cannon in 1380. A rising demand from competitive national armies and navies (and later geographical explorers) caused European metal-workers to create the smallest, most mobile and accurate artillery pieces in the world.

Greater quantities and qualities of iron had spill-over effects for other industries, including ship-building tools and printing. In the German town of Mainz, Johannes Gutenberg, who had learnt about metallurgy from his father, a goldsmith, adapted the new metallurgical possibilities to another Chinese innovation, printing. He invented the printing press with movable type that made books cheaper and more available to a wider audience. By 1480, there were over 380 working presses in Europe. Printing greatly expanded the possibilities for recording and distributing ideas and was a vital factor in the European technological revolution. A technical literature emerged, written by engineers for engineers, and as this knowledge became diffused, more and more people contributed to the advance of technology. In this way, European technology advanced like a cumulating snowball.

Europeans developed a respect for machines, innovation and the people who made them. The greatest minds concerned themselves with production technology. However, progress was not systematic. There was much duplication and time wasted on alchemy. Yet, by

1500, Europe had achieved a position of technological parity with the rest of the world.[10]

These processes of imitation and innovation strengthened the European economic system, providing surpluses for trade, education, demand and capital for investment. It provided the conditions under which entrepreneurs could invest in shipping and trade.

In the early Middle Ages, as in many other areas of technology, European shippers were well behind the Chinese and Arabs. The Vikings had crossed the Atlantic, but as opposed to being a transoceanic venture, theirs was more of an island-hopping venture which leapt from Europe to Iceland to Greenland before finally arriving at North America. It did not lead to the development of new trade routes. The voyages of Leif Ericcson became obscure folklore, unheard of by anyone outside Iceland.

European ships were neither capable of facing severe storms at sea, nor of driving effectively against contrary winds. Limitations in ship strength and navigation technique meant voyages were made by sailing close to the coast, rather than across open seas. Pilots were guided by experience and knowledge of landmarks. However, hugging the coasts brought with it dangers of piracy and the risk of destruction against rocks in a south-westerly wind. Consequently, mariners spent a great deal of time waiting for favourable winds and, at the first sign of bad weather, would duck into the closest safe harbour. Voyages that should have taken only a few days could often take many months. Long voyages pushed up the cost of transport, forcing up wage bills, victualling costs and port charges. Variations in voyage length made it difficult to calculate freight costs and respond quickly to market opportunities.[11] European shipping was a high-cost/low-quality service limited to regional routes.

Improved navigation could greatly reduce the cost of transportation and a series of tools and methods were introduced to achieve this end. The Chinese compass, which was a primitive pointer, was introduced and improved by placing the needle on a dry pivot, and a card was placed underneath indicating the wind directions. By the end of the thirteenth century this improved compass was being used in conjunction with portolan charts (charts with sailing directions). In the north, where there was greater tidal variation, mariners were using tide-tables by the late fourteenth century.[12] These improved navigational methods made sailing safer and more productive. Voyages became more predictable, the number of shipwrecks was reduced, and it now became possible to sail in winter, extending the sailing season and earning more from the capital invested in the ship. Seamen were still wary of winter storms but, with the new methods, they knew the distance to the nearest safe harbour. Safer voyages also lowered insurance premiums. These advances reduced the cost of shipping which further fuelled the expansion of trade.

For centuries, European shipping had been evolving in two distinct spheres. In the north, the roughness of the Baltic and North seas created a demand for a heavier ship, and the cog eventually evolved to sail in these conditions. The cog's design was also determined by economic conditions. Falling grain prices associated with the Black Death meant German exporters needed to improve shipping to become competitive. The cog was the solution. Its hull had a rounded shape with a broad flat bottom, creating greater carrying capacity. The ship's shallow draught reduced its vulnerability to tidal change. It had one mast with one square sail. This made it easy to handle with low labour requirements, labour being expensive after the Black Death. Its high sides were good for defence and positioning archers. A descendent of Viking and Celtic traditions, the cog was clinker-built, which meant the sides were built of overlapping wooden planks.

Southern ships from the Mediterranean area were more exposed to Arab shipping influences and developed very differently. They adopted the lateen sail with which sailors tacking a zig-zag course could make progress against the wind that a square sail could not achieve. In contrast to northern construction, southern ships were built first by constructing a skeleton frame on which planks would be added to the outside. The internal skeleton added greater strength. The planks would not overlap but were placed edge to edge in a process known as carvel construction, saving wood in the Mediterranean area, which had smaller wood supplies. Southern shipping also differed in rigging, keel and the method of supporting the mast.

As trade grew between northern and southern Europe in the last quarter of the thirteenth century, it opened interaction between shippers from each region and provided an introduction to each other's ship types. Over the next century, the best features of the two shipping traditions were combined and by the closing years of the fourteenth century, the carrack had evolved. The earliest carracks were two-masted, a square mast as per the north, a lateen sail as per the south. Eventually, captains and shipbuilders realized that adding a third mast allowed captains to balance the wind forces on different sails, giving greater control of the ship.[13] With the addition of the third mast in the early fifteenth century, Europe had its first vessel capable of long ocean passages.

The carrack was Europe's first fully rigged ship. It was developed over time through a process of imitation and internal evolution. The result was a fast, strong, seaworthy ship that could also sail close to the wind, and be more easily manoeuvred than any of its predecessors.[14] Unger refers to full-rigged ships as the 'great invention'. However, this was no technological leap. This was a slow and gradual process of improvement in which designers responded to environmental opportunity and constraint, but at the same time were limited by previous knowledge. Eventually, a threshold was reached in which they could venture out on to the great oceans. As trade grew, a more established demand for cargoes allowed ship-builders the luxury of building larger ships.[15] Traders in Genoa, with their high-priced cargoes, were more able to accommodate the expense of experimentation in ship design and were early movers of the carrack that, by 1500, constituted 90 per cent of Genoa's merchant fleet.[16]

Advances in metallurgy resulted in better quality tools.[17] It was now possible to produce saws that could effectively cut hardwood while the introduction of the brace made it possible to bore holes for nails. Stronger ships could be built more quickly. Governments intermittently contributed to technical advance and greater efficiency,[18] although some of the directions that governments took led to extreme waste, particularly when monarchs wanted to build big ships as a sign of prestige.

The last important transformation of European shipping was the placement of artillery on board. The competitive structure of the European state system had resulted in reliable guns that, although small, had a force equal to monster iron siege guns of earlier days. Their placement on ships changed naval defence, as their ability to cripple or even sink an enemy vessel dispensed with the need for the assailants to board ships.[19] This would give Europeans a strong advantage when they ventured into hostile waters. It reduced the risks to shipping and the costs associated with piracy and hostile governments. With these improvements, Europeans had the capabilities to sail their local waters profitably. However, in the fifteenth century they were still a long way from developing the skills that would enable them to cross the oceans. These capabilities would eventually be acquired by Spain and Portugal, who created new economic waves that would propel them into global leaders.

★ ★ ★

The countries of the Iberian Peninsula possessed two vital advantages over the states of northern Europe. They benefited from a geographic position that overlooked the Atlantic and also backed on to the Mediterranean, a handy position from which to absorb the expertise of the nearby Italians.[20] The Genoese were especially valuable, providing both capital and maritime expertise. Italians from the city of Genoa had dominated the officer corps of the Portuguese navy since the time of King Dinis (1279–1325). Portugal's first colonial possession, the Canary Islands (later claimed by Spain), was a discovery of Genoese seamen in the service of the Portuguese government.[21]

Both Spain and Portugal had also previously been occupied by Islamic rulers, an experience that filled them with a crusading zeal. In the eighth century, a Moorish army from North Africa had conquered the Iberian Peninsula. For the seven centuries that followed, the Christians of Portugal and Spain had fought to gain their freedom. These were societies where military men, fighting in the name of Christianity, fought the infidel and earned their place in nobility. Initially, Spain and Portugal fought the Muslims on their own territory, but eventually the reconquista mentality evolved into a Christian imperialism that would lead them on to the high seas. The reconquista value system was embodied in the key institutions of the time: the crown, the Church and military orders.

In 1415, this reconquista mentality led the Portuguese king to attack and capture the Morrocan fortress of Cueta. This involved fitting and organizing 100 transport ships, a task that fell to the king's third son, Henry. After the fortress was taken, Prince Henry was given the responsibility of ensuring the defence of the now Portuguese town. This included funding, organizing and arranging the flow of supplies shipped there. These activities were conducted at the newly created Casa de Cueta in Lisbon, a purchasing, distribution and shipping agency. It also came to include potters and coopers, who made products for export to Cueta, and a range of ship-builders.

Henry wanted the capture of Cueta to be the first stage of a Morrocan conquest in which he would star. However, his military exploits were disastrous. Throughout his life, Henry continued to earn his reputation as a rash and poor military planner, and many around him questioned his judgement.[22] However, once Henry obtained success, chroniclers and historians described him as being astute and full of foresight, the evidence being in his achievements.

His first shipping enterprises were directed towards colonizing the Atlantic islands, the Azores and Madeiras, where sugar plantations were established.[23] Sailing to these islands gave the Portuguese experience of the Atlantic wind system and ocean-going voyaging. From here, Henry sponsored a series of expeditions down the African coast to harass the Muslims living there. Developing new routes was fraught with danger. It was reported that if a ship went past Cape Bojador it would be overcome by a number of possible disasters, for beyond it lay boiling seas in which terrifying monsters lurked and, if the tropical sun did not burn the sailors black, Satan himself lay waiting.[24] These tales of dread were supported by currents and northerly winds that made returning difficult. Such tales presented a huge barrier to entry into the African trade.

In 1434, Prince Henry's sailors passed the Cape without being burnt, boiled or consumed by subterranean monsters. Nonetheless, Henry's success was not immediately applauded. He faced all the criticism of an entrepreneur-dreamer spending resources on an untried project, as the chronicler records:

during the first years, seeing the great number of ships that the Prince fitted out for the purpose at such expense . . . they

81

gave themselves up to criticising something of which they had little understanding. The longer it took for the enterprise to produce results, the more their criticisms grew. The worst of it was that not only the plebian people but also those of higher rank spoke about the issue in a contemptuous way, believing that no profit would come from so much expense and effort.[25]

Henry's motives for exploration were not just the pursuit of gold.[26] Henry saw himself as a crusader and his caravels were sent to do as much damage as possible to the Moors along the African coast. His missions were led, not by merchants, but by squires from his household. His ships' sails were adorned with the cross of the Order of Christ. However, in 1447, the military nature of the voyages came to an end when they reached black Africa. Here, they encountered poisoned arrows and lances, so decided trade alone would be a safer option. Initially the Portuguese traded horses for slaves, but as they went farther down the African coast new markets were opened, in particular gold and pepper. These provided the earnings and incentive on which further voyages could be based.

Trading in slaves opened up a new economic path inconsistent with Christian values and demanded legitimization. A new spin was given to the trade. Henry was now presented as saving the souls of heathen Negroes, as the fifteenth-century chronicler Zurara records:

The only thing that concerned your generous heart was not the thought of the small material gain . . . Instead of that, you were moved only by your pious intention to seek salvation for those lost souls . . . That is why, when you saw the captives displayed before you, so great was the pleasure the sight of them gave you that you reckoned as nothing the expenses you had to lay out on this enterprise.[27]

State-sponsored research continued after the death of Prince Henry. In 1486 King John II appointed Bartolomeu Dias, superintendent of the royal warehouses, to head an expedition. Dias had been on earlier trips down the Gold Coast so was experienced in navigation along the African coast. In 1487 Dias became the first European sea captain to round the Cape of Good Hope. A decade later, Vasco da Gama sailed completely round the Cape into the Indian Ocean and, with the aid of a Gujarati navigator that he picked up in Africa, reached as far as Calicut, India.[28] Another Gujarati, Malemo Cana, showed da Gama nautical instruments and a chart of the Indian Ocean, and explained the winds and currents that determined navigation in the ocean. The lesson did not stop the Portuguese from making mistakes on their return trip but it did provide an introduction to Indian Ocean navigation that trial and error would enhance. The Portuguese advances in international trade owed much to what they had learnt from the Italians and Islamic nations. However, they were encountering problems that prompted them to develop their own technologies. The voyages down the Atlantic required them to work out how to establish their position at sea. At a time when the rediscovery of classical books on geography had given the study of navigation more importance and respect, mathematicians, cartographers and astrologers[29] were equipped with the leading knowledge from the East. Prince Henry had brought together experts in these fields who eventually developed the *altura* system of navigation, in which the latitude of the ship was determined by examining the height of the sun at midday. This was made easier by the use of more reliable instruments, the quadrant and tables that related the height of the sun to degrees of latitude. By the sixteenth century published guides and tables for pilots were widely available. Such changes placed new demands on captains who now had to have knowledge of astronomical observations for finding positions and be able to do some mathematics. While these technologies were new to Europeans, Arab, Indian and Chinese pilots had long used similar methods. Europeans were only slowly catching up.

The expansion of knowledge was cumulative. As new navigation techniques allowed ships to travel farther, the resulting discoveries allowed cartographers the opportunity to make more reliable charts. This in turn gave captains greater confidence to sail out of sight of land. In this way the Portuguese built up capabilities and confidence in long oceanic ventures.

In the 1480s King John II of Portugal received a proposal from Christopher Columbus to finance a trip to India by travelling west across the Atlantic. After some consideration, he decided not to finance the project, so Columbus then made his offer to Spain where Europe's competitive political scene once more assisted technological advance. Ferdinand and Isabella were won over on the basis that, if they didn't support Columbus, he would go to a foreign power. They did not want to lose the possible benefits to a rival.[30]

Columbus's eventual success was a direct result of his native environment. He came from Genoa, a leading Italian mercantile city that gave him some of his earliest maritime and business training. He then lived in Portugal for some years from where he had travelled to the Madeiras and the African Gold Coast. In Portuguese caravels he had gained knowledge of currents and winds, islands and shorelines that was not available to an earlier generation.

The new age of printing had allowed Columbus to read Marco Polo and he had used the wealth of Asia as a selling point in his proposal to the king of Spain. He would also have known of a work by Silvio Piccolomani (later Pope Pius II) that summarized the rediscovered Ptolemy's *Geography* but rejected the idea that the Indian Ocean was a closed sea. He had also read *Imago Mundi* by Pierre d'Ailly, which suggested a westward voyage from Europe to Asia was possible, and it was on this that he based his calculations.[31]

Columbus also benefited from the huge advances in shipping technology that had occurred in Europe over the previous century. The ships that he took with him across the Atlantic, two modified caravels and one carrack, embodied the latest European technology. Columbus was in the right place at the right time.

Columbus was not the only European to venture out into the Atlantic. Between 1452 and 1487 at least eight commissions were issued in Portugal, and from Bristol English seafarers were searching the Atlantic for the mythical island of Brasille, which according to Irish legend lay west of Cornwall. But it was the Spanish who first won the conquest of the Atlantic, not without luck. Spain had already developed the Canary Islands as its first maritime colony. By good fortune, the Canaries were close to the prevailing north-east winds. Columbus reached America because, in having a starting point at the Canary Islands, he was closest to the trade winds that could power him across the Atlantic. Unfortunately, Columbus's goal was Asia, not America. Columbus's venture had failed to find a route to Asia, and the wealth he found in the Indies was not enough to compensate for his failure. It would take another thirty years before the New World would yield substantial returns.[32]

The Spanish and Portuguese had now achieved more than any seafaring nation before them. Aware of the possibilities of destructive rivalry, Pope Alexander VI in 1494 divided the world into Spanish and Portuguese spheres of influence. Unfortunately, sixteenth-century maps were very inaccurate and left open potential areas of conflict. Nevertheless, the Treaty of Tordesillas became the basis of a power-sharing document. The implication for shipping was that the world was divided into a quasi market-share agreement. Portugal had Brazil and the route to Asia via Africa and the Indian Ocean, while Spain had most of the Americas.

Spain also wanted to trade with Asia, but the Treaty of Tordesillas put the Indian Ocean route firmly in the hands of Portugal. So they were naturally interested when the Portuguese seaman Ferdinand Magellan arrived at the Spanish court suggesting another route to Asia across the Atlantic. An excellent Portuguese navigator, Magellan had travelled to the East Indies in his youth and had widely read the geographical theories of the day. Discharged from Portuguese service after being accused of treachery, he travelled to the Spanish court where he offered his services. He was convinced that the only reason Columbus and Cabot had failed to find a route to Asia was because they had yet to discover a way through the Americas.[33] The Spanish government agreed to sponsor Magellan. Although he did not survive the voyage, his men were to complete the first circumnavigation of the world.

En route, Magellan saw the Luzon Islands, which were later colonized, and named the Philippines in honour of Prince Philip. These islands were to play a key role in a new trade route and commercial system not imagined by any of the visionaries. Once experience taught the Spanish the nature of the wind system in the Pacific, a trade link was built between the Philippines and the Americas, the famed Manila Galleon. This new trade route saw Spanish galleons taking large amounts of silver to the Philippines from America. In Manila, they were met by Chinese ships and traders and skilled artisans who went to the Philippines to take advantage of the trade. From here, silver was distributed throughout Asia, while the galleons returned to America with produce from the East.

Iberian maritime research had opened trade routes and revolutionized commerce, creating a new pathway to wealth. However, the first enterprises were very expensive. Vasco da Gama's first journey to India lost 65 per cent of its tonnage and 63 per cent of its personnel. The cargo of pepper they carried home only amounted to six tons.[34] The Portuguese soon learnt from experience and dramatically reduced these costs. By 1500, they had learnt the need to schedule sailings to fit in with the monsoons. While da Gama's ships took between 733 and 804 days, the next fleet led by Pedro Alvares Cabral took between 471 and 505 days.

It took a century of trial and error for the Iberians to acquire the knowledge of trade routes that was vital for success in the industry. Of particular importance was their knowledge of the Atlantic wind systems. On voyage, pilots were required to keep daily logs and make records of the position of the sun, wind and weather patterns, the course they sailed and any noteworthy signs.[35] On return the pilots gave the logbooks to the authorities, who used them to upgrade their charts and sailing instructions. In this way, the governments acted as store-houses of knowledge and issued instructions to ships before departing, that included the sea route, geographic and technical instructions, as well as rules to ensure on-board cleanliness, order and discipline.[36]

Portugal went further with the creation of a school for navigation in the early sixteenth century. Portuguese pilots were required to read and write, and master the astrolabe, quadrant and other navigation advances. With the added benefit of experience and interaction with locals in the various regions they travelled, the Portuguese became navigators par excellence. It is significant that the percentage of tonnage lost on the route to Asia declined from da Gama's 65 per cent to an average of 5.4 per cent in the 1570s.[37] Such was their reputation that other European governments did all they could to tempt Portuguese navigators into their service.[38]

★ ★ ★

The Portuguese reaped the returns from their large investment in technology, skills and knowledge. They complemented these with investments in forts and trading posts throughout Asia. With superior skills and infrastructure they developed a reputation and aura of supremacy that further protected them from any challenges.

The commercial revolution that occurred with the opening of the trade routes simply would not have occurred without government patronage. Private investors shied away from such high-risk projects. Columbus and Vasco da Gama both had difficulty obtaining private funding. However, private backers were prepared to lend to the crown who would then bear the risk. Consequently the state played a key role in mobilizing finance, and the officers on Portuguese ships were not merchants but aristocrats.

Since the times of Prince Henry, Portugal's African trade had been a state monopoly and this was also important for the industry's development. Early advance incurred huge costs with little return, so the monopoly was important in that it reduced the risks of competition. This encouraged the prince to invest as it increased his chances of obtaining a return. However, the monopoly did create some opportunities for private entrepreneurs. At times, the route was contracted out. For example, in 1469 Fernao Gomes was given a five-year contract by King Alfonso V in which he was required to discover a minimum number of leagues of coast each year and pay the crown 200 milreis per annum in return for the trade monopoly in those areas.[39] Contracting out expanded the resource base the crown had access to and reduced the risk for the crown.

Following the death of Prince Henry, the African trade came under the control of the Casa da Mina. The Casa consisted of an office and warehouse situated on the ground floor of the royal palace by the waterfront of the River Targus, where later King John could personally watch the loading and unloading of ships.[40] Once the

Asian trade was opened, the palace also housed the Casa da India to oversee the crown's trade with Asia. It administered two enterprises; the Carreira da India, which served the Cape route to India and the Estado da India, which handled the trade within Asia.

Each year, the Casa organized and sent a fleet to Asia, where a network of factors (or trading posts) was responsible for the king's trade. Each factor consisted of clerks, a treasurer and a superintendent of weights. Factors were located across the Indian Ocean and were responsible for buying and selling cargoes on behalf of the crown. The king forbade any individuals other than his representatives or licensees from dealing in pepper, cloves, nutmeg, mace, cinnamon, pearls and elephants from Ceylon. When the fleets returned to Lisbon, the spices and other cargoes were stored and registered by the Casa da India, after which their distribution throughout Europe was handled by private traders.

Once the trade had become established, private investors became interested in investing in it. But the crown jealously guarded its revenue flow, even though removing the monopoly might have increased income through tax on an increased private trade. Nevertheless, private traders became significant features of Portuguese trade, despite the monopoly. Aristocrats, captains, pilots and crew were all awarded some cargo space on crown ships to transport their own goods. Some conducted their own trade but more often they sold these rights to merchants. For example, Duarte Gomes Solis loaded cinnamon and cloves on carreira vessels under the Duke of Braganza's trading concessions.[41] Many of these merchants also traded in areas beyond the reach of the royal estado. Initially, a number of officials, soldiers and other Portuguese citizens based in Asia invested small sums in these private trades but eventually the bulk of the trade came into the hands of a half dozen Lisbon-based families. While the royalty clung to the tried and true cargoes, in particular pepper, these merchants expanded into more diverse products such as diamonds and textiles.

While the eastern trade route to Asia was firmly in Portuguese hands, trade within Asia was a very different story. The Portuguese had hoped to establish another monopoly on trade within the Indian Ocean. The merchants of Gujarat who originally welcomed the Portuguese found themselves fighting for their livelihoods. The Portuguese could not shake their *reconquista* mentality. For them, trade and religion were two sides of the same coin: to deprive the heathens of trade profits and to kill them as enemies of Christianity was their passion.[42] With the support of the Pope, they believed they had the God-given right to half the new world.

With their age-old methods of ramming and boarding, the Asians were no match for the powerful artillery of the Europeans. Asians might be able to muster fleets of ships full of fighting men, but the Portuguese would simply blow them out of the water. The Portuguese won the naval battles but they quickly discovered that it would be very expensive to maintain a monopoly over an area the size of the Indian Ocean. The cost of maintaining a chain of fortifications and large fleets to intercept trade cut deeply into profits. The Indian Ocean was simply too large for a small country like Portugal to control. The vast distances made effective control impossible, and this led to corruption and insubordination.[43]

Nevertheless, the Portuguese did achieve some measure of trade control by imposing a system of passes. If Indian ships wanted to sail unmolested by the Portuguese, they would have to buy the passes (*cartazes*) or face having their ships and cargoes seized.[44] Under this system, the more the Gujaratis traded, the more passes were sold. Consequently, it was in the interests of the Portuguese to encourage Gujarati shipping and Gujarati sea trade prospered under the Portuguese. While the pass system raised the price of shipping and diverted some trade to Portuguese ports, the protection racket did in fact provide proetction.[45] It reduced attacks from robbers and pirates.

Gujaratis retained their pre-eminence in the Indian Ocean. While much trade was diverted to the Portuguese centre at Goa, the Gujaratis were not going to go out of business while they produced the cargoes to be shipped. Consequently, the Portuguese played a secondary role to the Gujaratis, who were secure in their competitive strengths based on their cargoes, strategic location and superior experience. However, one vital change was a decline in the importance of Malacca. The Portuguese captured Malacca early in the sixteenth century, gaining control of what had been the greatest trading emporium in the world. However, Gujaratis and other local traders responded by deflecting their trade to a wider area, and ports such as Acheh and Bantam rose in importance.[46]

Nor did the Iberians displace Chinese shipping in the Far East. In fact, they provided a new sense of dynamism to Chinese trade in the East. When the Portuguese arrived in China in the 1540s, the Ming ban on private shipping was still in force. Although trading illegally, they were welcomed by local merchants and eventually established an authorized merchant colony on the island of Macao. When the Chinese lifted their trade bans in 1567, they maintained a ban on trade with Japan, a long-standing source of pirates. Consequently, the Portuguese became key intermediaries in the China–Japan trade, establishing a permanent colony in Nagasaki in 1571. The trade link became one of the most profitable for the Portuguese. It is this route that formed the basis of James Clavell's book, *Shogun*.

In the sixteenth century the Portuguese focus was on Asia and little attention was paid to Brazil as it lacked the products and markets of the East. But Brazil offered some advantages. The route to Brazil was shorter, less dangerous and less dependent on wind patterns, and the sparsely inhabited tribes could not offer the resistance of the mighty civilizations of Asia.[47] Colonials began developing Brazil's untapped resources, exporting products from the region's rich forests using coerced native labour. In the late sixteenth century, sugar plantations were established, becoming the most valuable of Brazil's exports, and, in the seventeenth century, tobacco was also cultivated. As colonization grew, it provided a growing market for traders to import products from Europe. In the process, the Portuguese built an agro-maritime economy linked by shipping.

In contrast to the state-driven commercial enterprise in Asia, the economic development of Portugal's American territories was characterized by private enterprise. The trade between Portugal and Brazil included many small traders, merchants and ship-owners running small caravels from a number of ports in Portugal. There were few barriers to entry to this trade and the small ships were fast and flexible.[48] Private enterprise was also important in developing the plantations and sugar refineries that supplied the ships with their cargoes. The Brazilian trade furnished the government with a 20 per cent tax on imports and exports.

Spain's trading empire was also driven by private enterprise. From the time of Columbus's second voyage, Spanish ships began to shuttle back and forth across the Atlantic. The Spanish crown had hoped to impose a monopoly on trade to America similar to the Portuguese monopoly to India, but it soon found that the colonies had needs that government resources could not provide. The trade was thrown open to private traders, and the government's role was as a regulating, not a trading body.

The Spanish empire has been described as 'a vast contracting out system'.[49] The crown contracted out the extraction of minerals and other key activities, taking a one-fifth return on all profits. Even the conquistadors who conquered South America were organized on a partnership basis in which they paid a 'royal fifth'. Diego Velasquez and Fernando Cortés established a partnership contract with the object of conquering Mexico, in which each was to furnish half what was necessary and take half of any gains (with the king getting an obligatory fifth). Similarly Francisco Pizarro, Diego de Almagro and Fernando Luque formed a company to explore Peru. Luque acted as a stay-at-home partner, providing the money, while the other two conquered an empire.[50]

This arrangement had a marked effect on the *reconquista* mentality of the Spanish, but the desire to serve God was not the sole motive. Bernal Diaz del Castillo, who participated in the conquest of Mexico, stated: 'We have come here to serve God and also to get rich.'[51] Similarly, when a priest reprimanded Francisco Pizarro for maltreatment of Indians and failure to teach them the gospel, he was told: 'I have not come here for any such reasons. I have come here to take away their gold.'[52] Christopher Columbus had been driven by both incentives, but he was very clear on which was the most important. 'Gold,' he said, 'is a wonderful thing! Whoever possesses it is a master of all he desires. With gold one can even get souls into paradise.'[53] One clear incentive for all the entrepreneurs across the Iberian peninsula was the desire to become a gentleman (or *hidalgo*).

To govern the Spanish empire, a Council of the Indies was created through which university-trained lawyers governed. It was a change that recognized that the maintenance of the empire required different skills from those that constructed it. The battle-scarred conquistador was replaced by the official and the lawyer in the administration of the Indies[54] and an immense body of secretary officials (*escribanos*) came into being. Spain was creating its own mandarins.

The Casa de Contracion de las Indies (House of Trade) was also created in 1503 to regulate and encourage commerce in the newly discovered regions. The Casa was a revenue-collecting agent for the crown, so it checked ship's cargoes and collected the appropriate customs duties, especially from those carrying precious metals. It registered all cargoes and passengers going to the Indies, activities that not only kept the crown in touch with trade developments but also provided clarity in freight contracts between ship-owners and merchants.[55] Although these activities were introduced to protect crown revenues, they had the additional effect of reducing transaction costs for private shippers, although imposing compliance costs. The Casa exercised a considerable degree of control. It was responsible for fitting out fleets sailing on behalf of the crown, imposed safety requirements and inspected privately owned vessels to ensure their seaworthiness. The Casa licensed navigators and its technicians kept a systematic record of all discoveries in the Indies on a standard chart, the *padron real*. Charts of ships sailing to the Indies were inspected to ensure that they conformed to the most recent knowledge. The Casa appointed a chief pilot under whom a navigation school developed. In time a hydrographic bureau, a school of cosmography and a nautical school were added. Although criticized for its restrictiveness, in the early years of development the Casa performed essential services for the expansion of the trade.[56]

Under the Casa, trade was restricted to Seville (later extended to Cadiz). The logic of restricting trade to one port was that it gave the greater ease in maintaining control. However, it had the added benefit of providing economies of scale through the facilities based there. Seville could serve all the needs of the trade, including the machinery of dockyard services and financial and commercial organization. The port was safe and had easy communication with the hinterland. These forces combined to make the Seville monopoly both legal and effective.[57]

Initially, merchants preferred to arrange their own transport between Spain and the Americas, but, after 1526, merchants' ships were forbidden to sail alone to America[58] and a convoy system was introduced to protect ships from pirates, as well as to enforce the port monopoly at Seville. By the 1540s the fleet sailed once a year in a convoy to the Caribbean where it would divide into two: one half sailed to New Spain (Mexico), the other to Tierra Firme (northern South America) and Panama. As time progressed two separate fleets served the two destinations.[59] A guard squadron was provided to accompany the fleet, six to eight galleons for the Tierra Firme fleet, two for the fleet to New Spain. The system was highly effective as, in the 300 years of its existence, only once was a fleet lost to foreign attack.

As resources and markets were developed in the Americas, a new wave of growth provided opportunities by which entrepreneurs could make their fortunes. Migration to the Indies made it possible for artisans to become merchants. A good example of this can be seen in the career of Francisco de Esquivel Castaneda who operated at the beginning of the sixteenth century.[60] Francisco was the son of a guild-certified silk-master and trader in Granada. His family circle was composed of silk weavers, dyers and merchants. He emigrated to New Spain and established himself at Mexico City where he began exporting cochineal and indigo, products used as dyes in the textile industry. He also purchased Chinese silk brought to Mexico on the Manila Galleon and exported it back to Spain. His background in textiles, knowledge of dyes and family contacts were obviously an advantage. South American resources allowed him to become more entrepreneurial and embark on a new path of development.

When merchants first started in the Atlantic trade, they initially sent goods on a speculative basis to be sold at fairs in the principal ports of America. The heads of merchant houses in Seville could not leave their businesses for any length of time so would send confidential agents with whom they formed company contracts. In this way the bold entrepreneurs who risked their lives venturing to the new land gained access to capital and entrepreneurial activity that was otherwise inaccessible. As these merchants established themselves in America on a more long-term basis, connections were formalized in which the American contact undertook to sell merchandise sent from the house in Spain and purchase metals or products for the return voyage.[61]

Although South America was closer than Asia, these contracts still gave birth to organizational problems. In the Seville–America trade, European capitalists might offer the travelling partner a quarter of the profits made on 2,000 ducats of goods but provide him with goods to dispose of far in excess of that value.[62] On the other hand, European houses complained of agents not sending in accounts or misbehaviour in the dealing with funds. As in the East, this principal-agent problem was a prime reason for choosing family members as partners and agents, and the family was the dominant form of business organization.

The family firm of Alvaro Jorge, an ex-silk mercer, provides a useful example. They were active in the Afro-American slave trade and owned several of their own vessels. They maintained a network of agents in the New World and these normally were staffed by younger family members (sons or nephews). If it was necessary to employ someone from outside the family, someone with similar origins would be sought. Being *conversos,* Jews who converted to Christianity to escape persecution, this meant other converted Jews. Many business associates were related through marriage.[63] This reliance on family trust for commercial control also reflects the limits of the Spanish legal system.

Small merchants built shipping enterprises that by the mid-sixteenth century had become large merchant dynasties. These merchant houses developed an extensive agency and commission business importing and exporting throughout Europe and the New World. Many of the merchants were *conversos*. An example of the richest Sevillian business- men was Ruy Diaz de Segura who learnt his business skills as an old clothes dealer (*trapero*). He owned three ships involved in the Indies trade: the caravel *Santa Maria del Cabo*, the *Santa Maria de la Consolacion*, and the *Santa Maria de la Regla*, which he owned with his cousin.[64]

The new economic system increased social mobility and revolu- tionized social values.[65] However, the rise in commercial values was not always welcomed. This is reflected in the comment by Cervantes, author of *Don Quixote*, who complained that 'money is prized rather than worth'. The Spanish aristocracy did not approve of rewarding merit ahead of noble blood and proven lineage. The playwright and poet Lope de Vega believed that 'states are destroyed through men wishing to change their status'.[66] To such nobles, status should not be gained through non-military means. They emphasized the old values of virtue, service to the crown and the exclusive power of the prince to create nobility.

As the century progressed, more institutions were created that increased the efficiency of the Atlantic system. As trade with the Indies expanded, the number of commercial lawsuits increased and the Casa de Contracion became choked with business. In 1543, after repeated petitions, the merchant houses who at that time dominated the trade had been legally incorporated in a *Consulado* or merchant guild. The guild simplified and shortened legal proceedings, which led to an increase in efficiency in commercial jurisdiction, but at the cost of establishing a closed monopoly for the merchant houses that dominated the business. The guild became a rich and powerful stakeholder that could defend its privileged position by litigation and pay for it through the loans it made to an impecunious government.[67]

Another key institution created at the time was the Jesuit order of priests. The Jesuit order had initially been created in response to the Protestant attacks that exposed many weaknesses of the Catholic Church. Although the order was not created to serve the trade, it did become an important part of the economic system, buttressing the *reconquista* promise of conversion and profit. Jesuit missions (and the Council of the Inquisition) accompanied the trading stations around the world, and, while they imposed an added cost, Jesuits did at times play an important diplomatic role in getting preferential treatment for traders from local rulers.

The Jesuit order also stimulated intellectual and technical advance. There was a clear need for more qualified priests and a number of higher educational institutions were created, in particular Jesuit colleges. The Jesuit education system was built on the latest knowledge and had obvious benefits for the economy. It led to an increase in the quality of administrators and promoted scientific advance. It also helped to feed the bureaucratic needs of the state with educated professionals. During this time, Iberians gained a growing appreciation of the benefits of higher education and merchants sent their children to the colleges in an attempt to raise their status. It resulted in the founding of a number of new universities. To the four *estudios generales* in 1450, twenty were added in the sixteenth century.[68]

When combined with the stimulation that the American discovery provided, education improvements propelled Spaniards into the forefront of scientific adventure. They stimulated research into all aspects of natural science, including geography, navigation, engineering and medicine. The first ship-building treatise was published in Mexico in 1587. This was a period of scientific and technological leadership in Spain that helped to develop the nation's productive capabilities. The government was another key factor in providing innovation in ship-building. The Spanish government kept close control of its ship-builders so that any private ships built would also be suitable for state defensive needs. While the government dictated a number of requirements it was forced to consult ship-builders about these. The state showed a willingness to experiment[69] and ship-builders had considerable freedom of action. It was a period of experimentation, with some bizarre results and some great successes. Examples of this include the work of Menendez de Aviles and Alvaro de Bazan, who developed the *vesselei,* a narrower and faster ship than had previously existed in the Spanish fleet, and in the 1550s strenuous efforts were made to develop the galleon, also under Admiral Alvaro de Bazan.[70] Encouragement by the government did much to develop the science of naval architecture and, as a consequence, Spanish ships were better than those of other European nations.[71]

The other key supporting industries were those that filled the hulls with cargoes. From Spanish America, cargoes included hides and tallow, sugar, indigo (a blue dye made from vegetables), cochineal (a red dye made from small insects), exotic woods and medicinal plants. However, the most valuable of the exports were the gold, silver, pearls and precious stones from the Indies. In the 1540s and 1550s silver mining leapt in importance with the discovery of the Potosi mine in Upper Peru (present-day Bolivia) and a number of mines in New Spain (Mexico).

At this time, the earlier investments in African trading stations made by Henry the Navigator proved of great benefit. A labour shortage on Brazilian plantations was solved by importing slaves from its African colonies. Spain did not have African trading posts, so gave a contract (*asiento*) to Portugal to supply slaves to their colonies. Portugal held this contract from 1573 to 1676, thereby gaining a strong boost to its shipping.

The complementary demand patterns for these cargoes enabled the Iberians to carve out a global economic system. From Africa slaves were transported to South America where they worked the mines and plantations. Bullion and other produce from South America was shipped to Asia and exchanged for goods that would then be shipped to South America and Europe. At the same time bullion, sugar and other produce from South America was shipped directly across the Atlantic to Europe.

While this new economic system unleashed previously undeveloped resources, this was no free market.[72] Certainly, when in China and the Indian Ocean, the Iberians had to accept the market price, but the key cargo of bullion was extracted using slaves who had been taken from Africa by force. The main source of income in Asia for the Portuguese was the enforced sale of passes to local shippers. The Iberians gained no competitive strength from the products they personally made, apart from ships and mining. Given that their wealth and resources were based on conquest, it helped to cement the *reconquista* mentality and value system. The economy was personified by images of militant knights, not industrial captains.

Throughout this process, the Iberians developed new ways of thinking that built on the old *reconquista* values. In so doing, they built a new economic system with its own sense of what was rational. To the old *reconquista* paradigm of fighting Muslims was added the desirability of improving shipping technology and developing the resources of South America. But the prevailing rationality meant that the Church and nobility still took prime place over merchants and their trading. The crown, which had steered much of this advance, remained in its central position. The most extensive trading empire the world had thus far seen was built on an aspiration for conversion and conquest. Once established, maritime and organizational efficiencies helped to create an enduring monopoly. For a century, the Spanish and Portuguese nations faced no serious competition on the trading routes they had built.

4

NORTHERN INDUSTRIALISTS

By the end of the sixteenth century the oceans of the world could be characterized as a series of regional markets dominated by regional shipping leaders. The Chinese dominated the China Sea, the Gujaratis the Indian Ocean, and the Iberians mastered the Atlantic and the ocean routes linking these areas of activity. It is hard to say which of these nations produced the greatest output. Historical figures of this age are riddled with inaccuracies and can only be taken as indicative. In terms of value, Gujarat's oceanic trade would appear to be the greatest. On the basis of customs receipts, the value of Gujarati sea-borne trade has been estimated at 40,000,000 cruzados. By comparison, the value of Iberian trade was only half that. Spanish trade across the Atlantic was valued at 7–10,000,000 cruzados and the Manila Galleon 3–4,000,000. At the same time, the Portuguese carreira trade was valued at 5,000,000 cruzados.[1]

Unfortunately, we have no values for Chinese trade and no numbers for Gujarati shipping in this period. We do know that 137 ships legally traded from China in 1597[2] and this compares with a peak of 200 Spanish westbound ships of similar size (approximately 200 tons) visiting the Americas.[3] Records suggest Spain and Portugal had a greater transoceanic fleet in terms of numbers, but it should be stressed that China had a phenomenal coastal trade. China's coast line is so long that some voyages considered international by Gujaratis (and Europeans) would only be considered domestic in China. Finally, if leadership was judged in terms of ocean-miles travelled, the Portuguese and Spaniards were clear leaders.

Despite this relative equality, Europe was producing maritime and related innovations at a faster rate than its eastern neighbours. Asian shipping now appeared to be experiencing technical stagnation. Many economists believe declining innovation is linked to reduced levels of competition, but both China and Gujarat possessed very competitive commercial environments, but did not produce technological advance. One area where Europeans were experiencing greater competition was in naval warfare, and many of the technical developments that occurred in Europe were spin-offs from naval technology.

The Chinese and Indians did not seem to experiment in sails and rigging as much as Europeans. They were happy to maintain the junk and dhow which were faithful workhorses in their respective conditions. By contrast, ships were designed in Europe with increased manoeuvrability. In the second half of the sixteenth century, Europeans changed from having a few large sails to having many smaller sails, a development that was associated with changes in rigging. This generated huge improvements and, once started, the process became self-reinforcing as success led to greater experimentation.[4]

Eastern merchants seem to have been happy to use the tried and tested: seeking profits, not through technical innovation, but through commercial strategy; getting the best blend of cargoes for their respective destinations. These were the strategies that were considered rational in their economic systems. Chinese commercial strategy was driven by market-based solutions and the need to have good relationships with mandarins. In the Indian Ocean, Gujaratis had the most market-driven economy of the lot. Their commercial rationality was driven by the need to anticipate and link the supply of goods with those in demand. By contrast, European traders and shippers seem to be the most open to the possibility that technological changes could advance their profitability.

All merchants had to make political, technical and commercial decisions. However, the merchants in each nation seemed to have differences in the level of emphasis. Europeans seem more inclined to consider technical changes, a reflection of their environment where a new respect for technology was emerging. The improvements might only be marginal with little effect on a daily basis but, over a century, they accumulate. In the early sixteenth century, the Europeans gained no advantage in trade from their shipping technology but, in time, this difference would be felt.

In 1580, the Portuguese king Dom Henrique died without an heir. This led to a succession crisis that the Spanish king solved by annexing Portugal. The Spanish King Philip II now ruled two of the most powerful seafaring nations in the world with a trading network that stretched from China to Peru. The Spanish and Portuguese completely dominated the Atlantic Ocean. The Portuguese were the only traders regularly linking Asia and Europe, while Spain's Manila Galleon was the only regular route across the Pacific.

The rest of Europe stood in awe of this maritime and economic giant and many states wanted to replicate the Iberian success. Spain's success provided a demonstration of what was possible to achieve. But, more important, Spain posed a significant threat to the security of many nations in that it linked military and Catholic values, and had the wealth with which it could finance considerable military and naval action. The Protestant nations in the north were worried.

England was a backward nation. It looked upon the strength and wealth of its southern neighbours with a mixture of fear and envy. It possessed only one significant industry and only one significant enterprise engaged in international trade. That industry was woollen cloth, and that enterprise was the Company of the Merchant Adventurers who exported the cloth to Antwerp.[5]

Although surrounded by sea, Britain had nothing to compare with the fleets of the Spanish and the Portuguese. The English had earlier made a number of exploratory voyages in an attempt to find a westward route to Asia and the mythical isle of Brasille,[6] but their attempts achieved little. It took an Italian to give them their first transoceanic success. John Cabot (Giovanni Caboto) was the son of an Italian merchant who traded spices in the Mediterranean. This gave John the best seamanship pedigree that Europe could provide. About 1490 he moved to Spain hoping to tap into its exciting enterprises. He offered his services to the Spanish court, but they were not interested. So he moved to England and settled in Bristol where he gained support for a trip to Asia by sailing west across the Atlantic, a voyage similar to Columbus's but a more northerly route. Like Columbus, he failed to reach Asia, but he did discover a 'newe founde launde'. Unfortunately, Newfoundland did not have the gold and silver deposits that were so accessible in the south and the only gain were the cod fisheries off the coast. Sixteenth-century economic and maritime development would have been very different if Newfoundland possessed the same resource base that Spain had found in the south.

England's weak state and vulnerability to attack provided the impetus for the government to embark on a development programme for the shipping industry. With little difference between merchant and naval ships, merchant ships played a key part in warfare. The Tudor monarchs actively encouraged the development of a merchant class and shipping industry. Henry VII introduced protective legislation that reserved certain cargoes for British ships.[7] In an effort to build up a navy, Henry VIII recruited shipwrights from mainland Europe, thereby gaining the latest capabilities in fully rigged ship technology. He also established Trinity House for the Advancement of Navigation and Training in Pilotage.

The Iberians provided the model by which the English developed their maritime capabilities. Books on sailing and navigation were translated, such as *Arte del marear* by the Portuguese Ruy Faliero and *Arte de navegar* by the Spaniard Pedro de Medinas.[8] To advance navigation technique, Queen Elizabeth established a position of 'chief pilot' in imitation of the chief pilot established at the Spanish Casa.[9] The poor state of English industry meant that all the country's shipping supplies had to be imported. This could be a huge weakness in time of war, so assistance was extended to target naval supplies. French and Italian experts were imported to teach gun-founding while the state encouraged research in the use of domestic iron to replace imported bronze.

Outside of state support, two growing industries helped to spread basic seaman skills: fisheries and coal. Once the potential of the Newfoundland fisheries was realized, fishing boats helped to train many seamen in the skills required for ocean voyaging, while the fish they caught provided the basis of an export trade to Spain and the Mediterranean. The domestic coal industry also stimulated maritime progress. Coal, carried south by sea, was responsible for turning many landlubbers into seamen.[10]

A key influence in the development of seafaring capabilities was Sebastian Cabot, the son of the Italian merchant who discovered Newfoundland for the English. With his Mediterranean connections, Cabot introduced an array of maritime and commercial techniques. He advised the nation's first venture in long-distance trading, which occurred when a group of businessmen pooled resources in hope of finding a northern route to the riches of the East via the Arctic Sea.[11] The venture was entitled the Mysterie And Companie of the Merchant Adventurers for the Discoveries of Regions, Dominions,

Islands and Places Unknown. Unfortunately, the company's ships did not make it past the Bay of Archangel in Russia. Although they failed to make it to China, the Russian tsar, Ivan the Terrible, had a soft spot for lowly men such as merchants and granted the Englishmen permission to trade.

About the same time, English merchants developed trade with North Africa. The Moroccan trade was established by James Alday, one-time servant of Sebastian Cabot. Together with Henry Ostrich (who married one of Cabot's daughters) and two naval commanders, he established the trade using Jewish intermediaries who arranged the exchange of English cloth, ironmongery and other goods for highly valued Islamic sugar. Thomas Wyndham also led a syndicate that opened up trade to the Guinea coast, using a Portuguese Jew for a pilot.

Although commonplace to the Portuguese, these long-distance ventures were more ambitious than anything the English had ever tried before and taxed the nation's limited resources. Shipping to these distant lands required more capital and sophisticated organization than anything they had ever done. They required more ships, bigger ships and investment in stock levels large enough to cover the long periods involved. These trades were also much riskier. Not being rich in capital, merchants had to pool their resources together, giving birth to a new organizational form, the joint stock company. This structure had the added benefit of spreading risk among investors.

Risk was further reduced when the state gave these companies monopolies in their respected trades, increasing the chance that a profit would be returned. The monopolies were not popular with smaller private shippers, and interloping was common on the Russian and Baltic trades. When six interlopers tried to break the Russian Company's monopoly in the 1560s, the company had to justify why it should be given preferential treatment. The company included in its defence the role it was taking in advancing the nation's seafaring capabilities, stating that it retained a number of skilled pilots and masters in its employ and paid a man 'learned in cosmography' twenty pounds a year to teach its mariners.[12] The company was investing in a knowledge base of the routes, by which they could increase speed, reduce costs and bring new captains into the trade. As a result of these arguments, the English government confirmed and extended the company's monopoly.

In the meantime, chance political events helped to shape the industry's development. In the last quarter of the sixteenth century, the Protestants in the Netherlands revolted against their Catholic rulers in Spain. The conflict brought an end to Antwerp's role as a commercial centre and the biggest market for English woollens. With the fall of Antwerp, English merchants were forced to find new markets and establish new distribution systems. A number of new chartered companies were created. The Eastland Company was created in 1579 to seek trade in the Baltic, followed by the Turkey Company (1581), the Venice Company (1583), and, in 1585, the Barbary Company was created to exploit the trade first opened by James Alday. In 1592 the Turkey and Venice companies merged to form the Levant Company, bringing currants, wines and silks from the eastern Mediterranean. These early companies were all export-orientated in an attempt to find markets for English woollens and on their return voyages brought exotic imports back to England.[13] Another effect of the war in Flanders was the flow of refugees it released. These people brought skills into England that allowed the nation to create new woollen products of superior quality. These 'new draperies' provided a valuable cargo that helped English merchants enter markets where there was little demand for their old product.[14] Consequently, the loss of the Flanders market was a blessing in disguise that delivered a window of opportunity. With the Dutch occupied with their war with Spain, the English gained a foothold in the Baltic and Mediterranean trades, and English ships now brought back goods that had previously come through Antwerp.

The cold war atmosphere between Spain and England gave birth to another activity that contributed to the growth of English shipping: commerce raiding. Pirate raids (and the officially sponsored privateering) expanded the skill of many seamen and could be highly profitable. Privateering was as significant to the economy of Elizabeth I as automobile production was in the early years of Elizabeth II. Profits from privateering were used in the founding of the East India Company and the first American colonies.[15] Commerce raiding also expanded the market and capabilities of those onshore industries that fitted out ships, including carpenters, ship's chandlers, rope-makers, sail-makers and suppliers of victuals, stores and armaments.

This branch of maritime industry is best represented by Sir Francis Drake. Drake's father had been a Protestant vicar and the young Drake grew up with a fervent hatred of Catholics. After an apprenticeship sailing in a bark to France and the Netherlands, Drake joined his relative John Hawkins who in 1562 established a trade shipping slaves between Africa and the Caribbean, a market dominated by the Portuguese. This provided Drake with the navigational knowledge he would put to good use when he diversified into pirating, a career made possible by the political climate existing between Spain and England. This new line of activity was highly profitable for Drake who used his new-found wealth to invest in property and a fleet of ships.

In 1577 Drake diversified his activities once more and set off on a venture that would greatly assist the English catch up with the Spanish and Portuguese. With financial backing from Queen Elizabeth he commenced what would be the first trip around the world by an

Englishman. This was a deliberate intrusion into a world that the Spanish and Portuguese believed was theirs by divine right. Drake left England with five ships. First heading to Africa, he then crossed the Atlantic, sailed through the Straits of Magellan into the Pacific and ventured up America's Pacific coast to what is now the Canadian border. He raided Spanish settlements at Valparaiso, Lima and Arica, and captured a number of ships. The biggest prize was the *Nuestra Señora de la Concepcion*, a ship used on the Manila Galleon run between America and the Philippines. This ship alone netted eighty pounds of gold and twenty-six tons of uncoined silver, among other cargoes. Given the state of English shipping, Drake was reliant on foreign input for success. His crew included foreigners with specialized navigational skills,[16] and Magellan's route was used as the blueprint for the voyage. When he captured Spanish ships, he sought their nautical charts with as much fervour as he did their gold, as these were valuable in teaching the ocean routes.

After three years at sea, the man the Spanish named the Dragon (El Draque) returned to England. He carried with him the largest treasure ever seen in his native land. With spices bought in Ternate and bullion stolen from the Spanish, his investors made a 4,700 per cent return from their original £5,000. The queen's share alone was £300,000, enough to pay off the national debt and still leave £42,000 to invest in the Levant Company. Drake was knighted for his efforts. The voyage revealed both the wealth and the vulnerability of the Spanish empire in the East, and provided England with navigational skills and knowledge to enter the East Indies market. Most important, Drake had shattered the reputation that had left many northerners in fear of their Iberian competition. It seemed the market was now open for all. Unfortunately, the English were about to learn the difficulties of long-range oceanic trading the hard way.

The next voyage to the East was led by Edward Fenton who was to take a fleet to the East Indies.[17] Unfortunately, en route he decided not to go the Indies, but to stop at the island of St Helena on which he intended to make himself king. However, his regal dreams were not supported by his crew and the fleet returned to London without having left the Atlantic.

In 1591 another voyage left under the competent leadership of James Lancaster. However, nothing Lancaster had ever experienced could prepare him for the long periods in unknown seas without fresh food and water. Sailing to Ceylon, the ship got lost in the Indian Ocean and, with many of the crew sick and dying, the voyage was brought to an end. Of the 198 men who rounded the Cape only twenty-five returned and two of the three ships that left England were lost.[18] Through this experience, London merchants learnt that the spice trade was a high-risk investment which, with their current level of expertise, they could not afford to enter.

Problems like these were not confined to the Indian Ocean. In the same period, an attempt was made to settle North America with the establishment of a colony at Virginia. The colony was promoted by Sir Walter Raleigh, who found investors among London's richest merchants. Whereas Spain's colonies had been based on mineral wealth, income sources for the English venture were less forthcoming. Raleigh was transplanting an English village into a wilderness of which he knew little. Within three years, the colony disappeared without trace and Raleigh personally lost £30,000 in the project. It would be another three decades before the English developed an ocean-going trade with North America. Other failures included a number of exploratory trips to find a route to the East via the Arctic.

Despite these failures, the English had gained some vital capabilities. They had companies regularly trading to the Levant and Russia and now possessed scores of seamen with technical expertise, nautical ability and experience.[19] Nevertheless, Spanish and Portuguese merchant shipping stood secure in its competitive strengths on the long-haul routes. However, a more aggressive challenge was about to come.

If, in the middle of the sixteenth century, economists were to choose the next global leader, the Netherlands would have been very low on their list. It possessed few important merchants or financial facilities, and was reliant on Antwerp for most of its international trading requirements. The Netherlands were the lowlands of Europe. Built on a swampy river delta, they seemed to possess nothing that suggested future greatness. Dutch people were hard-working, but much of their energy was spent fighting the forces of nature. Their low-lying land was vulnerable to flooding, a vulnerability that created a healthy respect for the hand of God. Simon Schama[20] describes it as a 'flood society', and only through hard work and with God's help could the Dutch overcome the forces of nature, but if they displayed too much gluttony, vanity and sin, divine wrath would punish them.

Over the next half century these vulnerable swamp-dwellers transformed their economy in a way that was miraculous. As in China, where mandarins had to tame the river systems, the Dutch also had to master the forces of nature that taunted them before economic take-off could occur. This was an on-going process that had been occurring for centuries. Ditches and watercourses were constructed providing better drainage and opening up new areas for agriculture and settlement. As settlers moved on to these reclaimed lands, they created a new social structure unique in Europe at the time. This new society did not inherit the feudal institutions that dominated the rest of Europe. It developed a more equal society, aware of the needs for mutual cooperation.

Despite these improvements, the low-lying lands were still vulnerable to rising sea water and it proved almost impossible to grow crops such as wheat and rye on the peat soils. Many farmers reverted to cattle farming. In this way, nature forced the Dutch to specialize, the result being they had a huge surplus of dairy products to export but were dependent on imports to meet their grain needs. Dutch cheese captured the Belgian market, while Dutch merchants and cargo ships began to play an important role in the Baltic grain trade. As trade grew, the Dutch gained more opportunity to observe and learn southern business methods. Marine insurance, partnerships, use of factors, agents and correspondents were all practices that arrived in the northern Netherlands. With industrial growth and diversification came increased specialization and the arrival of the merchant marine, with the jobs of sailors and captains becoming full-time occupations.[21]

Growth in the shipping industry was also helped by developments in the fishing industry. The inland rivers, lakes and canals of the Netherlands provided plenty of opportunity for fresh water fishing. Eventually, the Dutch took their boats on to the Zuider Zee and the North Sea where the herring fisheries could be exploited. Once the nearest fisheries were depleted, the Dutch were forced to go deeper out to sea to search for fish. This required their sailors to develop deep-sea sailing skills and strong boats.

Fishing was a seasonal activity and during the off-season, Dutch boats entered the carrying trade. With fully rigged ship technology, the Dutch wrested the Baltic trade from the Hanseatic nations who had previously dominated shipping in the region.[22] One of the sources of Dutch competitiveness in this route was the more southerly location of their ports which became free of ice earlier. This meant they could pick up cargoes in France, take them to the Baltic and be back home before the winter set in. However, the main factor behind Dutch competitiveness was their low cost. The Dutch use of out-of-season fishing boats and low-cost labour gave them a competitive advantage with which the Hanseatic nations could not compare. By 1532, the Dutch had some 400 ships entering the Baltic on an annual basis.[23]

Despite achieving significant economic growth, by the 1570s, the Netherlands still possessed no industrialists or merchants of international stature.[24] However, political changes sparked a new stage of economic growth when the war in Flanders broke out. In 1585 the Spanish captured Antwerp, causing a flood of refugees to the north and England. Textile workers from Flanders and Brabant arrived in Leiden and Haarlem. The consequent growth in textile production provided the shipping industry with another cargo and reinforced the Dutch position in the Baltic carrying trade.[25]

The Dutch first gained the capabilities for deep-sea sailing by imitating southern navigation and ship-building methods. In time, Dutch ship designs began to evolve from the southern pattern, responding to local demands and geographic conditions. The first successful independent design was the *buss*, designed to meet the needs of Dutch fishermen. In the off-season fishing boats looked for cargoes, for which the buss was particularly good as it could weather northern storms. Eventually, boats were designed exclusively with cargo in mind. Modifications led to the evolution of the *boyer*, a flat-bottomed boat of shallow draught that enabled it to travel with ease in the internal waterways of the Netherlands. In the sixteenth century it was taken on to the sea and, as a consequence, ship-builders had to make a larger boat, building up its sides and expanding the rigging.[26] The *vlieboot* (or flyboat) was designed even more specifically for bulk carriage, rather than speed. It had a square stern and a broad beam that enhanced carrying capacity. Experience with the flyboat led to the evolution of the cargo boat par excellence, the *fluyt*.

First constructed at Hoorn in 1595, the fluyt's hull design had a low centre of gravity that was excellent for riding out bad weather.

The ship's sail area was kept small and its masts were short relative to its carrying capacity. This meant it did not need a large crew to handle the rigging. However, it also meant a slower ship, but as long as the ships were fast enough to conduct the Baltic run before winter came, extra speed was not an advantage. Although longer voyages increased crew wages and victualling costs, they were more than offset by the reductions in crew size achieved through the use of labour-saving devices such as pulleys and blocks. Ease of handling, small crews and large cargo space gave the fluyt a huge competitive advantage in ocean-going trade. It enabled the Dutch to undercut the French and English carrying trade by 30–50 per cent.[27] As Sir Walter Raleigh explained, the Dutch built vessels 'to hold great bulk of merchandise, and to sail with few men for profit'.[28]

Labour-saving devices found in the fluyt reflected many similar improvements that occurred on land at the time.[29] Key among these were developments in windmill technology, an old power source introduced from the East many centuries earlier. The Dutch needed efficient windmills to help drain lands for farming.[30] Their contribution to windmill technology resulted in the *bovenkruier*, a cap at the top of the windmill which could be rotated so the sails could be turned towards the wind. This meant large windmills became an efficient energy source. In 1592 Cornelis Corneliszoon van Uitgeest took out a patent for a wind-powered sawmill. At first, wind-powered sawmills were resisted by the guilds, so the industry located itself in the Zaan region north of Amsterdam where no guilds existed and there were no buildings and few trees to impede the wind. Once wind-powered industrial production began, other producers developed in the region.[31] Over time, windmill technology was applied to various industrial uses, including fulling cloth and hulling rice.[32]

By 1600 the Zaan had become an industrial zone which included sailcloth-weaving and cutting which employed as many as 1,000 people, whale fisheries (employing 2,000–2,700), the baking of ship's bread, compass-making, block- and mast-making, rope-making and certain metal trades such as nail- and anchor-making.[33] These industries developed into what we would today call an industry cluster in which companies draw competitive strength from related producers. The free-flow of information between them made it easier to innovate and improve the quality of their products. It also made it easier to gain access to supplies. In the process, the Dutch were building an industrial base with the most advanced practices.

A vital industry for the development of trade was the ship-building industry, and it too enjoyed improvements in efficiency. As the industry grew, specialization became more common, and some builders began to contract out work such as mast-making and block-making. Builders began to standardize components, a practice common in modern factories but in the seventeenth century it was a huge leap in efficiency. A relatively standard ship design with some standardized parts reduced the cost of ships and repairs, giving Dutch merchant shippers an advantage when competing with the Spanish and Portuguese. As a result of these changes, and the introduction of labour-saving devices, the ship-building wharf changed from a workshop to something more like a modern factory.

Another boost to the maritime trades came from policies on the Iberian peninsula. In Spain and Portugal, the reconquista mentality frequently gave rise to bouts of anti-Semitism. Many Jews expelled from Portugal fled north to Amsterdam. These immigrants possessed productive and commercial talent, wealth and international financial connections with which the Dutch could exploit longer sea voyages. In the early 1590s, trade with West Africa and the Caribbean was launched.[34] At first, growth was slow, but this changed in 1598 when Spain placed an embargo on Dutch ships visiting Spanish and Portuguese ports. Philip II of Spain was concerned that commercial expansion was strengthening the ability of the rebel provinces to keep fighting against him. The Dutch had previously got many of their foreign products through Lisbon, such as salt that was needed for the herring trade. Given the alternative of bankruptcy, the Dutch were forced to enter the long-distance trades and obtain colonial products at source. The political war that had been going on for three decades now became a commercial war. The Dutch aimed straight for the Spanish and Portuguese offshore bases, with the intention of usurping their trade and destroying them.[35]

Long-haul ocean shipping is not easy, even for a nation that possessed a large number of sailors and strong ships. Dutch experience had been limited to trade close to Europe, and they knew little about the Atlantic, the routes to Asia, and monsoon wind systems. Nor did they understand trading behaviour in the East. To make matters worse, the northern novices faced formidable competition from the experienced Iberian sailors.

Gaining the necessary skills was aided by the fact that a number of Dutchmen had sailed in the Iberian fleets including Jan Hughen van Linschoten who was born in Enkhuizen, a town closely connected with the herring industry. At the age of seventeen, he went to live in Seville where his two half-brothers worked as merchants. As their apprentice, he learnt Spanish and the rules of business and, after eight months, went to Portugal where he learnt the art of merchandizing. In 1583 he acquired a post as clerk to the archbishop of Goa and sailed on the *San Salvador* to the Indies where he gained great insight into the Portuguese maritime tradition.[36]

Linschoten spent five years at Goa where he wrote about his experience and incorporated extracts from Portuguese historical, geographic and ethical works that he had access to. When he returned home, his writings were published, complete with sailing directions to the East. The book became compulsory reading for all captains sailing to the East. Linschoten advised the first Dutch fleet to the Indies on the nautical secrets of the Portuguese. However, he suggested that, when going to the Spice Islands, they should not sail north to Goa as the Portuguese did, but sail straight east. Although this meant a longer time at sea, they could use the prevailing westerly winds to get to the islands without having to rely on the patterns of the monsoons. In this way, the Dutch had a shorter and less costly route that provided them with a dramatic strategic advantage over the Portuguese.

Another who helped raise Dutch skills was Plancius, a minister in the Dutch Reformed Church from the southern Netherlands. In 1585, he fled north to escape persecution where he translated and published Spanish and Portuguese *rutters*, sailing directions and maps. Plancius was paid 500 guilders to provide pilot navigation methods for the fleet that left in 1600. He was also responsible for the quality of charts and navigation instruments they used.[37]

Despite his advice, the first fleet to the Indies suffered from inexperience and poor management. Of the four ships and 289 men that left, only three ships and eighty-nine men returned.[38] However, the modest cargo of pepper they brought with them more than covered their costs and inspired others to follow in their wake. The following year, five companies were created, sending out twenty-two ships. The Dutch quickly moved up the learning curve and within only six years of the creation of the first company, Dutch trade to Asia had already outstripped that of Portugal.[39]

The large number of Dutch companies that initially appeared trading to the East Indies created unhealthy competition. At Indonesian ports, they would bid against each other and raise the prices of their supplies, which dramatically reduced profits. In 1602, after the political intervention of the States General and Prince Maurice, a merger was agreed and the Dutch East India Company (Vereeigde Oost-Indische

Compagnie or VOC) was created. Seventeen directors (Heren XVII) sat on the company's board representing the various regions contributing to the original trade. The government gave the company a charter that included the right to attack the power, prestige and revenues of Spain and Portugal and the company soon became a national champion in the Asian trade and was highly successful, growing to become the largest commercial organization in the world, with a payroll that at times included 40,000 employees.

The amalgamation of many companies into one resulted in a company very different to anything that had existed before.[40] The company owned not one vessel but a fleet, and combined shipping, freighting and ship-building under one corporate structure. The trade with Asia placed special demands on the organization. Normally, each voyage undertaken by a trading company was financed separately with a different list of shareholders. However, the large scale of operations, long distances and lengthy times voyaging from Asia to Europe meant a more permanent commitment to the trade. As a consequence, in 1612 the company changed to providing a permanent capital base committed perpetually to the enterprise. Shareholders bought shares in the company and this covered all voyages.

The first Dutch voyages to the Indian Ocean proceeded by trial and error, gradually building up a store of knowledge and expertise. Ships' logs from these early voyages were studied and, in 1617, the company issued its first sailing orders. By 1627 they had more than mastered the routes and the Amsterdam charter of the company published extensive instructions. With some modification and improvement, these instructions steered Dutch navigators for the seventeenth and eighteenth centuries.[41]

In many ways the company's activities resembled those of today's multinationals in the way it utilized information to help plan and coordinate activities in various nations. From the company's regional

HQ at Batavia, in modern-day Indonesia, the company's international activities were monitored as if by an enormous radar screen.[42] From Japan to Arabia, trading depots and factories sent reports on the political situation and market trends. The information was assessed, along with the performances of the various trading posts, and was used to help prepare plans for the following year. Finance, shipping and other resources would be allocated to the various company activities, depending on the potential growth suggested by the gathered information. Before making purchases in Asia, it would take into account European stock levels and sales. This avoided situations of over or under supply, something only a company with integrated facilities and information networks could do.

The VOC also reduced another problem, which had long plagued the Portuguese, where agents in Asia enriched their pockets at the crown's expense, a problem contributed to by a lack of a decent financial reporting system. The Portuguese had not adopted the double-entry accounting system introduced into Europe by the Italians. The Dutch did not make this mistake. Jan Pietersz Coen, who later became governor general of the company, had himself studied double-entry accounting in Italy as a youth. The Dutch system was not foolproof, yet it provided information for decision-making and pricing far superior to that of their rivals.

The corporate structure of the VOC allowed management to make decisions at many different organization levels, providing flexibility on which a vast network of trading operations could be built. At the various factories around Asia, staff would deal with local merchants, order stock, maintain the warehoused stock, inspect quality of stock and maintain accounting records. During the busy season, employees were occupied with loading and dispatching of ships, though during the off-season there would not be so much to do.[43] In a busy entrepôt such as Batavia, the staff kept regular office hours from seven to eleven in the morning and one to six in the afternoon. However, in a more remote port, life could be exceptionally dull waiting for the next ship to arrive. For example, in Ceylon the Dutchmen were described as beginning their day with gin and tobacco and ending it with tobacco and gin.

In the Atlantic Ocean, the organization of Dutch trade was very different from the VOC's operations in Asia, and was dominated by small-scale joint stock companies. In the early days, there were few Dutch merchants big enough to finance ocean-going ventures, which meant that small merchants would have to pool resources and share the ownership of ships and trading ventures. As a consequence, ownership of merchant ships was spread between timber dealers, ship-builders, sail-makers, brewers, millers and such like, in shares of $\frac{1}{16}$, $\frac{1}{32}$ or $\frac{1}{64}$.[44] A company would be based around a single ship, each ship having its own list of shareholders. Although one person would not by themself own a ship, as people became richer they might have shares in a number of different ships. This spread had the added benefit of reducing risk and consequently encouraged investment.

These young Dutch companies invigorated the Atlantic trade with their youthful energy in contrast to the Spanish who showed little originality. Spanish trade had become concentrated into a handful of merchant houses that were members of the privileged Consulado. Safe behind their protective status, this small group charged high prices and restricted their shipments to goods they could sell without difficulty. They were slow to exploit new products such as tobacco, a commodity that became fashionable under the Dutch and the English. Because the state was dependent on credit provided by these rich merchants and because the state itself possessed monopolies in salt, mercury and other products, it felt no need to break up this monopoly. Spanish trade persisted with tried and tested methods.

Dutch enterprises in the Atlantic were both young and competitive, albeit vulnerable. Operating in places like West Africa, Brazil, Venezuela and North America left them exposed to aggressive political and military action from Spain and Portugal.[45] This vulnerability gave rise to the suggestion that a single chartered company be created, like the VOC, with sufficient military strength to defend their trade. However, when a twelve-year truce was signed with Spain in 1609, the concept was shelved. When the truce expired in 1621, the idea was raised again and the West India Company (WIC) was created, amalgamating smaller companies into a monopoly. Many experienced investors stayed away from this new company out of fear that the military effort of battling both Spain and Portugal in the near Atlantic would be a harder task, and more costly, than that faced by the VOC in Asia.[46]

The West India Company was never as successful as its eastern counterpart. Its creation in 1621 was not welcomed by those independent merchant houses trading in the Atlantic and it would be thirty years before the company offered anything new.[47] Much of its time was devoted to military activities that undermined its profitability. By the time peace came it had been forced to sell off many of its monopoly privileges. It is questionable whether the monopoly structure that was so valuable in the riskier Asian trade was as useful in the Atlantic. The defensive abilities of the WIC were only important during the war with Spain, after which smaller shipping companies could operate in a lower-risk environment but with greater flexibility. It was also more difficult for the WIC to maintain its monopoly in the Atlantic, which was more accessible and contained fewer risks than the more distant Asian trades.

The Dutch introduced a number of other institutions that facilitated the growth in trade.[48] In 1609, the Wisselbank (Exchange Bank) was founded in imitation of the Giro Bank at Venice. Its function was to control money changing and settle bills of exchange. The Chamber of Insurance was set up by the Amsterdam City Council to resolve disputes and increase confidence by registering and processing policies. In 1614 the Amsterdam Loan Bank was created to help finance trade. These Amsterdam financial institutions undeniably helped bolster Dutch trade by providing a resource and degree of specialization that none of their rivals possessed. In lowering the costs of obtaining finance, the institutions gave the Dutch lower costs than their rivals.

Vital to the operation of the market was information and, by the standards of the day, Amsterdam overflowed with information.[49] Ships brought in reports of produce availability and demand from around the world. Early newspapers were established: the *Amsterdamsche Courant* in 1618, the *Tydinghen* in 1619 and the *Oprechte Haarlemsche Courant* in 1667. These publications were complemented by the intelligence networks of merchants and companies that gave early advice on market conditions.

Another vital institution was the bourse, the forerunner of the modern stock exchange. The bourse was a natural evolution from the waterfront markets that all ports possessed. It brought under one roof a place where deals could be negotiated, finance arranged, and shipping and commodity news gathered. The Amsterdam bourse, built in 1611, was arguably the nerve centre of the whole economy.[50] It was a building of arcades around a central courtyard in which merchants and brokers gathered and traded literally in everything known to that society. The scope of Dutch commerce enabled the bourse to provide more investment options than any exchange in other nations, from commodities like pepper to shares in companies like the Dutch East India Company.

Amsterdam became an entrepôt with economic advantages similar to that of Surat in the Indian Ocean. The ease with which commodities could be found and exchanged dramatically reduced the costs of doing business and added another factor to the efficiency of the Dutch economy. New financial securities were born at the Amsterdam bourse. The practice of selling stock before ships arrived in port led to the development of a futures market. As can be expected, when wealth is reliant on future outcomes, much of the business conducted at the bourse was nothing short of gambling and the bourse gained a reputation as an undignified bazaar. Lords who participated in share trading refused to set foot in the place, preferring to use the services of professional brokers.[51]

An example of the instability of the market can be seen in the tulip crash of 1637. Tulips were an imported luxury brought back from Turkey, becoming in the 1620s an unrivalled flower in fashion. Initially, the trade was in the hands of gentlemen horticulturalists and their estate gardeners, and their intense interest led to a rapid increase in the price of the bulbs. This increase in price was noted by non-professionals and in the beginning of 1634 speculators entered the market. At first their interest was only in the rarer bulbs but, by November 1636, even the more common varieties were caught in the frenzy.

The flowers readily lent themselves to a futures market because of their seasonality. Buying in winter for a spring delivery was an acceptable practice and in 1636 a formal futures market for the plant appeared. Prices began spiralling before one bulb had begun to sprout. Orders for deliveries were like gold as investors had their eyes on the coming spring and the expectations of huge profits. In January 1637 prices for bulbs increased twentyfold. One bulb sold for 5,500 guilders, equivalent to US$74,000 at today's gold prices.

As prices doubled and trebled by the week for a stock still unseen, authorities became concerned that speculative fever might be getting out of hand. Complaints were also voiced by genuine tulip fanciers disgusted at the corruption of their once passive hobby. It seemed official intervention was just around the corner. There is some uncertainty as to whether the final crash came as a result of official intervention or vice versa but, needless to say, a hint is sometimes all that is needed. On 3 February 1637, the crash ploughed profits into the earth.

As the tulip mania illustrates, many of the activities on the bourse resembled nothing more than a speculative circus as investors manipulated the market to their own ends. Yet the bourse served a valuable function in making it easier to raise finance and was indispensable to the operations of the city's trade. It was one of many innovations with which the Dutch had built a wonderfully efficient economy, producing goods and services of high value and low cost. With new ways of creating wealth, it challenged the might of Spain and Portugal.

5

CRISIS IN SPAIN AND
A DUTCH GOLDEN AGE

The empire in the East is like a ship that is sinking. Everybody shouts we are foundering, but nobody pumps the water out.[1]

When the Dutch and English first entered the overseas trades, Spain and Portugal stood supreme. The Spanish and Portuguese had built a competitive advantage based on their superior knowledge of wind systems and routes. They complemented these advantages with investments throughout Asia and America, supportive government policies and efficient organization. The combined superiority in skills, infrastructure and reputation created an aura of supremacy that further protected them from any challenges. However, the Dutch and English had undergone a process of catch-up, gaining skills and experience needed to compete. Superiority in reputation and experience no longer presented barriers to new competitors entering the industry. The Iberians would never be able to maintain a monopoly that spanned the world once other nations had caught up with the necessary capabilities. To protect their monopolies, they would have to revert to military strength. Many years of war followed but these battles should not be seen as just a battle for trade. They were part of a wider political play-off that once again reflected the *reconquista* mentality. The Spanish king had been elected Holy Roman Emperor, responsible for lands in northern and eastern Europe. He took to this role a desire to promote Catholicism and defeat the forces of

125

Protestantism. This entangled Spain in a series of battles that drained the Spanish treasury. As early as 1598, practically all sources of revenue were mortgaged and American revenues pledged in advance.[2] This deprived the nation of resources with which it might have been able to defend its shipping from up and coming imitators, the English and the Dutch.

Not only were the Iberian nations entrapped by old 'rational' beliefs – beliefs that had steered them to success in the past – they were also entrapped by a sense of their own achievements.[3] They became arrogant and developed a contempt for other nations. In Spanish America, the leaders of colonial society regarded themselves as the heirs of the conquistadors. The Portuguese were also convinced that as descendants of the conquistadors who built their empire they were vastly superior to the upstart merchants from the north, however wealthy they might be. This sense of identity with the past, and resulting cultural arrogance formed a barrier to internal progression. It masked the fact that Spanish tactics and organization had, by the seventeenth century, become static and out of date. The Portuguese were worse than the Spaniards. 'They practised no tactics other than a disorderly charge to the war cry of St James and at them! (*Santiago e a elles!*)'.[4]

The Iberians also persisted with their old formulas for success in naval operations. The Spanish maintained the Mediterranean tradition of using artillery to hit and disorganize the enemy just before boarding, while the English, who were limited in manpower, relied exclusively on manoeuvring by the wind and delivering an artillery broadside. While the Spanish built galleons with a forecastle that made it easier to board an enemy ship, the English produced vessels that were very light and very well gunned.[5] The Dutch defeated the Portuguese for exactly the same reason. A contemporary observer recorded:

The Dutch vessels which are handier to manoeuvre by the wind, overcome the Portuguese galleons very easily. The Dutch can take to flight when the wind is favourable to the enemy and attack when the enemy is low wind. To the Dutch any small wind is enough, while for the Portuguese vessels a half gale is necessary for movement.[6]

The Iberians were unable to maintain their monopoly through military means and had to accept that new competitors were entering the market.

The main cargo on which Iberian trade was based was bullion. The volume of bullion arriving in European ports had created an inflation that reduced the value of silver. Consequently it became less profitable to operate the New World mines and production was cut back. From the decade 1641–50 through to 1671–80, the mining districts of New Mexico experienced a 21 per cent recession.[7] With less cargo, Spanish shipping declined. The number of registered ships crossing the Atlantic fell from 1,363 in 1621–9 to 722 in 1640–9. Other exports also declined, for example hides fell from a peak of 134,000 in the early 1580s to 8,000 in the late 1660s.

In theory, the Dutch should not have had access to the ports of Spanish America from where the bullion and other products came. However, the rules that the Spanish had introduced to reduce costs provided them with a window of opportunity. In particular, the Spanish fleet system made it easy for foreign smuggling to occur. The fleet system was introduced as a rational way of reducing piracy, but it totally ignored colonial desires for supplies. The fleet system meant ships arrived very infrequently. Consequently, colonial Americans were very receptive to Dutch and English boats arriving at their shores loaded with goods. Smugglers provided South Americans with a larger variety of goods at more reasonable prices than those available through the Spanish merchant houses.[8] The locals were not going to refuse them the right to trade and gain bullion.

From Asia, the key commodity carried in Portuguese ships was pepper, filling 65–89 per cent of the cargo space in carracks returning from the East.[9] When the Dutch and English East India companies entered the Indian Ocean with their lower-cost organizational structures, they provided further competition that helped fuel declining prices. The Amsterdam exchange reported that prices for pepper declined from an index of 145.5 early in the seventeenth century to 57.3 in 1680–4. Even the sale of protection to Indian shippers suffered from saturation as the Dutch and English became competing suppliers in the seventeenth century.

With the saturation of key markets, further growth would only come by the opening of new economic paths, and the Dutch put their faith in industrial advances. Through technical innovation and an increased use of machinery the Dutch achieved advances across the economy. These included textile machinery, copper stills, presses, multiple blade timber saws and grinding machines for processing coffee. In the Zaan industrial zone, new style paper mills appeared around 1670, using much heavier and more expensive equipment that produced a smooth, white, high quality paper. The Netherlands became the technical research laboratory of the Western world.[10] The new technologies created exportable products whose competitive advantage was not quantity, but quality.

The Spanish, on the other hand, had no industrial base equal to that in the Netherlands. In the early years, Spanish ships had carried some manufactured goods to South America in return for raw materials. However, Spanish-Americans eventually established their own production of manufactured goods, decreasing their need for Spanish imports. The imports now wanted by the immigrants were high quality foreign goods.[11] Some of these would be smuggled to America in Dutch and English ships, while others would come via Spain, imported through the connections of the Consulado.

The Dutch ability to combine industrial and maritime expertise created a new wave of economic prosperity along the Atlantic seaboards. By contrast, the Iberians seemed to have a contempt for manual arts particularly given the industrial crafts were dominated by Jews and Muslims. This contempt has been described as the principal cause of Spanish economic decline.[12] However, industrial advance was inhibited by a number of legacies of their past success, in particular the high cost of domestic production. Spain's wealth had made it a high-cost nation. So bad was the inflation that foreigners could import Spanish wool, create finished woollen products that they would send back to Spain and still make a profit. The only way to combat the rising prices was to offer higher quality, but this was undermined by a feeling of easy money and contempt for manual arts.[13]

In both Spain and Portugal, the social order was characterised by social values that discouraged productive investment. Money once earned was not invested in industry. Successful merchants preferred to buy their way into the nobility. Many took the opportunity to raise their status by putting their sons into the Church or army, and became major landowners. Their wealth went into buildings, jewellery and other accoutrements of status. Alternatively, it could be invested in unproductive personal loans and government bonds (*juros*) that paid higher interest rates than productive investments in agriculture or industry.[14]

The Spanish had once led the way in ship design, but it was foreigners who were now producing the best ships. Spanish shipwrights introduced few design improvements during the years 1590–1630.[15] The government had attempted to upgrade its shipping to the quality coming out of Dutch shipyards. It stressed the incorporation of the new expertise that was changing the face of ship-building in the north. For example, Thome Cano, an early seventeenth-century expert, stated that 'it is extremely necessary that the builder or master be an Arithmetician and know how to judge tonnage so that he might apply the rules to construction'.[16] However, Spanish ship-builders did not possess the mathematical expertise to do this. Incorporating scientific principles was a radical departure from the normal way a master built, which was through experience and observation. Consequently, ship-builders stuck to construction methods in which they had capabilities, and restricted themselves to small refinements. As a contemporary writer noted, Spain was suffering 'from making its ships without rule or reason, but by the eye and at the caprice of each builder'.[17]

Technical advance in the Dutch economy was aided by high levels of education. The Reformed Church that dominated the Netherlands insisted that its followers should be able to read the bible.[18] Church schools provided the Netherlands with the highest literacy rate in Europe, if not the world, an accomplishment assisted by the establishment of five universities between 1575 and 1636. Maritime expansion also increased the quality and quantity of knowledge available to the Dutch.[19] The literature on travel and voyages became the best available in Europe, a lead expressed in the navigating manuals and atlases emanating from Dutch print shops. In all the major seaports a number of teachers taught the science of navigation to aspiring young navigators. Some were old sailors drawing on their experience, while others were experts on mathematics and theory.

By contrast, the Spanish and Portuguese suffered from scientific and technical retardation. The Jesuit education system, which had once been the best of its day, became entrapped by formalism. When the Jesuit education system was born, its founders analysed the best existing universities and developed an innovative study plan. Once adopted, the education system stopped evolving.[20] Teachers and pupils were discouraged from advancing propositions that were not grounded in Catholic orthodoxy. While the rest of Europe was experiencing an intellectual ferment led by Galileo, Descartes, Newton and others, the Jesuits kept Portugal and Spain from this cumulative advancement of science.

The extent of the decline made it apparent that change was needed. While there was consensus on the need for change, agreement on the cure was harder to come by.[21] A number of writers in the 1620s wondered whether the Portuguese lost their empire in the East because they had not become proper merchants, driven by commercial logic or, alternatively, in becoming more like merchants, they had lost the knightly spirit that earned them the empire in the first place.[22]

The call for reform intensified when Philip IV (1621–63) came to the throne. He appointed the Count-Duke of Olivares as first minister, someone who brought with him a mandate for change. Lamenting the state of Spanish technology, Olivares embarked on a reform programme. However, he soon encountered many of the obstacles we associate with organizational reform today: uncertainty, distrust, and opposition by vested stakeholders. To improve the state of the trade in the Atlantic, attempts were made to reform the Consulado and Casa de la Contracón which had become riddled with corruption. However, the crown was dependent on Consulado members for revenue. This relationship of dependence weakened the power of the state to effect change and the inquiry into its operations was dropped in return for a fine of 206,000 ducats.[23]

Olivares also attempted to reform the navy. His naval reforms included a vigorous ship-building programme that played some part in the defeat of the Dutch in Brazil. But, once again, many of his proposals encountered institutional resistance based on the existing value system and vested interests. For example, he tried to break the aristocracy's hold on the highest positions of naval command. In 1624 he removed a top aristocrat from the position of captain-general and abolished the system of naval training for sons of the nobility. (The training consisted of little seamanship.) However, when Olivares fell from power, the system was reintroduced.

Not all Olivares's projects failed. The defence he organized in South America was highly successful. The Portuguese recovered northern Brazil and the Dutch were left only with Guyana on the northern coast. Consequently, the Dutch did not achieve the same success in the Atlantic that they achieved in Asia and, in 1648, they signed a peace treaty with Spain.

In the peace that followed, Dutch trading activities prospered. They developed the Caribbean island of Curaçao as a trading depot and gateway to South America, particularly for slaves, which the Dutch brought from their forts in West Africa. In Asia, the Dutch took over Portuguese forts, conquered Ceylon and south India and thereby obtained a monopoly in cinnamon and a large control of the pepper trade. In Japan, where the Portuguese were expelled because of the religious activities of the Jesuits, the Dutch claimed another monopoly. With elephants from Ceylon, Japanese copper and Spanish silver, they had the commodities by which they captured the Bengal trade. By 1648 the Dutch were indisputably the greatest trading nation in Europe. By contrast, the Iberian wave of economic growth had come to an end, unable to adopt the innovations of the Dutch.

When the Gujaratis first encountered the Dutch and English in the first years of the seventeenth century, they were unsure how to respond, and were reluctant to upset the Portuguese by trading with the new arrivals. Nor did they want to lose any of their own trade to the northern ships. The early period was therefore characterized by animosity. However, by the 1630s the Mughal court was convinced that, if kept within their bounds, the trade of the Dutch and English companies was beneficial to Surat. Although they might provide some competition for local shippers, they also provided access to European markets for local products. They were also good customers for local merchants needing credit and other trade facilities.

In the early years, the northern Europeans participated in the Indian Ocean trade as just another competing group. They offered nothing new in terms of commercial expertise. In fact, in the Indian Ocean, Europeans were poor relations, as borne out in the amount of capital invested. To give a comparison, in the 1620s the Dutch had 500,000 rupees (Rs5,00,000) invested in all of India. By contrast, some Gujarati ships trading to the Red Sea in the late sixteenth century were worth more than Rs10,00,000 each.[24]

No one illustrates the superior wealth of the Indians more than Virji Vora. With an estate of approximately US$107,000,000 in today's terms (Rs80,00,000),[25] Vora in the seventeenth century was the richest man in Asia and possibly the world. Virji Vora is believed to have been born to a well-established Jain family around 1594–5.[26] At the age of twenty-five, he had become a prominent merchant in Surat, and by 1625 the English were calling him the 'prime merchant of this towne'. He had agents throughout northern India and international interests stretching from Malaya and Sumatra in the south to Gombroom and Mocha in the north. He dominated the pepper trade with Malabar, traded with South-East Asia and was a major ship-owner.[27]

The extent to which Vora dominated commerce can be gleaned from the English East India Company's records. These state that Vora (and another merchant) were 'prodigious moneyed men, who having always vast treasure ready in house, doe esteeme it safer invested in solid unperishable commodities though they get but 4 and 6 per cent by them, then either cash or interest.' The English were often looking to him for a loan, but Vora was a merchant, not a shroff, and was not always tempted by the interest he might earn, much to English displeasure. 'Virgee Vorah is the only master of it [money at Surat], and he is so close fisted that for the consideration of no interest cannot yet be procured of him.'[28]

Vora frequently used his enormous financial clout in the age-old strategy of cornering the market. For example, in 1625 the English tried to buy pepper from Vora but baulked at the outrageous price he charged. To get around his monopoly, they sent their broker to the Deccan to buy pepper, only to find that Vora had already outbid him. The English had no choice but to deal with him.[29]

Vora freely played the Dutch and English East India Companies off against each other and both learnt that they could not afford to offend him. The English found they were dependent on the agents of Virji Vora for goods and were frequently in debt to him. This dependence was such that he could force the English to carry his goods on their ships.[30]

The area where Europeans did have supremacy was in their naval and military technology. In the 1640s, the Dutch attempted to impose their naval power on Gujarat by forbidding ships leaving their ports from sailing to South-East Asia. The Mughals retaliated on land against the Dutch factories. Europeans soon learned that as they increased their land investments in the East Indies, they became more exposed to Mughal control and the possibility of having their assets seized if they harmed local shippers. So Dutch molesting stopped and Indian shipping grew significantly from the middle of the century.[31]

The one trade in the Indian Ocean on which the Europeans did have a significant impact was spice. The Dutch, like the Portuguese before them, sought a monopoly in the spice trade but were far more successful.[32] Through a combination of ruthlessness and superior military strength they seized the key strategic assets in this trade, the Spice Islands of Indonesia. In 1605, the VOC conquered the Portuguese fort on Ambon, thereby gaining control of clove production on the nearby islands. They then imposed treaties on the ruler of Ternate, Tidore and Bican by which they were allowed periodically to destroy the young clove trees in their area in order to reduce the supply and maintain their monopoly. Similar treaties were enforced on the Banda Islands, the only areas in the world where nutmeg and mace were produced. When locals tired to resist these treaties, the VOC, under the leadership of Jan Pietersz Coen, reduced the population of approximately 15,000 to several hundred. Although it took time to plug all the holes in the monopoly, by the 1630s and 1640s the Dutch could claim complete predominance in the waters around the Spice Islands.[33] However, as valuable as spices were to the Europeans, they were only one of many commodities exchanged in the Indian Ocean and Dutch power did not extend outside Indonesia for many years.

From time to time, Europeans dominated particular markets, but on the whole, trade in the Indian Ocean remained in the hands of Indian ship-owning merchants.[34] Gujarati shipping was still firmly based on key sources of competitive advantage: flexible organization, excellent skills, light mobile ships and close relationships with the markets and produce of the Mughal empire. These gave Gujarati shippers the strength with which they could repel competitors. It was a golden period for Indian maritime trade and textiles.[35]

The focus of Gujarat's maritime trade changed during the seventeenth century. Gujarati merchants cut down on the long-distance trading to South-East Asia and they abandoned their settlements in South-East Asian ports. This no doubt was contributed to by the

Dutch seizure of Malacca and the Spice Islands. However, opportunities for growth were occurring to the west, a reflection of the development of Mughal power in the west and the economic directions of the empire. This included the growing Red Sea trade and the political stability in the Ottoman and Safavid empires of Turkey and Persia which were contributing to an increase in trade.[36]

While Gujaratis basked in the increased trading opportunities provided by shorter journeys to the west, they were cutting down on long-distance trade at a time when, outside the Indian Ocean, long-distance ocean routes provided the greatest potential. These fast-growing routes were being seized by the Europeans.

In the China Sea, the arrival of the Dutch did not dramatically change the nature of trade and the Chinese retained their pre-eminent position. One key contribution was the development of Batavia as a base for South-East Asian trade. Batavia was the Dutch headquarters in what is now Indonesia. The Dutch pursued a policy of encouraging Chinese vessels to visit the port in order to exploit the Chinese trading networks in the China Sea. The Dutch hoped to gain a monopoly in the south-east, not through its shipping but through the port, and to do this, they welcomed Chinese shipping.[37]

The Dutch replaced the Portuguese in the Japanese trade. The Portuguese had been ousted by the Japanese government for their Christian evangelizing and were replaced by the Dutch who took a more secular approach to trade. However, even in Japan, it was the Chinese who dominated, particularly after the 1630s when the Japanese government restricted all Japanese from sailing overseas. From that point, the Chinese came to handle the vast majority of Japan's foreign trade.

Although the Chinese still dominated regional trade, some warning signs were beginning to appear. Chinese shipping was losing its advantage in shipping technology. Dutch vessels sailing from Batavia to Nagasaki routinely took less time than the Chinese.[38] European fully rigged ships could complete three voyages between Canton and Batavia per year in comparison with only one for the junks. Compared with the new designs coming from Europe, junks were unwieldy and could sail in a smaller range of conditions. They did not attempt to tack against the wind or sail at unseasonable times, but simply sailed with the reliable monsoon winds. This put a limit on the growth prospects of Chinese shipping, so we might expect the Chinese to adopt European construction methods. However, this did not happen.

One reason why the Chinese did not copy European designs may be that they lacked the opportunity to see how European ships were built. A second reason may simply be that they provided formidable competition without it. The Chinese could still out-trade Europeans in the Far East, even with inferior ships. They had greater experience of the regional trade and knowledge in handling regional products. They also kept a strong control of their own trade. European ships could only trade at Canton under much difficulty and with the burden of very high tariffs. Another advantage for the Chinese was their peaceful record of trading which stood in sharp contrast to the aggression of the Europeans. As a consequence, Asian rulers raised tariffs and other obstacles against European shipping, while the Chinese were freed of such constraints.[39]

Although Chinese traders experienced a number of difficulties over the following century, including a government ban in 1717–27 and a massacre of their community in Batavia, they always proved themselves to be flexible to the changing fortunes thrust upon them. The Chinese continued to dominate East Asian trade. Up until 1842, they were principal carriers not just for Japan and their own country, but also Vietnam, Siam and Cambodia, as well as a substantial proportion of other nations in the region.

6

THE WEALTH OF THE DUTCH

Amsterdam has arisen through the hand of God to the peak of
prosperity and greatness . . . The whole world stands amazed at its
riches and from east and west, north and south, they come to
behold it.[1]

Melchior Fokken

By the mid-seventeenth century, Amsterdam had become a global
centre of trade. Ships sailed to and from Africa, South America, Asia
and the Baltic, building a world trade system based on Amsterdam.
Spices brought from Asia were exchanged at Amsterdam with ships
sailing to the Mediterranean or South America. In return, vessels
carrying silver from the Americas could make a return trip with
spices and other eastern goods in their hulls. In this way, the trade
routes complemented each other and reinforced the success of other
parts of the economic system.

Products brought in on the nation's ships provided the basis of a
number of growing industries.[2] Sugar imports provided the raw
material for refineries and, by 1662, half the sugar refineries in Europe
were based in Amsterdam (approximately fifty), with another dozen
or so located at Rotterdam, Middelburg, Delft and Gouda. In the
Zaan industrial belt, imported ingredients were manufactured into
processed foods, including biscuits, spiced cakes, chocolate, mustard
and exotic liquors made from tropical and sub-tropical fruits. Imported
tobacco from America also stimulated local industry. Tobacco arriving

138

in Dutch ships sourced a tobacco finishing industry in which local and American leaves were blended to create a cheap flavoursome product. By 1700 twenty-three tobacco-spinning and blending establishments were located at Amsterdam. An offshoot of the tobacco industry was the manufacture of clay pipes, which became the main industry at Gouda. Imports also stimulated the diamond industry. Imported diamonds were processed by Sephardic and Ashkenazi Jews who developed intricate skills that were not easy for would-be competitors to replicate, giving the Dutch a clear advantage.

Another industry related to the growth of shipping and trade was delftware, a ceramic product made in imitation of Chinese blue porcelain. A window of opportunity to enter this trade opened when the VOC had trouble obtaining supplies due to political upheaval in China. In the absence of what had been overwhelming competition, local producers took the opportunity to develop their productive skills and seize the market.

This revolution in trade and production could not occur without associated changes in consumer taste. However, Europeans were not always quick to appreciate the new products unloaded at their ports. Imports such as tea and coffee were hard pushed to break the long established tastes of beer- and wine-drinkers, especially given the high price of the imported goods. When coffee originally arrived in Europe, it was seen as possessing medicinal properties. Coffee was the healthiest drink in the world, according to the writer Blankaart who drank no fewer than twelve cups a day, and especially fine for staving off 'mouldy joints' and scurvy. Yet it took some time to catch on and early market growth was slow.

It was not until the 1690s that coffee became a profitable market for the VOC. In the early eighteenth century, coffee clubs were established where aficionados could drink a brew spiced with cloves, cinnamon and ginger, and sweetened with honey.[3] A rapid growth in demand created a scramble for supplies from their source at Mocha. To relieve this situation, the Dutch decided a new source of supply was needed and established new plantations in Java. The VOC were acting like a modern international, regulating production in one part of the world to satisfy demand in another.

Tea and tobacco were also claimed to have medicinal properties and this helped their growth in popularity. Tobacco became very popular. Travellers of the day commented on the habit that filled every tavern with a smoky hue. The Frenchman Grosley claimed that the fumes from travelling barges was so bad that it drove foxes from their lairs as they passed.[4]

The strongest advocate for tea was the physician Cornelis Bontekoe who in 1678 wrote *Treatise on Tea: The Most Excellent Herb (Tractaat van het excellenste kruyd thee)*. The treatise suggested that tea was a panacea for ailments. Bontekoe suggested a minimum of eight to ten cups of tea a day should be drunk for the good of one's health and 50 to 200 cups was not unreasonable. He was such a strong promoter of tea that it was suggested he was in the pay of the Dutch East India Company. However, he genuinely seems to believe what he wrote. He followed this advice so strongly that in 1696, it was reported his joints rattled like castanets.[5]

Trade not only changed what people consumed but how they consumed it. With tea and sugar coming into Europe, it was only a matter of time before the two were consumed together, this contrasting with the situation in China where sugar is never put in tea. In the seventeenth century, these items became a sign of status and fashion as only the well-off could afford to consume these exotic imports regularly.

New patterns of production and consumption occurred as the economy expanded. The growing wealth created an upper class with the resources to purchase the imported Turkish carpets, Persian silks and Japanese lacquerware that were now arriving in Dutch ports. For those who could not afford the imported originals, local craftsmen turned out imitation mirrors and lacquer boxes at cheap prices. At Delft, the imitation of Chinese porcelain became an export industry in itself. The city's wealth provided a ready market for painters such as Rembrandt and Jan Steen. Melchior Fokken, who in 1662 published a *Description of the Widely Renowned Merchant City of Amsterdam*, described the most fashionable of addresses:

> the houses are full of priceless ornaments so that they seem more like royal palaces than houses of merchants, many of them with spendid marble and alabaster columns, floors inlaid with gold, and the rooms hung with valuable tapestries or gold- or silver-stamped leather worth many thousands of guilders . . . You will also find in these houses valuable household furnishings like paintings and oriental ornaments and decorations so that the value of all these things is truely inestimable.[6]

The labouring classes also benefited from the rising wealth. They enjoyed a variety in diet that was beyond the reach of their European counterparts. Farmers and fisher-folk could regularly dine on fresh and cured meat, fish, fresh vegetables and fruit, butter, eggs and cheese.[7] Trade and industry provided the working class a life that other parts of Europe could only dream of.

The new economy provided growth on which entrepreneurs could rapidly raise their wealth and social standing. For example, Jan Pietersz Coen was the son of a fishmonger from Twist who learnt double-entry bookkeeping and rose to become the VOC's most successful Governor General. His career illustrates that education and training were becoming more important as tools of social advancement. The same lesson can be seen in the career of Pieter Stuyvesant (whose name graces so many cigarette packets). Stuyvesant was a pastor's son and received a middle-class education before rising to the position of Director General of the WIC (a company whose cargoes included tobacco).

This growth in materialism did not go uncontested, and the Church did not approve of over-indulgence and the new consumer society. It succeeded in imposing some acts of petty suppression. For example, in 1663 the sale of dolls was proclaimed to be 'idolatrous' and a three guilder fine imposed for its violation. In 1607 gingerbread was banned. Some moralists and Calvinist preachers thought some imported foods were dangerous, especially exotic Indian spices whose heady fragrance and pagan origin were likely to lead men away from morality. Brazilian sugar, which found its way into waffles, pancakes, cakes and biscuits, was also suspected of leading men astray. The level of anxieties aroused depended on how exotic the item was, and was fuelled by word of tropical diseases such as beri-beri. The pineapple, with its exotic appearance, was one item singled out as a potential carrier of oriental infections.[8]

Calvinists were also against the vanity and materialism associated with money-making. But these factors were never enough to constitute a strong level of resistance to economic development. Even for the Church, the growing trade presented opportunities, as Dutch expansion came at the expense of the Catholic Portuguese and Spanish. It provided an opportunity to defeat the Antichrist and bring the gospel to distant lands.[9]

Dutch success was not always appreciated across the English Channel. 'I think the Devil Shits Dutchmen,'[10] was the verdict of William Patten, Surveyor of the British Navy. The English were jealous and resentful as the Dutch conquered one market after another. Many in England believed their markets should be protected from Dutch competition. British clothiers were particularly resentful of the Dutch who bought English woollens, finished them in Holland, then sold them as Dutch goods. Even the trading companies were in favour of some sort of protective legislation. The Eastland Company had always played second fiddle to the Dutch in the Baltic, while the Levant Company was watching its trade to Turkey wither under Dutch competition. Even in Britain's own American colonies, Dutch ships deprived the English of tobacco cargoes bound for Europe. The English could not compete with superior Dutch skill in commerce, ship-building and shipping management.

In Dutch eyes, the British were poor losers, unable to match Dutch resourcefulness and technical ingenuity. However, there were serious principles in dispute. For example, the English resented the activities of Dutch fishermen who operated in what they considered their territorial waters. The Dutch naturally refuted any thought of protectionism or claims on the sea. They believed the sea was free to all nations, a *mare liberum*. This notion was championed by Grotius who asked:'Can the vast boundless sea be the appendage of one country alone, and if not the greatest? Can any one have the right to prevent another from bartering with one another?'[11]

As strong as these arguments for free trade and open seas were, they ignored the fact that the Dutch had used military force to protect their monopoly in the Indies. Such hypocrisy is a recurring feature of economic history. The English responded to the situation by proposing an alliance between the two nations. When the Dutch rejected this, the English in 1651 introduced a range of protectionist measures and an economy-wide process of imitation. The government introduced a series of navigation ordinances to restrict English trade to English ships or ships from which the cargo originated. The government also offered export bounties for wheat and other grains, paid only if they were exported in English ships. They made it impossible for foreign ships to compete in these trades. However, the most telling form of assistance was a stinging export duty on coal carried on foreign ships. This was effective in ending Dutch competition.[12]

These Navigation Acts, together with other disputes, formed the grounds on which the two nations went to war. Over the following twenty years, there were three 'Dutch Wars'. English motives in the wars were very clear, as the Duke of Albemarle stated: 'What we want is more of the trade the Dutch now have.'[13] The wars achieved this end. The Dutch colony of New Amsterdam, which had been a notorious loophole in the Navigation Acts, was captured by the English and renamed New York. The English also captured a number of Dutch bulk-carriers which expanded the range of ships in the English fleet. These provided a balance to the strong and defensible English ships that were only superior in the more dangerous long-distance trades.[14]

The wars illustrated the importance of English naval power in cementing English commercial activity in the North Atlantic, a protection without which they would have had trouble competing.[15] With Royal Navy protection, the Navigation Acts gave English shipping a monopoly in the North Atlantic just as population growth in the colonies created a significant market for outward shipping. The colonies also possessed important raw materials for the return voyage. Timber came from the north, while the southern and Caribbean colonies developed plantations from which English ships could transport tobacco, ginger, cotton, indigo and sugar. English shipping entered a period of rapid growth between 1660 and 1689, as London established itself as an entrepôt: importing and re-exporting goods from its colonies to Europe.

Imitation of Dutch techniques occurred in ship-building. In the 1660s, the Navigation Acts were extended to limit the use of foreign-built ships (other than prizes captured in war), hence protecting English ship-builders from imports of Dutch-built fluyts. Dutch ships captured during the Dutch Wars had provided the English with bulk carriers, but as these ships aged and needed replacing ship-owners demanded replacements of a similar quality. Ship-builders were forced to respond to these higher standards of demand and reproduced something resembling the Dutch ships. It was in the northern ports at Whitby and Scarborough where this was most successful, fuelled by a demand for ships to transport coal. The old ship-building centres on the Thames seem to have found it more difficult to change building techniques, given the skills they had built up over time. By contrast, Whitby and Scarborough had not made the same level of investment in old techniques and were unrestrained by the ship-building traditions of the southern ports. This process of adopting Dutch hull design has been described as the main technical development in English ship-building of the early eighteenth century.[16]

Imitation also occurred on the Asian trade routes where the Navigation Acts had less impact. The English created their own East India Company in 1600, after the Dutch established their direct trade with the Spice Islands. The company quickly grew in significance and showed great flexibility, expanding into a number of new cargoes and routes. However, throughout the first half of the seventeenth century, the English East India Company continuously suffered at the hands of the Dutch, who had superior resources and organization. In times when competition reached a level that required an aggressive response, English fleets were always outnumbered. The Dutch could provide local merchants with consistent demand based on regular ship visits.[17] By contrast, there might be up to four years between English visits at an Asian port.

The English also suffered from poor organization. Although all

English voyages to Asia sailed for the same company, in reality each voyage was financed by different groups of subscribers. Consequently, each voyage paid its profits out to different people and calculated its profit separately. The result was intense inter-group rivalry and a lack of cooperation between voyages. For example, for some years the company had two groups of factors at Bantam, one representing the company's sixth voyage which left England in 1610, the other representing the eighth voyage from the following year. Not only did this double the necessary expenses, but also the factors would compete for goods, bidding up the price. This dramatically affected profit levels.

In 1657 the English company reorganized in imitation of the Dutch model. However, it was still less rigidly controlled than the VOC. The EIC allowed its crew and citizens based in Asia the right to engage in inter-Asian trade as long as its own interests were not affected.[18] Initially, this involved clandestine loading of private goods on company ships but some started operating as private traders, chartering or buying locally owned ships. In time, these shippers began carrying cargoes for Asian merchants, competing as equals in the Asian markets. English trade in Asia now operated on two levels: an overseeing company, which provided stability, political security and some degree of cooperation, as well as a flexible private trade. After the reorganization, English trade grew dramatically. From 1640 to 1690, sales volumes grew from practically nil to 3.4 million pesos, while the Dutch company only grew from 3.2 to 3.9 million.[19]

The dominant figure in the East India Company in the last quarter of the eighteenth century was Sir Josiah Child. Born in 1630, Child was the son of a London merchant, who provided him with an apprenticeship in the conduct of trade. Josiah Child's own business activities started in Portsmouth where he amassed a fortune providing victuals to the navy. His brother served in India, and no doubt contributed to Josiah's interest in the East India Company. Child began buying stock in the company and by 1673 had acquired £12,000 in shares, making him the single largest shareholder. The following year he became a director of the company, the beginning of a career in which he became deputy governor, then governor.

Despite English growth, the Dutch were still the main European players in Asia, secure in the fact that they controlled the Spice Islands. The English company could make little inroads into the spice trade and the English were forced to be flexible and carve out new markets, the most important being textiles. From the 1660s onwards, the EIC began to import Indian cotton textiles into Europe. This required a change in consumer habits in England where wool was the norm, but the product soon gained popularity as it allowed people the chance to wear lighter clothes in summer, and could be more easily modified as a fashion statement than the woollen products available at the time.

Growth in the textile market was not even. By the 1680s, when the trade to India was well established, many private traders began to challenge the EIC monopoly by illegally interloping on the trade. The response from the EIC was a strategy devised by the director, Sir Josiah Child, a trade war dramatically stepping up imports so that the 'unreasonable itch of the interlopers might be put to an end once and for all'. To prevent the market from being glutted, Josiah Child also embarked upon a policy of diversification and market segmentation. He ordered his factors in India to send a variety of products to cater for different markets. For seamen and ordinary workmen, he wanted strong blue and white cloth, for citizens he ordered 'white middling', and for ladies and gentlewomen he requested fine white cloth. The strategy worked in eliminating the interlopers but overstretched the company's resources. The company warehouses were full of unsold stock. As a result, the company's credit collapsed and Sir Josiah Child was forced to stand down from his position.[20]

Between 1560 and 1689 shipping was one of England's fastest growing industries, and tonnage multiplied nearly sevenfold.[21] However, the English were not going to supplant the Dutch unless they could replicate the broader commercial–industrial base that underpinned their success. The Dutch had gained so much competitive strength from their commercial and industrial base that much of the English literature of the day promoted a deliberate imitation of the Dutch. Sir Josiah Child listed several points where the English should follow Dutch economic practice, including their encouragement of innovation in industry and trade, liberal fiscal regulations and, above all, their banks and financial institutions that generated low interest rates and reduced costs for Dutch businessmen. In 1693, he wrote:

> the prodigious increase of the Netherlanders in their domestick and foreign trade, riches, and multitude of shipping, is the envy of present, and may be the wonder of all future generations. And yet the means whereby they have thus advanced themselves are . . . imitable by most other nations but more easily by us of this kingdom of England.[22]

Imitation of the Dutch occurred across the nation. At Jonathon's Coffee House in Change Alley, a market for financial securities developed along similar lines to the Dutch bourse. Investment options included shares in companies such as the East India Company or stock issued by the Bank of England and, by 1694, there were fifty listings on the exchange.[23] In 1694, the Bank of England was created in imitation of the Bank of Amsterdam, providing a new level of stability in the financial environment and helping to reduce interest rates.

Imitation did not occur without problems. The engine-loom (or Dutch loom) had been invented in the Dutch town of Leiden. With this machine one man could make ribbon equal to that previously made by four. This ability to replace labour did not endear it to organized weavers in England who resisted its introduction for decades. In London these looms were the cause of street riots in which they were burnt. However, in Lancashire, where there were no well-organized craft groups to oppose its introduction, it was in common use by the 1680s.

Over time, the English mastered the industrial and commercial techniques of the Dutch. Contemporary observers made comments about the English that we in the twentieth century were used to hearing about the Japanese during their process of economic catch-up. For example, the Swiss calico printer John Ryhnier wrote in 1766 that the British 'cannot boast of many inventions but only of having perfected the inventions of others . . .'.[24]

Within a relatively short period, England had developed an industrial base that could fill its ships with a vast array of cargoes. Throughout the same period, the population of the North American colonies grew rapidly from 300,000 in 1700 to 3,000,000 in 1776, providing a welcome market for the new industrial goods. British ships took cargoes of cordage, hats, leather, linens and silks to the markets in the west.[25] On the return voyages, hulls contained products from American forests and sub-tropical plantations.

Shipping's expansion also reflected a growing demand for raw materials and foodstuffs at home, a reflection of the nation's growing wealth.[26] The West Indies and Far East provided a new range of commodities (rice, tea and coffee) to import and re-export, but the fastest growing trade was with America. By the middle of the eighteenth century, the transatlantic trade accounted for nearly half of all British shipping. Through a process of imitation, buttressed by protectionist legislation and superior naval power, the British built the capabilities by which they rode a new wave of growth.

The battle for trade supremacy in the North Atlantic was not based on commercial superiority. If it had been, the English would certainly have lost against the Dutch who were secure in their commercial skills and industrial base. The English could only develop the skills to compete with the Dutch behind a screen of protection that the Navigation Acts provided. The battle for trade supremacy in the North Atlantic was a naval, not commercial battle. Britain won the battle on the basis of its naval superiority.

In many ways, Britain's naval strength was a consequence of its favourable geography and resource development. A large natural endowment of Sussex iron meant the British could make guns at a quarter of the price of bronze. Consequently, English ships were all well equipped with a 'heavy weight of broadside'. Perhaps the biggest geographic advantage was its physical separation from its European rivals by sea. Britain did not need a large standing army and could channel most of its defence into shipping. The Dutch could not afford this luxury, since they shared a border with France and Spanish territories.[27]

Enforcement of the Navigation Acts was not the only economic benefit provided by the Royal Navy. The navy also reduced costs for British shippers by eliminating piracy. In the early Atlantic trade, few individual shippers would take action against pirates because of the risk. Merchants pressured the government to provide protection and it fell to the navy to suppress piracy.[28]

However, it was not in the government's interest to pay for naval intervention unless trade reached levels that justified those costs. These levels were reached in the eighteenth century and had dramatic effects on the productivity of shipping. With protection from the navy, shippers could spend less money on armaments. For example, in 1729–30 the average ship operating in the Jamaica trade carried thirty-four guns per 100 men. By 1768 this had fallen to five. The declining need for defence similarly reduced the manning requirements on board. It also allowed shippers to use ships more specifically devoted to carrying cargo. Finally, with fewer losses due to piracy, insurance costs fell, the 1770 rate being two-thirds of the 1635 rate, and they continued to fall throughout the first half of the nineteenth century.

The Navigation Acts were only one part of a huge wave of protectionism that characterized the economy in the late seventeenth century.[29] The government provided subsidies to industries, bounties for exports, prohibitions of imports and protective tariffs. The government also introduced an array of supportive legislation. To protect ship-owners, the death penalty was introduced to deter masters from deliberately destroying their ships. In 1730 attempts were made to regulate wages and conditions of merchant seamen and put an end to destructive squabbling. In 1735 restrictions were put on the liability of ship-owners whose cargoes were embezzled by their crews (if the owners themselves were innocent parties).

As trade developed on the North Atlantic, there were also a number of improvements in productivity.[30] With growing markets, ships carried more cargo, making fuller use of their shipping capacity. This allowed them to reduce the prices they charged. The growth of a regular and stable trade also increased the flow of information on markets, increased the experience and knowledge of seamen and, as markets became better organized, ships spent less time in port and more time carrying cargo. Specialist shipbrokers evolved to arrange freight, and shipping agents to organize the loading and discharge of cargoes. This cut turnaround times and delays, which decreased the costs of transactions.

With greater experience of geographic and navigation requirements, ships could make faster voyages, while traders learnt to time their voyages to maximize buying and selling opportunities and reduce time spent in port. As knowledge of the trades was disseminated, it contributed further to the industry's expansion. Publications assisted this process and included such titles as *Lloyd's List* (1734), Murray's *A Treatise on Shipbuilding and Navigation (1765) and The Shipmasters' Assistant and Owners' Manual* (1778). The effect of greater precision in navigation was faster, safer voyages that reduced costs and maximized the use of shipping capital at the time.[31] Ports such as Liverpool, Hull, Bristol and Exeter grew into major cities, each with their growing arsenal of docks, shipyards, wharves and warehouses. In 1707 the Act of Union was signed and Scottish ships and ports, particularly Glasgow, also contributed to the growth.

A number of technological innovations were also introduced which had the effect of reducing costs and improving the productivity of British seamen. Changes in rig design meant that, instead of a few large sails, more smaller sails were used, making it easier to sail against the wind. The development of the jib, head sails and helm wheel made it possible to sail into westerly winds, opening up shorter routes across the Atlantic. The improvement in rig design also reduced labour requirements and costs. At the same time, improvements in packaging reduced costs of some commodities, in particular tobacco.[32]

The overall effect of these changes was a dramatic increase in efficiency. For example, freight rates in the Atlantic tobacco trade experienced a 1.4 per cent average annual decline over 150 years during the seventeenth and eighteenth centuries. To provide another comparison, at the end of the sailing era European shipping had reached a man-tonnage ratio of one man per 9–14 tons, a two- to threefold gain over the Indian dhow system (and 15- to 30-fold over Saharan camel caravans).[33]

Several institutions were created to promote the advance of technology in other industries. In 1662 the founding of the Royal Society of London grouped together scientists with a prime objective of advancing technological prowess. Of its eight committees, the Mechanical was the largest, followed by the History of Trade.[34] Industry became the subject of intense scientific investigation. Robert Boyle examined mining and metallurgy, while Robert Hooke and William Petty investigated ship-building, pumps and various kinds of engines. All three presented papers on textile dyeing.

Of more direct importance to shipping was the appointment of the Astronomer Royal and the founding of the Royal Greenwich Observatory in 1665 to solve problems of navigation and, in particular, the determination of longitude, one of the most pressing problems for trade and shipping. The government established a Board of Longitude, which oversaw a reward offering £20,000 to whoever developed technology that could measure longitude at sea.

The key to solving the longitude problem required an understanding of time. Time moves back every hour for every 15 degrees travelled west (15 degrees of longitude). Therefore if we know the difference between the time in London and Jamaica, the difference in time can be used to calculate the distance. This required a clock reliable enough to tell ships what the time was in London, even though they might be thousands of miles way. The problem was that changes in humidity and temperature and the motion of the ship all affected the effectiveness of clocks at sea.

John Harrison, who had a background in clock-making, gathered detail about the reward on a trip to London in 1730. Harrison devoted his life to the task and over the next forty years presented the Board of Longitude with five clocks with their financial support. However, when he finally presented a clock that was durable enough to keep accurate at sea, the Board were reluctant to reward him. Harrison had to petition government for the prize which he eventually received in 1773. The clock, or chronometer, dramatically improved navigation, and the East India Company soon insisted that all their ships carry one.

In 1768 the Royal Society persuaded the crown to finance an expedition to the Pacific from where the transit of Venus could be observed. This could provide valuable data that could aid navigation. The resulting voyage of James Cook, in his Whitby-built colliers, also opened up commercial possibilities in the Pacific. The sextant also came out of the British hot-bed of innovation and helped to measure latitude with more precision.[35]

Equally important were James Lind's efforts to combat scurvy. Lind was trained at the College of Surgeons in Edinburgh and in 1739 became a surgeon's mate sailing to the Mediterranean, Guinea and West Indies. Lind was disgusted that most of the doctors writing about scurvy had never been to sea. He wrote: 'before the subject could be set in clear and proper light, it was necessary to remove a great deal of rubbish.'[36] In 1747, while sailing on HMS *Salisbury,* Lind took twelve men suffering from scurvy and divided them into pairs. As a dietary supplement, they were given either cider, sea water, vinegar, a mixture of garlic, mustard and horseradish. But those that recovered from scurvy were fed on citrus fruits. The realisation that feeding sailors citrus fruit dramatically reduced the costs of labour as fewer men fell sick and died.

In the Asian trade, the English Navigation Acts had little effect on the Dutch. This was a region where the Dutch gained much competitive strength from their organization and control of the Spice Islands. However, from the second half of the seventeenth century, the VOC faced an increased level of competition. The English, French, Swedish, Danish and even Brandenburg set up companies in competition to the VOC. Many of these firms were set up by expatriate Dutch merchants attempting to side-step the VOC monopoly. This suggests that with the initial trading risks overcome, the monopoly no longer served the nation's best interests. However, no changes came in industry as they stuck to the old ways of doing things.

As a response to the surge in competition, the Dutch strengthened their commitment to their old formulas for success, in particular the wealth gained from their control of the Spice Islands. The VOC reinforced its monopoly by closing down an emporium at Bantam from which other countries were getting their supplies. They also closed other market gaps on the Coromandel coast of India. By 1689, the VOC had achieved substantial control of the spice and pepper trade. In doing this, the Dutch were escalating their commitment to their old markets at a time of change. Spices, which once dominated European trade with Asia, were no longer a growing market. Between 1680 and 1720, the tonnage of cargo returning on Dutch ships grew by 125 per cent, but revenue rose only 78 per cent. The growth had not contributed to increased profit.[37] The spice trade had reached its limits to provide future wealth.

While the Dutch escalated their investment in a market with little potential for development, the English were forced to try something new and diversified into tea, porcelain, saltpetre and other goods for which European demand was beginning to appear. Most important was their bold but risky attempt to market Indian calicoes in Europe. In taking a lead in developing these markets, the English were gaining early expertise in a new and growing economic wave.

There were a number of areas where the Dutch stuck to their old ways of doing things. One of these was their preoccupation with military expenditure. Forts and garrisons had always been a vital component of Dutch activities in Asia, a way of thinking that had its origins as trading warriors going to battle the Spanish and Portuguese.[38] Maintaining forts and garrisons was expensive, but a decision to demilitarize would not have been an easy one. Sir Josiah Child had even suggested the English company should increase their military presence in Asia on account of the advan-tages it gave. It is yet another example of the difficulty of finding correct solutions when an economy goes into decline.

The Dutch had always controlled their Asian activities very strictly from their headquarters in Batavia. This tight control was vital if they were to maintain their monopoly. However, it meant their operations were less flexible and this was a barrier to the development of new markets during times of change. By contrast, the English faced fewer restrictions and operated a decentralized decision-making process which made it easier for their traders to seize opportunities as they arose. This aided their manoeuvrability in the complicated and volatile textile market. The English company went as far as supporting private traders who complemented its own operations. In this way, the English acted with greater flexibility and promoted the raising of capital from new sources.[39]

The directors at Batavia were not unaware of the deteriorating situation. In the early years of the eighteenth century, they wrote:

> The profits have turned into losses, trade is declining, the competition of the English, French, Portuguese, Chinese and Moors cannot along this extensive coast-line be checked, the spending capacity of the population is diminishing, the sale of cloths . . . is not one fifth of what it used to be.[40]

This situation was made worse by the fact that Dutch naval technology was no longer in the forefront of labour-saving devices, nor navigation. In the early seventeenth century Dutch map-makers and publishers had provided their captains with the best literature and charts in the world. Dutch publishers continued to reproduce these old masters, while the French and English began producing globes, maps and charts of greater accuracy.[41]

Much of the blame for the stagnation in the VOC has been attributed to the low level of interest in improvements in navigation by the company's directors. The directors in Amsterdam operated far from the company's core activities and relied on the old rules and methods to generate profit. Navigators frequently complained of the restrictions placed on them, especially when deviations from the rules resulted in faster voyages.[42] Tight control also restricted innovation in ship design. With management making the final decisions on the ship design, the master builder at the shipyard had less opportunity for spontaneous innovations and experimentation was much reduced.

This situation was not restricted to shipping. Across the Netherlands, industrial technique stagnated. In 1779 one industrialist stated:'One cannot refrain from observing that there are very few industries or trades here which are not in need of improvement.'[43] In Leiden, which once led technological advance in textiles, industrialists and employers were now criticized for the lack of initiative and aversion to new methods.

Like Spain and Portugal a century earlier, the competitiveness of Dutch industry was restricted by high wage levels. For example, at the end of the seventeenth century, Pieter van Dam complained that, while in the early days the VOC could enlist seamen for eight or nine florins a month, it now had difficulty attracting staff with rates of ten or eleven florins with a bonus of one month's wages thrown in.[44] Previously, the high cost of wages had been a key force in developing labour-saving technology, but now foreign nations were catching up faster than labour-saving solutions were being found.

The problem was made worse by the fact that industrial power had become concentrated in the hands of a few. By the eighteenth century, society had a static class structure with an urban patriarch entrenched at the top. The great 'family' of Dutch culture was in the course of breaking into poor and rich kin.[45] This situation stood in sharp contrast to the early days when the Dutch economy was characterized by equality and social mobility, with new paths opening opportunities for economic advance. After 1680 there was a growing rentier mentality. The business class, who in previous generations pioneered aggressive new ways of thinking, were now gentlemen of leisure, happy to live off their investment incomes. Members of the Regent class, who once relied on monitoring trade to draw their revenue, could now live off the incomes provided from land, investments and annuities.[46] They might still possess ties to trading activity but the close association of the past had gone.

Compared with the social petrification in the Netherlands, England was a picture of social and economic mobility. New industrial technologies and trading opportunities provided a platform by which many Englishmen managed to break through social barriers and improve their status. Merchants and bankers such as William Cockayne, Josiah Child and Charles Duncombe bought large estates, acquired titles and married their daughters into the aristocracy. At the same time, the younger sons of gentry, who did not receive inheritances, often entered trade to make their fortunes. The result was a 'marriage of town and country, of merchant and landed wealth', a relationship which would come to dominate the British economic and social system.[47]

In the Netherlands, it was not just the rich who were protecting their position. Workers were bound together by guilds, the equivalent of modern unions. In times of growth the guilds had been a key institution in promoting ship-building technology, but during stagnation and decline their goals changed. They became more protective of their market, defending their interests in the face of decline out of fear of unemployment. Interest in building facilities took second place to sickness, accident and old age funds for members.[48]

Decline spread throughout the economy like a disease.[49] With fewer ships bringing in sugar from the West Indies, the number of sugar refineries in Amsterdam declined from thirty-four in 1668 to twenty in 1680. By the 1720s and 1730s the Dutch were experiencing a serious collapse in their industrial sector. By the second half of the eighteenth century, the industrial decline was widespread, although some industries such as diamond-cutting and paper-making survived on the basis of the high quality of their output.

If new companies had been established by younger men with new ideas, the country might have enjoyed more growth but a number of forces prevented this from happening. In the ship-building industry, ships had become so large and expensive to build that new players could not raise the capital to start a business. Those already in the industry cemented their position through their connections and superior organization skills that gave them better access to resources and labour. By 1750 it was almost impossible for new blood to enter the industry. Ship-building came to be controlled by older families with established wealth who were more concerned with reducing costs and ensuring rules were followed.

The Dutch experienced many of the same problems that modern organizations face as they grow larger. The first of these is how to generate innovation while keeping control. For example, at the VOC yards, standardized ship design had been adopted to reduce the cost of ship-building and repair, but these rules and regulations took away the master shipwright's opportunity to experiment and introduce innovations.[50]

The second of the problems caused by growth comes from increased specialization and division of labour. In the early days, ship-building companies were small and the manager would have an understanding of both production and contracting requirements. As ships became larger and more complex, managerial tasks became more important and the distance between the contractor and skilled carpenter increased. The industry which, before 1600, had little in the way of hierarchy was, by 1700, characterized by strict class divisions. As owners became increasingly divorced from the master journeymen, who were now only employees, a vacuum emerged with no one responsible for improving the technical quality of the ships.

The Dutch wave of prosperity had begun on the basis of new ship designs, industrial technologies and organizational forms. It was based on ways of thinking that included securing the Spice Islands' monopoly, use of military force and the production of standardized ship designs that reduced costs. However, once competitors adopted the Dutch innovations, the Dutch were denied many of their competitive strengths.

The Dutch had begun their wave of prosperity with an unbridled energy and enthusiastic belief that the world offered endless possibilities. By the eighteenth century, these characteristics were missing. The nation still had a wealth of capital and financial expertise, but industrial decline did not make the domestic market a preferred target of investment. Investors sought the safest options. They invested abroad, not locally, and, as with Spain before them, many preferred the security of public funds.[51]

Once decline had set in, it gave birth to mistrust and jealousy.[52] Political divisions that had always existed now deepened and undermined attempts at reform. For example, inter-provincial jealousies sometimes prevented agreement on improvements of road and canals that crossed boundaries, while pro- and anti-Orange factions blocked each other's sensible suggestions for reform.

By the end of the eighteenth century, the Dutch Golden Age had truly ended. James Boswell, who visited the Netherlands in mid-century, described a very different picture from the century before: 'Most of the principal towns are sadly decayed, and instead of finding every mortal employed, you meet with multitudes of poor creatures that are starving in idleness.'[53] It reflects a recurring pattern of economic systems: catch-up by imitating nations and entrapment.

7

BRITANNIA RULES THE WAVES

At the beginning of the eighteenth century, the Mughal empire possessed a wonderfully successful economy. A century of conquest and territorial expansion provided the empire with enormous resources while buoyant local and regional markets increased the wealth of the region. The economy possessed many of the factors we currently associate with success: a small government provided political stability yet gave businesses high levels of independence; a flourishing market economy was based on competition and individualism; and a number of commercial institutions reduced the costs of performing transactions. Most importantly, natural resources and skilled producers gave northern India highly competitive producers in the most important industry in the world at that time, textiles.

The merchants of Gujarat benefited from being part of this successful system. Gujarat was the busiest and most active trading region of India and entered the eighteenth century with 'the strongest export and import trade, shipping and merchant entrepreneurship in the Indian subcontinent'.[1] However, the tide was about to turn. In 1701 the number of ships based at Surat reached an all-time high of 112 and tonnage of about 20,000 tons,[2] but this would be its upper limit. 'The entire Indian Ocean was suffering from over-trading and prices were depressed in every market.' Markets were suffering from saturation. The economic path Gujurat was travelling, based on textiles and maritime supremacy in the Indian Ocean, could not generate future growth. In 1701 it seemed the limits of the Gujarati growth path had been reached.

The Mughal empire was primarily a military machine. With the best artillery on the continent and well-handled cavalry, it gradually expanded its borders. The officers who carved out these conquests were rewarded with their own share of land to rule (*jagir*). But after 1689 expansion came to an end. The mountains in the north provided a natural limit to expansion, while in the south the natives of the Deccan provided heavy resistance. Inside these military frontiers lay a peaceful arena in which merchants built connections with the producers of the hinterland.

In many ways, the empire resembles a modern organization. Built by dynamic men with an interest in technology, it grew and acquired more resources, but eventually organizations grow to a point where the leaders become distanced from their core activities. Throughout Mughal history, the emperors became more distant from the military technologies that created their empire. While early emperors such as Akbar had shown an active interest in weaponry, in later years official interest was occasional and haphazard at best.[3] The Mughals seem to have been content with the military technologies that brought them success in the past. Consequently in the seventeenth century the Mughals began to fall behind other contemporary powers.

With stagnant technology, expansion came to an end and this led to a squeeze on incomes. With no expansion, there was less new land available to reward the mensabdars who now struggled for jagirs. As their income declined, they put more and more pressure upon the *zamindars*, that is the class of gentry who actually and permanently held much of the land in the empire. The zamindars then passed this pressure on to the peasant. It was a recipe for instability.

This reached a tipping point in 1707 with the death of the emperor Aurangzeb which led to a series of bitter conflicts over succession to the throne. All this weakened the central authority, undermining the whole system of revenue collection and security. Regulations preventing abuse of revenue collection fell into disuse as regional lords resorted to open tax farming. Nobles became increasingly more corrupt in their capture of income. Merchants were squeezed and increasingly unable to raise the business capital of earlier days.

At Surat, the crisis came in the years 1730–32. The governor at the time was a man named Sorab Khan.[4] Attacks from the Marathas in the south had deprived the governor of income, and he found he did not have sufficient revenue to pay for his soldiers and associated retinue. Receiving no support from the disintegrating imperial court, he became heavily in debt to the leading merchant in the city, Mohammad Ali, the son of Abdul Ghafur.

Mohammed Ali inherited a fortune from his father. It included a garden house to the north of the city, a somewhat mouldy residence in the town and a wharf in the south. One of Mohammad Ali's first ventures with his acquired wealth was a massive property development around the wharf. He purchased land around the area and built on it, transforming the old landing place into a magnificent suburban complex. Another venture was the establishment of his own mint, with imperial permission.[5]

Ali's wealth saw him constantly being approached for loans from the governor, Sorab Khan. When this line of credit reached its limits, Sorab Khan began the squeeze on other businessmen in the town. In January 1730 he seized Rs22,000 in bullion from the shroffs of the mint by force. On 21 March a merchant was fined Rs700 but not told what the fine was for. On 10 May he fined a Muslim merchant Rs6,000 for having relations with 'girls of pleasure', a pastime that was generally taken for granted by the merchants. Even the arrival of a famine in 1731, did not stop the governor's search for money among the mercantile community. Before long, the merchants revolted and raised their own army with which to defend themselves. Mohammed Ali contributed 2,000 troops to the defence, while even the British and Dutch East India Companies joined in. The governor was eventually replaced, but Mohammed Ali was arrested and died in jail, with much of the family fortune plundered by the new governor. The fall of Abdul Ghafur's family symbolized the fall of a great merchant city.

The system was imploding and, with a weaker central administration, came a rapid decline in law and order that hit trade hard.[6] Caravans organized by private merchants could no longer travel from Surat to Agra in safety. As conflict riddled the trade routes, the port of Surat was increasingly cut off from the markets and production centres in the hinterland. A key source of competitive strength was lost. To make matters worse, in subsequent years key Indian Ocean trading partners became rattled by political unrest, including instability in the Ottoman empire, civil war in Yemen and the collapse of the Safavid dynasty. These had been key markets for Gujarat. The old shipping routes on which Gujarat had been so competitive were falling apart. This decline can be seen in the number of ships based in Surat. In 1701, 112 vessels were based in the port. By 1750, there were only about twenty.[7] The total trade of Surat, which measured approximately 16 million rupees at the beginning of the century, was down to 5 million rupees by 1740, and half of this trade was now being carried by the British, another tenth by the Dutch.[8] Local ship-owners had virtually been wiped out.

In times of uncertainty, the well-defended British ships became a more attractive option to Asian merchants wanting to transport goods. British ships were stronger and with more armaments than the light and flexible dhows, but they were also more expensive. In the political climate of the eighteenth century more and more Asian merchants were prepared to pay that price.[9]

The decay in the western Indian Ocean occurred at a time when the eastern Indian Ocean was experiencing a growth of activity bolstered by a growing trade with China. However, it was not the Gujarati shippers who reaped the benefits of this growth but the British who created the trade connections that provided growth. These long-distance routes were more dangerous and the Europeans had the strongest ships to cope with these conditions. Consequently, it was British ships that took Indian textiles to England and China, not those from Gujarat.

The British also benefited from the fact they had created territorial enclaves separated from the declining and corrupt Mughal empire. Over the previous century, the EIC had developed a number of fortified enclaves. The first was Madras, founded on the southeast coast in 1639. It was a strange location to build a trading post. All that existed was a small village and a few acres of surf-swept beach which were unsuitable for shipping. However, the EIC agent, Mr Francis Day, insisted on the location, even threatening to resign if his plans weren't accepted. He had a mistress at nearby St Thome and nothing would stop him from getting closer to her.

The second EIC territory was Bombay, an island on the west coast not far from Gujarat. However, the most important of the three territories was Calcutta. In 1690 the EIC bought the three villages that would grow into Calcutta for Rs1,300. Here they built a fortified factory enclosing warehouses and residential areas for both Europeans and Indians.

The fortified towns and soldiers employed by the EIC meant that British traders were in a better position to deal with political pressure than Gujarati merchants, many of whom moved to the British settlements to escape the political instability and tax farming in their home towns. For a short time, even the grandson of Abdul Ghafur retired to the British settlement at Bombay. Many Gujaratis moved to European ports on the Coromandel coast, serving as financiers and brokers in direct competition with the local Chetty sub-castes. As they took more to onshore positions and left the shipping to the British, they lost what naval experience they had and their investment in shipping declined.[10]

British expansion in the Indian Ocean was also a result of new companies being created. In the 1670s, the English East India Company made a deliberate decision to concentrate on the long trade routes between Europe and Asia, allowing private merchants to participate in the intra-Asia trade if they chose to. Many servants of the EIC chose to take the opportunity this trade presented and, using their savings and loans from local merchants, they started businesses which initially resembled those of the locals.

During the eighteenth century, the organization of British private traders became more sophisticated. They established agency houses in various ports, between which representatives (supercargoes) travelled with the ship, taking commercial decisions anywhere on a voyage.[11] This ability to make decisions on the spot gave the decentralized structure of the smaller agency houses great flexibility in responding to changing market and environmental forces, something the highly centralized English East India Company could not do.

One of the most dynamic private companies was Jardine Matheson & Co, formed by a Scottish doctor William Jardine and a trader from Sutherland. Jardine was introduced to the Asian trade in 1802 when he became a surgeon on East India Company ships sailing between Calcutta and Canton. At that time company servants were allowed some space on ship to carry goods of their own to trade. Jardine used his space to trade in narcotics and soon found it was more lucrative to do this than practise medicine. In 1818 he met James Matheson who had recently arrived in Canton, having spent some time working for his uncle in Calcutta. In 1832, they formed their company, initially trading between Bombay, Calcutta and Canton. Later they added a run to London.

Private companies like Jardine Matheson had a symbiotic relationship with the EIC. The EIC managed the opium production in India, but because of its contraband nature, played no part in the shipping or sale of the drug to China for fear of losing its trading rights. To overcome this problem, the EIC sold its opium crop to agency houses in India who then forwarded it for resale in China. The EIC provided protection and, in return, companies like Jardine Matheson distributed opium.

British private traders and agency houses transformed the structure of Indian maritime commerce in the eighteenth century. As Indian opium and textiles were taken to markets in Europe and China on an unprecedented scale, the individual Gujarati merchants of the Indian Ocean could no longer compete. The Muslim *nakhuda* and the *baniya* of Surat were replaced by the agency houses of Calcutta, Madras and Bombay, integrated into a broader global commerce. In the western ocean, the magnificent Gujarati fleet gradually dwindled into insignificance, while in the east the Calcutta fleet of private British merchants won the supremacy of the Indian.[12] However, the Indians could take comfort that they were still the world's greatest producer of textiles, but not for long.

While British traders were changing the face of the Indian Ocean, industry was changing the face of the British landscape.

Every new view of Great Britain would require a new description; the Improvements that encrease, the new buildings erected, the old buildings taken down; New discoveries in metals, mines, minerals; new undertakings in trade; inventions, engines, manufactures, in a nation, pushing and improving as we are; These things open new scenes every day, and make England especially shew a new and differing face in many places, on every occasion of surveying it.[13]

This description was written by Daniel Defoe, author of *Robinson Crusoe*. In his *A Tour Through England and Wales*, Defoe describes a country transformed by imitation and industrialization. The backward England of old, with its single woollen industry, was buried under layers of commercial and industrial activity. This was an age of innovation and the development of new productive capabilities.

Industrialization progressed with the same processes that we have witnessed in earlier chapters; farmworkers who previously produced many of their own supplies moved to the cities and gained specialist jobs in the new factories. They now had to buy some of the products they had once made at home, and items like soap became specialized industries. The difference between this period of specialization and those of countries we looked at earlier is that the British developed a broader range of production technologies.

The domestic market grew as productivity improved, and the expanding market, in turn, provided a healthy environment for entrepreneurs to introduce new technology and new products. A growing economy is good for entrepreneurs as it reduces the risk of failure and provides a quicker pay off from investments. The result was a cumulative industrialization, producing a new variety and quality of products. In this way, growing prosperity fuels further prosperity and innovation. Eighteenth-century Britain experienced an explosion of new products and production techniques, and increased incomes with which they could be bought.

As in previous episodes of rapid growth, the Industrial Revolution changed consumer patterns. This was a result of the new products available for sale and the increased incomes that people had to spend. Consumers could buy cottons from Manchester, cutlery from Sheffield and crockery from Staffordshire, while Birmingham let loose a range of products from buttons to buckles and candlesticks.[14] Consumers could also select from a wide range of leisure activities. By the 1720s horse-racing was advertised, followed by cricket soon after. Theatres, concerts and the reading of fiction became popular. This rising demand created a golden age of English literature, harnessing the talents of Jane Austen, Byron, Blake, Shelley and many others.

The consumer revolution also resulted in an explosion of marketing techniques. For example, Martin von Butchell, who had a practice as a doctor/dentist/medicine-seller, promoted himself by riding a white pony which he sometimes painted all purple and sometimes with spots. It was a sight that astonished those who saw him, but must have attracted attention for his practice was described as lucrative.[15] Another form of promotion that became common between 1730 and 1770 was the use of trade cards. The trade card of John Spilsbury, the original jigsaw puzzle inventor, described himself as a 'Map dissector in Wood'. Elainor Brainiff found a market niche providing key services to her clients. Her business card read:

> Daughter and Successor to her late father
> George Bridges,
> BUGG DESTROYER TO HIS MAJESTY

Advertisements became commonplace in newspapers and journals. For example, Mr de Chamant sold IMPROVED MINERAL TEETH that 'had the opprobation of all the learned Societies of Europe and that of the most emminent Medical gentlemen of Europe'. Such recommendations proved 'the superiority of his teeth . . . over those taken from dead bodies, or those fabricated of any other animal substances which are always corruptable and occasion a very offensive smell'.

The entrepreneur par excellence was Josiah Wedgwood, born in 1730 to a Staffordshire potter. Wedgwood learnt his trade at a time when Europeans were trying to imitate high quality Chinese porcelain. In his desire to match Chinese quality, Wedgwood searched for improved materials, techniques and standards of design. His explorations led to the development of a number of new ceramic techniques, including green glaze, cream-ware, black basalt and jasper. He also experimented in the types of product he made. His product line included cameos, tea trays, snuff boxes and knife handles. His long list of innovations helped to raise the quality of his products to the point where he could confidently offer the first recorded example of a satisfaction or money-back policy.

Having achieved perfection in production, he then focused on his sales and distribution. Wedgwood was aware of the marketing leverage that fashion provided. He claimed: 'Fashion is infinitely superior to merit in many respects, and it is plain from a thousand instances that if you have a favourite child you wish the public to fondle and take notice of, you have only to make choice of proper sponsors.' Wedgwood was a pioneer in celebrity advertising, making goods for society's elite in full knowledge that ordinary consumers would crave the same products. An object made for the Queen would soon spark orders. Through the use of ambassadors and envoys, Wedgwood's products were promoted throughout Europe and, by the end of the century, Britain had become a substantial exporter of ceramics.

Britain was an economy in ferment, and foreign visitors marvelled at the unprecedented wealth. In the 1770s the Gottingen Professor Lichtenberg said that 'the luxury and extravagance of the lower middle classes had risen to such a pitch as never before seen in the world.'[16] In the 1780s the Russian writer Karamzin noted:'Everything presented an aspect of . . . plenty. Not one object from Dover to London reminded me of poverty.'

This consumer revolution dramatically changed the economic status of the lower classes. Prior to industrialization, lower-class consumers had only modest possessions. The poorest families owned no table linen, little pottery, cutlery and furniture and the purchase of a garment or cloth was a luxury that common people could afford only a few times in their lives. Even the clothes of plague victims were eagerly sought by their relatives. In the eighteenth century this changed with the availability of cheap products and high incomes.

The lower classes bought things they could not previously afford and this was not universally welcomed by the upper classes, who saw a dangerous process of social levelling:

Our servant wenches are so puffed up with pride nowadays that they never think they go fine enough. It is a hard matter to know the mistress from the maid by their dress; nay very often, the maid shall be much the finer of the two.[17]

Even tea consumption reflected the changing economy. Once an exotic luxury that only the rich could afford, Jonas Hanway wrote that he was shocked to find that even labourers mending the road began demanding their daily tea. This increase in tea consumption was a direct result of increased imports by the East India Company that reduced the price to a level that even the poor could afford. Given that Jonas Hanway was a shareholder in the East India Company, his disgust would have been tempered by the dividends he earned. One important group that successfully opposed change were those associated with the woollen industry. This powerful group did not appreciate the imports of cheap cotton that the East India Company was bringing into the country. In 1701 and 1721 they persuaded the government to impose barriers on the importation of cotton. This protection of the wool market had unexpected consequences. The resulting gap in the local market for cottons encouraged local people to take up cotton production in imitation of the Indian product. Being a new industry, it was not restricted by guilds and other vested interests and became one of the most dynamic and technologically responsive industries in the country.

The most consistent feature of the British economy in the late seventeenth and eighteenth centuries was continuous improvement. Up until 1760 improvement was achieved by imitating foreign techniques; after, the English developed new ways to reduce costs, add value and create new products, a process aided in no small part by the widespread acceptance and promotion of innovation in the earlier phase. This wave of industrial innovation coincided with the foundation of a number of institutions devoted to the development of science and technology. In 1754 the Society for the Encouragement of Arts, Manufactures and Commerce was established. In the north, the Manchester Literary and Philosophical Society and the Birmingham Lunar Society became institutions by which technical ideas and information were exchanged. There was a high level of interaction between engineers, scientists and businessmen. Thus industrialists such as Matthew Boulton and Josiah Wedgwood included mathematicians and scientists among their friends.[18]

Technical advance gathered apace with the publication of journals, encyclopaedias, dictionaries and yearbooks. However, it would be wrong to overemphasize the importance of science in industrial development. Britain's early advances were made by 'tinkerers' who had little formal technical schooling. Advances in the cotton, iron and machine tool industries did not require a high level of scientific understanding but a high level of aptitude by mechanical amateurs.[19] Nevertheless, there is no doubt that innovation was assisted by the nation's high levels of education and, by the end of the eighteenth century, England had one of the highest literacy rates in the world and Scotland was even higher.[20]

One of the most dynamic industries was the textile industry and the names of a number of tinkering inventors have come down to us. First was John Kay, an apprentice to a reed-maker. The reeds made by Kay were used in weaving looms to keep the warp threads separated. The loom in use at the time had a shuttle that was kept in place by human hands. Kay invented a more efficient 'flying shuttle' that replaced human labour and doubled the productivity of loom weavers. However, such an invention was not appreciated by those workers replaced by the machine. John Kay's home was attacked in 1753, his loom was broken and he only just escaped.

Once initial resistance was overcome, the new loom led to a leap in efficiency but caused bottlenecks in other parts of the production process. Now five spinners were needed for each loom. A machine was needed that could spin cotton at the same speed as the loom wove. The Society of Arts put up a prize for an inventor who could create a machine that could spin six threads at a time but require only one person to man it. The solution came in 1761 when James Hargreaves, an illiterate but ingenious textile worker from Lancashire, invented the 'spinning jenny'. This breakthrough was greeted by workers in the predictable way. In 1768, Hargreaves' house was attacked and scores of the machines were smashed.

The next major breakthrough was by a barber and wig-maker, Richard Arkwright, who invented the water-frame. This machine made it possible to power textile machinery by a waterwheel. Factories were now built next to streams and rivers that powered the wheels.

However, the breakthrough did have the negative side effect of tying textile workers to the discipline of factory life. In 1779 Arkwright's Lancashire mill was also attacked by workers.

In the same year Josiah Wedgwood personally came across a crowd of 500 workers who told him that 'they had been destroying some engines & meant to serve them all so through the country.' The fact that Wedgwood felt no fear for his safety illustrates that they were no unwieldy mob. Their violence was targeted on the machines that threatened their livelihood. Wedgwood, who pioneered so much industrial innovation, did not see them as enemies. In fact, he voiced his displeasure on hearing that troops would be used against the crowd. To Wedgwood the protesters were merely deluded.[21]

The inventors described so far were only the most famous of numerous tinkerers who sought to improve machinery in a manner that reduced costs and increased quality. Scores of inventive minds tinkered with their machines, modifying here, adapting there, making small contributions that would rapidly be adopted by the industry.[22] The result was a massive leap in efficiency and industrial growth. Fifty years after the 1780s, the cost of yarn had fallen from thirty-six shillings to three shillings and the British could beat any competitor in the world, including India who they first imitated.

The expansion of the British economy inevitably increased pressure on the country's own limited resources. A major problem area was the growing demand for wood. As the economy expanded, more wood was needed for fuel and as a building material. As the country's forests were depleted, it became more reliant on wood substitutes: coal and iron. Britain had huge supplies of coal, but not all of these were easily accessible. Eventually, the surface coal deposits were depleted. The country still had plenty of coal at deeper levels but the deeper pits were susceptible to flooding. The most urgent technical problem of the time was the need for a machine that would raise water from the pits.[23] In the same way that the Dutch solved their production bottleneck with technologically advanced windmills, the English looked for a technical solution.

The problem attracted the talents of many ingenious inventors, including Thomas Savery, who patented a pump driven by a steam engine in 1698, but it was not until the development of a stronger engine by Thomas Newcomen that the problem was solved. However, this machine needed a lot of coal to power it and was very expensive to run. Further refinement by John Smeaton (1724–92) decreased the fuel requirements of the machine, then James Watt, an instrument-maker at Glasgow University, introduced a separate condenser that reduced the machine's fuel consumption by two-thirds. The effect of these improvements was a huge leap in efficiency of the steam engine. Between 1718 and 1834, improvements in the pumping engine meant the amount of water raised per weight of coal leapt from 4.3 to 109,000,000 pounds.

Improvements in the steam engine reflected the growing interrelatedness of technologies, as advances in one technology relied on advances in others. For example, the steam engine made it easier to extract coal for use in the production of iron, while improvements in iron production increased the efficiency of the machines extracting coal. The result was a cumulative path of development that fuelled economic growth. Key innovations in iron production included the smelting process introduced by Darby and the processes of puddling and rolling introduced by Henry Cort in 1783 and 1784. Throughout this whole process, British workmen gained a greater awareness of the potential of mechanics, developing their skills in the creation of modern mechanical engineering.

Before long, this technology was applied to other areas of the economy. Iron, as it became cheaper, could replace wood in water-wheels. It extended the life of wheels, reduced maintenance costs and increased their efficiency. Most importantly, it made it possible to build bigger wheels, generating a dramatic increase in horsepower. By 1780, the cost per unit of energy from a wheel had declined 20–30 per cent over its cost thirty years earlier.[24] British industry now had a power source more powerful and cheaper than any it had previously known.

That energy source had the potential to revolutionize industry, a reality that came about once Arkwright created his water-frame. This machine increased production and further reduced the need for labour. A child working on one of these machines could produce as much as ten adults previously. As a result of the increased efficiency from factory production, the price of cloth declined 85 per cent between 1780 and 1850.[25] Britain was opening a new wave of economic growth based on coal, iron and steam. Machines, fuelled by steam or waterwheels, could do the work of many men and dramatically reduce the costs of manufacturing.

Richard Arkwright, the inventor of the water-frame, was one of many entrepreneurs who enhanced their social position in this period. He built several factories and dramatically raised his wealth from the five pounds he began with. When he died in 1792, *The Gentleman's Magazine* claimed his estate was worth £500,000. Factory-owners like Arkwright also provided employment for many women and children. John Reed who worked in Arkwright's Cromford factory explained how:

> I went to work at the cotton factory of Messrs. Arkwright at the age of nine. I was then a fine strong, healthy lad, and straight in every limb. I had at first instance 2s. per week, for seventy-two hours work. I continued to work in this factory for ten

years, getting gradually advancing wages, till I had 6s. 3d. per week; which is the highest wages I ever had.

But Reed's income came at a price. Working with the machines had made him a cripple. Business was changing Britain and not all of these changes were welcome. For centuries, people would produce textiles in their homes. Now production was done in factories with the use of machines under the control of the factory-owners. One observer noted that:'At the same pace that mankind masters nature, man seems to be enslaved to other men or to his own infamy.'[26] That writer was Karl Marx, whose observations led him to become the father of communism. But Karl Marx was not the only writer to note the negative changes. Much criticism came from champions of the new age such as John Britton, who had a passion for industry and actively promoted the railways. Even he could not fail to notice the deteriorating physical environment.

From Birmingham to Wolverhampton, a distance of thirteen miles, the country was curious and amusing; though not very pleasing to eyes, ears or taste . . . a region of smoke and fire filling the whole area between earth and heaven . . . the surface of the earth is covered with its own entrails, which afford employment and livelihood for thousands of the human race.[27]

Eventually the new technologies were applied to shipping. It took some time for the cost of iron to decline to a competitive level, so iron did not become the dominant material until the mid-nineteenth century. The replacement of wood with iron in the shipping industry opened up many new possibilities. The most important advantage of iron was its strength. Stronger materials meant bigger ships could be built. It also meant thinner and lighter hulls could be constructed, leading to increases in dead–weight cargo capacity of up to 35 per cent.[28] (The later adoption of steel would decrease hull weights by another 15 per cent.)

It also took some time before the steam–engine was used on ships. The first experiments were not restricted to Britain. In the United States, John Fitch began experiments with a steamer on the Delaware during the mid–1780s. In France, trials were conducted on the Saône near Lyon in 1783. The French, with their superior scientific base, could have established a lead in steamship technology, but their industrial and scientific advance was stunted by political turmoil associated with the French Revolution.[29] Consequently, leadership fell to Britain, which had the skill and knowledge base that most complemented the new technologies. With its lead in coal and iron resources, entrepreneurial engineers and experience of steam technology, it took the lead in steamship development and, in so doing, developed productive capabilities that other nations lacked.

Steamship technology developed in three stages. Each stage went through a process of development until a plateau was reached at which it seemed the technology could go no further. This was followed by a period of experimentation until finally a breakthrough was made.[30] The first breakthrough was the paddle steamer that by the middle of the 1820s was operating on short sea, river and lake services in British, European and US waterways. However, the paddle steamer had limited applications for ocean-going transportation as undulating ocean swells could leave the paddle out of water, rendering it momentarily useless. Secondly, the depth of the paddle in the water would vary in the course of a voyage as its load of coal was used up. A more reliable form of propulsion was needed.

The second stage was the replacement of the paddle with a screw propeller. The concept of screw propulsion grew from an idea of Archimedes, two centuries before the Christian era. It involves shifting water with a screw in the same way using a modern screw-driver shifts wood and sawdust. The Dutch had used a similar device to raise water to higher levels centuries before. There were at least five attempts to apply steam technology to the screw before 1836, but the existing engine and boiler technology was not then up to the job.[31] The breakthrough finally came in May 1836 when Francis Petit Smith, a tinkering farmer, built a two-foot long boat which he tried on his farm pond. With the financial support of a wealthy banker he built the *Archimedes*. (In July of the same year a Swedish army officer, Captain Ericsson, who had lived in England for some time and was also working with a two-foot model boat, had similar success. Ericsson had the backing of US Navy Captain Robert F. Stockton and together they sought to capture the US naval market.)

With his financial backers, Smith formed the Screw Propeller Company to exploit the patent he had taken out and to develop a product that he hoped to sell to the Admiralty. However, it can be dangerous to rely on one target customer, especially when that customer is a government department vulnerable to the swings of party politics. While the Whig elite supported the technology, the Tories offered little support, and a change of government in 1841 worked against the project. To make matters worse, the Admiralty delayed purchasing the screw until its technical success could not be denied, but by this stage the company had fallen apart.[32] The Admiralty then picked up the technology at a cheap price. They had used their market power to break down the value of the patent. Pioneering does not always pay and the company collapsed. It is noteworthy that the great engineer Brunel, who picked up on the technology, saw no point in patenting ideas at the time.

Isambard Kingdom Brunel was born in Portsmouth in 1806, the son of a French civil engineer. He was sent to France for his technical education where he studied at the Lycée Henri Quatre and the University of Caen. At the age of twenty, he returned to England to work with his father. His first major project was a tunnel under the Thames, assisting his father who was chief engineer. In 1833 he was appointed chief engineer of the Great Western Railway, building a line from Bristol to London.

Brunel suggested to the directors of the Great Western Railway that they start a transatlantic steam service. This would mean the railway company could offer a total transportation service that ran from London to New York. However, using steam-powered shipping to cross oceans was a great departure from the prevailing rationality of the day. Even Brunel's father had previously stated his lack of faith in the technology. Not surprising, when Isambard Brunel put forward his suggestion, it was met with a combination of silence and uneasy laughter. The suggestion shared the absurdity of Henry the Navigator's ideas four centuries earlier.

The key problem was fuel. Steam-engines used a great deal of coal and were uneconomical for use on long voyages. On long-distance ocean voyages, the ship would need constant refuelling points or carry large quantities of coal. Not only was the large amount of coal required expensive, but storing the coal until it was used took up space that would otherwise be used to carry cargo. The obvious answer might seem to build a bigger ship but any rational person of the time realized a bigger ship required more fuel. Brunel broke the bounds of this rationality. He realized that as a ship grew bigger it would need proportionally less fuel. His observation was based on the fact that the carrying capacity of a ship was determined by its volume but the resistance that a ship encounters from the sea (and hence its fuel requirements) is determined by its surface area. In other words, an economic steamship could be built as long as it was built to the correct proportions.

The first steamship built by Brunel's company was the *Great Western*, a paddle steamer that did not prove a commercial success. After seeing the earlier success of the *Archimedes*, Brunel decided that the next ship must be powered by a screw. Screw propulsion works by forcing the water out behind the ship, thrusting the ship forward. Brunel hired the *Archimedes* for some months and conducted tests on it, using eight experimental screws. The results were incorporated in the building of the *Great Britain*. Being the first screw propelled transoceanic ship, and the first made out of iron, this giant heralded a new age of shipping.

Unfortunately, his company, the Great Western Steamship Company, also had limited success and was wound up in 1852.[33] The technology was still too limited in its applications. Of the 9,934 vessels listed in Lloyds Register in 1853, only 187, a mere 2 per cent, were steam vessels.[34] Fuel continued to be the problem.

More economical engines were provided by the last important breakthrough, when the process of compounding, which had been used on land, was applied to the marine steam–engine. The process of compounding expands the steam twice, therefore getting more use from the coal and reducing coal requirements (and costs). Once again this process relied on advances in different technologies. Maritime use of the compound engine had been limited by the weakness of existing boiler design and materials.[35] Eventually, advances in the making of steel meant that stronger steel boilers could be made to withstand higher pressures. By 1874 the first deep-sea commercial steamer fitted with a triple expansion engine was built. It presented a new age of sea power in which steam technology finally proved more economical than sail.

As marine technology developed, it became a contributing arm to the industrial cluster already blossoming on land. The engineers who designed machines for use at sea cooperated and formed learned societies with their railway and general engineering counterparts, providing a cumulatively growing pool of knowledge and experience.

With steam power, shipping was freed from its reliance on winds and ocean currents. Ships powered themselves; they could travel where they wanted, when they wanted. This made it possible to develop a new kind of shipping service: liners. Liners sailed to a regular schedule, thereby increasing the value they provided to customers with a regular and reliable service. The idea of running at a specific time, regardless of whether the ship had a full load, involved considerable risk but it was hoped this would be more than offset by attracting better paying cargoes such as mail and cabin passengers, attracted to a fast regular service.[36]

In the early days, steamships involved a substantial investment that was beyond the small player. For that reason, the principal mail and passenger lines were created as chartered companies. Probably the most famous of the new liner companies was P&O. The company was started by Brodie McGhie Wilcox, a shipbroker, and Arthur Anderson, who had spent time in the British navy before joining Wilcox's company. The two formed a partnership and became ship-owners in 1825, sailing a schooner to Portugal. In 1834, they issued a prospectus for the Peninsular and Oriental Steam Navigation Company and in 1837 gained the contract to carry mail to the Iberian peninsula. The contract was eventually extended through the Mediterranean. By 1840 they owned seven ships, growing to twenty-three in 1850 and fifty-one in 1867.[37] A major factor in the growth of the company was the growth of the British empire. Two-thirds of its passengers to India were government employees, the company to a large extent being an unofficial arm of the Raj.[38]

P&O was one of many companies that grew in the wake of the East India Company, which had been stripped of its monopoly in 1834. Earlier, Adam Smith, the father of modern economics and author of *The Wealth of Nations,* had attacked the privileged position of companies like the East India Company who used their monopoly to restrict the volume of commercial activity and get higher prices for their products.[39] The EIC had hotly defended its monopoly, but political forces were shifting as the new economy gave birth to new stakeholders. Industrialists, in particular the cotton kings of Lancashire, were frustrated with the company's inability to sell British goods in India and China, the largest markets known to man.[40] Their stance reflected a new confidence of the manufacturers in the competitiveness of their product. (Until this time, their attacks on the company had actually been the reverse: attacking imports of Indian textiles into Britain posing an 'unfair' competition for the domestic product.) The power of the industrialists helped to bring the monopoly to an end and the Asian trade was thrown open. By the time the EIC's monopoly was reviewed, the risks of trade to Asia had been long overcome and the economic security provided by a monopoly could no longer be justified. The nation possessed a wealth of navigators with experience in these trades. Unleashed, they contributed to a dramatic growth in shipping in the region.

Over time, steamship technology improved, reducing the costs and increasing the range of the new technologies. Improvements resulted from a number of factors, including more efficient machinery which reduced coal consumption and the number of staff required to stoke the engines. Improvements also resulted from the building of larger ships, which meant bigger loads could be carried without a corresponding increase in labour requirements, and advances in the iron industry, which reduced the price of iron and the cost of building ships. As a result of these advances, between 1873 and 1901 the cost of the coal used on the London to Bombay route declined from 21s to 13.55s per tonne, the size of the crew was reduced and the ships themselves became cheaper to buy. When combined with cheaper port rates, these economics of scale enabled shippers to reduce their costs from forty-six to sixteen shillings per ton.

However, steam was not the most suitable form of power on all routes. On longer voyages, sail was still the most economic form of shipping.[41] In fact, competition from steam technology and new areas of research associated with the new boats, such as in hull shapes, actually helped to inspire technological advance in sailing ships.

Other developments continued to reduce costs and advance the possibilities of trade. The opening of the Suez Canal in 1869 reduced the London to Bombay trip from 10,667 to 6,274 miles, and this reduced the coal requirements for steamships on the longer routes. Costs were reduced with the introduction of mechanical appliances for loading which reduced time in port and enabled ships to make more voyages. The development of refrigeration meant that perishable goods such as meat, fruit and dairy products could now be transported in a fresh state. These advances helped to fuel an expanding international trade and the world was more and more becoming a global market.

The arrival of steam and iron totally changed the nature of ship-building. Previously, ship-building had been spread over a large geographical area, nearly every port having its own repairing and building facilities. With the new technologies, the industry was defined by access to supplies of iron and coal, and became concentrated in three areas, the Clyde, Tyneside and Belfast. The industry had acquired a totally new skill base, and the old timber and sail craftsmen-based industry went into obsolescence. People came to the industry, not with a background in shipping, but with new iron and coal engineering skills. As British pioneers developed their capabilities, they built up knowledge, experience and a reputation that other nations lacked. Consequently, anyone wanting to buy a steamship would think of the British yards.

David and Robert Napier were pioneering entrepreneurs who arrived in the industry with backgrounds as blacksmith and ironfounder. They built their first marine engine in 1816, which they followed with the *Rob Roy*, the first steamship to cross the channel between the Clyde and Belfast. Their first ship-building yard was on the Thames, but in 1841 they moved to Govan on the Clyde, launching the region's great tradition of iron ship-building.[42]

The Napiers provided their employees with the engineering capabilities required in the industry and a number of them eventually formed their own companies. David Todd and John MacGregor had been managers in David Napier's works before opening their own yard in 1836. John Elder, who patented the marine compound engine, had been employed as chief draftsman with Robert Napier before commencing his own business (later becoming the Fairfield Shipping and Engineering Company). Also from the Napier yard were J. and G. Thomson who founded their own shipyard at Govan in 1851, later known as the Clydebank Shipbuilding and Engineering Company. William Denny came from a family of ship-builders, but it was after working in Napier's that William Denny and Brothers of Dumbarton was created.

The growth of many firms in one district led to the creation of external economies. Regions with many firms could share infrastructural and transportation facilities. They also developed highly trained pools of workers that employers could take on or lay off as demand required. The concentration of so many firms in a region meant that common standards of worker training and qualification would be available to all employers. Given the high quality of labour and the fact that training and organization was performed by senior workers, administration costs for the various firms were very low. Employers did not need to invest in managerial or planning skills. Firms remained relatively small and were family-owned and managed. The low capital requirements of firms made entrance to the industry relatively easy while competition between firms helped to maintain standards.

This was a pattern of industrial development found in many industries throughout the country. Industries might originally grow at a location because of their access to raw materials, for example steel for ship-building or clay for ceramics. As the industry grew, a pool of skilled workers emerged who would move from employer to employer in the region as demand dictated. These districts became known as Marshallian districts after the economist Alfred Marshall, who recognized that firms gained these external economies if they existed in the same area. If an entrepreneur wanted to be in the industry, it made sense to go to those regions where these economic advantages could be gained. By 1850 the reputation of the Clyde was attracting ship-builders from other places. By 1876 there were more iron ships built on the Clyde than in the rest of the world put together.[43]

The head start obtained by the British also enabled them to build up economies of scale that made it hard for foreigners to compete. The steel industry could make longer production runs, thereby reducing costs.[44] The large market made it possible for ship-builders to specialize in certain types of ships, particularly in the building of tramps. This allowed ship-builders to economize on the equipment they needed and allowed them to build even before orders had arrived.

Many of the new steamship companies formed strong associations with ship-builders, which strengthened the profits of both companies. Ship-builders gained repeat orders and an opportunity to specialize in certain types of ships. In return, the ship-owners received vessels at lower prices; for example, the White Star Line completed an agreement to have all their steamers built and designed by Harland & Wolff in Belfast.[45] The ship-builders, for their part, offered not to build ships liable to compete with White Star services. The two co-operated with their ideas. The flow of information contributed to the line's ability to meet the market with hitherto unknown standards of comfort.

Cunard obtained financial backing from the engine builder Robert Napier.[46] In return, Napier gained a guaranteed market that must have encouraged him to invest further in the new technology. The relationship led to a flow of information including, for example, what size ships would be needed, given the necessity to store coal on board. However, Cunard was rather conservative in developing new ideas, preferring to let others take the risks.[47] While many pioneering companies went bankrupt, Cunard would only adopt an idea once its success had been proven. The failure of many individual first movers illustrates the dangers of being a pioneer. However, the environment of expanding global trade did much to favour early movers adopting the technologies in a growing market and the industry as a whole could override the failures of a few.

The British had created a new economic system driven by steam and coal. British steamships travelled to foreign ports where British-built railways opened up the hinterland of places like Canada and India. From India came jute, indigo, hides, tea, rice and raw cotton. From Canada came lumber and grain, while South Africa gave diamonds and gold. Rubber, first found in Brazil and West Africa, was distributed throughout Britain's tropical colonies and became a major export for Malaya and Ceylon. Sheep were introduced into Australia and New Zealand, providing a new source of wool and meat, once refrigeration was invented. Many companies born on this growing wave are still in existence today. They include Cadbury, Lever Brothers and Bovril, companies that invested in foreign plantations, agencies and trading companies to ensure the supply of necessary resources.[48]

It was through this process that the world divided into industrial and non-industrial nations, taking a shape that would remain for the next century.[49] Industrial exports flowed from Europe in return for commodities. As the colonies became richer from their exports to

Britain, they in turn could afford more of Britain's manufactured goods. The resulting commercial system developed reinforcing arms of commerce, industry and shipping, the lead in one field reinforcing its strength in the others.

British rule enhanced the ability of colonies to obtain capital on the London markets, by promoting law, order and stability, thereby reducing the investment risk (although often the benefit went to the white elite in those countries). However, it was not necessary to be ruled by Britain to be part of this process. The infrastructure of the United States was developed largely with finance from Britain. Similarity in language, culture and institutions helped to reduce the risk of investment, although shipping between the two nations remained in the hands of the British. Argentina also became an extension of this structure in that it was a provider of primary products, such as beef, to Britain.[50]

While the growth of the British empire helped fuel the growth of trade and shipping, this was not a protected arena. In 1849 the Navigation Acts, which had protected British industry during its early growth, were repealed. This opened colonial shipping routes to competitors from foreign nations. Not only did the repeal do away with the inefficiencies of the legislation, it also reflected the confidence of English shipping in its ability to defeat the competition. Britannia ruled the waves and could comfortably take on all comers. The nation became a disciple of free trade, forgetting the role protection had played in its early growth.

British advances in railway, steamships and iron hulls provided the technologies by which trade volumes soared. But large-scale enterprises like these could not be built without capital and here the City of London came to take a central place. Wealth generated by the Industrial Revolution found its way to London's capital markets where it was lent to foreign governments who wanted to develop their nations' commercial infrastructures.

Limited liability legislation introduced in 1855 made it easier to raise capital as it reduced risk. This changed the nature of ship-ownership, and the old companies of many partners became a thing of the past.[51] The new law gave birth to scores of one-ship joint stock companies, often owned and managed by small groups of investors. Entrepreneurs with capital, connections or experience in trades (perhaps from serving in the East India Company) seized the opportunities the new technologies and legal protection gave. Many investors established family firms, some with partners.

Small family companies were very common in the tramp ship-ping market. Tramp ships did not sail to a regular schedule like liners. They travelled the world, where and when the cargoes dictated. It was a form of shipping made possible by the development of tele-graph technology that informed shippers in advance where cargoes lay. Telegraph and cable made communication easier and took a lot of the risk out of business, as goods were sent less by speculation and more to order. It also allowed an increase in contact between the buyer and seller, with the elimination of the middle man. This led to reduced prices and increased business. Brokers had almost complete knowledge of the rates being paid in the main chartering centres for the various trades and the ships receiving those rates. This open information, large number of firms and relatively low costs of entry made the tramp market highly competitive, perhaps the closest thing we have seen to perfect competition in the industry. In this fiercely competitive environment, tramp-owners were characterized as hard-driven businessmen fiercely competing with other ship-owners.[52] Tramp shipping enjoyed an annual growth rate of 7 per cent between 1870 and the First World War,[53] by which time they constituted 60 per cent of the nation's fleet.[54]

As British industry rode an increase in world trade that it was doing so much to shape, the profits were reinvested in the latest sophisticated technology, skills and experience, allowing the British to defeat foreign competition. By the middle of the nineteenth century Britain produced about two-thirds of the world's coal, about half its iron, five-sevenths of its steel, two-fifths of its hardware and about half its commercial cotton cloth. Its iron and coal-driven merchant fleet, which carried manufacturing goods out and raw materials in, was by 1890 larger than the rest of the world's fleets put together. In London, the City's financial institutions provided the capital by which the system advanced. The result was a buoyant economic system in which related commercial and productive activities propelled each other forward to a position of global eminence.[55]

8

CHANGES IN THE WEST

In 1776 the North American continent was still dominated by the most primitive economic system, hunting and gathering. Over most of the continent, native Americans gained their resources by hunting and gathering, as did the few hardy Europeans who ventured west of the Appalachian Mountains. The only place where the economy reached any level of sophistication was confined to a narrow strip of land along the Atlantic coast. It was here that the vast bulk of the European population lived.

In New England small family farms produced goods for their own consumption. Further south, in the Middle Atlantic States, the economy became more market-orientated and grain produced on large home-steads formed the basis of prosperous market links with the West Indies. However, it was in the American South that the greatest links with the international market were formed. Here, the huge tobacco, rice and cotton plantations, worked by slaves, produced exports that were marketed to Europe. The common characteristic of all these economic systems was their basis in agriculture and raw materials. In the coastal towns and cities, some small crafts and manufacturing had developed but generally there was little industry, with most manufactured goods imported from England.

A number of towns grew in the wake of this market activity, notably Boston, Salem, Newport, New York and Philadelphia. The shopkeepers and ship's captains who handled the imports and exports eventually expanded the distribution of their products, becoming petty merchants in the process. As the domestic economy grew, some of these merchants came to acquire greater wealth and influence. However, compared with activity in other parts of the world, their scale of business was not great. The population was small, transportation was difficult and the nation had an inadequate money supply to lubricate transactions.[1] The market did not provide opportunity to specialize and the merchants normally performed a small number of transactions covering a wide range of goods.

Before the United States gained its independence, its ships flew under the British flag, so received some benefits of protection under the British Navigation Acts, as well as advantages in being tied to the strongest merchant navy in the world. They could actively participate in British colonial trade and many New England shippers gained their first experience of international trade carrying grain to their British colonies in the West Indies.[2] However, the vast bulk of American domestic and international shipping at the end of the eighteenth century was conducted by foreigners, in particular the British.[3]

By the 1760s the leading merchant in New England was Thomas Hancock, a shrewd and bold operator who distributed goods to storekeepers in Massachusetts, but earned most of his fortune supplying the British army during the Seven Years War (1756–63). The war was primarily one between European powers but, because Britain and France had colonies overseas, battles were waged around the world. It ended in 1763 with Britain claiming French territories in North America and India.

Thomas Hancock did not live to fully enjoy his wartime profits. He died the following year and his fortune was inherited by his nephew John who overnight became the richest man in New England. On a global scale, his fortune of £70,000 was modest compared with Richard Arkwright's £500,000 in England or Abul Ghafur's £1,000,000 at the beginning of the century. Yet Hancock was six times richer than the richest merchants in Philadelphia.[4] North America was a commercial backwater, lacking the environment that created millionaires elsewhere in the world.

John Hancock lacked the commercial ability of his uncle. To some degree he suffered in taking over the business when peace returned, depriving him of lucrative army supply contracts, but the activities he did start were not successful. In particular, he attempted to corner the English market for whale oil, but found he could not compete with the more experienced oil merchants from Nantucket.

Financing the Seven Years War had been expensive for the British government and much had been spent protecting the North American colonies from French troops. To the British, it was only fair that the Americans contribute to the costs, especially given they had a continuing need for a military presence. The French in Quebec had the potential to rebel at any moment, while native Americans in the Pontiac threatened colonists at the border. The Pontiac threat was very much one of the colonists' own making. While the British government had made pledges to the indigenous people which it intended to keep, land-hungry colonists felt no restraint in taking land in regions occupied by native peoples. As the future president George Washington put it: 'those seeking good lands in the West must find and claim them without delay'.[5]

To pay for military expenses, the British government placed taxes on a series of goods from tea and sugar to playing cards and dice. The Navigation Acts, which were originally introduced to encourage trade, were also more rigorously enforced to increase the revenue from trade duties. Much of the colonial trade was done with places like the French West Indies which were outside the imperial system, so the new trade restrictions hurt merchants like John Hancock who increasingly reverted to smuggling to evade the taxes. In 1768 his sloop *Liberty* was impounded by British customs officials for tax violations. This led to a riot by those Bostonians expecting the cargoes it carried.

It was a cargo carried by the East India Company that provided the final spark to rebellion. A tax on tea had been a source of grievance for the colonials and, on 16 December 1773, a mob dressed as Indians climbed aboard a ship and poured its cargo of tea into the ocean. The act, immortalized as the Boston Tea Party, heralded the beginning of the battle for independence. When the Declaration of Independence was drawn up, John Hancock was the first to put his signature on it.

Britain's loss of its American colonies was not so much a case that its claims were unfair, for many in North America were willing to contribute to their share of costs. It was more a case of how things were done. In many ways forces were at work similar to those in a modern company that grows too quickly. Those at the top had become out of touch with those on the ground. They had become rigid in their decision-making and failed to consult or understand what they were dealing with. The lack of voice for those on the ground is embodied in the revolutionary rallying cry: 'No taxation without representation.'

When the United States gained its independence from Britain it did not lead to a dramatic change in its international economic relations with the world. The United States economy was still strongly shaped by the British imperial trading system. The South was still tied to European markets, while northern fish, farming and forestry products found their primary market in the British West Indies.

The American continent possessed a wealth of untapped resources, so it was inevitable that the nation's first wave of economic growth was based on trade and the exploitation of those resources. This gave plenty of opportunity for entrepreneurs, one of whom was John Jacob Astor.[6] Born in Germany in 1763, Astor emigrated to the United States at the age of twenty where he got a job beating furs for the New York merchant, Robert Bowne. Before long, Astor was making the long and fatiguing journeys inland to meet and bargain with the tribes who provided the furs for his employer. By 1786 Astor had earned enough money to start his own fur business in a small store on Water Street. Every penny he earned was invested into the company's expansion and soon he had scores of trappers and agents ranging the wilderness in search of furs. By 1800 he had amassed the colossal sum of a quarter of a million dollars at a time when an average family could live comfortably on $800 a year. With such wealth, it was not difficult for Astor to purchase ships and transport his own goods to Europe. When his ships arrived in Britain, they were reloaded with manufactured goods for sale in the United States, thereby expanding his profit.

Astor's climb was not smooth and included moments of bad luck. In 1808 he incorporated the American Fur Company with the intention of gaining furs from more remote areas of the continent, but the War of 1812 hampered his hopes. Fortunately, the war was short-lived and Astor eventually established a monopoly in the fur trade, which he protected through a number of means, including government favouritism, fraud and force. Any individual who dared to threaten the monopoly was exposed to the most severe of reprisals, including the possibility of murder. Astor's company also violated federal laws by plying native Americans with drink and swindling them out of their lands and furs. However, Astor's millions could always afford him the best lawyers and the support of powerful people in the Senate. His monopoly was secure and highly profitable. The company had capital of $1,000,000 but returned $500,000 per year, a massive profit of 50 per cent.

Astor was not the only entrepreneur to invest in ships during this period. The Napoleonic Wars gave a great boost to US shipping as it distracted European competition and, for a time, gave American shippers the chance to enjoy the benefits of neutrality. This protection, and the opening of new markets with China and Russia, turned the shipping industry into one of the most profitable avenues for investment. It became the focus of all the nation's risk capital and provided the basis of many American fortunes.[7]

It is common to see this period as a time when the great houses of American commerce were built, but most businesses at some time either failed or came close to the brink of disaster. Nathaniel Griswold, who became a successful tea merchant and ship-owner, said that, of the hundred merchants he had known over a fifty-year span, only seven had avoided bankruptcy.[8] But it was a period when the United States, as a nation, built significant skills and abilities in business.

This early period of capability building was followed by a process of advance as Americans innovated to meet the particular needs of their industry. For shipping in the North Atlantic, heavily built packet ships were designed with reasonable speed and good cargo-carrying capacity. For the fast developing trade to China, a line version of the packet was employed, the progenitor of the 1840s' clipper, built for speed. The bulk of the US fleet in the nineteenth century were schooners with gaff sails and two or more masts. These were fast ships but had less carrying space than square-rigged vessels. During the nineteenth century Americans added more masts that could propel faster, bigger ships. On the back of growing trade and innovative technology, the nation by 1850 had succeeded in building the second largest mercantile fleet in the world.

However, many believed the economy should take new directions. They wanted the United States to become a strong nation, truly independent of Britain, and this meant developing the nation's industrial base. The first US Treasury Secretary, Alexander Hamilton, released a *Report on Manufactures* which strongly argued for the introduction of protectionism to support local industry. He also established the Society for the Establishment of Useful Manufactures. He had earlier visited the Great Falls on the Passaic River, which he thought could be used to power industry and, through the society, founded Paterson in the vicinity with the intention it should become an industrial city. While the society's efforts to build its own mills failed, its management of the falls and real-estate sales spurred investment and, by 1815, thirteen water-powered cotton mills were operating in the region.

In the South there was no need for industrialization. It produced one of the key cargoes for Britain's Industrial Revolution. Cotton plantations provided the raw material for Britain's textile industry, and wealth poured into the South. So prosperous was the region that, as late as 1860, it would have been the world's fourth richest nation if it had seceded from the United States.[9] But Southern wealth was not equally distributed. Slaves, who themselves had been treated like cargo on the Atlantic run, did not share in the economic value they created.

The desire for industrialization was far from universal, and encountered resistance from powerful opponents, including Benjamin Franklin and presidents Jefferson and Madison. It might seem strange that Benjamin Franklin, a man at the forefront of science and innovation, opposed industrialization, but this was an issue that struck at the heart of American values. The Declaration of Independence was influenced by John Locke's ideas of natural rights and philosophies which stressed private property, the Protestant work ethic and individual rights. Franklin believed that industrialization would lead to disparities of wealth and power, and this would be a formula for social unrest. Like many others, Franklin believed the United States should be based on a simple agricultural economy of individual producers.

Some industrial enterprises were started during this time, but the main engine of growth was agriculture. Before 1840 agriculture enjoyed a rapid growth as immigration increased the manpower available to develop the new land.[10] After 1840 other factors contributed to the growth of agriculture, in particular the new technologies and methods of production which were coming into practice. Between 1845 and 1855 the rate of investment in farm machinery jumped from $11,000,000 to $23,000,000.[11] In 1843 the first commercial sales of fertilizer appeared. It was a period of growing demand where the market rewarded practical invention.

Throughout the nineteenth century the country experienced large-scale immigration from Europe. As the population migrated west, previously underutilized resources were opened for development, while the burgeoning population created new markets. It was a process of economic development with similarities to Sung China during its southern migration, and the integration of Gujarat into the Mughal empire. Accompanying the migration west were two new transportation systems that facilitated the flow of labour and resources. A canal-building boom in the 1820s and 1830s helped facilitate early trade, but it was the railroads that came to perform the key role. The first tracks were built by the Baltimore and Ohio Railroad in 1828. By 1850 tracks were crossing the Appalachian Mountains and, within the decade, had reached the Mississippi River.

The railroads integrated the vast nation into one large market in the same way that the river system had done for China during the T'ang and Sung dynasties. Local producers began to make products for markets many miles away. For example, Texas cowboys brought their cattle to the railheads for transportation to the markets in the eastern cities. An eight-dollar cow in Texas could go for forty dollars in the East, so there was a strong incentive for cowboys to get their stock on the trains. Cattle from Texas would be driven north through the Indian Territories to railhead towns like Dodge City, Abilene and Wichita. Having spent weeks on the trail, the cowboys would be let loose on the pleasures that the rail towns provided, gambling, drinking and whoring. To deal with the drunkenness and disorderly conduct, these towns appointed marshals. Wild Bill Hickok was marshal of Abilene, while Wyart Earp spent time as a lawman in Wichita. The activities of the cowboys contributed to the reputation of the Wild West, a reflection of how economic systems shape the social system and culture. Even the name 'cowboys' is derived from the commodity they took to market.

While the cowboys were spending their money on drinking, gambling and prostitutes, at the other end of the railroad tracks an economic transformation was taking place. The huge volumes of cattle arriving at the Chicago slaughterhouses placed great pressure on them to increase production. The response was the assembly line. Meat-packers invested millions in large mechanized packing-houses that enabled them to process the vast quantities coming through. The new business environment created new rules and rituals for the slaughter of fatted calves. The new gospel was mass production and would soon be adopted by the rest of the economy.

Such changes in the economy did not occur without pain. For example, John Burrows, a leading merchant in Davenport, Iowa, underwent economic dislocation with the arrival of the railroads. Burrows had built a successful business investing in relationships with wholesalers and suppliers, warehousing and transportation facilities. The arrival of the Chicago and Rock Island Railroad in 1854 offered speedy regular services to Chicago, not St Louis where Burrows had established many contacts. Because small quantities could now be transported with ease, many small competitors arrived and Burrows' large warehousing facilities, which had been an asset in the pre-rail days, became an expensive liability tying up money. Burrows tried to adapt by diversifying into flour mills, a sawmill and a reaper factory, but nothing worked. The new environment brought by the railroad required business methodologies too alien to Burrows' familiar way of doing business. He went bankrupt within five years of the railroad's arrival.

As in all the economies we have looked at where a market is made, a number of auxiliary institutions are required that make it easier to perform transactions and smooth the flow of capital. In the United States, new banks, insurance companies and mercantile exchanges emerged where contracts were made and deliveries arranged. The first Stock Exchange was created at Philadelphia, followed by Boston and New York.[12] The earliest dealings at the Exchange were in government bonds, banks and insurance companies.

After 1812 transportation became the largest growth sector in the American economy and the popularity of stocks and bonds in railroad companies helped fuel the growth in capital markets. The large amounts of capital required were beyond the reach of small entrepreneurs, and rail companies were dependent on external finance from the very beginning. Sometimes rail men went directly to London where specialized investment bankers existed with the levels of capital necessary. But, eventually, demand from the rail companies enabled US investment bankers to become established. The pioneer was Nicholas Biddle who in 1823 became president of the Bank of the United States in Philadephia.[13] During the 1830s, he and his brother Thomas, whose own company marketed securities in railroads, helped finance all the major railroad companies of the time. Biddle had placed an agent in London to raise finance that would be funnelled through the bank to the rail companies.

Biddle's bank failed in 1840 and the centre of investment activity shifted from Philadelphia to Boston, which was flush with funds from shipping, whaling and textiles. Here, during the 1840s, a close-knit circle of mercantile and manufacturing capitalists emerged, including John Murray Forbes and John E. Thayer. Forbes and his cousin J.P. Cushing earned substantial wealth trading with China. They exported pelts from Oregon, sandalwood from Hawaii and opium from Turkey in return for Chinese tea and silk. In China, Forbes formed a trading relationship with Howqua, once the richest man in the world, whom he also convinced to invest in American railroads.

However, the rail industry demanded more capital than the personal connections of the Bostonians could muster. By 1850 there was only one city in the country that could mobilize the necessary large-scale funds for railroad construction. New York was enjoying prosperity as the nation's leading port. Profits from the expanding import trade provided New York merchants, bankers and brokers with funds for long-term investment. The American–European trade also provided the city's merchants with commercial contacts in Europe from whom capital could be raised. Wall Street brokers became specialists in marketing railroad securities and by 1860 held undisputed dominance in this area.

Between 1849 and 1860 American railroad mileage jumped from 7,000 miles to over 30,000 and railroad companies reached a size not previously seen. To provide an example, the largest manufacturing enterprises were textile mills, but the initial costs of the biggest mills in the 1850s rarely reached $500,000. By contrast, at the same time, five railroads had issued stocks and bonds of over $190,000,000. By 1873 the costs of building and equipment for the Pennsylvania railroad were $400,000,000.

This wave of economic development provided by the opening of resources and development of markets gave huge opportunities for entrepreneurs. No one illustrates the ride to prosperity more than Cornelius Vanderbilt. Vanderbilt was born in 1794, the son of a Staten Island farmer who also ran an irregular ferry service across New York

Bay to Manhattan Island. Vanderbilt junior found ferrying more attractive than farming and in 1811, with $100 from his mother, he bought a piragua (a shallow boat) with which he hauled freight and passengers across New York Bay. As more and more immigrants came to the region, Vanderbilt rode the wave of a growing market. He gained a reputation for reliability and in the second decade of the nineteenth century began operating schooners on both the East and North Hudson Rivers.

In 1818 Cornelius Vanderbilt was hired to pilot a steamship in return for the substantial sum of $1,000 a year. He also took over a dilapidated inn where his passengers rested en route. His wife ran the inn, making a healthy profit. Eventually Vanderbilt started building his own steamships and ran lines to Albany, New Haven, Providence and Boston. New York at the time was enjoying rapid population growth and provided a soaring customer base. By 1835 Vanderbilt was worth half a million dollars, ranking him among New York's wealthiest. In tribute to his nautical skills, people began to refer to him as 'the Commodore'. He went on to establish maritime links with the West Coast (through Nicaragua), and ran steamships across the Atlantic with the aid of mail subsidies.

Cornelius Vanderbilt's son, William Henry Vanderbilt, became interested in railroads, buying the Staten Island Railroad, which, at the time, was having trouble surviving. By cutting expenses and linking the railroad with a line of ferries, William Henry turned the railroad around. This success inspired his father who began investing in the railroads that linked with his ferries. This was a time when investment opportunities on the New York Stock Exchange were dominated by the stocks of railroad companies and Cornelius Vanderbilt seized the opportunities available. In 1858 he sold his West Coast shipping link for $20,000,000, and invested in railroads, particularly those entering New York. He stopped trying to compete with British steamships on the Atlantic, and eventually divested from all his maritime activities. In 1867 he became president of the New York and Hudson Railroad. He then purchased the New York Central Railroad which he merged into his previous acquisition. The 'best steamship manager of the time'[14] was becoming a railroad king. By the time Cornelius Vanderbilt died, he was the richest man in America. His fortune of $90,000,000 was more than twice the size of his nearest rival's. Born to the sea, his wealth matured on land, a reflection of how the US economy had turned from the sea to its heartland.

9

CHANGES IN THE EAST

In 1793 the British government sent a mission led by Lord Macartney to Peking. Loaded with gifts for the Chinese emperor, the purpose of the mission was to increase the trading rights of British merchants in China and establish a British representative at the Chinese capital. However, the mission did not receive the response it had hoped for. The resulting edict from the emperor to King George III read:

> We, by the Grace of Heaven, Emperor, instruct the King of England to take note of our charge . . .
>
> As to what you have requested in your message, O King, namely to be allowed to send one of your subjects to reside in the Celestial Empire to look after your country's trade . . .
>
> The Celestial Empire, ruling all within the four seas, simply concentrates on carrying out the affairs of government properly, and does not value rare and precious things. Now you, O King, have presented various objects to the throne, and mindful of your loyalty in presenting offerings from afar, we have specially ordered the Yamen [government department] to receive them . . . Nevertheless we have never valued ingenious articles, nor do we have the slightest need of your country's manufactures . . . Hence we have issued these detailed instructions and have commanded your tribute envoys to return safely home . . .[1]

This condescending response to the English king reveals much about the Chinese view of the world at the end of the eighteenth century. It highlights arrogance and an ignorance of the changes in the world. The Chinese still saw themselves as rulers of the four seas while the Westerners were mere barbarians. The edict reflected the prevailing belief that China was the centre of civilization, to which all other nations owed their loyalty. However, China no longer ruled the waves and was losing its technical supremacy in the cargoes that filled the boats and the knowledge that had generated maritime innovation. Worse still, no one in China had any idea of the developments that Europe was making.

At this time the Chinese still had some reason for their high sense of self-belief. Throughout the eighteenth century Europeans certainly viewed China with enormous respect. Philosophers during the enlightenment saw China as a utopian state that they thought European governments should emulate.[2] The Chinese economy, with its hydraulic projects and national network of canals, was still generating wonderful levels of wealth. Agricultural production, which as late as the eighteenth century accounted for most of a nation's productivity, was higher per hectare in China than in the West,[3] albeit with a more labour-intensive method.

The Chinese economy showed a continual ability to adapt and grow. Between 1600 and 1850, the amount of land under cultivation doubled, and new crops were introduced, including fresh strains of early ripening rice and American crops like potatoes and peanuts.[4] These crops could be used in dry land areas not previously exploited, expanding the nation's agricultural frontier. As a consequence, Chinese society became more rural and even more market-orientated. There was a rise in the number of goods traded and the number of market towns.

As private enterprise expanded, merchants and guilds rose in power. Entrepreneurs developed relationships with other merchants and built networks by which they could gain supplies and distribute their output. This was an efficient market structure in which industries and merchants responded to the ebbs and flows of market forces.[5]

Not only did the economy show flexibility, but also high levels of social mobility. During the Ch'ing dynasty, social relationships in the countryside were changing. One cause of this was the peasant rebellions. Sparked by famine, flood, drought, rapacious officials or usurers foreclosing on mortgaged land, there were frequent occasions when the peasants reached boiling point. The possibility of being murdered caused recurring discomfort to landlords who gradually decided owning serfs was not an attractive option, and serfdom came to an end. This, and the practice of dividing land estates on death, resulted in a society which has been described as 'one of the most fluid in the world, lacking any of the status or caste restraints which typified late pre-modern Japan or India'.[6]

This was an economy displaying all the pillars of growth that modern economists seek, a wealthy, socially mobile, market-driven economy. One source suggests that the per capita income at the beginning of the nineteenth century was equal to or greater than European levels, even though Europe was in the process of its Industrial Revolution.[7] This may be overstated as another source[8] states that the per capita income of Europeans was double that of China at the time. Nevertheless, the Chinese economy seemed to be based on solid economic fundamentals.

The economy still provided opportunity for entrepreneurs. In fact, the richest man in the world is said to have been living in Canton Harbour. This was Howqua, whose wealth in 1834 was estimated at $26,000,000, the equivalent of $3 billion in the year 2000.[9] Howqua profited from the emperor's decision not to open China to trade, which meant European traders had no option but to do business with a guild of thirteen merchants who had been given permission to trade with Westerners. Howqua was the leading merchant of this guild (or *cohong*) and had grown phenomenally rich from his position. Tea and silks provided by Howqua were sold to British companies like Jardine Matheson who carried them to England where companies like Twinings had established themselves in the British tea market. The British passion for tea had helped make Howqua a wealthy man and a global capitalist. His wealth was invested on the London stock market and he bought shares in the burgeoning US railroads.

Chinese officials had given the merchant guild in Canton a monopoly on trade with Westerners. In return for this privileged position, the merchants collected tax on the trade for the government. The merchants also had to tolerate frequent 'squeezes' from government officials whenever funds were required for public works. In the Chinese business culture, maintaining good relationships with the local mandarins was a key commercial strategy, something that did not impress the British merchants who felt that Howqua's 'natural timidity of character' made him vulnerable to the demands of government. His wealth was 'always an object of attention to the government, eager to inculpate him whenever an opportunity presented itself, causing his entire submission to all their requisitions'. Nevertheless, the British traders at Canton praised Howqua for his 'great command of capital and superior intelligence'. Unlike Abdul Ghafur who gained his market power in Gujarat through aggression, Howqua was generous. His success allowed him the luxury of a palatial home with 500 servants and a pleasure garden of 10,000 pines. He dressed in the finest silks and satins and dined on the finest foods.

Howqua's wealth was acquired through time-old patterns of commercial behaviour. He built relationships with merchants who distributed his products in the Chinese hinterland and also built symbiotic relationships with officials. The products he carried might change and he might have been particularly astute, but he was still a merchant riding the old wave of prosperity. He was very different to the industrialist–entrepreneurs who were building new waves of growth in Britain. Entrepreneurs developing new products and new production techniques were very rare in China.

These later years of prosperity mask the fact that something was wrong with the Chinese economy. Although vigorous economic growth occurred between 1500 and 1800, it was not accompanied by a per capita increase in income.[10] The average person was no better off. There was extensive growth but not intensive. The economy experienced growth within the established paradigm with existing patterns of behaviour, relationships and productive activity, but there was a notable absence of invention.

The lack of significant innovation in the techniques of production suggests that there was something wrong with Chinese science, which failed to advance at the rate achieved in the West.[11] In Europe institutions such as the Royal Society and the Royal Observatory at Greenwich had contributed to growth. China also had institutions devoted to scientific advance, such as the Imperial Bureau of Astronomy and, from as early as 1645, a Catholic missionary had always been in charge of the bureau.[12] However, astronomical advances were not widely distributed in China as they were in the West, and advance in China endured a stronger process of censorship.

Educated people in China devoted less time to practical problems and this had serious implications for technology. Chinese thought and education were changing in a way which reflected the attitude that the economy had solved many material problems. Philosophers moved away from consideration of the material world to the metaphysical, exploring the mind and the spirit.[13] As the nation's top thinkers moved away from exploring the physical world, the growth of a European-type science, based on mechanistic and quantitative approaches to phenomena, was unlikely to occur, limiting the potential for science and technology.

This retreat from practical technological matters was another example of how those with power become distant from core productive activities. It could be seen in the long fingernails of mandarins who never saw manual work,[14] a visual symbol of the distance between those who worked and those with education and power. The consequence was a lack of attention to developing new production techniques. This stands in dramatic contrast to Europe where knowledge and education were increasingly applied to problems of industry, and institutions such as the Society of Arts were created to facilitate this link.

Another cause of technical stagnation was the formalized nature of Confucian education. Once a highly rational mode of thought, Confucianism had become traditional and conservative.[15] Schools did not encourage innovation but focused on reproducing the old classics. This emphasis on old values resulted in examinations becoming formalized with a preoccupation with style. An example of this can be seen in geography: while British mariners had mapped the globe from New Zealand to Greenland, the Chinese in the early nineteenth century still thought of the world as flat, with China located in the centre.[16]

However, the links between science and technology should not be stressed too strongly. It presupposes that industry in the West progressed on the basis of scientific advance, and this was not the case until the nineteenth century. Industrialization in Britain during the eighteenth century had only a weak connection with scientific thought[17] and most industrial advances were made by artisans with little scientific knowledge. These 'tinkerers' held no scientific advantage over Chinese artisans who were very capable of making the products of the early Industrial Revolution, and had already made their own water-powered spinning machines. A true technological gap did not open up until the arrival of advances associated with steel and electricity.

If Chinese businessmen were failing to innovate, a good place to search for an explanation was the market itself. Growth in the Chinese market had led to very high levels of specialization: artisans specialized in producing goods with little attention given to the workings of the market, while merchants specialized in distributing goods with little thought as to how the goods were produced. The result was a rising gap between producers and merchants and, in many cases, intermediaries increased this gap. The consequence was that those with capital and the keenest awareness of market forces had no interest in production technology. At the same time, producers lacked the capital and marketing sense to create any significant leap in production technology.[18] Consequently, no significant leap occurred. There was a similar problem in India, where market-based specialization stunted domestic innovation. By contrast, in Britain young industries were being created by men like Josiah Wedgwood, who had both craft skills and an entrepreneurial eye for the market.

Another barrier to innovation in the Chinese market was the mentality it bred. Under the market-based rationality, businessmen sought solutions to their problems in the market. If a merchant had problems getting supplies, he never sought a technical or productive solution, but sought solutions in the market place where he had developed his skills. For example, if demand was high for cotton, wages would rise and encourage some of the hundreds of thousands of peasant households to divert their labour from agriculture to the cotton industry, and, when demand fell, the peasants' labour would be redirected back into farming. The market was so efficient that it was unnecessary for merchants to become directly involved in production.[19]

One factor that had made Chinese merchants so efficient in the early days was the networks they made with other suppliers and buyers in the market. However, new forms of economic activity involved transactions between people outside of existing networks and few entrepreneurs were prepared to go outside the existing norms. It took time to develop a business relationship built on trust; to be too flexible and shift between new people with new ideas was dangerous and irrational. By contrast, Europeans had overcome this problem by developing a legal system that made it safer for merchants to do business with people they had no relationships with. European laws on contract encouraged commercial innovation, while intellectual property law encouraged technical innovation. China lacked these laws and this stopped the entrepreneur from safely going it alone. In addition, the rules and controls of guilds discouraged new ways of thinking, with the result that businessmen were entrapped within existing patterns of economic activity. This legacy still exists today, as Westerners doing business in the East know that building relationships is more important than any law or contract.

However, industries that were less reliant on the market also suffered, for example the centrally managed ceramics industry. Inside the kilns specialization had reduced costs and enhanced quality, but this technical perfection came at the cost of entrapment. Specialized craftsmen working under tight control from above had little opportunity for individual creativity and innovation.[20] While large-scale production reduced experimentation in China, the small state-owned factories in Europe were given regional monopolies, government support and freedom to experiment and innovate.[21] In Britain the industry was producing new products, such as bone china, and new techniques, such as transfer decoration. Europeans rapidly improved their productive capabilities to the point where they could more than match the Chinese and, by 1791, the British East India Company no longer found it profitable to import Chinese porcelain into Europe.

Many economists link technical stagnation to declining competition. They claim that the more producers there are competing in an industry, the more likely they will innovate and produce technological advances. However, there is no evidence to suggest that there were fewer kilns competing in China than in Europe where the industry was younger. Consequently, the decline cannot be attributed to a lack of competition. Nor can state control take the blame, as many of the kilns in Europe were state-owned. The cause of rigidity would seem to stem from the industry's investment in specialized routines and centralized control. In the past, this form of operation had been a factor in the industry's success, but led to inflexibility in times of change. The fact that both market-based and centrally managed producers had become entrapped shows the importance of historical investment in skills, rules and procedures.

It is common to blame the Chinese government for the lack of technological advance. It is claimed that because the Confucian government gave merchants a low ranking in society, it did not create a positive environment for investment. When combined with the riots and uprisings that posed a constant threat to merchants' assets, the long-term strategy of merchants was to invest wealth either in the safety of land or in education, so their families could obtain a higher social standing and perhaps enter the bureaucracy themselves.[22] Consequently, they did not invest in proto-industrial development as did the merchants of the West. However, the theoretically low ranking of merchants was misleading.[23] When the government sold degrees to raise money, wealthy merchants could buy into the gentry, and merchants' guilds experienced a rise in status and power over this period. The Ch'ing dynasty (1644–1911) was a period in which markets were growing and businessmen became respected and influential citizens.

The Chinese government was not as restrictive as some authors have suggested. It appears the state actually reduced its role in the economy during the Ch'ing dynasty. Government revenue figures at the end of the eighteenth century show that the share of the economy in the hands of the government had actually decreased. In fact, the government's share of gross national product (GNP) in China was 5 per cent, compared with 10 per cent for the United Kingdom.[24] This illustrates that, by the Ch'ing dynasty, the Chinese government was not as all-pervasive as previously thought and cannot be seen as the main barrier to advance. It also seems merchants benefited far more from contact with officials than they suffered from taxation or periodic special exactions.[25] Officials showed an increasing appreciation of market forces and a symbiotic relationship developed between the two. They recognized the role of merchants in the economy and their importance as a source for revenue.

However, one negative effect of the Confucian bureaucracy stands out. To succeed in this environment, Chinese merchants invested their energies and capital into building relationships with scholar-officials. Strong relationships with mandarins overcame the vagaries of political control and the possibility of legal bans on trading, and increased the chance of obtaining official favours. This diverted their energies away from technology and innovation. So, while political obstacles to economic growth in this late period may have been minimal, the incentives generated by the scholar-officials continued to shape business behaviour within the same old patterns. Cultivating relationships was more profitable to merchants and hence a more rational area of development than improving techniques of production.

Perhaps more telling than the size of the state was its changing role. In the earlier Sung dynasty (960–1279) the government took a leading role in diffusing innovations, but during the Ch'ing dynasty 'the Chinese government ceased almost entirely to provide any kind of public services'.[26] This could reflect a perception that the most obvious techno-economic advances under the Confucian paradigm had been achieved, and there was little left for the scholar-officials to do but sit back and take their share of the distribution of wealth. The government became an entrenched stakeholder, taking revenue but offering little in the way of infrastructure or services. The imperial system had become a sort of protection racket, a ritualized arrangement whereby the elite lived off the people.[27] Unfortunately, no individual or group stepped into this void to help the advance of technology, and the government was content to let the old economy ride its old, once successful growth wave.

As the government retreated from economic activity, it was left to the guilds to perform the bureaucratic and legal functions of commerce.[28] The guilds were closer to activity and in a better position to control what happened. With power decentralized to the guilds, we would normally expect an increase in competitive innovation, but the guilds had their own set of rules and they were ruthless in administering them.[29] Through coercion and the practice known as 'cessation of all business' (i.e. refusal to trade) they could impose their will on traders both inside and outside their membership. The resulting tyranny restricted freedom of enterprise and individual initiative. Guilds allowed industry to grow but not at the expense of another member's income. Their concern with market share and corporate welfare meant they had become entrenched stakeholders in the existing system. By restricting competition they restricted innovation.

Probably the worst example of how guilds restricted growth comes from the gold-beaters guild which produced gold leaf for the emperor. The rule of this trade was that no employer could have more than one apprentice at a time, restricting the amount of work any workshop could do, and thereby ensuring work was spread around its members. So, when one member received permission from the local magistrate to employ a number of apprentices, this did not make him popular with the guild. Soon word spread around the trade that 'biting to death is not a capital offence'. The guild spread this statement in the belief that no one bite would kill the man, but 123 guild members would certainly have an impact. Before long the man was dead and the law was brought in to inspect the teeth and gums of all the guild members. The man who took the first bite was discovered and executed. In this instance, the man who had broken guild rules had been creating product for the emperor and had had the magistrate's permission to hire more apprentices, but even this did not stop the guild from seeking a reprisal. It illustrates just how vigorously guilds could act to stop behaviour that upset the status quo.

The economy of the Ch'ing dynasty was caught in a 'high level equilibrium trap'[30] in which the high level of agricultural and water transport techniques, and the near complete resource use gave the economy a structure that was almost incapable of change through internally generated forces. Its farming and transport technologies were so good that no simple improvements could be made. Its transportation and commercial system had reached the limits of efficiency from which no further reduction in transaction costs could be achieved within the existing paradigm. Agricultural productivity per acre approached the limits of what was possible without new industrial-scientific inputs. When combined with population growth, China actually experienced a decline in per capita production. Farmers had less additional output to trade and this reduced their demand for other products, reducing the opportunity for the market to reward innovation. At the same time, resources were becoming scarce, making it more expensive to produce capital goods, while labour, fuelled by population growth, was becoming cheaper. This provided no incentive to innovate with labour-saving machines or improvements in the manner of the Europeans.

Inevitably, this decline hit the shipping industry. The Chinese superiority in the industry had rested on a number of factors, including the experience and skills they had developed, their organization structure that helped raise capital and enforce transactions, superior technology in ships and cargoes, supportive government policy and, in the China Sea, the restrictions it placed on foreign merchants entering China. However, one by one, those sources of competitive advantage had been eroded. In the early nineteenth century the Chinese were still the leading shippers in the China Sea. The junk trade of the South China Sea is estimated to have measured 74,190–85,000 tons at this time (including those junks based in South-East Asia).[31] By contrast, prior to 1833 the British East India Company never had more than 30,000 tons in the region. However, the China Sea was just one of many markets for the British. As early as 1771–3, the British had more than double that tonnage in the Atlantic trade alone.[32]

While the British were carving out new markets and routes across the globe, Chinese sailors stuck to their age-old routes in the China Sea. The decision to concentrate on the China Sea and meet traders at midway points had been a rational decision. It was on these routes that Chinese shippers had developed skills, experience and contacts. New trades were risky. However, while the Chinese continued with their old ways, Europeans were developing new waves of prosperity, sailing every ocean in the world and developing new markets in each. Western organizations developed complementary tentacles and economies of scale with which the Chinese family firm could no longer compete. For example, British private traders could borrow EIC funds at Canton and repay them in London, while the joint-stock financial structure meant British firms could assemble capital from an array of sources, from civil servants to army officers.[33] It may have taken centuries, but it was the Chinese who were now the poor cousins.

The Chinese had also lost their edge in shipping technology. Even before the age of steam, European fully-rigged ships could complete three voyages between Batavia and Canton each year, compared with only one for the junks.[34] Eventually, Chinese merchants began to use European ships instead of those of their countrymen, but this was not well received by their compatriots. In 1844 a Chinese merchant who accompanied his cargo on a European ship was nearly seized by the authorities on his arrival home for 'patronising a Foreign Vessel to the detriment of his own countrymen' and spoiling the junk market.[35] In response, the British government issued a statement saying that all Chinese merchants living in the Straits area (Singapore) were British subjects and it gave them documentation to confirm this. These documents became tradable commodities among the Chinese merchants who now regularly used European ships to transport their cargoes.

Eventually, Chinese shippers lost their most valuable competitive strength, the superiority of the cargoes they carried. This edge was lost in the nineteenth century as the economy suffered from technical stagnation. In 1800 China was still producing 33 per cent of the world's manufactured goods but, by 1860, their share had fallen to 19.7 per cent, and by 1900 it was down to 6.2 per cent. During the same period, Europe's share had grown from 28.1 per cent to 62 per cent.[36]

★ ★ ★

China had been the centre of world knowledge and technology for so long that it was virtually impossible to believe this situation could change. It was an irrational thought that went against everything they had learned. It took an external threat to wake China up to the new reality and the need for reform. The first realization of any European supremacy came with the Opium Wars, which ironically were seeded in China's lack of interest in Western imports. At the time, the British were importing huge quantities of Chinese tea, but found that their own manufactures made little headway in the Chinese market. To overcome the trade deficit, the British resorted to importing opium from India.

The British were not the only ones participating in the drug trade.[37] The first Americans to engage in it were James and Benjamin Wilcocks who in 1804 purchased opium at the port of Smyrna in Turkey, which was carried to China on the brig *Pennsylvania*. Americans were cut off from the supply of opium in British India, so the discovery of the Turkish product led to an opium rush that provided several American fortunes. However, the vast bulk of the opium trade was in British hands.

Chinese efforts at ending the drug trade were hindered by the fact that many in the administration benefited from the cargo. The commander of the anti-opium fleet drew a levy on imports and is reported to have actually carried the cargo. The web of corruption may even have reached the imperial palace in Peking. In 1839 Lin Tse-hsu was made Imperial Commissioner and sent to Canton to bring an end to the trade. Lin Tse-hsu was governor general of Hunan-Hupeh and had a reputation for justice and humanity. Known as 'Honest Lin' (Lin Ch'ing-t'ien), he was seen as incorruptible, the right man to close the opium question for good.[38]

Lin decided to punish the thirteen Chinese merchants of the guild handling the trade with the West. The guild leader, Howqua, was locked in a *cangue* (a wooden frame with holes for hands and head) and marched to the British warehouses. A document posted on the cangue stated that he had been found guilty through association of the capital crime of smuggling opium. If the Westerners did not hand over their entire stock of opium, he would lose his life. The British agreed to save Howqua and relinquished their stock. Lin's burning of 20,283 chests of opium was a spectacular sign that a new force was in town. He also wrote to the British crown asking it to bring an end to the trade:

> The barbarian merchants of your country, if they wish to do business for a prolonged period, are required to obey our statutes respectfully and to cut off permanently the source of opium. They must by no means try to test the effectiveness of the law with their lives. May you, O King, check your wicked people before they come to China, in order to guarantee the peace of your nation, to show further the sincerity of your politeness and submissiveness and to let the two countries enjoy together the blessings of peace.[39]

It is uncertain whether Queen Victoria ever received the letter, but she certainly did not show her submissiveness. At the time, opium was sold in Britain without restrictions. In fact, many artists consumed the drug and many famous pieces of English literature had been created under the influence of opium. These include Mary Shelley's *Frankenstein*, Lewis Carroll's *Alice in Wonderland* and Samuel Coleridge's 'Kubla Khan' whose last words reveal much of the poem's influence:

> For he on honey-dew hath fed,
> And drunk the milk of Paradise.

With opium being so openly consumed at home, the British thought that Chinese opposition was merely an attempt by officials to milk more money from them. Others thought that the Chinese government was getting what it deserved, their restrictions on trade halting the development of commerce above board. Spiralling tensions led to the first Opium War which had an immediate effect on the price of tea in London. Gloomy news led to a tripling in the price, while news of victory saw prices plummet.[40]

The wars of 1840–42 were the first of a series of armed conflicts in which Western powers used their military and naval might to force unequal treaties on China. The Opium Wars revealed the huge technological supremacy that Britain had developed over the years. Chinese bamboo cannons and crossbows were no match for the modern weaponry.[41] The result was a humiliation for the Chinese who were at last forced to acknowledge the supremacy of western technology. The European victory led to the signing of a number of treaties in which treaty ports were opened where the British and other foreigners had unrestricted freedom of residence and trade. This was a total humiliation for the Chinese who could no longer deny the new reality. It was now apparent that they needed to imitate the technologies that made Europeans so powerful. However, this opened up a range of problems, including identifying what to adapt, overcoming vested interests and values, and dealing with the burden of insufficient skills and infrastructure. Finally, the Chinese had to confront the problems of managing change itself, something they had little experience of.

The suggestion that foreigners were in some way superior involved not only a new way of looking at technology, the Chinese also needed to unlearn many of the things they had previously taken for granted. They had to re-evaluate their view of the world and their position in it. In particular, the nation had to go through a process of accepting that it was in their best interests to imitate people that they thought were inferior. The new policy met with the inevitable resistance. Many of the problems in introducing change came because the new requirements confronted old aesthetics and much of the resistance was on ideological grounds. For example, Wo-jen[42] led the attack against changes in education, arguing that if their 'brilliant and talented scholars . . . change from their regular course of study to follow the barbarians, then the correct spirit will not be developed, and accordingly the evil spirit will become stronger'. An educational programme placing students in US schools came to an end when the students failed to kow-tow in front of a Chinese official in Washington. Such attitudes undermined the certainty that the new policy would receive ongoing support.

Another problem was deciding how far to go. Even among the proponents of change, there was not universal agreement about how much Western science, technology and institutions should be adopted. For example, Li Hung-chang (1823–1901), who was probably the least conservative high official of his day, thought Chinese political and social institutions were superior to those in the West.[43]

Many of the problems faced by the Chinese can be seen through the experience of shipping. From the outset, shipping had revealed itself as a key industry.[44] During the Opium War, British steamships had made a deadly impact, travelling with ease and terrorizing Chinese people who called them 'the demon ships'. No one was more aware of their importance than the officials in charge of military operations during the war. Lin Tse-hsu, whose anti-opium crusade had sparked the war, took an early lead in promoting technology transfer. He wrote to the emperor seeking funds to build Western-style ships and armaments so that China could 'learn the superior skills of her enemy and how to control her'.[45] However, he got little response. As in other successful economies, key decision-makers had become isolated from the country's core activities. The court had no idea of the significance of the new technologies and, with the emperor hearing only distorted reports of Opium War defeats, Lin Tse-hsu's memorandum came to nothing.

Without court support, Lin took the initiative and became the first official to persistently adopt Western means of maritime technology. From Canton, he actively sought information on Western commerce, geography and shipping and is thought to be the author of *Hai Kua Tu' Chih* (Illustrated Record of the Maritime Nations). The motive in this early phase of imitation was defence, so Lin's focus was not on buying ships but creating capabilities for building stronger ships. By 25 April 1840 his team had achieved some success. The Chinese *Repertory* reported: 'Two or three schooners have just been launched on the river at Canton; they are built after the European models, and are, we suppose, to be attached to the imperial navy.'[46]

After the battle of Amoy in 1841, the British found a shipbuilding yard containing a large amount of timber and a 300-ton European-style ship in the process of construction. The British reported that the Chinese 'had evidently made a great step in advancing the art of shipbuilding – indeed, the longer the war lasted, the more the Chinese found themselves led on by the "impulse of necessity" to attempt great changes'.[47] But these were wooden sailing ships. Building iron steamships would require skills and investments that China did not possess. Their attempts at building steamships achieved little as they lacked the necessary industrial infrastructure; as Yen P'ao T'u Shuo reported: 'Unfortunately the craftsmen at Canton possessing no machine to make machines, cannot build big ships.'[48]

Near the end of the war the central government finally recognized the importance of supporting the modernization efforts. Over

222

the next two years the imperial court issued about thirty imperial edicts on ships and guns. The edicts recognized British superiority, and phrases such as 'it is necessary to change' and 'must not follow old methods' were repeatedly used. Provincial governments were given instructions to improve and purchase ships, and continue the work made by Lin's men at Canton. Unfortunately, the edicts received blanket opposition and, once again, the opposing arguments were couched with a very strong rationale, in particular putting forward environmental barriers to adapting the technology. The province of Chihli reported that their local waterways were too narrow and shallow for the new ships. The province of Kiangsu noted that the ships were not suitable for their local conditions and added that, with a shortage of strong wood and skilled shipwrights, they would not be able to build ships hastily that were equal to the foreign ones. And, even if they could, they would be useless because nobody knew how to operate them. These reasons were all valid and nothing in their environments favoured the creation of this new industry. Eventually, the emperor had to give up the idea of introducing the new ships. Thus, for a year or so after the war, interest in modernization at the court and in the provinces continued but eventually, with no wartime pressure to upgrade, it became a low priority.

The pressure to modernize reappeared with the Taiping rebellion and, once again, it was those in the forefront of battle who pioneered change. The scholar-official Tseng Kuo-fan was 'captain of war' during the rebellion and developed a keen interest in modern weaponry, in particular steamships. This time the court was quicker to appreciate the need for modernization and gave instructions to proceed with plans for ship-building. However, with little experience, this was not going to be easy. The *Annals* describe the results from Tseng's first attempt to make rafts to carry guns:

Unfortunately the rafts made were useless and no one has ever seen warships or is able to take the initiative. They look at one another and are at a loss. Nevertheless Tseng labours day and night asking advice from them all.[49]

Although strongly motivated to imitate Western technology, nothing in Tseng's life had prepared him for the task. Luckily, he came upon two petty officials who knew something about ships and presented him with plans for several types of vessel. Tseng established shipyards at Hengchow and Hsiang-tan where experimentation proceeded but, as the following note to the court reveals, they still lacked the skills and capabilities to achieve their goals:

> several sample boats were built. None of them, on account of the lack of skill on part of the shipwrights, and the smallness of size, can surmount the waves of the Yangtse, nor can they stand the shock of the cannon.[50]

Tseng wanted to build a steamship, but while the British had developed their steamship capabilities gradually over a century, the Chinese had less time. In theory, a following nation can catch up rapidly without enduring all of the development costs; however, the Chinese had no opportunity to examine a steam vessel closely. Their efforts ended in failure. Eventually, Tseng Kuo-fan bought a ship which allowed his men the chance of further investigation. Unfortunately, he had no previous experience to tell him whether he was buying a mechanically sound ship and, as luck would have it, the ship was a lemon.

In 1861 Tseng moved his headquarters to the city of Anking where his mechanics and engineers worked on all kinds of machines, including a steam-engine which was successfully demonstrated on 30 July

1862. The engine was followed by the construction of a model steamship, after which Tseng instructed Hsu Shou to build a full-sized ship and, with opposition from local officials and no foreign help, he attempted to build a ship using Chinese tools and equipment. But advance was slow, as Tseng's own words to the emperor reveal:'Although a small steamer was built, its speed was so slow that it showed we had not yet learnt the proper technique.'[51]

The Chinese were learning the difficulty of grafting foreign technologies into a new environment. Before they could imitate, they had to learn how to imitate. They eventually realized that foreign machines and workers had to be used. This lesson was put into practice at a newly established machine shop at Shanghai in 1864. They recruited Yung Wing (a graduate of Yale and the first Chinese student to return from America) to go abroad and buy foreign machinery. A foreign machine shop was rented and strengthened by the arrival of the new machinery. Six or seven French and British mechanics were employed to help with the process of modernization. The first steamship was completed in 1868 and named by Tseng *Tien Chih* (Calm and Prosperous). Four more were completed before Tseng's death in 1872.

To further assist this transfer of technology, foreign books were copied. Tseng established a translation bureau (whose first four books translated were *Treatises on Steam Engines*, *Catechism on the Steam Engine*, *Practical Geometry and Coal and Coal Mining*), and he inaugurated a scheme under which thirty Chinese students were sent abroad. At the now named Kiangnan Arsenal, he also established the country's first military engineering school where mechanics could learn Western techniques with the assistance of foreigners.

Importing foreign workers and machines still left many problems. These are expressed by Tso Tsung-t'ang, a modernizer who attempted to establish a modern ship-building yard:

First, the difficulty of selecting a place for a shipyard; second, the difficulty of finding and buying steamship machinery; third, the difficulty in engaging head mechanics; fourth, the difficulty of raising and accumulating a huge amount of funds; fifth, the difficulty that the Chinese are unaccustomed to navigation and that after the completion of the ships we would still have to engage foreigners; sixth, the difficulties of the numerous requirements of expenditures for coal, salaries and wages after the ships have been completed, all of which would have to be paid every month, in addition to which from time to time the ships would have to be repaired. Seventh, in this unusual enterprise it is easy for slander and criticism to arise: one person initiates the plan, another carries it out, while a third is a mere bystander; and if the enterprise fails near its completion, then both public and private loss will result. With these several difficulties, it is no wonder that there is no man who cares to take the responsibility . . . At the beginning they will worry about the lack of accomplishment; then they will criticise the expenditure as being too much, and will probably also say sarcastically that we have lost our national dignity.[52]

Beyond resource constraints and the problems of acquiring capabilities were a host of other problems, including the need to compete with the British who could benefit from their first mover advantages. The chance of failure was high and exposed the modernizer to ridicule. It is not surprising that people erred on the conservative side. Finally, it reinforces the fact that no industry is an island. It requires a supporting infrastructure that trains staff and affords the necessary supplies.

In the meantime, a technology gap was opening between China and the Western nations, but the Chinese experience must be put into perspective. Technological adaptation is not a simple process and

the United States was also having difficulties adopting British technology, even though it had a modern iron industry and could easily
recruit immigrants speaking the same language. It should also be noted
that Britain had developed its expertise over a century and, although
some of the development costs might be avoided by imitation, the
task of 'catch-up' would involve many complications. The Chinese
government set up a steamship company, but it also had only limited
success. In 1872 the China Merchants' Steam Navigation Company
was created in imitation of the foreign companies, as a joint-stock
enterprise with shares issued to private individuals. However, as much
as they tried to adopt the latest methods, they could not shake off their
old ways of thinking. The company was operated under the traditional
government supervision and merchant operation system, under which
the security of the manager's posi-tion and the existence of the enterprise was tied to a particular group of bureaucrats.[53] This made it
difficult for managers to take a long-term view of their position and
everyone involved took the opportunity to profit while they could.
This short-term thinking accentuated the already bad tax-farmer spirit
typical of Chinese government-business relations. Government officials
continuously meddled in company affairs; nepotism and corruption
were rampant. By the early 1880s, the Chinese company's offices and
warehouses employed two or three times the number of men actually
needed. Cheng Kuan-ying, a manager in the company, described the
problem:

> The personnel recommended by the officials are neither scholars,
> nor farmers, nor artisans, nor merchants. They are men who
> have never had any sort of experience. Some of them want to
> be secretaries and receive a salary without doing any work.
> Others seek posts as pursers on board steamers, the actual work
> being done by assistants while they themselves sit and wait for

their share of the spoils. Still others become assistant managers at the branches of the company. They frequently entertain the local authorities and wastefully incur expenses without contributing anything to the operation of the company.[54]

The industry may have fared better if other private companies were started and, in 1877 and 1882, two attempts were made to establish private steamship companies. However, on both occasions the official patrons of the government-sponsored company opposed any new competition. Steamships were seen as too important to be in private hands. It is notable that in the treaty ports, where compradors were free from mandarin control, Chinese shipping companies were established by compradors who had gained the necessary management capabilities from their experiences working for foreign companies.[55] For example, the Ningpo Steam Navigation Company was established and registered as an American firm in 1877. The treaty ports provided experience with Western techniques in a different commercial environment, and here the Chinese could shine. Unfortunately, the treaty ports were mere blips on the Chinese economy which rolled along like a dinosaur on the path to extinction.

The Chinese had at one time possessed the world's largest and most successful shipping industry. Chinese shipping rode a wave of prosperity based on features of its domestic environment that could not be found in other parts of the world. These included wealthy domestic consumers, sophisticated industries which provided cargoes to export, leading shipping technologies which reflected the high level of education in the domestic economy, and the Confucian bureaucracy which underpinned the success of the whole economy. But the old ways no longer brought success.

With the exception of compradors who had worked for foreign

companies, Chinese merchants showed a strong reluctance to enter new fields.[56] Even when they became aware of superior Western technologies, few traditional merchants invested in industrialization. It would take a brave man to risk large sums of money and time on production techniques he knew little about, so the attitude of the Chinese merchant was 'stick to what you know'. There was some good economic reasoning behind the conservatism.[57] Western-style industrial projects took a long time to generate a return that matched traditional commodity trading and money-lending. Chinese businessmen were driven by market forces and a rationality that told them to stick to their existing path of development.

The Chinese decline sheds light on the importance of the environment and the fact that, as we have already noted, no industry is an island. It requires supporting industries to provide capital, machinery and demand. It also needs educational facilities to provide skills. To try to create an industry without these ingredients is laden with difficulty, as China discovered. It took so long that, in the meantime, the West leapt even further ahead. Change was also limited by uncertainty; uncertainty over what was required and whether support for change from the imperial court would continue. The balance of power between the proponents and opponents of change was determined by the circumstances at the time. War increased the pressure to modernize. With the peace of the 1870s and 1880s, the pressure for reform cooled in favour of the conservatives, who preferred to use government funding for their own purposes. A policy of self-strengthening of the state was replaced by self-profiting individuals. The empress dowager provided the worst example of this when millions of taels of silver raised to build a Western-style navy were redirected into the rebuilding of her Summer Palace.[58]

By the end of the nineteenth century even the tea industry was having trouble competing. New supplies were coming out of India and Ceylon (Sri Lanka) and the quality was excellent. When Thomas Lipton made a revolutionary decision to bypass the normal distribution channels and set up his own operations, he chose Ceylon and quickly became the largest tea-grower on the island. Producers in India and Ceylon put an emphasis on getting their product to market in top condition. They took greater care in cultivating, collecting and packing. While the Chinese took their time putting together large orders that varied in quality and were frequently stale, the new competitors rushed smaller orders to market that arrived fresh. By the 1890s, only 7.5 per cent of tea sold in Britain came from China.[59]

It would take action either from outside or from the top to shake China off its path of development. Change from the outside did occur in the form of foreign investment but the levels were simply too small to have a major impact. Change from above was attempted but had its hands tied in a number of ways. The policy was placed in the hands of mandarins who were limited by their own value system and skill base. Any policies or solutions were interpreted within their pre-existing outlook and needed to fit within the Confucian framework and patterns of administration. This tied the new enterprises to a bureaucracy that did not fully understand the motives of businessmen or the importance of costs, prices and the market. It also saddled the enterprises with traditional bureaucratic behaviour, including nepotism and the fleecing of funds by officials.

Finally, the Chinese experience illustrates the difficulty of imitating after a long period of success. Success strengthens the entrenchment of values, methods of business and vested interests. The longer that success exists, the deeper the resistance to change. The Chinese economy, which once provided a wonderful environment for entrepreneurs, had reached the end of its growth wave. It had become entrapped by the legacies of its past success.

10

THE LAND OF THE RISING SUN

With China open for business, the world had become increasing bound by ties of trade and commerce, but one nation lay mysteriously out of reach. For two centuries Japan lay isolated from the rest of the world.

During the sixteenth century Japan was plagued by civil wars from which the house of Tokugawa emerged as the new ruler, or shogun. In theory, the shogun owed allegiance to the emperor, whose family had ruled Japan from time immemorial, but the emperor lived in seclusion in Kyoto and played no role in the country's government. Power lay with the shogun who ruled the country as a military dictator.

About the same time as the Tokugawa clan were cementing their position, the Portuguese succeeded in establishing trading links with clans in the south-west. But Portuguese success was undermined by the work of the missionaries who travelled with them. Their active conversions and politicizing attracted the attention of the country's rulers, made worse by internal bickering and finger-pointing between Jesuit and Franciscan priests. The shogun introduced a series of measures banning Christianity, but the final act came in 1639 after a peasant rebellion near Nagasaki. The revolt was fuelled by the heavy tax burden, but Christians figured prominently. The shogun lost 10,000 troops putting down the revolt, which he was determined would be his last. The Portuguese were expelled and the nation's doors were shut to foreign influences. Japanese were forbidden to travel offshore, and the building of vessels large enough to make overseas voyages was banned. The only foreigners allowed in the country were a small number of Dutch and Chinese traders who occupied the tiny island of Deshima, off the coast near Nagasaki. For the next 200 years, Japan remained isolated until, in the nineteenth century, the United States began to look its way.

Americans had their eyes on Japan for several reasons. First, they hoped they could use Japan as a coaling base for ships on the way to China. Second, they wanted to ensure that any shipwrecked sailors landing in Japan were well treated. This concern was raised after an American whaling ship was wrecked in Japanese waters and the sailors were treated cruelly. Finally, Americans were aware of the benefits that could come from trading with Japan. With these goals in mind, Commodore Matthew Perry, a sixty-nine-year-old with long experience in high-level naval diplomacy, was chosen to lead an expedition and agree a treaty between the two nations.

Perry's fleet arrived in Edo (Tokyo) on 8 July 1853. Enforcing the 200-year-old law prohibited any dealings with foreigners, the shogun instructed Perry to go to Nagasaki, where the Dutch and Chinese traders were encamped. But Perry refused to go. This refusal to obey the shogun's orders caused a furore in the capital where news of China's defeat in the Opium Wars was widely spread. The populace expected arson, pillage and massacre at the hands of the 'red hairs from the West' and many fled the city.[1] Perry's four black ships, with smoke belching, posed a fearsome threat to the shogun's authority.

Perry was aware that the Japanese would use any device or deception to get rid of him and he was determined to stand firm. He made it very clear that, although his hand was extended in friendship, he was prepared to make war if his terms were not accepted, and falsely boasted that he could rally a hundred warships to win it. The Japanese did not call his bluff and reluctantly agreed to deliver a letter to their emperor from US President Millard Fillmore. The letter requested 'friendship, commerce, a supply of coal and provisions, and protection for our ship-wrecked people'.[2] With the letter delivered, Perry left, saying he would return the following year.

Perry returned to Japan in February 1854 and landed for talks on 8 March. He soon received the good news that the Japanese agreed to let foreign ships purchase supplies and to treat crews humanely, but gaining permission to trade was not so easy. The Japanese negotiator explained that 'we are not discontented at being without the products of other nations'.[3] Perry was prepared for such a statement and had brought gifts with him to whet their appetite. In the following days a number of crates were unloaded from the ships containing items of Western manufacture. The exhibition included perfume, books, rifles and carbines, a printing press and photographic apparatus. A telegraph was set up and runners were challenged to carry a message to the Treaty House half a mile away faster than the new appliance.

The item that generated the most excitement was a quarter-scale locomotive intended as a gift for the emperor. Passengers sat on top of the train and screamed in delight as it made its way round a circular track at twenty miles an hour. Some days after the exhibition closed, the Americans received gifts of silks, kimonos, bronzeware and an immense supply of rice carried by sumo wrestlers who also put on a display. But the best gift of all came on 31 March when the Japanese signed the Treaty of Kanagawa opening two ports to trade. Four years later, the British, French and other nations also gained permission to trade.[4]

At that time Japan seemed like a land from the Middle Ages with sword-wielding knights, subservient peasants, merchant guilds and haughty feudal lords.[5] This backwardness was reflected in its international commerce: Japan did not possess a single ocean-going ship.[6] With a modicum of trade carried out by the Chinese and Dutch around Nagasaki, the country was woefully inexperienced in international commerce.

Any attempt at modernization had to contend with a number of institutions that riddled the economy. The most important of these were the samurai, who had been the nation's warrior class. During Japan's long period of peace, they had had no opportunity to function as warriors. Forbidden to become involved in industry and commerce, they became a ruling intelligentsia, performing a similar role in society to the mandarins in China. As a consequence, the sword was replaced by the writing brush as the instrument of power in Japanese society[7] and, like their counterparts in China, their ideas and ethical norms were shaped by Confucian philosophy, whose values permeated society. And, as in China, society reflected the same four-fold class structure: samurai, peasants, artisans and merchants, in this order of ranking.[8]

Another barrier to economic change was the restrictive nature of social relations. Japanese society was characterized by a commitment to loyalty and obedience to superiors. This hierarchical obedience was reinforced by powerful peer pressure. All individuals in society belonged to some group: samurai, guilds, merchant houses and family groups involved in rice cultivation and delivery. Peer pressure was a powerful force in these groups, for a behavioural discrepancy by any individual could bring shame on the whole group, so individuals were forced to comply with group interests. Enforcement was achieved in a number of ways, but the most powerful tool was fear of expulsion from the group. Under such pressure, individuals found it preferable to suppress their own ideas and decision-making came to be based on consensus as opposed to majority. The individual counted for little and this could stifle initiative.[9]

Despite these rigidities, Japan in the nineteenth century possessed some key differences from China. They had learnt it was possible to import technologies and improve their quality of life. (For the Chinese, foreign ideas and technologies had always been inferior and this would make a key difference in their attitude to imitating foreigners.) Since the eighteenth century, several internal factors were working in Japan to undermine the existing socio-economic structure. These included a growing interest in Japanese ancient history and literature and the publication of *History of Great Japan*, which informed the literate classes of a time when emperors, not the shogun, ruled Japan.[10] This was combined with an increased sense of nationalism. Many scholars wanted to cast off foreign Chinese and Buddhist influences, and promoted nationalistic virtues, including a return to beliefs associated with the Shinto religion and the divinity of the emperor. This *kogugaku* (national scholarship) was particularly popular among the western clans who had been subdued by the Tokugawa clan from which the shogun came.

At the opposite extreme to the nationalists, another restless group of intellectuals was the school of Dutch studies (*Rungaju*). Western books, with the exception of those dealing with Christianity, had been allowed into the country since 1720, imported through Dutch merchants based at Nagasaki. By the end of the eighteenth century, Dutch studies had been added to the curriculum in most schools and provided alternative models to the existing regime; it also provided an awareness of the superiority of Western technology.[11]

Economic factors also worked to undermine contentment with the current regime and created a desire for change. The ruling shogun ran a system in which feudal lords were forced to spend a large amount of their time at the capital in Edo (Tokyo). While in the capital, the lords competed with one another in displays of prestige that required great sums of expenditure.[12] This put pressure on them to raise their incomes and some responded by creating industrial and trading enterprises in their *hans* (feudal domains). Others resorted to raising loans and became indebted to merchants. At the same time, a series of natural disasters undermined agricultural output. These two factors meant that feudal lords had less money to pay their samurai, who had to shoulder a cut in income. Many impoverished samurai were forced to pawn their swords, armour or insignia of rank, or even worse, take up occupations below their status. When a series of crop failures hit the peasants, these impoverished and dissatisfied samurai were instrumental in leading peasants in revolt.

This situation stood in stark contrast to China, which still enjoyed a prosperous standard of living and consequently felt less need to change. In reference to China between the 1830s and 1850s, Robert Fortune stated 'that in no country in the world is there less real misery and want than in China'.[13] Clearly, there was a big difference in the level of satisfaction with the existing regime. Another contrast between China and Japan was a subtle difference in education of the key stakeholders. Although both focused on the Confucian classics, samurai had a more practical approach to learning:[14] samurai never forgot their role as warriors. They still learnt martial arts and still saw their role as protectors of the nation. While both nations realized that industrial power was the basis of Western military strength, the samurai were quicker to take the lesson to heart. All in all, imitating the West was more consistent with the values of Japanese stakeholders and therefore less likely to engage resistance.

Impoverished samurai were very aware that their nation's defences had been run down. They deeply felt the humiliation handed out by Commodore Perry and the US Far Eastern Squadron. After Perry's visit, the central government and some of the domains quickly seized opportunities to grasp Western technology. For example, the domain of Fukui began building small guns, batteries and gunpowder after the Western model and, in 1857, built a two-masted schooner after Dutch and American models.[15]

At the national level, the shogun also realized the need for greater openness to catch up with the West, and began to seek advice from the lords whom he had previously kept in a state of weakness.[16] He bought weapons from the Dutch and lifted the ban on the construction of deep-water ships. Samurai advised the shogun to establish an institute for Western studies which later became the nucleus of Tokyo Imperial University. The British were encouraged to establish an English school at Nagasaki in 1858; the French established the Yokosuka naval complex in 1865 and a French language school at Nagasaki.[17] The government sponsored diplomatic missions to the United States in 1860, Europe in 1862 and France in 1864–7. Although their purpose was principally to foster foreign relations, the visits also served to investigate institutions and culture.

Students were sent to Holland in 1862, Russia in 1865 and Britain in 1866 to study navigation, naval affairs, and foreign relations.[18] International travel was liberalized and many samurai went overseas to study as private individuals, particularly to America. Between 1868 and 1902, 11,248 Japanese went overseas to study. On their return, the young Japanese students found it was not plain sailing trying to establish themselves, particularly given the importance that society placed on seniority, but, generally speaking, the pipe-line for introducing Western knowledge and technology was open in Japan and returning students played a major role in bringing new technologies into the country.[19]

As in China, the shipping industry was an early focus of attention. After all, it was the superiority of Commodore Perry's 'black ships' that had so badly humiliated the nation. The ships came to symbolize the power of the new scientific age.[20] Japanese officials realized very early that there was a need to build Western-style vessels. The Mito han (domain) was ordered to start constructing a Western-style ship, with the result that the Ishikawashima shipyard was opened in 1853. However, the following comment from the man who drew up the plans exposes the nation's lack of experience: 'On order of the government I translated a book on shipbuilding, and theoretically I know how to construct a ship, but of course I have never before built one nor even sailed in one.'[21]

The Japanese were clearly experiencing the same difficulties that the Chinese experienced in trying to imitate a technology from a starting position of complete ignorance. In this instance, the task was made worse because the book that the Japanese builder translated, and on which he based his plans, did not describe a modern ship. When the builders completed their first Western-style ship, the *Asahi Marua*, they found they had constructed a seventeenth-century East India ship, which is what the book had described. Nationalistic hans, such as Satsuma, also embarked on ship-building programmes, but they too were stifled when they realized the sailing ships they were building were out of date. Realizing the technical difficulties in building steamers, the han eventually put an end to its ship-building programme.

An opportunity for a more direct lesson about Western ship construction was provided in 1854, when a visiting Russian frigate was shipwrecked and the Japanese were asked to build a replacement.[22] The offer was eagerly accepted and officials, carpenters and blacksmiths were sent to assist and learn modern ship-building technology. This experience showed the Japanese that direct learning from foreigners was an efficient method of gaining technology, and a naval school was established at Nagasaki using Dutch instructors. A shipyard was attached to the school and in 1857 a small steamer was successfully built under Dutch supervision. This programme was augmented in 1862, when the government sent naval officials who had studied at the Nagasaki naval school and other workers to Europe for the purpose of studying ship-building technology. As a consequence of these experiences, the Japanese were quick to develop methods in which foreign technology could be imported.

The process of change was not without pain, and economic and social dislocation became a fact of life for many groups. For example, with the opening of trade, the export of raw silk hurt local weavers as the price for their raw material rose. Many craftsmen experienced hardship as cheap imports entered the country and deprived them of markets. Merchants enjoyed a rise in status, but this incurred the jealousy of samurai who felt a loss of social and economic position. The new economy was distributing resources in a way that undermined the old social order and the legitimacy of the shogun.[23]

These difficulties contributed to revolution in 1868 when the shogunate was overthrown by samurai from the clans of the west. In the hans of Satsuma and Chosu power had fallen into the hands of samurai groups intent on destroying the regime. In 1866 Saigo Takamori of Satsuma and Kido Takayoshi of Chosu formed an alliance with the express purpose of challenging the shogun and restoring the emperor to power. In the Bochin War of 1868 the alliance defeated the Tokugawa's forces, bringing an end to the shogunate. The emperor was taken from Kyoto and made the figurehead of the new regime. Although the conspirators acted in the name of the emperor, they retained political power and an oligarchy of ex-samurai from Satsuma and Chosu now made decisions in Tokyo.

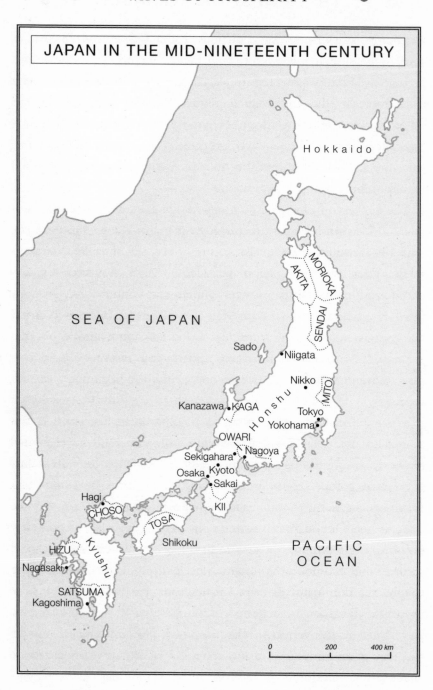

JAPAN IN THE MID-NINETEENTH CENTURY

Hokkaido

SEA OF JAPAN

MORIOKA
AKITA
SENDAI

Sado
Niigata

Nikko
MITO

Kanazawa KAGA
Honshu
Tokyo
Yokohama

OWARI
Nagoya
Sekigahara
Osaka Kyoto
Sakai

Hagi
CHOSO
KII

TOSA
Shikoku

HIZU
Nagasaki
Kyushu
PACIFIC
OCEAN

SATSUMA
Kagoshima

0   200   400 km

From this description, it is obvious that the shogun was not over-thrown because he was resisting change.[24] In fact, the government that replaced him was initially more nationalistic. It ordered all students sent abroad by the shogunate to return home and wanted to expel all foreigners working in Japan. However, the government soon realized that these activities played an important part in strengthening the nation. They expanded the overseas study programme, but their overall modernization programme was far more nationalistic in nature.[25]

In 1871 members of the oligarchy went on a trip around the world that would dramatically affect the course of Japan's development. The Iwakura mission included over a hundred scholars, administrators and students who toured the United States, Europe and other Asian nations to gain information on technological, economic and social systems. Among their number was Okubu Toshimichi who had earlier played a major role in the Meiji restoration. Okubu was particularly impressed with Britain, its railways, canals and the industrial enterprises he found in every city. He felt that Britain set a precedent for Japan to follow, as, like Japan, it was once a small insular country with small harbours and some natural resources. He noted that Britain had grown by protecting its industries from competition though laws such as the Navigation Acts. Only after gaining world leadership did it adopt a policy of free trade. When Okubu returned home, he was made head of the newly created Home Ministry. The ministry was concerned with national security and promoting economic development, a role which made Okubu the dominant figure in Japanese politics. It also gave him the chance to direct Japan's economic development.[26]

The Japanese government played a key role in introducing change, mobilizing resources and using them to create new organizations needed for development.[27] Western organizational models were

241

examined in order to find those most suitable for Japan. The navy and communications system were modelled on the British; the police on the French; the banking system on the American; and the legal system was based first on the French and then the German. The whole feudal system was dismantled and hans lost their independent administrations, which were replaced by a system of prefectures around a stronger centralized government. The move to centralized government was made easier with the introduction of three key Western technologies: railways, telegraph and postal systems. These improved communication and transportation, making it easier to coordinate control for the central government.[28]

The government created two key departments to promote the industrialization process: Kobusho (Ministry of Engineering and Public Works), established in 1870, and Naimusho (Ministry of Internal Affairs), which oversaw agriculture and textiles. Kobusho (sometimes referred to as the Ministry of Industry) was given the responsibility of building pilot enterprises and promoting industrial enterprise by the private sector[29] with an emphasis on heavy industry: mining, ship-building, railways, machinery, construction and armaments. The overriding goal was national defence and the establishment of transport and communication systems.

The government also realized the value of using foreign workers and that, instead of wasting time with local experiments, it could pay high salaries to foreign technicians to teach the Japanese their technologies. Over 500 foreigners were employed by the Ministry of Industry in its initial years, passing on their skills through on-the-job training as well as formal training in enterprise schools.[30] However, in areas where foreigners were used for their expertise, the ministry made it clear that Japanese were to eventually learn their skills and assume full operation.

The process of transition needed to be financed, but Japanese traditional values regarded loans from foreigners as shameful. Yet foreign exchange was needed to pay for the much needed imports of machinery and raw material. In this area, Japan had luck just when it needed it most. In the early years after the Meiji restoration, silk crops in Italy and France failed, leading to a high demand for Japanese exports.[31] Silk became the principal export for Japan (ahead of tea, rice and the less important craftwork such as pottery, fans, Japanese-style paper, lacquer and bronzeware).

The second financial problem was accumulating capital and channelling it into industrial enterprises, a problem augmented by the Meiji government's nationalistic character that would not tolerate foreign investment. The initial intention of government was to rely on private enterprise but the results were disappointing. Outside of government four groups existed that had the potential to supply capital for industry: the traditional merchant houses, the former feudal classes (high-class samurai and nobles), the landlords and the new rich who were prospering from the newly created export opportunities. Each of these groups was held back for the same reasons that traditional Chinese merchants failed to invest in Western technologies. That is, they lacked experience and were not going to risk entering an activity of which they had had little knowledge.

The government tried to encourage investors into new areas of production, but the level of capital was too weak, and technical and managerial difficulties too great.[32] Given that market incentives would not create the necessary systemic change, the government found it had to perform the role of entrepreneur and began to invest in industry directly. Many of the samurai who made up the new bureaucracy had gained some experience of administration and Western technology during their time administering their domain governments. Many had personal experience of industry and almost all had at least some exposure to Western studies. The scale of government investment in industry, however, was not large and their achievements were modest. As in China, many of these enterprises suffered from bureaucratic inefficiency and inexperience, with the result that many were managerial and financial failures.[33] Despite these failings, the nation had acquired capabilities in modern industrial enterprise, something that would not have happened if left to the market. State enterprises became a model that the private sector could imitate. Government patronage also helped to overcome some of the initial technical difficulties and set-up costs which private enterprises would not have been able to endure. However, these enterprises were at the start of their learning curves and their poor profitability placed a heavy financial burden on the government.

In the 1880s, as the financial burden of these fledgling enterprises grew, the government decided it should sell its factories, mines and other enterprises. This was not an unwelcome move, as the government had always believed industry should be in the hands of the private sector. The enterprises were sold at low prices that reflected their poor performance, and also made it easier for new owners to start in the industry. The prices were determined by officials who worked closely with the new owners who included ex-officials and old merchant houses. These close political ties saw the industrialists receive blatant favouritism that was bordering on the scandalous yet, despite the favouritism, the new owners proved to be worthy entrepreneurs.[34]

Clearly this system was not too different from the 'government supervision merchant operation' programme in China. However, as lavish as Japanese subsidies were, they were used for productive investment, and owners did not extract funds on the same scale as in China. This different use that businessmen made of government funds probably reflected old behaviours, as 'milking' had always been a more legitimate practice in China. The higher level of reinvestment in Japan also reflected the greater confidence that Japanese entrepreneurs had in the long term. Japan approached Westernization on a broad scale and this must have helped individuals have greater confidence. This commitment to Westernization could be seen at the top where the Japanese emperor changed into military uniforms in the style of Western monarchs, something that would never happen in China. If businessmen in each nation needed confidence in the change process before they invested, the Japanese were clearly at an advantage.

With political support, the young Japanese companies established quasi-monopoly positions in their local markets and, although orthodox economics chastises monopolies, it has been argued that Japan needed to go through a monopolistic stage if it was to build up its capabilities.[35] Given the technological gap vis-à-vis the Western nations and the limited purchasing power in the Japanese market at the time, local monopolies made the transition easier. Raising tariffs on imports might have been another option, but these were denied by the trade treaties the government had been force to sign under military pressure. Consequently the government supported a small number of large enterprises. To help them survive, these companies were furnished with lavish subsidies, privileges and strong government purchases.

The process of imitating the West continuously confronted the values of the old regime's stakeholders, which were either discarded or remodelled to fit the needs of the time. The new sense of materialism stood in sharp contrast to traditional values and led to a call to combine Western technology with Eastern morality. Attitudes to business needed redefining and, through a promotion campaign, the government attempted to create an acceptable face for businessmen as the nation's new samurai. Entrepreneurs now did 'business for the nation and not for profit',[36] while company officials rose in prestige and were treated as the new gentry.

245

Some aspects of the old regime actually helped the process of imitation. The fact that transformation was performed in the name of the emperor (and thus in the name of ancestors) meant that loyalty to Japanese values strengthened the process. The nation's hierarchical social structure also made the lower social classes receptive to instructions to modify. Basic attitudes, like loyalty to community groups, dedication to hard work, and respect for authority, helped smooth the transition.[37] But the process of change did not occur without resistance. The education system was one area of opposition. Conservatives lamented what they saw as moral degradation and sought a return to moral education in schools. The Emperor Meiji himself, after a tour of schools in 1878, was so alarmed by the extent of Westernization that he commissioned *The Great Principles of Education* (1878) to increase Confucian morality in the curriculum.

Although samurai were in the forefront of change, transformation on this scale rarely occurs on a balanced front and many samurai suffered during the process. Many lost their jobs when the feudal domains were broken up, depriving them of their positions and income. To make matters worse, the creation of a Western-style conscript army deprived them of their status as the nation's warriors. Opportunities for samurai might be opening in commerce, but earning money from commerce and industry had always been considered below their class. A number of revolts broke out, as portrayed in the movie *The Last Samurai*, featuring Tom Cruise. The most important of the rebellions was the 1877 Satsuma Rebellion.

In the early 1870s, the three great nobles of the Meiji restoration, Saigo Takamori, Kido Takayoshi and Okubu Toshimichi were still in power. However, not all were happy with the direction the country was taking. Saigo Takamori was at heart still a samurai and despaired as funds were poured into railroads when they could have been used

246

to modify the army. When Korea refused to recognize envoys representing the new government, Saigo wanted to lead a military campaign to Korea. Not only would this avenge the insult, it would provide much needed employment for thousands of out-of-work samurai. Others in the government were more cool-headed, recognizing their budget constraints and the weak state that the army was still in. Saigo resigned in disgust and returned to Satsuma where he established a number of military academies. Fearing a rebellion, the government sent warships to seize a military arsenal in Satsuma, but this only provoked open conflict. The resulting Satsuma Rebellion lasted nine months and pitted 60,000 imperial troops against 30,000 rebels who were annihilated.

The Satsuma Rebellion taught the government an important lesson. Like modern-day organizational change practitioners, the Meiji government learnt it had to accommodate key stakeholders. From this time on, increased effort was made to absorb the samurai class into the new economy. To compensate for their loss of income, the government gave samurai interest-bearing bonds which many invested in some kind of business venture. The government provided these ventures with loans and guidance but, with little business experience, some very bad results eventuated. Samurai made more valuable contributions to education and administration, which were closer to their previous professions.

Samurai had qualities that could be of use in the new regime, such as discipline, education and a belief in public service. A period of change and uncertainty favoured men with confidence, strength and optimism. It favoured strong men who could operate fast and efficiently, brandishing their abacus like a sword in battle.[38] Many educated lower-class samurai were aware they were entering an era of great possibilities where effort and ability would be rewarded. Educational achievement was encouraged by parents who saw the possibilities that could open for their children. However, individual success still paid homage to old values. While the graduate could now rise quickly, he still needed to display submission to the group and the principle of human harmony.[39] Rules of merchant houses might change to reflect the times, but obedience to the old rules and ancestral line were as important as ever.

The years 1860–87 represent a period of change with little economic growth. Clearly, the economic transformation did not occur without difficulties. These included the conflicts of values and stakeholders associated with the old economic system. Many mistakes were made during the process. However, a greater systematic effort was made to absorb the new than in China, and this created a more favourable environment for industrial expansion. After an initial period of confusion and reconstruction, the economy entered a period of expansion. Between 1889 and 1938, per capita national expenditure grew at an average of 2 per cent.[40]

The pattern of development and change outlined above shaped the growth of the shipping industry. When the Meiji government came to power in 1868, it regarded maritime industries as a pivotal industry for the advance of foreign trade, balance of payments and defence. The authorities were also well aware that loss of control over domestic waterways had spelt disaster for other Asian nations.[41] However, a huge technical gap existed between Japan and the West. For more than two centuries, Japan had no ocean-going shipping, so had to build its industrial capabilities from scratch.

The initial focus of maritime policy was to create a modern shipping organization as quickly as possible,[42] and as early as 1869 a decree was issued allowing Japanese to possess Western ships. However, it only produced one noticeable undertaking as the nation still lacked the capabilities to launch such enterprises.[43] The skills and infrastructure required for ocean-going shipping were very different from those in traditional coastal shipping based on tiny wooden ships. The industry required managerial skills, educational arrangements, physical facilities and a market that just did not exist. The tiny group of entrepreneurs interested in operating ships were not capable of introducing such large-scale systemic and institutional changes, so it was left to the government to effect a change that the market could not generate.

As in China, the government established the first domestic steamship company, using government-owned vessels under the supervision of state officials. The company, Kaiso Kaisha, was established in 1870 to operate on coastal routes around Japan. Reorganized in 1872 and made semi-public, under the new name of the Nippon Postal Steamship Company, it attempted to provide a liner service between Osaka and Tokyo. Although it had been given the very lucrative shipments of rice and other government privileges, the company suffered from bureaucratic inefficiency: its vessels were uneconomical, its seamen and engineers were unskilled and its management was poor.[44] The company did not prove viable and was dissolved in 1875.

The government changed its policy: it would leave private enterprise to own and operate the businesses, but provide protection and support. The government transferred its ships to the only company in Japan capable of running a fleet this size, Mitsubishi Shokai.[45] Mitsubishi was started by Iwasaki Yataro (1834–84), a lower grade samurai of the Tosa han. The Tosa han had been in the forefront of modernization before the Meiji restoration. While working in the han, Iwasaki had been given responsibility for armament procurement (including ships) in the han's Nagaski and Osaka offices. In 1870 he used the han's ships to enter the coastal trades. The following year, the hans were abolished and their enterprises were transformed into an independent company. Iwasaki became its manager. He eventually took over the company, bringing to it a samurai mentality, promising that no other enterprise in Japan would surpass it.[46]

In these early days, all Japan's foreign trade lay in the hands of foreign ships and the young Mitsubishi Shokai was only involved in coastal shipping. However, with government help it quickly expanded. In 1874 government demand pulled the company onto the ocean highways when the Japanese embarked on a military expedition across the seas in Taiwan.[47] The government bought thirteen steamships from abroad and Mitsubishi was given the task of managing them. The military campaign was a success and, on its conclusion, Mitsubishi was allowed to retain the ships in return for a nominal fee. As part of the deal, the government instructed Mitsubishi to use these vessels between Yokohama and Shanghai, thus launching Japan's first ocean-going liner service. This, however, brought Mitsubishi into competition with foreign liners, in particular the American Pacific Mail Steamship Company. Mitsubishi won this struggle when, with the aid of the state, it purchased its rival's ships and shore facilities.

The Yokohama–Shanghai line was the first of a number of government-ordered routes which gave Mitsubishi experience on ocean liner operations with the protection of government subsidies. In this way, Japan built up its experience and expertise of operating ocean-going liners. In an effort to build up domestic expertise, the government gave additional payments for the training of seamen, and established a number of educational establishments to meet the needs of the growing industry. The close relationship between Mitsubishi and the government continued during the Satsuma Rebellion, when it was contracted to carry troops and war supplies.[48]

The government's motive in supporting Mitsubishi was to build a strong company that could compete with foreigners. In the process, the company had developed substantial market power in the local coastal trades, much to the dissatisfaction of small ship-owners and the general public. A chorus of disapproval forced the government to create a new company. The government provided half the capital to create Kyodo Unyu Kaisha, a company based on a combination of existing smaller firms. The new company provided direct competition on all Mitsubishi's domestic routes.[49] However, aggressive competition in a small market was destructive and both suffered serious losses as they reduced their freight rates to compete.[50] Eventually, in 1885, the government ordered the companies to amalgamate. The new company, Nippon Yusen Kaisha (NYK), was now the only state-aided shipping firm, to which the government guaranteed an 8 per cent dividend.

NYK's first attempt to open a long-distance service was the Japan–Bombay line. Opened in 1893, NYK sought to carry raw cotton at rates cheaper than those provided by the existing shipping conferences led by the British firm P&O. The entrance of a new competitor was not welcomed by the conference and two years of cut-throat competition ensued. However, NYK had the support of the Japan Cotton Spinners Association, the people who bought their chief cargo, their action highlighting the importance of supporting industries in industrial development. NYK survived the competition and was admitted into the conference in 1896, hence establishing Japan's first ocean liner service. Trade between India and Japan soared, growing fourfold in the ten years prior to 1902.[51] NYK grew hand in hand with this trade, and eventually expanded into other distant routes, including Europe, North America (Seattle) and Australia.

As the Japanese economy was restructured and new productive skills developed, the country entered a new era of economic growth that opened up opportunities for entrepreneurs. In particular, growth in demand provided opportunities for small shippers to begin tramp services on Japan's coastal routes. However, they lacked the skills and capital to operate steamships, so plied their trade in wooden sailing ships.[52] In

1885 the government prohibited the construction of large-scale sailing ships, which led to the gradual replacement of virtually all the fleet by steamships and, before long, these small companies expanded into international waters, crossing the short distance to Korea and China.[53]

The growing wave of economic activity also created opportunities in the liner market, and a second major company was born in the west of Japan. Here, many small companies were engaged on coastal routes using second-hand steamships. Their numbers increased significantly during the Satsuma Rebellion, creating excessive competition once the rebellion was over.[54] To remedy the situation, the government recommended amalgamation, so in 1882 fifty-five small firms joined together to form a new joint stock company. Initially, the Osaka Shosen Kaisha (OSK), as it was to be called, with its small-scale wooden steamships, was no match for NYK and only operated in the coastal trades. However, with government assistance the company eventually acquired a number of steel steamships and in 1890 it commenced its first ocean-going liner service to Korea.

Both of the liner companies were strongly dependent on the government. For example, the gross profit of NYK in the financial year ending September 1893 was only about 930,000 yen. The government subsidies it received amounted to 900,000 yen, or 97 per cent of its profit.[55] Government demand during the Sino-Japanese War of 1894–5 was another key support. At the outbreak of the war, domestic shipping still accounted for only 10 per cent of the nation's ocean-going services,[56] but nevertheless the country now had two companies with experience and capabilities in ocean-going steamships, something it had not possessed before.

Having created two major companies, the government continued to encourage an expansion of capabilities, and its attention turned to developing specific routes.[57] From this point, the government awarded subsidies, not for any particular company, but for the routes and mileage they covered. This led to the introduction of the Navigation Promotion Law and Shipbuilding Promotion Law in 1896. These laws offered a break from past policy in that the assistance was open to all companies, not just those previously supported by the government. Inspired by the new legislation, a third major company was created by Asano Soichiro, a prominent businessman with experience as an operator on coastal routes. His decision to enter ocean-going shipping led to the establishment of Toyo Kisen Kaisha (TKK). In 1898 the company began a service across the Pacific Ocean to San Francisco.[58]

Some shipping companies were created as a result of integration with other industries, the most prominent of which was Mitsui Bussan. Mitsui was an old merchant house founded by Hachirobe Takatoshi, a masterless samurai, in the seventeenth century. Hachirobe had become a key player in the Edo retail textile market, eventually building up a chain of shops and expanding into wholesale and banking. In 1872 Mitsui established a general trading company that traded items such as rice, coal, raw silk and tea. In 1876 the company took up an offer from the government to export coal to China from the government-operated Miike mines. At this time, the British company Jardine Matheson had the largest share of the Shanghai coal market, but by 1880 Mitsui's shipment surpassed them.[59] This introduction to foreign trade led to an expansion of its shipping operations and the opening of branch offices in Shanghai, Tientsin, Hong Kong and Singapore. By 1890 Mitsui Bussan had emerged as a substantial operator of merchant shipping.

Mitsui was one of a number of large diversified general trading companies, a unique organizational form, given the extremely diverse range of activities in which they operated. The government encouraged these giants, as foreign trade was new to the country and small

Japanese manufacturers found linguistic, cultural and geographical barriers daunting. The general trading companies had economies of scale and scope which allowed them to carry risk, diversify their product range and spearhead the nation's exporting effort. Controlling both imports and exports meant their ships could carry loads on both legs of the journey. In this way, the dispersed range of their activities increased the economic viability of their shipping and, by 1900, Mitsui Bussan handled about one-third of Japan's total foreign trade.[60]

The shipping departments of trading companies such as Mitsui and Suzuki played a key role in developing the nation's maritime skills. They acted as incubators for talented individuals who later became top managers of lines that included Kawasaki, Kokusai and Daido shipping.[61]

Japan's merchant marine grew rapidly during this period. Not only did this reflect its increased maritime capabilities but also the growing capabilities in other industries that provided the cargoes for the ships. On the back of this industrialization, Japanese exports tripled in the late 1890s alone.[62] Cargoes included exports of cotton cloth and yarn to Korea and China, silk and silk cloth to the United States, and coal throughout Asia. Imports included raw cotton, sugar and rice from India and America, and ironware, plastics and manufactured goods from Europe and the United States. The most important of the exports were the textiles coming from the large cotton mills established in the 1880s with government loans. During the first thirty years of the twentieth century, the textile industry would account for over half of Japan's exports.[63]

By 1912 NYK owned 280,000 tons of shipping, OSK had 130,000 tons and TKK more than 70,000 tons.[64] The industry had advanced with strong aid from the government which, by 1913, provided a fourteen-yen subsidy for each ton operated by the principal firms. This compared with the three or four yen that some German and British liners received.[65] Europeans might accuse the Japanese of cheating with this extra help, but the Japanese could equally claim that the Westerners had a head start. Government policies were not free of errors, and policies required continual adjustment through a process of learning. However, within sixty-five years, they succeeded in building the third biggest maritime fleet in the world, and the nation had begun to ride a new era of economic prosperity.

11

THE CORPORATE AGE

In its early years, the United States government had played only a minor role in the US economy. It coined money, established postal and road services and created a system of patents and copyrights which encouraged innovation. It created a legal system to deal with commercial disputes and the law courts made decisions that showed a strong sensitivity to commercial interests. It was through the market, not the government, that the nation's resources were allocated. This changed with the Civil War.

The Civil War of 1861–5 is commonly described as a fight over slavery, but this is an oversimplification. A number of factors led to war, and the changing nature of American business played an important role. The South had a buoyant economy based on the export of cotton to Britain. By contrast, the North was trying to develop an industrial base and wanted to impose tariffs on imports of competing products arriving from Europe. The South gained no benefit from tariff protection. In fact, by raising the cost of the products they bought, the tariff was an additional tax. Naturally, southerners preferred to buy the cheap, high-quality products coming from Britain.

The debate on tariffs reflected very different views of the role of government. The North wanted the central government to play a key role in industrialization. They believed the nation would advance if the government aided the development of roads, railways and canals. By contrast, the South believed that most power should lie in the hands of the individual states. If Washington took a stronger role, the southern states feared they would become dominated by the North, where the population was growing, and southern interests would be overlooked. Slavery was one of those interests. The South believed that the North, which did not rely on a plantation economy, had a distorted understanding of the importance of slavery. They believed that if northerners were reliant on plantations, they would not be so moralistic. When the Republican party came to power, its new leader Abraham Lincoln made no statement that he intended to abolish slavery, but he did oppose its extension to the new territories opening up in the west. To the South, this indicated that federal power was falling into the hands of northern industrialists, unsympathetic to southern needs, and the South wanted out.

With the outbreak of war, southern politicians were absent from the halls of Congress, and the northern states immediately introduced a new political-economic direction. The government now took a key role in the economy and introduced legislation to achieve its goals. In 1862 the Morrill Land Grant College Act granted land for the building of colleges devoted to agriculture and the mechanical arts. In 1863 the National Banking Act created a national banking system and currency. Federal income tax was introduced, as well as several bills which gave grants for rail expansion. A number of new federal bureaucracies were created, including the Department of Agriculture, the Bureau of Printing and Engraving, the Office of the Comptroller of Customs, and the Office of Immigration. The National Academy of Sciences was created to boost technological development. Most importantly, the government, particularly the military, became an important consumer of industrial products.

The government also introduced a protective tariff policy, starting with the Morrill Tariff of 1861. Shielded from foreign competition,

Americans began imitating foreign production technologies. This legislation played a key role in developing the nation's industrial capabilities. In fact, the most rapidly expanding industries between 1870 and 1914 were those protected by the 1870s' tariff structure.[1] The transfer of industrial technology to the United States occurred in those places with similar environmental conditions to the original European production centres. Particularly important was access to raw materials. They also relied on skilled immigrants from Britain to help develop their capabilities. For example, at Trenton, New Jersey, immigrants from Staffordshire found suitable clays to build a ceramics industry. At Waterbury, Connecticut, copper and zinc deposits provided the basis for an industry which attracted skilled brass-workers from Birmingham. Iron production grew at Albany, Troy and Buffalo, but it was at Pittsburgh where iron ore and coal deposits provided the bedrock of the US steel industry. Ninety-five per cent of the nation's anthracite coal was located in eastern Pennsylvania and here a number of centres grew, first as coal mining and transportation centres, then attracting other industries that used coal for energy.

Ohio developed a number of industries reflecting its broad resource base, while Chicago developed into a great trading city. With its good water and rail links, Chicago redistributed agricultural products from the west and industrial products from the east. It was all part of a process in which the nation developed a number of industrial centres in the north-east.

It would be wrong to say that all new industries were imitative. American entrepreneurs also seized opportunities made available by the latest developments in science. For example, in the mid-1880s, at Rochester, New York, George Eastman perfected a small hand-held camera (the Kodak) which provided the base for the world's largest manufacturer of photographic equipment. It was at this time that advances in electricity and steel were changing the possibilities of what goods could be made and how people made them. Americans seized opportunities stemming from this new technological wave. George Westinghouse invented an air brake for trains before founding the Westinghouse Electric Company to manufacture electrical generators and appliances. At the same time, Thomas Edison, who began as a telegraph operator, started experimenting with telegraph technology before inventing the phonograph and building the nation's first electrical power station in New York. These examples aside, the leading American businessmen and firms were rarely the pioneers in technology.[2]

The American industrial environment was much larger than Britain's and it was railroad expansion in the nineteenth century that linked this vast continental land mass into one huge market. In the process, the economic system had been reshaped and a new economic paradigm appeared. It favoured mass production, large integrated organizations and the gospel of scientific management.

The railroad was the first big US industry, and provided an organizational model on how large-scale business could be done. Initially, these companies were run by merchants who divided managerial functions between themselves. However, as the scale of business grew, it was no longer possible for owner-operators to control such vast commercial activity. They found they had to hire others to do the job for them, and as the railways got bigger, different levels of managers were required.[3] The first managers were recruited from construction, machine and engineering trades but, as organizations grew, they were able to recruit from inside, creating a career ladder which enhanced management loyalty. The corporate ladder was born.

One of the main problems faced by these giant companies was how to build an organizational structure that allowed business to be conducted efficiently. These companies were larger than any commercial organization ever seen before, and there was a big distance between top management and workers. To overcome problems of distance, clear hierarchies, rules and procedures were created for workers to follow. To overcome problems of size, the companies were divided into smaller managerial units. A manager of these units would be responsible for the company's operations in a certain geographic area or product line. These managers were close to the daily operations and could quickly solve problems as they occurred. While these regional managers focused on day-to-day problems, a central staff at head office provided overall coordination and planning with a focus on future developments. To improve decision-making and information flow, sophisticated forms of cost accounting were introduced. These structures provided the model for other large industrial enterprises that followed.[4]

By improving national transportation, the railroads transformed the US economy. Before the railroads arrived, a firm might have been the sole supplier of goods to a town or region because there was no way a competitor could get his products there. The local producer often had a monopoly, but the railroads broke down the geographic barriers that created these monopolies, allowing firms the opportunity to invade other firms' territories. This increased competition caused many businessmen to defend their position by integrating with their competitors to form larger companies. Another defensive strategy was to integrate backward with suppliers in an attempt to control their supply of raw materials. Some companies integrated forward with distributors in an attempt to control their marketing effort. These amalgamations created large powerful corporations.

Amalgamations became very common during the depression of the 1870s when producers, who had previously increased their production potential, found themselves in dangerous positions of excess capacity when the market went into decline. The result was ruthless price competition in which many businesses went bankrupt. In the period 1871–5 the rate of failure doubled, with similar episodes in the 1880s and 1890s. Competition had turned into destructive rivalry.

The first solution to the problem was the formation of pools in which producers agreed to fix prices and reduce output. However, pools could only work if members refrained from producing at their full potential. Sooner or later, one party would give in to temptation and sell below the agreed price, causing the whole agreement to fall apart.[5] More enduring solutions to the problems of excessive competition came with the trust and the holding company.

The most famous trust was that of Standard Oil, led by John D. Rockefeller. Rockefeller grew up in up-state New York where he spent his boyhood raising and selling turkeys and hoeing potatoes. Being very frugal, he saved diligently and eventually ended up lending money to the farmers who employed him. When his family moved to Cleveland, the young Rockefeller studied bookkeeping at school and worked as a clerk for a produce merchant. By 1859 he had saved $800, enough to start his own business buying and selling grain and other provisions to rural customers.

When the Civil War arrived, Rockefeller earned a small fortune selling provisions to the Union army at high wartime prices. This provided Rockefeller with investment capital just as the nation was about to embark on a new wave of industrialization. Sensing growth in the oil industry, he used his earnings to build the largest refinery in the country. However, as we have seen throughout this book, new growth paths invariably attract many people wanting to cash in. Rockefeller soon realized that this increase in competition would result in lower prices and smaller profits. To counter this, Rockefeller developed a strategy that involved not just technological and organizational improvements, but also removing competition. It was a strategy that we have seen time and time again, from Virji Vora in Gujarat to the East India Companies.

With the help of a few partners and Cleveland bankers, Rockefeller purchased fifty competing firms. This made him the largest player in the industry. He exploited his market power to negotiate low rates from the railroads that carried the oil to the cities. This in turn allowed him to charge cheaper rates to his city customers, further expanding his market share. Rockefeller continued his policy of reducing competition and invited his rivals to join him in business. In 1881 he formed the Standard Oil Trust in which forty different companies (controlling 90 per cent of American oil refining) turned their stock over to nine trustees in return for a share in the combined companies. The trustees managed the combined operations and were given the power to close down any plant should they desire. The Trust successfully brought stability to the industry and, in the 1890s, Standard Oil was earning impossibly large profits of $45,000,000 a year.

Much of the success of Standard Oil relied on the economies of scale its huge refineries could deliver. In 1885 the average US refinery produced 1,500–2,000 barrels of kerosene a day at a cost of 1.5c per gallon. By contrast, Standard Oil's refineries could produce 6,500 barrels a day at a cost of 0.452c a gallon. These low costs provided Standard Oil and Rockefeller with huge profit margins. Rockefeller's strategy brought stability to the industry, but it was achieved at a cost to the consumer. Standard Oil had amassed substantial market power by which it could influence prices. There was a popular call for the government to regulate the company. This call was based not just on economic grounds, but also on social and ethical concerns. By this time, free competition had become an entrenched national value. To Americans, the advantages of competition were too self-evident to be debated and it was naturally assumed that eliminating monopolies would lead to competition.[6] The government responded by introducing a range of anti-trust legislation, including the Sherman

Act which outlawed 'combinations in the form of a trust or otherwise in restraint of trade'. It was now illegal for firms to collude with one another to manipulate the market.

Ironically, as the anti-trust laws outlawed combinations of businesses or cartels, firms realized their only safe response was to merge completely into new single corporations. A merger frenzy ensued, with 131 occurring at the peak in 1894–1904.[7] In this way, the corporation became a dominant feature of the American economic system. Of course, larger companies could not swallow the smaller ones without the finance to make the acquisitions, so Wall Street and the financial sector increased its importance in the American economic system.

The leading light of Wall Street was J. Pierpont Morgan, who had learnt about banking working for his father, a senior partner in the London office of George Peabody & Co. In London, Morgan learnt the mechanisms of the pipeline that pumped capital from the British financial markets into the expanding American railroads. Eventually, Morgan extended his banking activities to provide finance for consolidating industries. In 1892 he merged Thomas Edison's interests with rival Thompson Houston Electric Company to form General Electric. In 1901 he headed a group that purchased Carnegie Steel and merged it with the Federal Steel company to create the nucleus of the United States Steel Corporation, a giant responsible for 67 per cent of all the steel produced in the United States with an authorized capitalization of $1.4 billion. The investment banking fees for facilitating such a transaction provided a bonanza for Morgan and Wall Street. It was a new era for American commerce in which Wall Street banks earned huge profits advising and arranging mergers and takeovers.[8]

Although the objective of most integration may have been market power,[9] the resulting corporations evolved other economic advantages. Big companies could exploit economies of scale. This meant they could invest in large-scale machinery and equipment. With the high sales levels these companies achieved, the cost of building these plants could be spread over a large number of products, dramatically reducing unit costs. These giant companies could also exploit economies of scope. This meant expanding the scope of their activities and diversifying into related products and services that also used their core facilities. With greater use of their core facilities, manufacturing costs declined to an unprecedented level.

The increased use of large-scale plant and machines was also a response to limitations in the local environment. The US did not have the same number of skilled workers that Britain possessed. In fact, many of the immigrants coming to the United States from southern and eastern Europe were uneducated with few skills. In these circumstances, it made sense to increase the use of machines and simplify the jobs. The result was a dramatic change in the ratio of capital to human labour in production.

Companies could only justify investment in large plants if they had a steady flow of output. To ensure that sales kept up with the large-scale of output, successful organizations also had to invest in large marketing and distribution networks. Integration into production and manufacturing facilities also reduced transaction costs; when a company did its own marketing, it could save money on marketing to suppliers and the costs of making and enforcing contracts. This factor became more important as products increased in technicality. To sell a technical product, sales staff needed to be more familiar with their product, so if the company controlled its own sales effort, it could ensure the staff had the skills needed to gain a marketing edge.

Finally, these companies had to invest in management that would plan and coordinate these various production and distribution activities.[10] These managers created sales and organizational strategies for the new giants. They organized and administered accounting and production systems, company rules and regulations and reported back on results. The first movers who made these investments in production, marketing and management gained increased profits and experience. This provided competitive strength with which they could repel new entrants who threatened to take a share of the market.

The esteemed economist Alfred Chandler[11] called this economic system 'managerial capitalism'. It reflected the peculiarities of the American environment. These peculiarities included the large national market and resource base, and transportation and communication improvements such as the telegraph which allowed coordination over long distances. Not all industries were amenable to this new mass production technology. These new business methods were most suitable to industries where economies of scale and scope were possible. These big businesses included petroleum, chemicals, sugar, alcohol and metal production, industries that lent themselves to mechanical production and standardized goods. However, it was less suitable for the manufacture of textiles, shoes, furniture and printing, where small-batch custom orders still dominated due to the changing customer needs.

The new corporate age produced its own gurus and philosophers. Frederick Winslow Taylor took the lead after his experiments at Bethlehem Steel Works where he studied labourers at work. These men performed a basic job carrying pig iron, but Taylor analysed it scientifically. His researchers discovered that the most tiring part of the job was picking up the iron.[12] They also found that the men's work-rate was affected by the distance the iron was carried and the slope the men had to walk up. By analysing work scientifically and paying men on the basis of what they did, not the hours they worked, Taylor found he could increase daily output from twelve and a half tons per man to forty-seven and a half tons. Taylor suggested that men needed to be scientifically selected for the job and jobs should be divided into highly specialized tasks to maximize the benefits of specialization. This 'scientific management' did much to assist producers to shape their manufacturing processes to the opportunities made possible by the mass market. Taylor also contributed greatly to the increased efficiency of the US steel industry through the introduction of high-speed tools.

Taylor was not the American Confucius. Taylor's writings were specifically devoted to production, not social relations. Nevertheless, his work came to define American leadership. For example, in an article printed in 1901, Charles Schwab, the founding president of US Steel, stated that American industrial leadership was won by handling and transforming the raw materials of the earth in a 'scientific manner'. In so doing, costs were reduced to the lowest level, following the rule that the larger the output, the smaller the cost of production. This rule supported 'the science of business consolidation' as opposed to the wastefulness of the individualistic, competitive business system. In this way, the 'industrial combination' not the 'individual manufacturer' put the United States in 'industrial control of the world'.[13]

As organizations became bigger, they needed a steady supply of skilled managers, so education institutions started to provide courses in management. It became possible to get academic training in accounting and the first book on cost accounting was published in the 1880s.[14] The Wharton School of Commerce and Finance at the University of Pennsylvania was the first university to offer courses in business. In the decade after 1899 commerce schools were set up at the Universities of Chicago, California, New York and Harvard. Engineering graduates also flowed from the universities after the 1880s, when the Massachusetts Institute of Technology, Purdue, Wisconsin and the Stevens Institute of Technology all established mechanical engineering departments.[15] These institutions trained the American mandarins who would maximize the efficiency of the economic system.

Changing methods of production also had an impact on society. One change was a growing split between white-collar workers responsible for planning and decision-making and the blue-collar workers who carried out the orders.[16] As this new economic system became more established, it led to an increasing gap between the rich and poor. In 1890 the top 1 per cent owned 51 per cent of all property, while the bottom 44 per cent owned only 1.2 per cent.[17] This was a recipe for unrest and a group of female social justice activists lobbied the government for social policies, while the clergy and other socially minded writers also expressed concern for those at the bottom of the economic system.

This world of large corporations was a far cry from the small producers and individual liberties advocated by Benjamin Franklin and his contemporaries. In *Wealth Against Commonwealth*, Henry Demarest Lloyd wrote a blistering attack on corporate power which was soon supported by newspaper exposés of the practices of robber-barons and successful businessmen.

> The world, enriched by thousands of generations of toilers and thinkers, has reached a fertility which can give every human being a plenty undreamed of even in the Utopias. But between this plenty ripening on the boughs of our civilization and the peoples hungering for it step the 'cornerers', the syndicates, trusts, combinations . . .

Rich tycoons became common anti-heros in popular novels. Like Henry the Navigator four centuries earlier, the corporations needed to legitimize the new growth path they were building, and they did it in a way that distorted the original concepts put forward by the founding fathers. The new business leaders claimed their enterprises were the natural extensions of market activity. They stated that the competitive market was a survival of the fittest and their businesses were the fittest. They further legitimized their status by claiming to be champions of individualism and free competition, and it was the government that most threatened this natural process. They saw no irony in the fact that their oligopolistic corporations were reducing competition and the role of the individual in the economy.

While there was anger at the corporatization of the economy, more and more Americans found jobs in these enterprises. The world of small producers where men and women worked for themselves was replaced by one in which men sold their labour to corporations, while women stayed at home and did the cooking, cleaning, sewing and looking after the children. Economic growth did not desert these employees as real wages increased 70 per cent between 1865 and 1890. As one Italian immigrant remarked, in America 'work was rewarded with abundance'.[18] Although there were many who suffered misfortune, the common American story was one in which immigrants arrived with only the clothes they stood up in, and ended with bank accounts, pleasant homes and college-educated children. The American dream was built on an emerging economic wave.

From 1870 through to the First World War, GDP grew fivefold, compared with a mere doubling in the UK.[19] In a very short time, the country had been transformed from a predominantly agricultural and commercial economy to an industrial giant. This development did not progress smoothly or without problems. The nation encountered a series of economic disasters on its path to leadership, including depressions in 1857, 1873 and 1893. However, by the turn of the century, America was appearing as a land of economic giants, with an economic system based on mass production and distribution which exploited economies of scale and scope, standardization and the intensive use of natural resources. It had successfully adopted many European innovations and, with its own distinctive system, was generating a far higher level of output than anything the world had ever seen before. The world of big business, skyscrapers, telephones and automobiles had arrived.

There are numerous examples of European innovations progressing further in the United States because the local environment could accommodate greater economies of scale, but the best known was the automobile. The automobile was built around the internal combustion engine invented by a Belgian, Etienne Lenoir. However, Lenoir's engines were expensive to run and needed improvement before they would have a commercial use. It was a German, Nicholas August Otto, who eventually came up with a design that could be produced economically. Karl Benz took one of Otto's engines and built what is now considered the first petrol automobile, a motorized tricycle.

It was in France where the automobile industry first took off, as evidenced in the words we now associate with the industry: 'garage', 'chauffeur' and 'automobile' are all French in origin. There are a number of reasons why France was the cradle of the industry. First, the French government had built fine roads to transport its armies. These roads made driving far more enjoyable than in other countries. Second, Paris at the *fin de siècle* was the most vibrant city in Europe. It attracted Brazilian playboys, Russian grand dukes and English younger sons all wishing to enjoy the *joie de vivre*. They created a healthy market for fashionable novelties, of which automobiles and aeroplanes were the latest. With this market in mind, many French metal-working shops began producing cars as a sideline to their existing business.

While Brazilian playboys took their vehicles on to the streets of Paris, Henry Ford was working as chief engineer at the Edison Illuminating Company in Detroit. In his spare time he tinkered with gasoline engines and made his first car in 1896. His first entrepreneurial venture was the Detroit Automobile Company. He hoped to capitalize on the growing interest in motor cars, but the company failed. His next venture was the Henry Ford Motor Company. However, after only four months, he had a fall-out with his partners and was shown the door. The company was eventually reorganized as the Cadillac Automobile Company, the flagship of General Motors Corporation. Ford's early entrepreneurial efforts were clearly unsuccessful. In 1903 he tried again by forming the Ford Motor Company with capital provided by a Detroit coal merchant. Finally, he had a successful enterprise under his belt, quickly becoming one of the nation's top four producers.

At this time, the automobile industry was characterized by batch production. This is illustrated by the large number of producers. There were 178 automobile manufacturers in the United States in 1904.[20] Although mass production had a long established tradition in American industry, it had not yet been used in automobile production. A car engine was still a crafted product built by hand. Parts could not be produced with consistent shapes so most parts coming from the machine shops would need to be modified to fit into a car. Eventually, work-study techniques of the type advocated by Frederick Taylor were applied to the industry and, with developments in machine tools, American firms gained the opportunity to produce accurate, standardized parts in large volumes.

Until this point, cars had been playthings for the wealthy. Ford realized that if cars could be produced cheaply, a whole new market could be opened up for people such as doctors, engineers and professional travellers. Ford's strategy was to produce one design. If large numbers could be built, costs would come down, allowing more people to afford them. In 1907 the average price of American-built cars was $2,150. The following year, Ford released the Model T for $850. The car was a great success and soon huge demand required faster production techniques. To meet the demand, assembly-line production was introduced into the Ford plants by Clarence W. Avery, a college graduate recently employed by the company. With higher output and greater economies of scale, the price of the car declined to $345–$360 in 1916, and further still to $220–$260 in 1926.[21]

Ford was a product of his environment. He rode a wave unleashed by new developments in engineering and the largest and wealthiest middle class in the world. These supported the introduction of mass-produced automobiles on a scale that no other environment would allow. Within fifteen years, Ford had built the world's largest and most profitable enterprise.[22] By 1915 the automobile industry was the third largest industry in the States. By 1923 it was number one, a position it held for fifty years.

Although Ford was later voted the entrepreneur of the twentieth century, he repeatedly made serious errors. In the 1920s, Ford clung to the Model T recipe for success for too long and failed to notice the market had changed. Whereas under the leadership of Alfred P. Sloan, General Motors introduced a new product policy, offering a number of different cars of different qualities and different prices to meet different consumer needs.

Sloan also gave General Motors a more efficient organization structure. Under the new structure, direction was set at the HQ while decision-making was decentralized at divisional level. By contrast, Ford failed to invest in a sufficient management structure. He had an uncompromising belief that businesses did not need managers, but, by the late 1920s, his company was a shambles and lost money

271

nearly every year until 1947. All that helped it survive were the company's cash assets. These carried Ford through a number of significant managerial mistakes.

Despite these failings, the US automobile industry remained the world's largest for decades to come. With hierarchical organizational structures, mass production techniques requiring low-skilled workers and large investments in machinery, the industry generated economies of scale that no other country could match.

In each chapter of this book to date, industrialization has normally provided ideal conditions for shipping entrepreneurs. Industrialization meant a nation gained cargoes, increased the capital available for investment, and raised demand for shipping services. In the first half of the nineteenth century, the US economy did develop a strong merchant marine, but much of this was destroyed during the Civil War, a period in which Britain leapt ahead with its steam and iron technologies. The age of steamships required different skills from the age of wood and sail and Americans were slow to rebuild their fleet with this new technology, and with good reason. American industry was growing so rapidly during this time that the domestic market provided far better opportunities for investment than shipping.

What international shipping did occur was still in the hands of foreigners, in particular the British. The US industry was burdened with high costs, such as high wage rates. The *Scientific American* reported in 1872 that the average American seaman earned \$40 per month, compared with \$12 for the British, while an American first class engineer earned \$240, three times that of his British contemporary.[23] The industry was also burdened with the high price of local ships. British ship-owners could buy iron-hulled steamers for one-third the American price.[24] Although Americans had developed a healthy iron industry, American expertise lay in rails, nails and structural shapes for bridges. Ships required shapes and plates that local mills did not have the skills or capabilities to produce.[25]

The high price of local ships could not be circumvented by importing because of the high tariffs protecting the local industry.[26] By the late nineteenth century, communication and transportation links were regular enough for US ship-owners to have easily bought British ships, but the law dictated that American companies buy their ships at home. This policy was designed to develop ship-building skills that were needed by the navy.

Earlier, we read that British ship-builders enjoyed a similar legislative protection during their early period of growth, but the people who bought and sailed those ships were also protected from foreign competition and so could absorb the higher costs. American shippers did not have the same protection, so they had to compete against the leading shipping nation with one hand tied behind their back. Government policy supported its ship-building industry at the expense of its ship-owners and operators. Paradoxically, the long-term growth of ship-building depended on the health of its shippers. In much the same way that protective legislation tied ship-owners to a protected and costly ship-building industry, ship-builders were also tied to a protected and costly iron industry. Protective tariffs gave iron producers the opportunity to charge high prices at home.[27] In this way, the multi-tiered protective legislation hamstrung American ship operators.

The problems with iron did not stop innovation in wooden ship-building. During the 1880s and 1890s four-and five-masted schooners of over 1,000 tons were common. One seven-masted ship was even built. However, this technological pathway held less potential than the iron steamship technology pursued by the British. On the positive side, a number of institutions were created to help improve US marine production technology. In 1874 schools were established in all the leading port cities, in the hope that effective training would provide competent crewmen and reduce the appalling number of groundings, collisions and fires that plagued American ships.[28] The United States Naval Institute and the United States Naval War College were founded to encourage thinking on naval and maritime problems. A major institutional advance was the creation of a Department of Commerce and a Bureau of Navigation within the Treasury. This provided the industry with the political and administrative organs in government to oversee the merchant marine and report on commercial conditions.

Although the profits paid by US flag ships involved in foreign trade were not attractive, some maritime activity still warranted investment. Americans made large investments on domestic shipping routes which were protected by cabotage laws that prohibited foreign competition on these routes. Tonnage in coastal and lake shipping increased markedly over this period.[29] The number of routes Americans could sail while protected from foreign competition increased as American territory expanded. Victory in the Spanish–American War gave the United States two new colonies in Puerto Rico and the Philippines. These both required shipping services. In the same year, 1898, Hawaii was also annexed. Routes to these new territories were now protected under US coastwise laws. This provided the opportunity for ship operators to build up their capabilities without having to face the all-powerful British. The Matson Navigation company started in the 1890s to take oil to sugar mills on Hawaii. The American-Hawaiian Steamship Company, created in 1899 with sugar plantation shareholders, also benefited from the exclusion of foreign carriers.

Many Americans who wished to invest in international shipping registered their ships in foreign countries to escape high US costs. Companies that invested into shipping in this way included Munson Steamship, Grace Lines and United Fruit, who established shipping services to the Caribbean and Latin America. These companies sailed under the British flag as local wages and ships were simply too expensive. By 1901 the proportion of international trading ships owned by Americans but sailing under foreign flags was 75 per cent of those registered as American.[30] Without a change in tariff policy, there would need to be a huge improvement in ship-building before ships would fly under the United States flag.

Many companies had previously invested in iron ship-building during the Civil War. Realizing the government would need iron-clad ships, they invested in new machinery and yard expansion. For example, the Philadelphian ship-builders W. Cramp and Sons converted from wood to iron during the war, building their first iron boat for the northern navy. However, the industry was far from competitive; inefficiencies in cutting procedures were so bad that Charles Cramp claimed: 'in the early days the scrap heap was the largest mound in the yard'.[31]

The father of iron ship-building in America was John Roach who had learnt the moulding trade at a pig iron works in New Jersey before buying his own company. Through a combination of acquisition and internal expansion, he built 'the finest marine-engine works in the United States'.[32] The Roach yard was pivotal to America's catch-up with the British: in 1881 it was the first to introduce pneumatic power tools and, in 1883, the first to begin rolling suitable plates. They were also the first Americans to build a tanker, the *Standard*, for the Standard Oil Company. In this way, the company gradually expanded its productive capabilities.

American yards were dependent on Europe as a source of technology transfer and productivity improvement. Charles Cramp took his supervising engineer on a fact-finding mission to Britain where their discussions included compound engineering technology. One of the people they spoke to was the chief engineer of the British liner *Italy*, whom they ended up employing and taking back to America with them. By 1872 the shipyard was building ships with compound engines for the American Steamship Company.[33]

The government also played a key role in the catch-up process in ship-building. When Congress ratified steel as the preferred material for warships, navy demand provided the opportunity for many to invest in the plant for steel-hulled ships.[34] This activity gave birth to a military industrial complex based on the Roach and Cramp ship-yards and the Carnegie, Midvale and Bethlehem iron and steel plants. The navy helped to facilitate technology transfer.[35] When it imported engine plans from Britain for the cruiser USS *Baltimore*, it gave the Cramp shipyard a chance to create more powerful engines based on the triple-expansion engine. The navy's policy of placing ordnance officers with European ordnance companies also provided a path for technology transfer as the officers gained experience and brought it back to the United States. Ship-building contracts with the navy also provided funds by which yards could upgrade their facilities.

As the ship-building industry increased its investment and experience, the price difference between American ships and British ships began to close. In the early 1880s the price differential was 25 per cent, and had closed to 15 per cent by 1888.[36] However, the industry still suffered from small demand that did not allow it to achieve the same level of specialization that the British shipyards achieved.

At the end of the nineteenth century, total tonnage flying under the American flag was substantially smaller than that of Britain. However, growth in the domestic economy increased the number of companies in the industry. Many companies started investing in shipping because they needed to transport their own goods. In the Pacific Ocean, the Oceanic Steamship Company was started by a San Francisco entrepreneur, Claus Spreckels, to carry sugar from his plantations in Hawaii to the refinery in California. The Great Northern

Railroad Company created the Great Northern Steamship Company in 1900, after its tracks reached Seattle, in the hope of establishing a Pacific-based carrying trade to complement its onshore transportation services. The Dollar Steamship Company was created to carry Dollar's lumber products.

Vertical integration also provided the industry with new companies on the Atlantic Ocean. The Pennsylvania Railroad was the biggest company in the world at the time and a leading example of corporate capital. Wanting to develop a continual transportation system from the mid-west of the United States through to Europe, the railroad started transatlantic links to Liverpool and Antwerp. So, together with a small number of investors, it created the International Navigation Company. The only other American company on the Atlantic was also started by a railroad company. The Baltimore and Ohio Railroad gave birth to the Atlantic Transport Company. It is no coincidence that railmen outside of New York took an interest in developing this route.[37] New York was emerging as a prosperous railhead with links to European shipping in the Atlantic. The southern companies had to develop ocean-going shipping from their ports in order to compete (although both companies eventually added New York as a terminal port for their operations).

These young US companies were small fish in a big pond. Unfortunately, increased competition from growing French and German shipping was taking the market towards an oversupply situation in which the weakest would lose. The great Wall Street financier J. P. Morgan considered the competition to be ridiculous. Ships rushed out of New York on the same day in an attempt to be the first to reach Europe. If they distributed their sailings more rationally, the result would be a more dependable and profitable service. Morgan had been responsible for many of the business amalgamations during this period and now weaved his magic on shipping. The two American companies were amalgamated and combined with the British White Star and Leyland Lines. The new company, International Merchant Marine (IMM), became the fourth largest industrial corporation behind US Steel, Standard Oil and the American Tobacco Company. With 130 steamers, it was the largest merchant fleet owned by any one company in the world, although most ships were still registered under the British flag.[38]

However, this great shipping combine was not as successful as the land-based combines. To finance the merger, the company had built up high levels of debt and the consolidation did not lead to a reduction in operating costs. In fact, some costs actually increased with attempts to improve coordination between the various units. The killer came when the company launched a new prestigious ship in April 1912. That ship was the *Titanic*. Not only was the sinking of the Titanic a human disaster, it was also a financial disaster. On the sharemarket, the preferred stock for IMM declined from $51 per share to $3, while common stock declined from 3\frac{3}{4}$ to $\frac{5}{8}$. The iceberg sank more than the *Titanic*.[39] By 1915, the company was in the bankruptcy court and was only rescued by the outbreak of the First World War.

The First World War dramatically affected global shipping by providing a form of infant industry protection. Britain and other European nations took their merchant shipping out of the market to use in their war effort. In their absence, Americans took the opportunity to enter those trades vacated by what had been superior competition. In so doing, American companies increased their knowledge, experience and investment in new foreign markets. Americans enjoyed the benefits of neutrality and very high wartime freight, and this encouraged investment into the industry. People like John D. Rockefeller and Averell Harriman (son of a railway magnate) were attracted to the industry by the high returns that were now being made.

In the Pacific Ocean, Japanese shippers also benefited from the First World War, as Asian markets were left entirely open to Japanese products. This created a huge window of opportunity for Japanese businessmen to increase their capital, skills and experience, and Japanese shipping went through an unprecedented boom. Its network of routes grew to include Africa, the east coast of South America and all the regions of South-East Asia. Japanese tonnage increased from 1,514,000 gross weight tonnes in 1913 to 2,841,000 in 1919, and the loading rate climbed to 70 per cent.[40] Japan now ranked as the third largest maritime nation behind Britain and the United States. This burst in Japanese activity was not driven by government but by entrepreneurs. After fifty years of government guidance, the country had acquired the capabilities in steamship technology with which the industry could now generate its own start-ups.

For the Americans, the First World War provided the long awaited alignment in military and shipping goals. President Wilson had long seen the merchant marine as an important pillar in global power and prestige.[41] He linked a decrease in tariff and expanding foreign trade to a policy of support for a strong American merchant marine. He initially came across strong resistance from the private sector, which was concerned that the nation was edging away from the principles of free enterprise. However, heightened wartime activity increased the demand for more shipping. These changed circumstances allowed President Wilson to pass the 1916 Shipping Act which established the United States Shipping Board 'to promote, investigate, regulate and administer the shipping industry'.[42]

One of the board's first tasks was the creation of the Emergency Fleet Corporation (EFC) which was responsible for meeting the needs of America's war effort. The resulting 'bridge of ships' to France became the largest industrial undertaking ever attempted in the United States. Meeting the shipping needs of a war across the Atlantic required a massive investment in new shipyards. Initially, the EFC was handicapped by lack of experience, and managers learnt as they went. It is hard to imagine this occurring in a competitive commercial environment without the protection of war and wartime demand. At the beginning of a steep learning curve, the scheme encountered delays, waste and numerous clashes of personality and policies.[43] Nevertheless, over time, they mastered the necessary skills and Americanized them with mass production techniques.[44]

The output on the Hog Island yard in Philadelphia was phenomenal. At its peak, it employed 34,000 workers and could produce more than all the yards in Britain combined. So great was the number of launchings at Cramps that, instead of bringing in dignitaries from town to launch ships, they would call the company's restaurant from where a brawny cook named Maggie would come, swing a bottle of champagne and send the ship on its way.[45] By the war's end, the United States had the world's largest merchant marine at 13.5 million tons.[46] However, it is one thing to have ships; it is another to be able to manage them competitively. With the war over, the amount of shipping needed in the Atlantic declined as European competition returned, and Americans had not developed knowledge of the markets outside the Atlantic where they operated during the war. To make matters worse, US seamen were still the most expensive in the world. Consequently, the British soon re-established themselves on their old routes.

The years that followed were years of excess supply. There were too many operators in the market and many companies went under. But now the US government recognized the value of a merchant marine and passed a number of laws to assist the industry and provide subsidies. These included the 1920 Merchant Marine Act in which private entrepreneurs were given the chance to charter surplus warships on 'essential trade routes', gaining experience, after which they could purchase them. In 1936 the Merchant Marine Act created the US Maritime Commission. Under Joseph Kennedy, the Commission administered cheap loans for construction of new vessels.[47] However, being drafted during the depression, the new act's principal concern was employment, so it included a requirement of 100 per cent American crews on freighters and 90 per cent on passenger vehicles seeking the subsidies. Working conditions of the crew were protected with a mandatory three-watch system and minimum standards for quarters. As welcome as these changes were to an under-employed labour force, US labour remained expensive and this undermined the competitiveness of the US fleet.

In contrast to the high-wage Americans, the Japanese were a low-wage/low-cost producer, and this gave them a particular advantage in a depressed market. The Japanese fleet consisted mostly of old imported second-hand vessels and the age of the fleet was the second highest in the world.[48] Japanese wages were also much lower than their main competitors[49] and growth in their domestic economy fuelled the demand for shipping services. Consequently, during the depression years 1929–39, when the US fleet shrank on average 2.4 per cent per year and the British fleet shrank 1.1 per cent, the Japanese fleet grew by 3.0 per cent.[50] Another low-cost operator to emerge in this period was Greece with 3.5 per cent growth. The Norwegians also continued a steady climb, based on a high level of flexibility to changing market conditions. Nevertheless, by the outset of the Second World War, the British still had the largest fleet in the world, followed by the United States and Japan. But things were about to change.

12

COAL, OIL AND A FASTER
RATE OF CHANGE

The coal – *il carbone!* I knew we were for it. England – *l'Inghilterra* – she has the coal. And what does she do? She sells it very dear . . . The price. The exchange! il cambio . . . I can't walk a stride without having this wretched cambio, the exchange thrown at my head . . . In Italy, there is no escape. Say two words, and the individual starts chewing old newspaper and stuffing it into you. No escape. You become – if you are English – *l'Inghilterra, il carbone* and *il cambio*; and as England, coal and exchange you are treated.

D. H. Lawrence, *Sea and Sardinia*

At the outset of the First World War, Britain was a phenomenally rich country. It possessed the largest empire the world had ever seen. It ruled a quarter of the world's population, 12,000,000 square miles of land,[1] and it was still growing. With the most sophisticated technologies, it had created an economic system that linked the world, and at the core of this vast system lay London, the centre of international finance and trade.

Coal was the fuel that powered the system. It provided the energy behind the iron, steel and engineering trades. It fuelled the construction of ships, the fuelling of ships, and gave Britain an export cargo that allowed it to charge lower rates on return journeys. Scattered around Britain were coal mines and industrial districts where family-owned firms employed highly skilled workers that moved from firm to firm as the market dictated. Their highly desirable products were carried to markets around the world on British ships. On the return voyage, these ships carried butter, sugar, chocolate, tobacco and meat to the spoilt British consumer.

Anyone living at this time could easily believe that the British were superior when they enjoyed such wealth and ruled a quarter of the world. The truth was self-evident and, like the Chinese before them, the British became arrogant. As Donald Hoare stated in *God is an Englishman*: 'it was not for what they did, but for what they were, that destiny had rewarded them so lavishly'.

It was an age that left an indelible imprint on the British psyche. It gave birth to a particular English view of the world that was carried forward in the nation's political, social and commercial traditions. Possibly the most important of these were the educational institutions. Britain's elite sent their children to public schools where they were educated in aristocratic ideals of honour and public leadership. Students received high moral training that prepared them for careers in the military, civil service, political life and the higher professions. Unfortunately, while they made excellent administrators for Britain's far flung empire, these English mandarins were not encouraged to develop an aptitude for business. The idea of maximizing individual or national wealth seemed mean-spirited when the country possessed such riches. This attitude to commerce can be found in the literature of the day. For example, in *Tom Brown's School Days*, the schoolmaster admonishes Tom:

> You talk of 'working to get a living' and 'doing some real good in the world' in the same breath . . . Keep the latter before you as your only object, and you will be right whether you make a living or not; but if you dwell on the other, you'll very likely drop into mere money making.

283

This aversion to 'mere money making' was even more pronounced at the universities. The curriculum at Oxford and Cambridge was designed to create a model gentleman who could give moral and spiritual leadership to the nation. It was an ethos that shaped business long into the twentieth century. For example, a study of executives at Shell Oil, mostly graduates from Cambridge and Oxford, found they were inclined not to talk of oil as a profitable fluid but as part of a public duty.[2]

These values of honour and public worth were not very different from those of Japan where they had been turned into an asset. In Japan, however, there had been a deliberate attempt to promote industry and commerce as honourable careers. Perhaps the biggest difference between the two nations was that in Britain there was little science in the curriculum. Science and working with one's hands to make money were not endorsed by a society that increasingly saw industry as an area unworthy of a gentleman. The problem would not have been so confining but for the fact that the public school formed the model for state schools.

This has been interpreted as Britain retreating from industry, a process that started in the mid-nineteenth century.[3] The engineer Brunel, who pioneered the use of the screw and iron steamships, sent his children to Harrow where the education would not prepare them to follow in their father's footsteps. After achieving success, businessmen bought land and retired to the country. Here they enjoyed the prestige of being a landowner and acquired the trappings of the gentry. It was a process very similar to that in China where successful merchants bought land and paid for their children to be educated as Confucian scholars. A similar process also occurred in Spain and the Netherlands in the eighteenth century, a process which recognizes that, after a level of economic success has been achieved, people seek non-material goals such as status. As a consequence, Britain's most able men became divorced from the world of commerce and industry.

In the cities, company directors became aloof from management, their boardrooms exhibiting a gentleman's club atmosphere that nourished cautious policies. Nowhere was this more apparent than the prestigious Institute of Directors, which inhabited three mansions in Belgrave Square. Its director general once explained that 'directors are a kind of aristocracy; they should be men of parts, and they should have interests outside business . . . you could say we have a gigantic old boys network.'[4] The goal of these gentleman industrialists was not the whole-hearted pursuit of economic growth, but gentility. The result was a conservative managerial culture which placed stability ahead of growth, and generally resisted institutional overhauls.

These values also reached the government. The Tories in particular believed that economic forces should be made to accommodate established patterns of social relationships. Conflict and uncertain change were to be avoided, and materialism should be minimized. In a desire for stability, regulation conquered laissez-faire. The comparison with China, where the mandarins sought to preserve social harmony, is striking.

It is easy to criticize this conservatism as being irrational, but the desire to avoid social disharmony and conflict was a very real issue. Economic change in Britain would incur social costs that Americans did not have to face. The United States faced shortages of skilled labour, so intense mechanization could occur without resistance. By contrast, Britain possessed highly skilled specialized workers who would have suffered very real dislocation from the change to unskilled mechanized industry. Consequently, in Britain, there was not the same push for large-scale mechanized plants. Both employers and employees showed some preference to try to squeeze more out of the existing technologies, with the inevitable reduction of incomes and in some cases, loss of quality.[5]

The suggestion that Britain retreated from industry and technology may be going too far. Britain was still turning out a number of significant innovations. If you had paid a shilling to enter the Olympia Motor Show of 1910, you would have seen many signs of British entrepreneurial activity. New vehicles were displayed by the twenty-nine-year-old H. F. S. Morgan who ran a motor works and bus company in Malvern Link. His three-wheel cars at the exhibition quickly secured orders that helped launch the Morgan Motor Company. Also on display was a car by Rolls-Royce, a company started four years earlier when Frederick Henry Royce who owned an electrical and mechanical business, made his first vehicle and approached Charles Stewart Rolls who sold cars in London. They pooled their commercial expertise into a new company, and before long their Silver Ghost was claimed to be the 'best car in the world' by *Autocar*, evidence of the quality of British manufactures.

At the same time, Courtaulds, the British thread and textile-maker, bought a little known American company that held the patent for making artificial silk. The idea of artificial silk was dubious, but Courtaulds were open to new ideas and were duly rewarded. Under the name rayon their $100,000 investment earned $100,000,000 in its first decade. Another dynamic industrialist was the British soap magnate, William Lever, who that year bought a company in West Africa to secure supplies of palm oil. His company already had soap factories in Australia, Canada, the United States, Germany and Switzerland.

Across the British economy, there were numerous signs of industrial dynamism, but while the economy was growing in absolute terms, its position relative to other nations was deteriorating. For example, while Britain had no shortage of entrepreneurs in the automobile industry, their largest producer, Wolseley, built 3,000 cars a year in 1913. By contrast, the following year Henry Ford's plant produced 1,000 chassis per day, a rate of production not achieved by European manufacturers for another forty years.[6]

The difference in attitude to technology can be seen in education. By the First World War, Germany was producing 3,000 graduate engineers a year and the United States produced 4,300 graduates from its engineering colleges. British universities were turning out only 350 graduates in all branches of science, technology and maths.[7] The world of technology and commerce was gaining pace and leaving Britain behind. While America and Germany were developing new science-based education, British talent was not given the skills to generate technological advance. An interesting illustration of this outlook occurred at the turn of the century when a donor offered £100,000 to establish a school of naval architecture at Cambridge, but eventually withdrew his offer in disgust after learning students would have to qualify in Greek.[8] Even the Royal Society, the British academy of science, became more distanced from industry and more concerned with pure science.[9]

The effect of this could be seen in the ship-building industry, which suffered from a woeful shortage of skilled scientific staff. While Japanese ship-builders received a flood of graduates in marine sciences, Britain's academic institutions produced few with similar skills. The result was reduced expenditure and commitment to research and development. Ship-builders showed little faith in the ability of scientists to contribute to ship-building. British ships had always been built by practical men with no scientific training and they had always produced the best ships in the world. In their eyes, scientists did not know how to build ships. It 'was felt that only people who had passed through a proper apprenticeship in the yards and shops were likely to know enough of the problems involved in shipbuilding to be able to arrive at satisfactory solutions'.[10]

British producers continued with the old recipes for success. While

Britain emphasized the values of the 'practical man' and technolog-ical levels that had brought them success in the past, other nations developed deeper understanding of maritime technology. An example of the limited scientific approach to ship-building can be seen in the development of the turbine by Parsons. The turbine was origi-nally a British invention, but development proceeded in a pragmatic way with no attempt to understand, for example, the fundamental physics and mathematics of blade design. New development was left to other countries, notably Japan, the Netherlands, Sweden and Germany. As late as 1958, expenditure on research and development in British ship-building was running at 1 per cent of net turnover.[11]

The British economic system had produced its own ways of thinking and this extended down to the workplace. American success was contrasted with a Britain founded on the values of humanity, honour and craftsmanship. Even leading engineering magazines objected to American ideas of scientific management with the comment that 'there are fair ways and unfair ways of diminishing labour costs'.[12] The British were proud of their success and the way they had achieved it. Wayne Harkin of Texas observed this pride when he inspected British shipyards:

> I found among these men a real pride in their accomplish-ments and indeed they have a right to be proud. Skilled craftsmen are in evidence all over the place. What amazed me was the fact that they had been able to turn out the quality of work with the facilities.[13]

At the outset of the First World War, Britain still enjoyed a healthy trade based on those industries that characterized the Industrial Revolution: textiles, coal, iron and steel still contributed to two-thirds of British export earnings.[14] The old economic wave still provided a high level of prosperity but the world was changing, markets were being lost, and nations like the United States and Germany were carving out new roads to development.

The industrial rise of such nations had begun after introducing trade restrictions that protected their markets from British competition. The United States, Germany and France all introduced tariffs in the nineteenth century. Even British colonies in Australia and Canada introduced protective barriers to promote domestic manufactures. Like the Dutch in the eighteenth century, the British now had to contend with declining markets and rising competitors from countries which had once been markets for their goods. However, Germany and the United States were not prepared just to imitate. They created new methods of organization, and developed new products based on technological breakthroughs in steel, chemicals and electricity. On the basis of these new technologies, these nations enjoyed an increasing share of world trade, while Britain's share continued to decline, as shown in the following table.

Percentage Share of World Industrial Output of Top Five Nations 1870–1938[15]

Nations	1870	1913	1926–9	1936–8
Britain	31.8	14.0	9.4	9.2
United States	23.3	35.8	42.2	32.2
Germany	13.2	15.7	11.6	10.7
France	10.3	6.4	6.6	4.5
Japan	–	1.2	2.5	3.5

Although British industry was strongly committed to the technologies, it did not completely ignore new opportunities. New industries were rising in importance in both foreign exchange and national income figures.[16] A number of enterprises appeared, based on new technologies and organizational forms; the Dunlop Rubber Company and Nobel Explosives (later ICI) were among the first to set up an internal management structure as found in the United States. Courtaulds was a company that grew out of new technologies and established huge economies of scale based on volume. These companies obtained a highly competitive position in the global market. However, generally speaking, the transition was too slow to reap the growth that others were achieving. Technology and commerce were now changing at a faster rate than the British had ever experienced. To get a foothold in the new opportunities they needed to respond at a faster rate than they were used to, but overcommitment to old industries and successful formulas of the past left Britain vulnerable to changes in the international economy.

There were several reasons for Britain's slow response. In some industries, American first movers established themselves so quickly in the British market that local firms barely had a chance.[17] In some instances, adoption of new technologies was hindered by environmental factors. Britain lacked a Niagara Falls or the fast flowing rivers of the European Alps that could generate hydro-electric power and allowed Germans and Americans to exploit electro-chemicals. Lack of water-based power also affected production of non-ferrous metals such as aluminium. This situation shows strong similarities to that 150 years earlier when the Dutch, who lacked coal, could not adapt to Britain's new production technologies.

One of the main barriers to change was, ironically, the high level of efficiency that existed in Britain. Britain possessed a labour market of highly skilled workers. This can be seen in the textile industry, where American and Japanese manufacturers faced a shortage of cheap skilled labour, so they adopted the ring spindle which could be operated by low-skilled labour. The new machine provided great savings to the new competitors. The British, who did not face problems of skill shortages, would not have achieved the same benefits from the new technology, so did not adopt it. This is an ironic situation because the British textile industry had surpassed Indian textile production two centuries earlier under very similar circumstances. India had skilled cheap textile workers, so did not mechanize as the British did. It is yet another illustration of the recurring nature of the forces of entrapment.[18]

The nature of the British market also created a barrier to the adoption of many of the new production technologies coming out of America. The United States could exploit new mass production technologies because it had the mass market to sell to. The British market was much smaller and could not generate the same economies of scale.[19]

Together these examples show the importance of the environment. No businessman or entrepreneur could change the business environment to the extent needed. They could perhaps have ignored the cheap efficient labour market and bought new machinery, but, if demand for their products turned down, they were left with expensive machines. Expensive machinery was a fixed cost that had to be paid for, regardless of income. By contrast, labour was a variable cost that did the same job. Labour could be hired and fired at will, depending on the state of the market. If the environment did not support these new technologies, it did not make sense to invest in them.

Adoption of foreign industrial techniques was also inhibited by the industry structure. British industry was characterized by small family firms that could not by themselves muster the capital necessary to invest in larger-scale production, management and distribution systems that were propelling the United States to industrial leadership. With less capital and a desire to keep family control, British firms were hesitant to risk investment in new products and processes.[20] Perhaps we might have expected them to join with each other, raise funds on the share market or seek bank loans, as the Americans did, but the desire for families to retain control meant they were reluctant to increase debt or seek funds through the share market.

With less capital, British firms never made investments that would allow them to benefit from economies of scale or scope. When changes were made, they were smaller, more evolutionary steps within the confines of the old organizational form. If British firms amalgamated, they still continued to use the same old plants that the old families continued to manage. There was no attempt to close them down and build new large plants that provided economies of scale. In the boardrooms of the new amalgamated companies, directors might negotiate price and output but little attempt was made to amalgamate facilities in a way that cut across the old divisions. The economies of scale behind American success remained an elusive goal.

The families that managed these companies became entrenched stakeholders. While managers in the United States were increasingly promoted by ability, British family members became hereditary leaders of the family firm. Nowhere could this be seen more vividly than the textile industry, which between 1880 and 1940, was the biggest industry in terms of output, assets and employment. Writing in 1928, John Maynard Keynes noted:

There is probably no hall in Manchester large enough to hold all the directors of cotton companies, they [run] into thousands. One of the first things should be to dismiss the vast majority of these people, but the persons to whom this proposal would have to be made would be precisely those directors.[21]

Families were not the only stakeholders in the economy. Stakeholders also became entrenched inside the firms. Skilled senior workers created strong unions that created a barrier to the adoption of automated production. This position was not helped by management's traditional reliance on the market for labour. Workers knew the market determined their future and they could be laid off at any time. Knowing their future did not lie with any one company, workers protected themselves by defining their jobs not in terms of any particular firm, but in terms of a right to work with particular types of machines or materials.[22] Unions organized to reinforce such rights and demarcation lines appeared. If an employer hired a non-union member to operate a machine, he would encounter industrial unrest on a major scale.

Demarcation lines were also the result of a high degree of specialization among the highly skilled workers, and in previous chapters we have seen that high levels of specialization can become a barrier when it comes to introducing technical change. These divisions make it difficult to coordinate labour as efficiently as in Japan, where workers identified with the company and cooperated with the various machines and materials they used. Demarcation lines also made technological change a long, difficult and costly exercise. As the economy declined and the position of workers became more uncertain, unions became more defensive, responding with vigour to even minor changes in machinery or materials.

The British were proud of their industrial heritage in which honour, humanity and craftsmanship were key values. Success had provided them with a healthy sense of self-belief and, like the Chinese and

293

others before them, it inbred a sense of moral superiority that created a barrier to adopting foreign ideas. They saw Americans as being obsessed with size, speed, mechanization and money. Gentleman-industrialists, like Peter Menzies of ICI, put down American materialism, saying it would be wrong to 'take up the American patter'. Samuel Courtauld (1876–1942), chairman of the company of the same name, admired the technical achievements of the Americans but even he confessed:

> I view the so-called Americanization of Europe with the utmost dislike. I doubt whether American ideals of living – purely materialistic as they are – will finally lead to a contented working nation anywhere when the excitement of constant expansion has come to an end.[23]

In the same period, Prime Minister Baldwin assured both business audiences and the general public that they need not abandon traditional standards in favour of apparently more successful foreign ones.[24] Once more there is a strong similarity with China where foreign production technologies were rejected in a desire to protect the nation's values.

However, the economy continued to decline. With the continual loss in economic standing, the need to change was apparent to everyone. The Atlee government (1945–51) was the first government to give a high priority to raising industrial productivity and it created a number of policy measures to effect change. The most well known of these was the Anglo-American Council on Productivity (AACP) established in 1948. The AACP was a non-governmental body and comprised members representing both management and labour, and included employers' representatives from the United States. It might seem strange that Americans were willing to help potential competitors, but, after the Second World War, they were keen to raise British productivity as part of their concern for European prosperity that gave rise to the Marshall Plan.[25]

The inclusion of Americans should have made the process of technology transfer relatively easy. The council certainly had open access to information. The programme included visits to American plants, exchange of production techniques, productivity measurement and other economic information. Forty-nine teams were created, dealing with specific industries, and another seventeen dealing with specialist subjects such as management accounting. They revealed many factors leading to high US productivity, including extensive use of mechanical aids, appreciation by workers of the need for higher productivity, and managerial techniques including modern methods of costing, production planning and control and work study methods.

Despite this free flow of information, the AACP failed to have an impact, for a number of reasons. Stakeholder resistance was one of them; the Federation of British Industries, the principal employers' representative, had initially welcomed the AACP as it believed it would clear it of many of the negative comments made about British management. Much to its dismay, the results actually confirmed the failure of management technique in Britain and this raised a defensiveness among employers. Some of their resistance to change was based on solid rationality. Much of the AACP's comments were devoted to spreading the gospel of scientific management which many saw as inappropriate to British industry as Britain did not have the mass American market that offered opportunities in the United States. A second reason for the AACP's minimal impact was many of Britain's smaller firms who were most in need of reform were not involved in the programme. These problems illustrate the difficulties in implementing change even when there is agreement that change is needed.

Unfortunately, the productivity teams and reports of the AACP were simply inadequate to deal with problems that were so deep-seated. Strong action by government might have helped, but for ideological reasons, the government was not prepared to take a more interventionist role in the workings of industry. Timing did not help, as the immediate postwar environment was highly profitable for British businesses who were operating in a seller's market and this must have undermined employers' sense of urgency. The postwar environment in Britain was also one which desired stability in preference to economic growth. This is in sharp contrast to France, which had recently been occupied by Germany and which seized the opportunity to upgrade its productivity with American techniques.

Commitment to reform was also undermined by uncertainty. The new American methods with high investment levels and bureaucratic administration were superior in times of stable growth and expanding mass markets, but there was uncertainty whether those conditions would continue. British producers had experienced protracted recessions in the past and they were concerned that, if the postwar boom was followed by a slump, they would be left with expensive large-scale investments. The old method of production, which relied on the market with low overheads, may have been more adaptable during periods of instability. This uncertainty undermined commitment for change.

The AACP did not achieve the desired results, but this did not stop the realization that change was needed. The loss of industrial leadership became undeniable. In many industries, declining profitability and the collapse of major producers eventually led to agreement on the need for serious reform. However, the same old barriers to change reappeared. Virtually every plan for rationalization in the ship-building, engineering and cotton industry floundered because conservative stakeholders could not commit to serious institutional reform.[26]

As the climate of uncertainty and mistrust became more entrenched, it undermined efforts to coordinate the various reform proposals put forward. This could be seen in the relationship between the Shipbuilding Employers Federation and the unions. Negotiations for reform operated in an environment of fear that the other side was trying to make changes that suited themselves. Consequently, results in most cases amounted to only local modification of the craft system.

During the second half of the 1960s, the matter became urgent and significant changes in work organization finally occurred. Local employers negotiated a series of productivity agreements offering greater job security in exchange for increased flexibility and inter-changeability among the skilled trades. Recognizing the severity of the crisis, ship-builders accepted the need for reform and the existing craft system was modified. But, even when both parties agreed, it was not replaced by the more successful bureaucratic administration of work. Once again, it only resulted in piecemeal adjustments to the existing arrangements, and did not lead to substantial improvements in competitive performance. Planning techniques remained rudimentary while skilled workers and shop-level foremen continued to play a key role in coordination of work. British employers could not implement change successfully because they lacked experience with more bureaucratic methods. Like the mandarins in China, their attempts at change were limited by their own skills base and capabilities, and again as in China, past investment in skills and established stakeholders kept Britain on the old economic pathway.

Britain had missed the economic wave that other nations were riding and became the 'sick man of Europe'. One of the nation's leading economists at the time was Sir Alec Cairncross, the Director of the Economic Development Institute. He summed up the plight of Britain in the period 1945–77, stating the country had become conscious 'of acute and apparently insoluble economic problems:

troubled by the consistent lag behind other countries in economic growth, lacking in pride and self-confidence and given to moods of frustration, despair and at times desperation.'[27]

These patterns of declining competitiveness can be illustrated by the shipping industry. In 1890, over 10,000,000 tons of shipping sailed under the British flag, a phenomenal amount representing approximately 50 per cent of the global total.[28] Yet over the next half century the British share of world shipping declined dramatically. By 1960 its market share had fallen to 16 per cent, soon to decline even further. However, it should be noted that, in this period, total British shipping had actually grown to nearly 21,000,000 tons. Unfortunately, other nations were growing at a dramatically faster rate. Britannia no longer ruled the waves.

British competitive advantage had been based on supportive government policy, superior technology and organization, supporting industries, skills, experience and reputation. The last three of these were lost as other nations caught up and acquired the skills and experience to compete. One by one, the other sources of competitiveness also fell over. There are two principal explanations for the British eclipse. One explanation[29] states that British shipping reflected the state of the British economy in general; the other looks at barriers to flexibility within the industry.

The first explanation of British decline is based on the fact that shipping was an integral part of a nation's economy and accurately reflects both its relative efficiency and its international competitiveness. The declining competitiveness of British ship-building did not help the plight of shipping. In theory, this should not have been a problem as, by now, it was relatively easy to buy ships from other nations. However, British ship-owners continued buying tonnage from British yards, even though better and cheaper ships could be obtained from overseas. The old relationships and ways of doing business were hard to change. For example, the knowledge that tankers could be built more cheaply on the continent during the 1930s did not lead to buying abroad; it was just another reason for not buying tankers at all. The owners would stick to their old behaviour and complain about British prices.

This way of acting ran against economic theory that suggests ship-owners should shift to cheaper, more efficient ship-builders. In reality, commercial relationships are enduring and ship-owners often bought British ships out of goodwill to their fellow countrymen, an expensive gesture for some. In the 1960s, P&O continued to give orders to Fairfield Shipbuilders, even though the Japanese could provide the ships much more cheaply. When Fairfields collapsed in 1965, P&O was burnt as an unsecured creditor. As Sir Donald Anderson, chairman of the company, stated: 'our gesture of goodwill towards British shipbuilding turned out to be very expensive for us, and of no help to the shipbuilding industry'.[30]

These close links between builder and ship-owner were born in the successful years when such relationships increased the flow of information and led to greater efficiency. Commercial ties such as these were investments that took time to develop and work effectively. However, close relationships can become a weakness if one partner becomes inefficient and weighs the other down, or if communication remains based around old patterns and does not change with the times. It was a particularly harmful linkage, given the integrated nature of the industry in Britain.

Shipping was also affected by the declining competitiveness of industries that provided cargoes, in particular coal. British shipping had derived a marked competitive advantage from the fact that it had an outward cargo like coal which, in the days of steam-engines, had a vast global demand.[31] Unfortunately, coal exports declined with the rise of oil, an increase in foreign output of coal, and more efficient use of coal which reduced its use. Between 1913 and 1938 British coal exports halved from 77,000,000 tons to 38,000,000, and further still to 7,000,000 in 1960.[32] The decline of coal was particularly damaging to Britain's tramp shipping, which was well adapted to the trade.

The effect of coal as a supporting industry is well illustrated by the Cardiff-based British Steamship Company. At the turn of the century, Cardiff was the largest coal exporting port in the world[33] and had a large tramp fleet going to the Mediterranean, the Black Sea and Latin America, where the return cargo was grain. The British Steamship Company was one of a number of companies founded by John Cory, a master of coastal traders.[34] In 1854 he started his own business, drawing on close association with Cory Brothers, coal exporters of Cardiff, and William Cory and Sons, who operated colliers. Cory used ships powered by sail until 1874 when he bought his first steamships and rode the wave of prosperity provided by the new coal, iron and steam technologies. By 1884 he had nineteen steamships in his fleet. Like other British companies at the time, this was a family owned and managed firm and his sons were brought in as partners in 1885, the eldest taking over the business on the father's death. By 1891 the company had become the largest importers of iron ore in South Wales. By the outbreak of the First World War, the company had twenty-three tramps and a world-wide market for its unique blend of coal.

The First World War cost the company dearly, with wartime losses halving the size of the fleet. However, worse was to come with the decline in coal exports. Cardiff shipping suffered greatly and in 1923 more than half of the city's tramp-owners crashed. Sound financial management enabled the Corys to survive, but other aspects of the company's business were declining, in particular imports of iron ore, which were stopped in 1927. By the Second World War, the company had just three tramps, only to lose all of them in the hostilities.

With experience being their only remaining asset, they survived by chartering ships and making the occasional purchase, including the company's only motor-ship in 1959. However, ships were getting bigger and more expensive and the family firm could not afford to build an expensive bulk carrier. In 1989 they were no longer a shipping company but operated as shipping agents under the name Raymond Cory. It was a well-managed company, rising and falling on an industrial wave of coal and iron technologies.

The rise and fall of the Cory family's British Steamship Company emphasizes the importance of environmental factors on a company's success, in particular supporting industries and consumer demand. However, there were also internal barriers to growth.[35] The critical period for British shipping was between 1920 and about 1958 when tremendous changes occurred in trading patterns, competition, ships, cargoes and passengers. The British industry was slow in adapting itself to these changes. It was an industry geared to maintaining its position of supremacy, not to meeting changes. When it woke up, the world had moved on.

One of the internal barriers was that recurring human trait, arrogance. Like the Dutch, Spanish and Chinese before them, the British had learnt from experience that they were the world's most competitive shippers. Having been in this position for so long, the generally accepted fact was that the British industry was best by definition.[36] By the time that international competition became serious, the idea was so embedded that the crumbling of that paramountcy occurred almost unnoticed.[37]

One of the key changes to occur at this time was the arrival of the diesel-powered motor engine, which challenged the supremacy of the steamship. The British were not averse to innovating with this technology and, in fact, played a significant role in the early development and application of marine diesel propulsion. The British built the world's first ocean-going motor vessel, a tanker ordered by the Royal Dutch/Shell Group.[38] However, British ship-owners were slow in diffusing the technology and clung to the steamship. In the early days, there was good reason for clinging to the steamship. The tramp steamer had been improved to the point where it was efficient, reliable and economical. In contrast, early diesel engines had a tendency to break down under less than ideal conditions. Even as technological bugs were removed, there still remained uncertainty over the availability of oil. For every person who asserted that the future would provide abundant supplies of low-priced oil, there were several to announce either the world's supplies of oil would shortly give out, or that the companies controlling its distribution would never allow the using public the advantage of low prices.

During the First World War, many navies around the world, including the British, turned to oil, helping to remove these uncertainties. However, this did not lead to mass conversion. One reason was timing. In the First World War, a large proportion of the British fleet was destroyed and British owners could have taken the opportunity to buy replacements with the new technology but, due to the shortage of ships, freight rates were very high and owners were keen to take the ships most readily available. That meant locally produced steamers, ships built during the war, and foreign acquisitions.[39] By the 1920s, when questions of oil availability and engine reliability had been solved, these businessmen found they had high levels of investment sunk in the old technology. Then, to make matters worse, the economy did a complete reversal and the industry experienced a depression. Few people were prepared to invest in new ships under such conditions. Consequently, in 1925 motor ships accounted for only 3.9 per cent of the British merchant fleet, compared with 21.4 per cent for Sweden, 18.1 per cent for Denmark and 12.9 per cent for Norway.[40]

Domestic resources supplies also contributed to British persistence with the coal-powered steam-engine. The principal economic advantages of oil were that it required less space and had lower fuel consumption.[41] Savings of 30–50 per cent in fuel made the new technology attractive, particularly for countries like Norway which had to import its fuel. Britain had its own high quality coal, but no oil, therefore the economic advantages were not so great. The British did not have to pay the transport costs of importing fuel and had a greater sense of certainty of on-going coal supplies.

As late as the 1930s the advantages of the motor ship were still not clear cut. For example, the Liverpool firm of T. & J. Harrison (the Charente Steam Ship Company) looked very carefully from 1925 onwards into the potential of motor ships to enhance their profitability.[42] Their research was highly professional and governed by the principle that any innovation must improve profit over the whole range of trades in which the company was involved. They conducted tests on a number of means of propulsion and applied DCF investment analysis, yet continued to order coal-fired steam-engines in the 1930s. They realized it was also necessary to consider, among other things, routes travelled. Motor ships were not always the best buy for all routes. In 1935 motor ships still only accounted for 16.6 per cent of the British fleet compared with 48.6 per cent in Sweden, 41.9 per cent in Denmark and 36.6 per cent in Norway.[43] Scandinavians were also using faster ships than the British, who seemed to hold a genuine belief that slower ships would provide a superior economic performance.[44]

In contrast to the hesitation of British businessmen, the Japanese government actively promoted the building of new 'crack ships' in yet another illustration of the key role that governments can play in directing technological advance. However, the building of new ships was not always beneficial to private enterprise and the government was sometimes more motivated by prestige than efficiency. The question whether to turn to diesel motor ships was widely discussed and, although it brought higher earnings and lower running costs, the higher initial costs did not always guarantee the expected profit.[45]

The first attempt by the Japanese to use diesel motors was in 1923 when OSK trialled one in a small vessel operating on an inland sea route.[46] This success led to their deployment on emigrant ships travelling to South America. In the following two years, Mitsui and NYK also began using diesel on some of their routes. The successful introduction of diesel by these companies was followed by the competitive introduction of large, modern, high-speed ships. OSK ships achieved record speeds to New York through the Panama Canal. The New York route was characterized by high-value cargoes and speed was a competitive weapon. Consequently, it provided a profitable service even in the midst of the depression.[47] However, not all routes benefited from increased speed.

Like the Japanese, the British government also introduced a number of initiatives to help their industry, including a scrap and build plan whereby ship-owners were provided with loans if they scrapped old tonnage and replaced it with modern ships. However, unlike in Japan where a similar scheme led to some fleet modification, English ship-owners were slow to respond and the scheme was abolished.[48] The British government also provided bounties to assist ship-owners and forced the industry to set up a Tramp Shipping Administration Committee to promote cooperation among shipbuilders. The committee had some success in limiting some of the negative effects of competition during the depression. However, the British government had less influence over its much larger industry than its Japanese counterpart, and forces of decline continued to set in.

Many of the industry's shortfalls can be linked to the structure of the industry. Once more, the shape of the industry was a consequence of its historical legacy that gave birth to two dominating forms, liners and tramps. Liners were ships that sailed to a regular schedule, between specific ports at specific times. At times in its history, the liner market experienced periods when competition was tight. As early as 1850, some liner companies felt the need to cooperate on minimum freight rates.[49] The movement to inter-company agreements gained pace in the 1870s after the opening of the Suez Canal. The canal dramatically reduced the length of voyages to the East, so reduced the number of ships needed to transport goods. There were now too many ships on the world market and many firms adopted defensive manoeuvres that involved cooperating with other lines. Competing companies frequently amalgamated, giving birth to lines such as Union-Castle, Shaw Savill and Albion, and Elders and Fyffe, their joint names evidence to this process of amalgamation.

A second defensive option was to limit the competition between companies by forming conferences. A shipping conference was a cartel in which shipping lines operating on similar routes agreed to regulate competition between themselves and restrict new entrants from competing on the route. Many customers of these companies were naturally discontented with this situation. The cartel nature of these agreements imposed restraints on trade that reduced competition, the very thing that the Sherman Act was introduced to combat in the United States. However, a Royal Commission on Shipping Rings conducted in 1906–9 (and other similar inquiries) found that conferences were necessary to assure stability of rates, regularity of service and improved facilities.[50]

Economists generally expect a decline in competition like this to lead to slower innovation and this appears to have occurred. The conference agreements provided stability but gave little incentive to break from conventional business behaviour. British businessmen in the liner market explicitly avoided aggressive competition and had an overwhelming tendency not to take any action which might invite reprisals. By contrast, foreign operators with little market share were not restricted by these fears, and enthusiastically seized opportunities to win trade from increasingly inefficient liners. While the British sought stability, foreigners innovated with cheaper and better value services for customers.

Flexibility was also hampered by past growth which had created large companies. With every increase in size, the ship-owners at the top of these companies became more distanced from their ships and the smell of salt. As they became isolated from the ship-master and their associated commercial intelligence, liner companies were run more and more by people with skills in accounting and negotiating. Working from offices, they increasingly judged operations through balance sheets rather than the detailed competitive problems on any particular route. A reflection of this change was the increased social position they now held; ship-owners became socially important figures, the purchasers of land and the recipients of titles. Through this process of gentrification, the business elite became distant from industry's core activities and problems.

Another aspect of the organizational management structure that hindered adaptability was the family-owned structure. As in other British industries, families had emerged as entrenched stakeholders. Family members still dominated the board of directors and would not be displaced by deserving talent. This made the industry less attractive to people who had ability and ambition, so the industry suffered from a shortage of good management.[51]

The process of amalgamation and conference-building that occurred in the liner market did not hit the tramp industry. Tramp ships did not run to a set schedule as liners did. They sailed anywhere in the world where there was a demand for their services at any time. This was the flexible market-driven side of the industry. Tramp-owners were individualistic businessmen who held a personal pride in the achievements of the ships that bore their family name. This gave them a personal incentive that the managers of large liner companies lacked.

The tramp market was a highly competitive arena of small competing firms. Orthodox economic theory would suggest that, given the high level of competition, British tramp-owners might have been expected to show more flexibility than the liner companies. However, competition did not lead to the rigour one might expect. In fact, British tramp shipping was routed, declining from 60 per cent of the fleet at the turn of the century to less than 20 per cent by 1960.

There are a number of reasons for this demise. But standing out is the fact that dogged adherence to old behaviours and beliefs proved a far stronger force on the industry than competition. In a high-wage nation, British tramp-owners needed to keep at least one step ahead of low-wage competitors in the adoption of larger and faster vessels, yet by 1914 advance had practically stopped. The industry believed the standard tramp ship coming out of British shipyards was the ideal ship required to compete in the market. The reliable tramp ship was to the English what the fluyt had been to the Dutch, an excellent trader with which they learnt to maximize economies. Ship-owners knew these ships well and built their strategies around them. The tramp-owners 'were cheese-paring by nature, meeting competitive pressures by continuous economies within traditional ship types, but rarely taking a longer view and endeavouring to reduce costs (or increase receipts) by spending money on ships designed for existing conditions'.[52]

While the British clung tenaciously to their all-purpose vehicles, other nations created more specialized vessels to meet the needs of particular trades. For example, Scandinavians made increasing use of refrigerated holds for the Mediterranean fruit trade and showed a flexibility and entrepreneurial attitude that stood in sharp contrast to the British who clung to traditional attitudes.[53] For the British, it did not seem rational to build specialized ships when flexible all-purpose vehicles had proven so successful in the past.

The fastest growing category of specialized vessels was oil tankers, a reflection of the booming demand for oil. Although world tanker tonnage soared from 11,000,000 tons in 1939 to 38,000,000 in 1960,[54] the British were slow to seize the opportunities this vessel offered. Tramp-owners were entrapped by the old beliefs of what constituted a good ship and to the British ship-owner, tankers weren't real ships, but floating pieces of pipeline.[55] Consequently, when the British oil company Anglo-Saxon sold off its tanker fleet to raise capital for exploration, few of its fellow companies showed interest.[56] This provided an opportunity for the Norwegians, who bought the vast majority of the ships and gained a strong foothold in a growing part of the industry.

One financial consideration which contributed to conservative decision-making was comparative profit. In the early days, the tanker market offered lower profit margins than the British were used to, so they did not consider switching. This left a window of opportunity open for a new competitor to gain an entrance into the industry. This conservative outlook also meant the British were slow to recognize the benefits of increased size. Size offered a number of economic advantages.[57] In 1968 a 5,000 ton ship cost £85 per ton to build compared with £35 for a 20,000-tonner. A large ship might require an engine ten times more powerful, but it could carry forty times the weight of cargo. Average running costs also declined with size. For example, above 65,000 tons crew costs remained static.

One possible explanation for this failure to enlarge is the small size of British ports, which limited their ability to handle large tankers and bulk carriers. However, management seemed overly conscious of the limitations of the British oil terminals in handling the biggest tankers. Given that a tanker on international routes might never visit Britain, it was a misguided perception, but businessmen make decisions on the basis of their perceptions and the local environment often distorts perceptions of global change.

Another reason why family tramp firms failed to up-size was they lacked the capital to switch to large ships such as tankers.[58] The possibility of raising money through debt or issuing shares existed but, like other British family-owned companies of the time, they avoided outside capital in order to retain control of the company within the family. The shunning of outside finance was also a reflection of old business practices. These companies had grown from small beginnings by reinvesting profit. External finance was never a key factor in their mental outlook. In fact, during the nineteenth century some companies did take the opportunity to borrow, but heavy debt left them vulnerable during the depression of 1904–11. Many lines failed and the industry took the lessons to heart. The unwritten rule became financial conservatism.[59] Consequently, the small owner of two or three tramps would not risk raising a loan to invest in large ships. He clung to what he knew he could do best and the lessons that history had taught him. These practices contrasted strongly with the innovative financial techniques introduced by foreign entrepreneurs like Daniel Ludwig of the United States and Aristotle Onassis and Stavros Niarchos of Greece. These entrepreneurs financed rapid expansion through very large loans. They obtained these loans after having signed long-term charter contracts with the oil companies. The contracts provided the cash flow to meet loan repayments.[60]

We must also consider the number of distractions, uncertainties and red herrings that abounded throughout this period of change. A number of factors existed that could have blurred British businessmen from seeing the need to upgrade. During and immediately after the First World War, British ship-owners could earn high profits without a technical change. This was followed by the depression that made new investment an unattractive option, then a postwar shortage of shipping and very high profit rates which once again seemed to endorse the correctness of traditional strategies.[61]

Change and uncertainty made efficient decision-making difficult. For example, in the inflationary period following the Second World War, there was an expectation that after the initial burst of activity, a slump would occur, as happened after the First World War. The effect of this uncertainty on decision-making is illustrated by Sir John Denholm of J. & J. Denholm who explains:

> When the second war was over, my brother and I decided we had either to get out, or go right for it. We'd have done nicely if we sold out then, but we made the decision, and we went ahead while other firms waited for the slump that never came . . . It seemed unfair to inflict the whole gamble on our share holders . . . by 1951 we had seven ships, all of them built or bought at prices we could never have hoped for if we had waited to see what would happen.[62]

J. & J. Denholm expanded but many other tramp-owners held off, waiting for the expected slump in ship-building prices, only to witness sixteen years of rising prices.

Britain's relative decline compared with other nations occurred during a time when world trade was expanding. This provided growth and stability in the cargoes that Britain carried but it hid the fact that faster paths to growth were being developed by other nations who were increasing their market share. The British had entered the twentieth century on the back of coal, iron and steam technologies, family firms developed skills, capabilities and ways of doing business. Success showed that British techniques were the best, and they were. But when superior techniques arrived, British industry was entrapped by belief systems and practices which slowed down the pace of change. Britain did not stagnate, as illustrated by the innovations that regularly appeared. The difference was that other nations were developing and diffusing innovations faster.

Although Britain was no longer the workshop of the world, in its period of eminence it had made one change that would later come back to help it. It had carried the English language to the four corners of the world. This advantage would later be exploited with the aid of information technologies initially developed by Americans. Britain's service sector reasserted itself and, at the beginning of the twenty-first century, the British economy was the fifth largest in the world.

13

PACIFIC TSUNAMI

I fear all we have done is to awaken a sleeping giant and fill him with a terrible resolve.

Tora, Tora, Tora

Although there is no evidence Japanese Admiral Yamamoto, standing on the deck of an aircraft carrier at Pearl Harbour, actually delivered that line from the film *Tora, Tora, Tora*, it seems to have captured his thoughts about war with the United States, which possessed a resource base that, once mobilized, could grind the Japanese to dust.

The Second World War had a profound effect on the US economy. It forced the nation to mobilize its resources in a spectacular manner. Factories sprung up all over the country producing steel, tanks, planes and ships, all utilizing the latest mass production techniques. Output sky-rocketed and the unemployment of the depression came to an end. In the five-year period 1940–45, the index of manufacturing leapt from 66 to 110, while GNP more than doubled.

The war also stimulated advances in science and technology. For example, shortages of rubber led to the development of synthetic rubber. New treatments emerged in medicine; jet planes were built that could fly at three times the speed of prewar planes and, in electronics, short-wave radio and radar (a British invention) were but two of many advances. This period provided Americans with a new respect for the power of science in a situation not dissimilar to that of Spain in the sixteenth century. Spain grew on the basis of natural resources, but the wealth it created allowed it to develop technology which further buttressed its competitive strength.

This new respect for science could be seen in the rapid growth in public and private research and development (R&D) spending. By 1969 American expenditure on R&D was more than double that of Britain, Germany, France and Japan combined.[1] Half of that came from the government through organisations such as the National Science Foundation, the National Institute of Health, NASA and, most important, the Department of Defense. From this nest, a number of new technologies were born. The computer was born from military expenditure and the research interests of MIT, IBM and AT&T. The semi-conductor was developed privately by Bell Telephone Laboratories in anticipation of the government market. NASA and the army were major early purchasers and provided significant funding for its development.

Although the percentage of engineers and scientists emerging from the universities was small compared with graduates in other disciplines, the sheer number of students ensured a steady flow of skilled labour. They found jobs in the cities of the south and south-west like Houston, San Diego and Los Angeles where the new industries were based. As a consequence of this wave of innovation, the United States now had two pillars buttressing its economic supremacy: mass production industries and high-tech industries. In the quarter century following the Second World War, the United States had the world's most productive economy, with a worker output 30-50 per cent higher than its nearest competitors.[2] The American economic system was generating output at a level no nation had achieved before.

More than ever, the United States was a corporate world. The nation's corporate assets of $598 billion in 1950 had more than doubled to $1,207 billion by the end of the decade. For more and more Americans the road to prosperity was occurring inside a corporation, not through entrepreneurship, and this affected the nature of American business leadership. The famed economist J. Kenneth Galbraith[3] noted that the entrepreneur of old, with imagination and courage in risking money, was a dying breed. The US economic system had matured and now required people with organizational skills. Leadership now fell to the 'technocrat', a highly educated manager who administered what was proven to be an efficient economic system. The technocrat was an American mandarin.

The corporate society provided unprecedented prosperity. The US consumer enjoyed bowling, 3-D movies, TV quiz shows, automobiles and home appliances, and could choose from a range of cars, ice creams and toothpastes. The number of families with televisions soared from 5,000,000 in 1950 to 45,000,000 in 1960. In the same period, automobile registration shot up from 40.3 million to 61.5 million.[4] With corporatization, the old values of individualism were dying but found new outlets in entertainment. The young found much appeal in Marlon Brando on his motor cycle, the rebellious rhythms of Elvis Presley, or the rebel without a cause, James Dean. Many rode this wave of prosperity, although its benefits were not evenly spread:

> The nation's affluence did not happen to go just to those who deserved it. Many people became rich as a result of luck rather than judgment, or selfish calculation rather than moral virtue. Others remained poor because they happened to live in the wrong part of the country.[5]

The spread of prosperity might not have been even, but the United States provided a level of affluence unmatched in history. No other nation could have dreamt of putting a man on the moon, but, for the Americans, it was only a matter of time and the correct application of their extensive resources.[6]

★　★　★

The forces that shaped American prosperity also affected the US shipping industry. During the Second World War, a War Shipping Administration (WSA) was established to ensure wartime shipping requirements were met. The war placed huge demands on shipping across the Atlantic and Pacific oceans and meant that the output from American shipyards needed to be raised and as a result the number of ships built reached staggering levels. Through the use of mass production techniques and contracts that rewarded perform-ance, 12.5 million tons of shipping was launched from American yards in 1943 alone.[7]

The WSA also undertook a huge training programme to provide the officers and men for the vessels. It included the establishment of the US Merchant Marine Academy, seven training ships and schools around the country. During the war these institutions trained 270,000 seamen, 10,000 officers, 7,500 radio officers and 5,300 pursers. The US mercantile fleet experienced a fourfold increase in size, while the fleets of America's competitors had been decimated. At the war's end, 130 shipping companies and 4,500 vessels gave the United States a staggering 60 per cent of the world's tonnage.

To complement this situation, the United States now provided the world's most advanced maritime technology. American scientists and engineers led with developments in ship design and improved components parts. The American Bureau of Shipping, a major insur-ance classifier, had its own research laboratories advancing technology in design, construction and machinery. The Maritime Research Advisory Committee (MRAC) was created by the National Academy of Sciences and National Research Council. In 1958 the Matson Navigation Company became the first to use computers in ship design. It then worked through MRAC to convince the maritime administration to conduct a broad study in operation research for better merchant ships.

It was an age of competitive and scientific advance. Americans were the first to apply nuclear power to merchant shipping in 1959, when the first nuclear-powered cargo ship, the *Savannah*, was launched. However, concerns regarding radiation and other environmental matters stopped this line of research. Americans also introduced innovations in cargo handling technology, including roll-on roll-off vessels and LASH (lighter aboard ship) technology in which a barge is used to carry cargo to the ship, giving the ship access to areas it might not otherwise be able to service. They also introduced the technology that would revolutionize shipping – containerization.

Containerization was an innovation born from the government, or, more particularly, the military. During the Second World War, the War Shipping Administration was overwhelmed by its vast cargo handling requirements.[8] To try to speed up cargo deliveries, it began to fill ships with similar size crates. This dramatically reduced cargo handling times and costs. The WSA distributed its results in many publications, but private enterprise was slow to realize the potential of the innovation. It was not until twelve years after the war when Sea-Land Service first used container ships between the Gulf Coast and New York. However, pioneering new technologies is never easy and the expense eventually undermined Sea-Land's financial position. Grace Line was the first company to adopt containers on international routes but ran into trouble when longshoremen in Venezuela refused to unload the vessels out of fear they would lose their jobs.[9] Spread of the new technology was also frustrated by government regulations, steamship conferences, technological problems and the sheer expense.[10] These experiences illustrate the difficulty of pioneering change, even after the government had overcome many of the early development costs.

The economic advantage of containers comes from their ability to reduce costs. Prior to containers, loading and unloading was very time-consuming. Half of a ship's time was spent in port, rather than on the high seas, and port labour costs accounted for 80 per cent of total voyage costs. With containers, the time in port was reduced by four-fifths, with a huge reduction in costs.[11] In 1966 the first containers appeared on the North Atlantic, their appearance illustrating that shipping, like other US industries, was a wealthy, innovative arena. Many US executives believed that because US companies had taken such a lead in container technology that subsidies were no longer needed to help them compete.

The ease of handling containers made it possible to create a fully integrated transportation system, as pioneered by Seatrain in 1971. As its name suggests, Seatrain combined container travel by train across the states, connecting with ships at either coast. The speed improvements were such that a New York–Tokyo route now took only twenty days, compared with the thirty days offered by the all sea route through the Panama Canal. This development was facilitated by the development of computers which helped track container movements.

While Britain was experiencing its relative decline and the United States stood like a colossus, Japan continued to imitate the leading economic technologies. The Japanese business environment was very different from that in Britain and the United States, so imported technologies had to be modified to accommodate local needs and behavioural patterns. In the process, Japan evolved a unique economic system that reduced costs and added value to these industries.

An important example of modification to suit the local environment can be seen in labour management. In the early days of Japan's industrialization, Japan faced a shortage of skilled labour. As a consequence, businesses raided each other for staff, creating a situation where all producers found it difficult to retain staff. To overcome this situation, employers decided to sign non-raiding agreements. However, pressure for staff inevitably led to new bouts of raiding. Some argued that the market would solve labour problems, as it had in the West, but this stood in sharp conflict with traditional values. Most employers believed that employer–labour relationships should be guided by traditional father–son principles. For these people, monetary principles and legally defined rights had no role, so the Japanese system of permanent employment emerged with pay based on seniority. This fitted comfortably with the workers arriving at the factories from the rural areas, as it reflected the permanence, hierarchy and sense of community that they were used to in their villages.

The need for skilled staff gave birth to another unique Japanese characteristic in the labour system. With few appropriate educational institutions, companies had to take responsibility for training staff. The development of in-house training became a characteristic of Japanese firms that has continued to this day.

The Japanese showed some ingenuity in overcoming weaknesses in their environment, and nowhere is this more apparent than in cotton, another industry that had grown with government support. The industry had trouble obtaining imported textile machinery due to the expense and the shortage of foreign exchange. Domestic manufacture of such machines could have relieved the pressure for imports but was difficult due to the shortage of iron. This problem was solved by a carpenter named Sakichi Toyoda (1867–1930). His solution to the problem was a wooden loom. Scraping together loans from various sources, he established the Toyoda Automatic Loom Works. He was so successful that he eventually sold his patent to Platt Brothers, the top loom manufacturer in the world at the time. The Toyoda family used the money from this sale as seed capital for their next idea, automobile production.

In the 1930s the Japanese army became interested in developing domestic motor vehicle production to ensure a supply for military transportation. At the same time, the Ministry of Commerce was concerned about the dominant position that GM and Ford held in the Japanese car market, and the effect it was having on the balance of payments. Both government departments believed the country needed a domestic producer of cars and asked the major trading companies, Mitsui, Mitsubishi and Sumitomo, to diversify into automobile production. However, all three believed it would be too difficult to compete with the American giants. Fortunately, two enterprising men were prepared to give it a go. Both were graduates of the technical engineering department of the University of Tokyo, and had companies that they wanted to become as big as the three *zaibatsu* (mega-corporations). They were also driven by a nationalistic desire to see Japan develop a strong industrial base. The situation is recalled by Eiji Toyoda:

> The government had repeatedly exhorted Japanese concerns to move into vehicle production, but almost no one was willing to raise his hand and say: 'We'll do it.'
>
> Then, just as the government was starting to think that it had no choice but to rely on GM and Ford, two men rose to the challenge: our Kiichiro and Nissan's Yoshsuke Ayukawa. They were called in by the government and told: 'Now that Toyota and Nissan are starting to produce motor vehicles, tell us what support measures you'd like us to take.' The responses made by Kiichiro and Ayukawa were essentially the same: 'Government support measures up until now have been totally worthless. My company needs no assistance.' Both agreed that it was better to go it alone without aid from the government.[12]

Despite this brave entrepreneurial spirit, Toyota and Nissan were fighting giants and didn't stand a chance. 'Toyota and Nissan might go in and work for all they were worth, but they'd never catch up with GM and Ford.'[13] Consequently, the government introduced 'The law concerning the manufacture of motor vehicles'. This legislation restricted the volume of output of foreign companies to 3,000 cars a year. GM and Ford were already operating near this level, so any future growth in the market would go to Japanese firms. Eiji Toyoda remembered: 'Looking back on it now, this was a very low blow by the government against foreign auto-makers.' However, even this wasn't enough to help Toyoda in those days as they were at the beginning of a very steep learning curve:

> For a short while, from the end of 1936 through early 1937, we had been unable to sell the vehicles we made. One reason, of course, was the depressed economy, but more importantly, our product just couldn't pass muster . . . unless we were able to fix whatever was wrong with our cars and trucks, we would never be able to sell them. But more was required than just turning a bolt here and there. And once we'd fixed whatever was wrong, we still had to go out there and regain the customer's confidence. If we failed to act promptly and effectively, the company would go under. It was as simple as that.
>
> Or so we thought. The situation changed abruptly when the war in China broke out and the army bought up all our trucks, cleaning out our entire stock.[14]

When Japan invaded China, the demand for military vehicles saved the company. In March 1937 the board at the Toyoda Automobile Loom Works decided to separate car manufacturing from the rest of the company. The company had earlier decided to replace the 'd' in Toyoda with a 't', and thus the Toyota Motor Company was born. The company's subsequent growth illustrated classic economies of scale. It aimed to make a car that could sell for 2,400 yen so it could compete with the American companies. In October 1936 Toyota produced 150 cars for 2,948 yen. The next month 200 vehicles were produced for 2,761 yen. Toyota was very aware that the more cars it produced, the cheaper it could make them, yet the existing factory only had the capacity to build 500 vehicles a month. Recognizing the importance of economies of scale, the company decided to build a new plant that could produce 1,500 vehicles a month so, working at full capacity, production costs would fall to 1,850 yen. Within the new factory, a number of key innovations were introduced by Kiichiro Toyoda. The first was a revolutionary new layout:

> Kiichiro's idea was to switch over entirely to a flow-type production system. He reasoned that this would eliminate large stocks of materials and parts, doing away with the need for warehouses. Cutting back running stock also reduced capital outflow. If, once this production system got under way, we were able to sell our finished product before payments were due on our materials and parts, we would no longer have any need for operating capital.
>
> What Kiichiro had in mind was to produce the needed quantity of the required parts each day. To make this a reality, every single step of the operation, like it or not, had to be converted over to his flow production system. Kiichiro referred to this as the 'just in time' concept.[15]

'Just in time' was an innovation that dramatically reduced costs associated with storing supplies. The other key innovation that would create an ongoing legacy was born from the poor quality of the cars:

> Each shop had three managers, of which one was responsible

for inspection. Kiichiro's intention here was to catch any defective product and correct whatever processes were at fault. The task of the inspection manager was not simply to differentiate between a good and a bad product, but to find a way to fix whatever had to be fixed – be it machinery, equipment or tools – to prevent defective products from arising.

After the war, we studied quality control and actively incorporated this concept into our operations. The basic idea behind QC of 'creating product quality within the process' is essentially identical to Kiichiro's thinking. This was an idea that would have occurred to anyone, and Kiichiro was certainly no genius for stumbling upon it. What set him apart was his initiative in putting the idea into practice.[16]

This focus on quality was not restricted to Toyota. Many Japanese were aware of their technical inferiority as their goods were perceived as cheap and shoddy. The pursuit of quality became one of the overriding themes in postwar Japan. As early as 1950, they invited W. Edwards Deming, a statistician from the US Census Bureau, to give lectures on methods for statistically monitoring the quality of companies' products. Japanese companies embarked on a crusade for quality, each trying to achieve the lowest defect rate. (A national award for improving quality of products since 1951 is called the Deming Prize.) In July 1950 Eiji Toyoda went to the United States where he had the opportunity to inspect the Ford plants. Although he learned a lot on the trip, it struck him that 'Detroit isn't doing anything that Toyota doesn't already know.' It brought the realization that catch-up was feasible. There are clear comparisons with the situation in the sixteenth century when the Dutchman Jan van Linschoten revealed the truth about Portuguese shipping methods and cracked the myth of supremacy. However, no matter how modern Japanese techniques were, they still

322

had a long way to go before they could match the economies of scale achieved by the Americans. Detroit's plants were producing huge volumes of output that Japan could in no way match. However, as the Japanese economy grew and the market for cars expanded, they too began to gain economies of scale in their production.

While visiting one of the car plants in the United States, Eiji was told 'nobody at Ford knows everything that goes on around here'. The statement illustrated just how specialized American production methods had become. American plants were full of specialized individuals who focused on their own jobs. No worker had a broad knowledge of the whole process. On hearing this, Eiji thought to himself, 'Maybe you don't have anybody like that at Ford, but we do at Toyota.' Of course, Toyota was smaller, so it was less difficult to have knowledge of the whole operations, but this difference also reflected what was becoming a distinctively Japanese approach to production. Instead of specialized workers, Japanese workers were expected to master a number of tasks. This gave employees greater understanding of their job and the way it affected other activities in the firm.[17] The result was flexibility and no demarcation problems. It also led to increased sharing of information and greater coordination, so problems could be addressed by individuals who cooperated and had a greater level of understanding of what was going on around them. For example, an engineering control room might be located alongside the engineering workshop and the staff rotated between the two to facilitate knowledge-sharing and discourage the development of isolated shop centres. As a result, workers were fully aware how their actions affected the whole operation and gained a higher sense of common objectives beyond their job. This flexibility was a clear plus for a company as the global environment entered a phase of increased instability.

Another consequence of the smaller size of Japanese plants was the close relationship between technology and management. Management preferred to work at a factory rather than in an office, which meant they were closer to problems as they occurred and could deal with them more effectively. It also helped to blur lines between worker and management, and led to a degree of cooperation that stood in sharp contrast to the West where blue- and white-collar divisions were the norm. White-collar managers in the United States, with their business degrees, operated in offices distant from the factory floor. They operated as dispassionate experts primarily concerned with finance and control, but lacked the hands-on expertise that Japanese managers possessed.[18] US managers exerted control necessary to ensure mass production methods were adhered to, but it came at the expense of flexibility.

Another key difference between the Japanese and American economic systems was the role of the government. Given that the Second World War had destroyed any remnant of market activity, the Japanese government resumed the strong planning and coordinating role it had taken in the post-Meiji period. In 1946 the Economic Stabilization Board was established to create plans for reconstructing the economy destroyed by the war, as it was obvious the market could not be relied upon under these circumstance. Later renamed the Economic Planning Agency, it set targets for investment, savings, employment, production and foreign trade, and created detailed plans for investment in the nation's infrastructure.

The Japanese government could strongly influence industry through its control of capital. Few enterprises at the end of the war had the capital to finance expansion, so they became dependent on banks. It led to an unusual situation where enterprises would borrow from a bank well beyond their capacity to repay, resulting in debt-equity ratios that Westerners would consider with some alarm.[19] Because of the high rate of lending (ratio of lending to deposits), the banks themselves became very dependent on the central bank (the Bank of Japan). This set of relationships gave the Bank of Japan powerful control over the nation's credit, and the government used it as a tool for direct investment. Through the bank, the government could choose what industries and enterprises received funding.[20] It created a list of industries that would get preferred access to credit, and supported this with generous depreciation allowances that stimulated investment in certain industries. When combined with the government's own investments, these policy tools enabled the government to profoundly influence the direction of investment in the economy.

The other key arm in Japanese economic policy was the Ministry of International Trade and Industry (MITI). The ministry's policies defied the conventional economic thought of the day that said a country should stick to what it does best, i.e. to its comparative advantage. At that time, Japan had developed a comparative advantage in low-tech industries like textile production, but MITI realized if the nation concentrated on its traditional exports it would confine the whole economy to slow growth. Instead of following the prevailing rationality and exploiting its strengths, MITI chose to move upstream into modern industries.[21] In this way Japanese industry embarked on a second period of catch-up with the West.

To assist the process of catch-up, MITI shielded its fledgling industries from foreign competition with a range of protective measures, including import control, a quota system, tariffs on commodity trade and foreign capital inflow regulations. They also provided subsidies, cheap loans and special depreciation policies.[22] The government was not the only force propelling catch-up. Companies and individuals also saw its merits. From 'the blue-collar worker to the company president everybody, in one way or another, was swept along with the zeal for innovation and education. American patents were bought, American management was studied; and American organizational forms were introduced.'[23]

MITI was very aware that a key factor in American success was the size of its companies and the economies of scale they generated. MITI also believed that large-scale enterprises could more adequately promote technical change. To create competitive strength, it encouraged mergers between leading firms, especially in capital-intensive industries where economies of scale had distinct advantage. However, as opposed to concentrating resources on a national champion, MITI promoted oligopolistic rivalry, where a small number of firms competed with each other. MITI guided investment in such a manner that excessive competition was avoided. Firms were not allowed to make an investment so large that it would destabilize the market.[24] The result was managed competition. The policy preserved competitiveness, as companies sought to increase their market share while reducing the risk of excessive investment. When combined with trade protection, which provided a captive home market, the policies provided Japanese companies with increased certainty and high profits. This enabled them to undertake higher rates of investment and improve the quality of their products. This would eventually lead them to capturing markets abroad.

MITI did not apply a blanket policy to all industries. It assisted chosen industries that it believed would generate a high growth path, and in the early 1950s it favoured rapid development of electric power, ship-building, coal and steel industries. Over the following years, other industries promoted included petro-chemical, heavy machinery, and auto industries. In 1957 it added the electronics and synthetic rubber industries and, in 1958, the airplane industry. Under MITI's guidance the nation's industrial structure was changed from light, labour-intensive industries to steel ships and automobiles, of which Japan became the world's leading producer.[25]

To accurately predict which industries to invest in involves a large degree of forecasting of social and technological change. In Japan, this occurred at a level not seen before in any other society.[26] MITI conducted open dialogue with industry, university scientists and technologists, becoming well informed of developments. The resulting visions of the future were not presented as accurate predictions, nor were they the basis of inflexible plans. They provided a broad direction of advance for the economy and technology, which gave companies a degree of confidence when making long-term investments in research, development, software, equipment and training.

The Japanese government did not dictate to businesses but operated through consensus. The goal was to support private enterprise, not supersede it. The result was a government–business relationship very different from that in the West. As one commentator observed:

> Efforts to produce new technology can often be made cooperatively rather than competing among enterprises. The government can guide such co-operative activity by selecting firms with suitable qualifications . . . such a relationship between the public and private sector is found in Japan.[27]

However, it took some time to develop an effective government–business relationship and MITI has frequently been criticized for going too far. This close relationship between government and business stood in strong contrast to the situation in the United States where there was little cooperation. The US government tied down industry with regulations in a relationship which lacked the close support found in Japan.

Japanese economy and society were overhauled by an influx of foreign production technologies. A key method of importing technologies was reverse engineering, in which foreign products were dismantled to see how they were made. As the products were taken apart, engineers thought about how the products were designed and the way they were manufactured. This led to a method of thinking about process design and product design in an integrated fashion. This was very different from the United States where product design and process were considered separate functions. Whereas in the West, product development went through a series of separate stages, the Japanese system was more flexible and different stages were inter-meshed depending on the needs at the time.[28]

As the Japanese developed more efficient and flexible manufac-turing systems, Americans were content to use their old methods. They did not close the door on innovation; in fact they welcomed it, but it was innovation in products, not how they were made. While Americans devoted two-thirds of their R&D expenditure to new products, Japanese concentrated their R&D efforts on the processes by which the products were made. The emphasis on manufacturing processes and facilities allowed the Japanese to substantially reduce production costs and increase competitiveness.

These different approaches were reflected in education. American business schools offered few courses on production.[29] In the late 1980s, only 6 per cent of American baccalaureates were in engin-eering, compared with 20 per cent in Japan and 37 per cent in Germany.[30] Like the British before them, Americans were falling behind the Japanese. American managers, once the best in the world, were not equipped with the skills to grasp the new directions in which global technology was moving.

In the early 1980s Robert Hayes and William Abernathy were professors at what was possibly the leading educational institution for business, Harvard.[31] They identified a number of weaknesses in American business training. They criticized US management educa-tion for turning out generalist managers with no expertise in any particular industry or technology. Business training enabled graduates to step into any unfamiliar company and run it through financial controls, portfolio concepts and a market-driven strategy. Lacking hands-on experience, they focused on short-term cost reduction rather than long-term development of technological competitiveness. This short-term vision meant that risky new ventures were not valued. As one manager stated: 'Why risk money on new businesses when good, profitable low-risk opportunities are on every side?' Effectively, the American mandarins learnt to maximize the existing system through financial tools such as return on investment (ROI) which were used to evaluate the performance of managers.

When faced with fresh Japanese competition, Americans clung to their old formulas of success, in particular the mass production systems, hierarchical organizations and a belief that market transactions were the best way to deal with outside suppliers. An MIT study of American productivity decline noted how managers continued to use the outdated strategies that had worked in the golden years:

> In industry after industry the commission's studies have found managers and workers so attached to the old ways of doing things that they cannot understand the new economic environment. Challenged by stronger foreign competition and stagnant productivity, they respond by clinging more tenaciously to the patterns of production and organisation they associate with the heyday of American economic primacy. To some extent, it is the very magnitude of past successes that has prevented adaptation to a new world.[32]

Like the Chinese and British before them, Americans had become arrogant about their achievements. 'The dominance of American science and technology in the early post-war decades was so great that companies could operate as if American laboratories were the only ones generating useful knowledge'[33], and this attitude blinded them to developments being made offshore. The old patterns of behaviour were played out in all parts of industry. US labour management relied on the old recipes for success: mass production systems that created highly specialized jobs with no flexibility. When skills became outdated, American managers relied on the market, placing discarded workers on the labour market where they sought more suitable workers. By contrast, Japanese companies dealt with skill problems in-house, and workers were retained and retrained. For example, when new mass production techniques were introduced to Japanese shipyards, it meant that some jobs became obsolete and new skills would be required. Instead of laying off workers, employers held training programmes for the workers who knew they were employed on a lifetime basis, so adopted the changes with little resistance. As a result, a 32 per cent reduction in man hours per ton of construction was achieved in 1953–6.[34] With less fear of losing their jobs, workers were less likely to oppose innovation.

Confrontation in Japan was also reduced by the fact that unions were organized on a company-wide basis. Unlike in the West, where unions were structured on the basis of their skills and professions, Japanese workers belonged to their company union, regardless of what job they did. This tied unions to the company and reduced fear that any skill was going to be made redundant. Consequently, there was greater openness to change, even if it made their old skills redundant. Such unions helped cement a realization that the company and workers were all in the same boat with similar goals.

By contrast, lack of cooperation was a prevailing feature of the US economy. The study on US industrial decline performed by the Massachusetts Institute of Technology found little cooperation between firms, within firms or between workers and management:

Individual enterprise and competition are the foundations on which market economies are built and anything that might undermine them tends to be viewed with suspicion. But co-operation and the pursuit of collective goals are essential too. A balance must be sought between the two poles. As the envir onment changes, sometimes too must the balance.[35]

Inside firms, the old organizational forms based on hierarchical control and highly specialized individuals did not help cooperation. Hierarchies made communication and coordination difficult, while workers focusing on their specialized tasks found it hard to see beyond their imme-diate task. An emphasis on multi-skilling was noticeably lacking. When innovations were introduced, they often became islands, isolated from the rest of the organization not involved in the initial development. It is easy to see the comparison with eighteenth-century India and nineteenth-century China, where workers had become so specialized that innovations were not introduced that required a broad vision.

The market mentality also shaped how American firms dealt with their suppliers. Relationships with organizations that bought and sold their goods were seen as market transactions in which suppliers received little help from their buyers and frequently involved competitive negotiation. By contrast, Japanese companies developed large enterprise groups in which companies formed cooperative rela-tionships with their suppliers which could involve sharing research facilities, support staff and production capacity. The core company might offer training courses to help raise skill levels or they might provide finance to help upgrading. These relationships allowed the core com-panies to implement innovations without enduring the restrictive weight of an administrative bureaucracy.[36] At the same time, the com-petition between the satellite companies raised the standards of producers.

The Japanese enterprise groups had a bank associated with them

331

which provided a number of advantages.[37] If a firm got into financial trouble, reorganization by the main bank could occur sooner than under the market-oriented financial system and this could help fend off bankruptcy. These banks have longer investment horizons than shareholders wanting a return on investment. They are more interested in deriving solutions that keep the company operating as a viable concern. This is in sharp contrast to the United States where banks operate through the market with distant and dispassionate interest.

There were other unifying features to the Japanese commitment to growth. The nation also possessed a sense of vulnerability in having a very limited resource base. Being born in a land of few resources has meant that the Japanese have had to manufacture and keep track of changes in the world market. Another psychological factor was patriotism. In the postwar years, economic performance was one way to restore national pride lost in the war. Japanese businessmen exhibited great patriotism and concern for the long-term good of the nation.

This patriotic attitude could be seen in the attitude of an auto-mechanic from Hamamatsu, Soichiro Honda. Mr Honda ran his own auto-repair business for twenty years, then in 1948 began producing motor cycles. On several occasions his company went close to failure but he persevered stating: 'Even if my company becomes bankrupt at the rate at which I expand my plant, the plant itself will remain to be used for the development of Japanese industry. So I will take the risk.'[38] The long-term perspective illustrated by Mr Honda stands in sharp contrast to the short-time horizons of American managers who were always conscious they had to provide a return to investors. This meant short-term returns were preferred over longer investments, a result of a market-based financial system.

The new way of doing business brought Japan success, as was apparent in the vibrancy of Japan's foreign trade. Japan's share of world exports climbed from 7.8 per cent in 1972 to 8.9 per cent in 1984. Most notable has been the spectacular climb up the rankings of car producers. In 1962 it overtook Italy. In 1964 it surpassed France, Britain in 1966 and Germany in 1967. Finally, in 1980, Japan emerged as the world's largest producer of autos, taking the crown that the United States had worn for fifty years. This success was based on government steering, cooperative approaches to shared problems, excellent management, and an entrepreneurial spirit reminiscent of the samurai. The end result was a considerable increase in product quality and productivity. New management techniques such as 'just in time', quality control techniques and the whole concept of *kaizen* (continuous improvement) enabled Japan to reduce costs and add value to products with which they took on the world.

By contrast, the United States lost leadership in many industries, entrapped by government rules, unions and a free market individualistic culture. This economy produced a rationality that emphasized return on investment, market-based relationships and vibrant competition. Americans born of the free-market philosophy threw scorn on government intervention. In their eyes, the Japanese were cheating with the amount of government help they received. They felt that this cheating would not lead to enduring success, and continued to believe that the old rules, like anti-trust regulation, would promote efficiency and therefore progress. However, this thinking ignores that their competitors were not tied to these rules or old ways of thinking.

I am often asked if it is possible to make a small fortune in US shipping and I always tell them, 'Yes – if you start off with a large one.'

Conrad H.C. Everhard, President Dart Container Line

The shipping industry provided the first battleground of commercial values: Japanese culture of cooperation versus the American culture of free-market individualism. Up until the 1930s the Dollar Line had held the predominant position on the San Francisco–Orient route using high-quality ships. The Japanese government had targeted this route and, to increase their competitive strength, had encouraged two of their companies, TKK and KYK, to merge. To make the merger more attractive, it provided a generous subsidy to enable them to finance the new crack ships necessary to win the route.[39]

At the time, the Dollar Line was suffering from wasteful management and soon wilted under the strengthened Japanese competition.[40] To stave off bankruptcy, the Dollar Line was taken over by the government-owned US Maritime Commission, which changed the name of the company to American President Lines. In the US free-market culture it was generally believed that government management would be inefficient. However, government management freed the company of the need to satisfy stockholders with immediate profits, and also eliminated any concerns with take-over fights. The company's sole concern was to provide a quality shipping service. With an injection of capital, sound management and increased demand from the war, the company emerged strong and profitable, producing an unbroken record of efficiency that stood in sharp contrast to most of the private operators.[41] It became the largest shipping operator in the Pacific.

This was not the only government-run company. During the depression, the government picked up the pieces of a number of ailing companies and turned them into profitable entities; however, the US government knew the electorate would not tolerate this for long and, when the war was over, went to great lengths not to antagonize private interests. When selling surplus wartime ships, the government gave private companies, including foreign buyers, first crack at the best ships. The American President Lines was only allowed a modest purchase programme after any hints of socialism were buried.[42] Recognizing that the line was shackled, one of the company's executives stepped into the breach and started his own company, the Pacific Far East Line, with staff milked from the government company. Japanese companies rejoiced that instead of facing a strong rival, they now faced divided American competition and an onslaught ensued so that by 1953 the Pacific Far East Line was forced to operate under subsidies in order to survive.

Another major US operator born from the free-market culture was Hans Isbrandtsen, a maverick who had little respect for government subsidies or conference agreements. In the years immediately following the Second World War, Isbrandtsen conducted a service from New York to Japan via the Suez Canal. He achieved a dominant position where his ships took 26 per cent of Japan's eastbound cargoes.[43] At that time, a number of European companies operated lines to the East under a conference agreement. Isbrandtsen believed in free enterprise and the competitive spirit. He ignored the price agreements and lowered his prices. The conferences responded by lowering their prices and Isbrandtsen lowered his again until he was trading close to his operating costs. Prices plummeted in a bitter rate-war and it reached the point where Isbrandtsen did not know if he was undercutting his rivals or not. In a desperate attempt to end the war, Isbrandtsen flew to Tokyo. The Japanese were receptive, but the European lines that operated in the conference were keen to bury the upstart. Isbrandtsen was defeated and died of a heart attack. The company's east-bound line from Japan was cancelled, a consequence of his aggressive independence and belief in fierce competition. Eventually, Japanese ships gained a near-monopoly position in sailings from their country, and soon rose to confront US ships in areas of the world previously considered the United States' preserve.

There were other examples where the culture of free competition created economic deficiencies. Market-orientated American companies frequently operated in response to short-term market signals that left them deficient in the long-term. For example, the Korean War provided a huge demand for tramp shipping and led to a rush in investment. Many US companies raised loans to buy ships, only to find that when the war ended, they were left with high debt and overcapacity. As the years went past and the vessels became more obsolete, shipping companies found they did not have the capital to replace their increasingly uncompetitive ships.

The boom–bust cycle generated by the Korean War also affected Japanese shipping operators but their government came to the rescue, offering low interest loans to approved shipping projects. Given the industry's level of indebtedness, the government became very influential in directing investment in the industry. The subsidies were tied to the purchase and building of new ships.[44] Consequently, despite dire financial conditions, Japan's fleet stayed at the forefront of technological advance. The subsidy scheme was operated with flexibility, catering to changed circumstances as they occurred. Top priority was initially given to liners, as it was believed these would best meet the export needs of Japanese light manufactures. However, as the domestic economy was restructured, its shipping needs changed. In particular, the heavy engineering and chemical industries were achieving rapid growth and this placed a huge demand for very large ships carrying bulk cargoes from iron ore to oil. Government policy changed to reflect these circumstances.

The Japanese trend towards larger and more specialized ships was strongly complementing events offshore. In 1956 hostilities in the Middle East led to the temporary closure of the Suez Canal so ships had to travel all the way around Africa to reach the oilfields of Persia and Arabia. This increased shipping costs, so larger, more economical tankers were built to offset the rising costs. Once the cost-reducing benefit of large ships was realized, a movement towards larger vessels gained its own momentum. Japanese government policies were sensitive to these changes. However, the wisdom of the Japanese government should not be overstated. The market was changing to a type of ship that the Japanese were beginning to specialize in. It was a form of favourable market shift not too dissimilar to that of the eighteenth-century Indian Ocean, when the market moved to a ship that the English specialized in.

While the Japanese changed with the times, American entrepreneurial vision failed to see the demise of passenger liners. Entrepreneurial vision was blurred immediately after the war by an acute shortage of passenger vehicles but, more importantly, Americans failed to see the shift in the market that resulted from a reduction in immigrants crossing the Atlantic and the advance of aircraft. A number of American companies, including American Export Lines, Moore McCormack and United States Lines, all suffered from their commitment to liners. Perhaps American business judgement suffered from experience. Passengers and immigrants had always been an important component of American shipping. The Japanese never had the same experience with immigrants, their concerns being to supply their islands' resources. (Fortunately, some use of the US liners could be made with the rising demand for winter cruises to the sunny Caribbean.)

One part of the industry where Americans had taken an early lead was the tanker market. During the Second World War, the US Maritime Commission built up the largest tanker fleet in the world and its market share was such that it could set its own high freight rates. Foreign competitors would prefer to let their rates rise upwards and meet the commission's price rather than attempt to undercut this strong leader.[45] The US Treasury was earning very healthy profits of $20,000,000 a month from this position. However, the operating strength, profitability and efficiency of the Maritime Commission were irrelevant in a culture based on free enterprise. Americans would not tolerate government-run companies. The government was forced to sell its ships to private enterprise (with the exemption of ships retained for naval support).

The task of defending the US share of the tanker trade fell to a motley group of newcomers who were referred to as 'the independents'. Foreign operators who had been hesitant about taking on the market power of the commission had no hesitation in knocking off their new US rivals one by one. With lower operating costs, the foreign companies reduced their rates to levels with which the Americans could not compete. In desperation, the independents, who had previously pressured the government to end the Maritime Commission's activities, now rushed to the government for protection. They eventually gained some reprieve by the Korean War, which raised demand for shipping services

It wasn't long before another instance occurred when the market failed to generate enduring efficiency. When the Suez Canal raised demand for tankers, a number of private investors in the United States rushed to order tankers to take advantage of the high rates, only to be caught in a tanker slump after the canal reopened in 1957. American investors continued to respond to market signals and, when the market turned sour, they blamed unfair government competition, the fleet that the navy operated for their own purposes becoming the scapegoat. As de la Pedraja, who studied US shipping during this time, states:

> The get rich quick speculators had little knowledge of or interest in the volatile history of tanker movements; once again providing capital when it was not advisable, while in other shipping situations it failed to invest in indispensable ships and facilities.[46]

The most successful independent was Daniel Ludwig. Born into a fairly prosperous family, his father, grandfather and several uncles had been ships' captains or ship-builders. Ludwig gained valuable industry experience working first for a ship's chandlers, then as a marine engineer. It is this experience that differentiated him from many other independents who were merely investors responding to market signals. He started his first business during the First World War, an ideal time given that high wartime prices were delivering healthy profits, but his early business attempts were not all successful. It was not until he neared his forties that he could draw on his experience to reap the growing oil market.

Ludwig was a pioneer of many new commercial practices. He was one of the first to build a tanker by getting a contract to carry oil for an oil company, and borrow money from banks on the basis of earnings from the contract. In this way, he acquired tankers without putting up a cent of his own money.[47] He was also in the forefront of many other new developments that the British were slow to touch. His company, National Bulk Carriers, had pioneered a new kind of vessel, the OBO which could carry ore/bulk/oil. At that time ore carriers had mostly been small vessels such as the faithful British tramp. Frequently, a shipper using these vessels would take a cargo to a foreign destination where it would unload and return empty. A more versatile vessel could return with different kinds of cargo, and hence the success of the OBO. This vessel enabled Ludwig to enter new markets, including the transport of coal, ores and grains. It also provided higher returns as the ship now carried cargoes on both legs of the trip. Ludwig strove to build bigger vessels, being fully aware that the bigger the ship, the lower the operating costs. By the end of the Second World War, his company had the fifth largest tanker fleet in the United States, and he owned a shipyard near Norfolk, Virginia.

Ludwig had also become aware that the biggest profits in the tanker industry were made hauling oil from the Middle East to the United States. The Greek shipping tycoons Aristotle Onassis and

Stavros Niarchos were doing well on these routes using surplus wartime ships brought from the US government, which they registered in places like Liberia to escape US regulations. Ludwig wanted to play catch-up with the Greeks, so transferred his ships to the Panamanian flag in the early 1950s, enabling him to reduce costs by employing foreign workers. The conditions on board his ships were atrocious and he became known for his stinginess; seafarers tried to avoid working for him if possible.

Ludwig's business activities did not stop with shipping. He branched into a number of international activities, including the construction of refineries and drilling for oil. His investments in oil enabled him to ride an industrial boom as more and more Americans relied on cars and trucks for transportation. Nevertheless, he closed down his American shipyard in Virginia and opened a new yard in Japan, once again to escape the high US costs. In 1951 he signed a ten-year contract with the Japanese government to take over the former naval yard at Kure in Hiroshima. The contract specified that Japanese ship-builders and engineers were to have access to the yard and be able to examine all aspects of their building processes. This played an important role in bringing Japanese yards up to date with the world's best practice in welding and block building techniques. Ludwig helped the Japanese gain skills with which they would later surpass the Americans.

Ludwig's decision to register his ships under foreign flags was soon copied by other tanker-owners, including oil companies. In a new phase of globalized business, these companies could buy their ships in Asia or anywhere they chose. They could employ low-cost labour from the cheapest provider, and were freed from the high standards of safety and design that the US government imposed on its vessels. Liberia, Panama and Honduras became flags of convenience under which US tankers now sailed. The share of oil imports carried by US flag tankers declined from 81 per cent in 1945 to 4 per cent in 1961.

The flight to these foreign flags might have been stopped if Americans had come up with innovations that reduced costs, particularly labour costs, but organized labour had become entrenched stakeholders in the industry, intent on getting their share of the pie. In 1936 American seamen earned slightly less than American factory-workers but, by the late 1960s, they earned nearly 200 per cent more than their factory counterparts. Onshore, unions also ate into the competitiveness of the industry and prevented US companies from taking full advantage of technological breakthroughs. For example, although only seven men are needed to load and unload containers, East coast shippers had to employ a gang of twenty-one.[48]

One technology that could have reduced labour costs was automation. Although Americans had a highly developed expertise in artificial intelligence, they were very slow in converting this to shipping. American slowness in adopting shipboard automation has been described as an 'incongruous conundrum'. However, in adopting marine technology 'attention must be paid to the environment in which the technology will operate' and union hostility was one factor that limited some advances, particularly cargo handling.[49]

It is perhaps worthwhile to compare the American adoption of ship automation with their similarly slow adoption of robotics technology in other industries. A major reason for the slow adoption of robotics by American companies was that they expected a 30 per cent rate of return from their investment, compared with the Japanese who were prepared to accept 20 per cent. If the Japanese had used the same requirements as the Americans, their investment in the technology would have been halved.[50] It illustrates yet again the weaknesses of relying on ROI. Not only can financial controls stifle innovation, but when new competitors arrive, the old stakeholders may have temporarily to accept lower rates of return.

Rising wage costs were also a problem faced by the Japanese,

although they succeeded in producing a number of cost-cutting innovations, in particular the world's first automated vessel in 1961. Although
both nations faced the same problem, the Japanese had success delivering this technology because of the nature of their economic system.
It was a result of the cooperative efforts of Japanese ship-builders,
ship-owners and unions who accepted the changes despite their labour-
saving nature.[51] Technological advance and amalgamation could not
have occurred without cooperation from the unions. Although the
seamen's union has a poor strike record compared with other Japanese
unions, it has generally been realistic in accepting technology and
rationalization measures, seeing them as an opportunity to bargain
for better conditions. This is aided by lifetime employment which
creates a strong basis for worker–company identification. Consequently,
Japan has achieved a faster reduction in manning levels than elsewhere, and the introduction of more sophisticated types of vessel.
This has allowed Japanese industry to maintain its international competitiveness, despite sharply rising labour costs.

In all areas of competition, the Japanese gained strength from
cooperating with one another. Japanese companies were in the habit
of enriching each other through mutual exchange and, as early as
1955, eight Japanese lines began quoting the same shipping rate.
Individual liners would claim that the same rates were a coincidence,
a mere consequence of using the same pricing techniques. They
might admit to having the occasional lunch meeting, but this was
simply the revival of a prewar custom 'to enrich our knowledge by
mutual exchange in a pure social gathering'.[52] To Americans, this
was cheating and, if they tried the same activities, they would be hit
with anti-trust injunctions.

The Japanese government recognized that severe competition could
be counter-productive, and encouraged the formation of associations
to rationalize marketing and sailings. At other times it promoted

outright amalgamation, although this was not always popular, as many of the firms wanted to retain their own identity and autonomy. The largest attempt to reduce excess competition came after 1962, when the Council for the Rationalization of the Shipping and Ship-building Industries produced a blueprint for reconstruction, influenced by the experience of British shipping firms in the early twentieth century when they merged into larger groups. The Japanese proposal was to form groupings of satellite companies around a nucleus company. Participation in the restructuring was encouraged through government financial assistance.

While the reconstruction meant some companies experienced unwanted restrictions, and led to some friction among merging workers, the amalgamations were successful. Ninety per cent of Japan's deep-sea fleet came together into six main groups (including NYK and Mitsui-OSK). Reduced competition placed the companies in a stronger financial position. The shipping companies that emerged were more diversified, operating a range of vessels from liners, tramps and tankers, to specialized carriers, giving increased flexibility to changes in trading conditions. It also strengthened the companies' hand with the unions, provided economies of scale and placed the companies in a stronger position to raise large amounts of capital at lower rates of interest. They could spread their risks more widely and had greater resources to access key clients. Finally, it enabled them to resource the large vessels that would shape the industry's future. These advantages put them in a strong position vis-à-vis their competitors in America who could not amalgamate due to anti-trust law. The restructuring of the industry was highly successful and by September 1967 all companies were paying dividends.[53]

The more stable and financially strengthened industry that arose was in a better position to cope with technological change and shoulder risks. One technological change that would not have been

possible without the reorganization was containerization, the introduction of which was once again characterized by government
direction. It established container groups to eliminate excessive competition and, once again, financial assistance provided the inducement
to cooperate. By 1973 container networks operated on all of Japan's
main routes. It was yet another successful example of government-
led cooperation.

While the Japanese government encouraged cooperation, the
American government encouraged competition. We have seen how
anti-trust legislation denied Americans the chance to create more
competitive organisations through amalgamation.[54] American law
was based on a rationality of free-market competition. As de la
Pedraja notes:

> An emotional attachment to an idyllic form of free market has
> kept the US from marshalling its resources in order to reap the
> commercial benefits that having a merchant fleet brings in the
> foreign trades. Instead, the government has preferred to subsidise
> competitors, squandering resources on a costly rivalry.[55]

The US government did not encourage cooperation or technical
upgrades and, as the years progressed, government administration of
shipping became increasingly inefficient. It played a great part in the
industry's decline. The government subsidy system quickly became
outdated and restricted recipients to outdated trade routes and modes
of operation. As Whitehurst states below, they also tied American
companies to restrictive conditions that increased costs and limited
competitiveness:

> First, US statutes require a continuous radio telegraph watch. This
> in turn requires employing two additional radio officers at a

monthly cost of $9,800. Carrying a doctor on a passenger ship is not required by international agreements. However, on US-flag ships carrying over forty-nine passengers, a doctor is necessary. Traditionally, when a US ship is certified as a passenger ship and carries over twelve passengers, a doctor is also carried. The additional monthly cost is $1,600.[56]

US regulations provided a historical drag that failed to recognize advances in navigation and communication. Ships were much faster and safer than when the legislation was first drafted, while computer-assisted medical advice and diagnosis had become available. US regulations had aged. By contrast, Japanese shippers achieved significant cost reductions in these areas. In conjunction with their unions, they removed the need for ships to carry a doctor on board in 1962 and reduced the number of radio operators from three to two. There was also a complete change in the way manning levels were determined. Previously manning levels were fixed for the whole industry depending on the size and type of ships. Now ship-owners determined levels in consultation with the unions.

In theory, government subsidies and favourable loans should have made life easier for US shipping companies, but they came with the restriction that the ships they operated were built in US shipyards. The value of this restriction was great, considering a standard US container vessel cost $118,000,000 compared to $61,500,000 for one built in Japan.[57] Government protection only reduced the need for US ship-builders to be efficient.[58]

The need for change resulted in the replacement of the US Maritime Commission by a number of boards that recognized the different functions of administration and regulation. But it did not stop the rot. The Federal Maritime Commission, created in 1961, became a lawyer's paradise with ever more complex regulations. The safeguards imposed to stop earlier abuses generated red tape and delays that partially negated the benefits of subsidies. Rather than providing swift and effective responses, it gradually sank into a quasi-judicial mindset with cumbersome judicial procedures.[59]

By 1966 the share of American ocean-borne foreign trade carried in US vessels was down to 7.2 per cent, from a high of 57.6 per cent in 1947. By the early 1980s, it was down to 4 per cent.[60] Americans still owned a large number of ships flying under flags of convenience but they were not registered in the United States and they did not employ American seamen. It was a new period of globalization in which high-wage nations now divided their productive investments around the world in order to maintain cost competitiveness.

Japan managed to retain its position longer, despite being a high-wage nation, using new patterns of production that gave substantially better value for money to customers. The new Japanese methods were applied to industry after industry, creating layers of industrial superiority. Japanese success in shipping was repeated in ship-building, steel, automobiles and consumer electronics. The Japanese had found new ways of creating value and reducing costs, and in so doing created a wave of economic growth that propelled the Japanese people to a new level of prosperity.

14

A RAPIDLY CHANGING WORLD

Global trade has changed the world forever, and the rate of change is growing exponentially. It has only been forty years since the esteemed economist J. Kenneth Galbraith wrote that the American entrepreneur was a 'diminishing figure' replaced by 'technocrats', organizational men and women. With the loss of these dynamic economic figures, American industry appeared to be in decline.

In 1979 Ezra Vogel released the bestselling book *Japan as Number One* that recognized a change of industrial leadership had occurred. Over the following decade, companies such as Sony, Honda, Toyota and Toshiba swept all before them. The Japanese had made the automobile, steel, ship-building and consumer electronics industries their own, while 'rust belt' became a new geographic term referring to the region that had once been the US industrial heartland. With their new-found wealth, the Japanese went shopping for American icons. Included on their list was Columbia Studios, Pebble Beach golf course and the Rockefeller Centre in New York. Japan seemed invincible.

But in the 1990s Japan's growth hit a snag, and two causes stand out. The first was the social structure that underlies its economy. Hierarchical relations and close-knit relationships have hidden a number of inefficiencies that need to be addressed, in yet another example of how the historical drag of social structures affects the path of economies. The second cause was also familiar. Every nation's wave of growth involves bubbles of speculation. We saw it with the Dutch in the eighteenth century where, instead of investing in productive ventures, many investors preferred to speculate on the rising prices of tulips, with devastating results for those involved. The United States has endured a number of speculative epochs, most spectacularly being the late 1920s when sharemarket speculation led to the 1929 Wall Street crash.

In the early 1990s speculative fever took hold of Japan, and investors speculated, not in shares or tulips, but in land. In 1985 the Japanese Ministry of Finance lowered interest rates, which made it easier to borrow money and buy property. With plenty of money to lend, banks were lax in their standards and many loans were made on the basis of social relationships. The Japanese borrowed heavily and, with so many buyers in the market, property prices soared. Property-owners enjoyed seeing the value of their assets rise and soon realized they could use these as collateral to borrow and buy more land. The result was a spiral of inflated land prices and indebtedness. Land prices escalated to the point where the gardens of the Imperial Palace in central Tokyo were said to be worth as much as the entire state of California or all of Canada. Of course, all bubbles eventually burst and the inevitable crash arrived. Japan entered an economic crisis with an over-supply of construction, high indebtedness and a shaky financial sector. It retained the productive capabilities it had built up, but its economic wave was derailed.

Economic waves are never smooth. They invariably involve bubbles and ferments of speculative investment that do nothing to improve the productive capabilities of the economy. As obvious as the waste is to any observer, it never fails to lure punters ready to play the markets. Humans are drawn to a new source of wealth like locusts to a wheat field, all intent on getting their share. In the process, much destruction can be wrought. It is notable that while Japan was enduring its crisis, the United States had its own bout of 'dot.com' sharemarket speculation. Fortunately, the Federal Reserve under the guidance of Allan Greenspan delivered an intelligent monetary policy that raised interest rates and stopped the bubble reaching the giddy heights of Japan.

In 2010 Chna passed Japan as the world's second biggest economy. Two old powers are once again on the rise. A 2003 study[1] acknowledged that a revitalized China and India could eventually replace the United States as the world's most powerful nations, and the United States would become a second-rank power. Two forces are behind this change: their larger populations and economic growth. This study, conducted by Emilio Casetti from Ohio State University, ran a number of projections and these showed that China would first become as powerful as the United States. The average American will still be much wealthier than the average Chinese, but because of the larger population, the Chinese economy will be the same size as that of the United States and will be able to afford a similar size defence budget.

More worrisome for the Americans was that, at some time, China will dramatically surpass the power of the United States. In the future, we could expect their positions to be reversed. Casetti ran a number of projections to determine when China will obtain a lead over the United States of similar proportion to that the United States had over China in 1995. A number of projections suggest that China could be number one as early as 2030. The idea that, within our life-time, the United States will no longer be the world's most powerful country has a number of implications for global dynamics, but it is not a given.

The growth of China is being driven by the same processes that we have witnessed throughout this book, a process of imitation and capability-building in which it is gaining the abilities to make products that will be carried to the markets of the world. Between 1978 and 1999 the Chinese economy grew on average by 9.5 per cent a year. The irony is much of this is actually being driven by Western nations setting up foreign production operations in China. At the beginning of the twenty-first century, China was the world's largest recipient of foreign direct investment, and this is fuelling its technological catch-up.[2]

For China to move dramatically ahead of the United States, it still needs to go through a process of innovation. This is not yet driving China's growth but the country is investing in capabilities that make this possible. In 1964 the rate of illiteracy in China was 52 per cent; by 1999 it was down to 17 per cent. Both public and private investment in education is growing, and once again foreign countries are helping this process, setting up universities in China and taking Chinese students in their homelands. In 2006 China was producing nearly twice as many science and engineering undergraduates as the United States. Although the quality of Chinese education is not at the same level, it reflects an increasing ability to produce and absorb new technologies.

Of course, there are other problems that could affect China's growth. First, it has a rapidly ageing population which will affect the productivity of its labour force. Second, it has limited natural resources. Third, moving to a more dynamic, innovative economy will require more institutional and legislative reforms that the government might resist, including in areas like intellectual property, liberalizing movement of people and resources, and the government structure itself. The Chinese economy will eventually reach a size that will demand changes in administration patterns as well. Finally, China will experience the growth pangs and bubbles that we have witnessed in this book. These will slow down the rate of advance.

Not all the changes inside China have been positive. Economic growth has not been even and the movement to a free-market economy has seen many former state employees lose their jobs, leaving the nation with an exceptionally high unemployment rate of 17 per cent. More alarming is the effect on the environment. In 2005 the Ministry of Water Resources stated that 70 per cent of China's rivers and lakes were polluted, and more than 400,000 people die each year as a result of air pollution. In 2006 China passed the United states as the world's largest emitter of greenhouse gases. The Chinese government is aware of these problems and has introduced programmes to address them, but much remains to be done.

The rise of China and India leads to the question of whether the West could fall to the levels of impoverishment seen in the East in the last century. Can the West escape the bounds of entrapment that have dragged other nations down? It seems a silly question to ask in a time when America has been revitalized by new industries that are propelling it on a new epoch of industrial advance. The 1990s were a period of healthy growth in the American and British economies as information and bio-technologies asserted themselves. The IT revolution helped boost productivity in a number of areas and increased access to information that made markets work more efficiently and reduced transaction costs. It boosted the efficiency of supply-chain management and improved communication between customers and suppliers. The IT revolution also gave birth to new products, most spectacularly the Internet; and entrepreneurs, whose demise was noted by Galbraith, have re-emerged.

In this light, some may argue that the decline of the American economy discussed in the last two chapters was merely a temporary adjustment, a reflection of free-market efficiency as the US discarded those industries in which it could no longer compete due to its high labour costs. However, there are a number of weaknesses with this argument. First, this argument ignores the fact that Japanese labour costs also rose substantially in this period. Japan still advanced and maintained its position in many industries despite its own high labour costs. This argument also ignores the most vital question: why did the United States stagnate in these industries when Japan continued to innovate and introduce new ways of adding value and reducing costs through a process of continuous improvement? The other point to note is that the US boom occurred in the 1990s after the collapse of many industries. It was not a situation where resources were taken out of sunset industries and transferred into sunrise industries as a result of market signals. US industries fell because of superior competition and the country suffered much dislocation in the process. Clearly, many American rust-belt industries collapsed because they were entrapped in their old patterns of behaviour at a time when competitors were undergoing a process of catch-up and innovation.

The fact that American economic strength has recently reached new heights based on new technologies suggests that the process of entrapment is limited. It would appear that the education system in the United States was not fully entrapped and showed an ability to adapt to the new. Perhaps American regeneration also reflects the diversity of the American economic system. The number of production technologies used and products made are far more numerous than those that existed, for example, in Gujarat. It is notable that the Japanese did not choose to compete in all the industries in which the United States participates. Japanese advance occurred in a limited range of industries, especially consumer electronics, automobiles and steel. The Japanese economy is nowhere near as diverse as the American economy, so a full frontal assault could not be made.

Other factors might be operating to reduce the chances of future entrapment, in particular our increased knowledge of change management. Within the last twenty years, the study of management has delivered a number of texts on how to implement change. Yet, even with the latest knowledge of psychological, social and organizational processes, the introduction of change is not free of pitfalls. For example, David Collins[3] identified difficulties that managers have imposing their ideas for change on others when those ideas conflict with embedded social processes. Change programmes confront beliefs and attitudes that have been imprinted on society through a process of cultural reinforcement. Behaviour that has been learned and reinforced over the years can be very hard to change, especially when that behaviour has helped to create strong cohesive groups.

Management of change is embedded with issues of politics, conflict and control. Protagonists for change are lined up against opponents in repeated struggles and shifting alliances. Underlying this landscape is uncertainty and distrust. There may be uncertainty over how enduring the environmental shifts will be and the need for change. There will also be uncertainty over which solution is most appropriate. Information flows during the change process can become riddled with rumours and tid-bits that shape and distort expectations. Distrust is fuelled with the fear that one party will gain from the change at the expense of others.

Even if management succeed in introducing appropriate changes, problems can still be carried forward from the old regime. These include resource constraints, the continued use of old knowledge and misaligned incentive systems. Finally, after change has been introduced, it can take years for the results to flow. It is a period of relative loss in which the old ways and glory days beckon a return to the past.

In 1995 John Kotter[4] of the Harvard Business School noted that of the more than a hundred US companies that he had observed trying to remake themselves, only a few had been successful. Underpinning the high failure rate was the difficulty of managing a change programme. At the end of the twentieth century, implementing change in a company was still embedded with difficulties, despite our greater knowledge.

These age-old problems are afflicting even the most modern of industries. In *Only the Paranoid Survive*, Andrew Grove, the CEO of Intel, gives an interesting account of changes that hit the computer industry. Intel had been a highly successful company making computer memories. However, new Japanese competition was knocking Intel off its perch. Grove describes many of the forces that acted to inhibit change. He described how CEOs are at the centre of fortified palaces 'and news from the outside has to percolate through layers of people from the periphery where the action is'. Consequently, the CEO is often the last person to know when change occurs. It was the same problem we saw in the Chinese court during the Ch'ing dynasty.

Grove also spoke of the rationalities and belief systems that pervaded Intel and made it hard to agree on the need for change:

> The company had a couple of beliefs that were as strong as religious dogmas. Both of them had to do with the importance of memories as the backbone of our manufacturing and sales activities. One was that memories were our 'technology drivers'. What this meant was that we always developed and refined our technologies on our memory products first because they were easier to test . . . The other belief was the full product line dogma. According to this, our salesman needed a full product line to do a good job in front of our customers.[5]

These beliefs were based on strong rationality and had been keys to past success. They determined the company's priorities in allocating resources and making decisions. As Grove states: 'Our priorities were formed by our identity; after all, memories were us.' Intel focused on these areas while the world was changing around it. There was a substantial shift in the competitive environment, and the CEO experienced a business crisis that took him through all the forces of uncertainty that have faced decision-makers in previous centuries:

> It's a very personal experience. I learned how small and helpless you feel when facing a force that's '10X' larger than what you are accustomed to. I experienced the confusion that engulfs you when something fundamental changes in the business, and I felt the frustration that comes when the things that worked for you in the past no longer do any good.

Fortunately for Intel, one part of their business was growing rapidly: microprocessors. Having divested themselves of memories, Intel became the leader in the microprocessor market. It opens the question: 'What would have happened to Intel if this option had not been available?'

How great is the power of one individual to resist the forces of change? It is tempting to read the exploits of Marco Polo or Columbus as individuals who can change the march of time, but this is an oversimplification. These individuals were products of the forces around them. Marco Polo could only travel to China because of the peace that Khubilai Khan had created on the trade routes east. Columbus could only travel west across the ocean because of the improvements in shipping technology that preceded him. Similarly, today's bio-tech and IT entrepreneurs are riding the wave of opportunity created by those who came before them. It is wrong to see history as a procession of great men and women. Entrepreneurs are like drops of water: they get carried along in waves and, in so doing, they contribute to the force of that wave. So, if the question is asked, 'Do entrepreneurs ride or make waves?', the answer is they do both.

One factor that could reduce the chances of entrapment on a national basis is globalization, as companies will be less dependent on their domestic environment. In a global economy supplies can be acquired from the most efficient provider in the world leading to a far more efficient use of resources. A ship-owner can obtain finance in London, build the ship in Korea, install American navigation equipment, hire a crew from the Philippines and register the ship in Liberia or Greece. The ship might then be put on service between the Middle East and Japan.

The development of a global economy suggests that national economies will be less important in shaping the path of industrial growth in the future. While there certainly will be greater flexibility, it would be foolish to overstate the effect. This ignores knowledge of how an industry develops. The home economy is very important in helping a nation gain the initial capabilities to succeed in an industry. The domestic market is where the infant industry learns to walk. An industry is an offshoot of other industries, consumer demand, military demand and a myriad other factors that might or might not exist in the local environment.

Although the domestic environment is reducing in impact, it still appears to be an important factor in a nation's industrial success. Consider the example of Norway, a shipping nation that appears to excel on routes that go nowhere near its home base. Consequently, we would think its domestic environment is irrelevant. However, Norwegian shipping draws strongly on its home-based industrial cluster which includes 20 per cent of the world's ship insurance market and 15 per cent of the world's fleet classification, ship-gear producers, educational facilities and brokerage houses. The domestic economic system still appears to be playing a large role, albeit at a reduced level than that in the twelfth century.

In welcoming the impact of globalization and its effects on flexibility, we must also acknowledge many negative impacts. In removing tariffs, globalization reduces options for many nations. For example, it takes away the chance for a nation to imitate a market leader under trade protection. Of course, there are other support options available. Japan's initial industrial development did not occur under tariff protection, although after the Second World War its trade barriers became legendary. Without some form of protection, globalization will favour those nations who already possess the leading production technologies.

There are other worrying factors associated with globalization and, once again, shipping is probably the best industry to illustrate these. In an international market, customers can buy services from the cheapest supplier and this puts pressure on operators to reduce costs, including the reduction of safety standards. In 1959 the percentage of ships lost at sea was only 0.28 per cent. Twenty years later, the figure had doubled to 0.56 per cent.[6] Given the huge advances in safety in navigation and construction, this is a dreadful figure, and its explanation is not hard to find. The worst offenders are the low-cost flags of convenience. For example, in 1978, 473 ships were lost. Of these, Greece lost eighty-seven (2.3 per cent of their total shipping), Cyprus lost thirty-one (3.21 per cent) and Panama lost sixty-two (1 per cent). These figures are dramatically higher than the world average of 0.42 per cent and the world average would be lower still but it includes these nations.

In response to market pressure, ship-owners reduce crew numbers to unsafe levels, use old ships that are barely seaworthy, overload the ship, skimp on pollution control and hire staff with low skill levels. Unfortunately, the costs of ship loss include not just the loss of life and cargo but also the effect on the environment from oil spills and other damage.

In most countries the government imposes controls so the market does not push safety to the lowest common denominator. However, in an open global market, contracts go to the cheapest supplier. Some of the standards that result are deplorable. The *Pacific Charger* was a 10,000 ton ship registered in Liberia and owned by a combination of Japanese, Hong Kong and Taiwanese interests. On its maiden voyage it ran aground in New Zealand and it was discovered that the ship's master held a master's certificate without being examined. He bought his Liberian master's certificate for $20. No one on board had any radar qualifications. In another reported incident, a ship tried to navigate to Bermuda using nothing more than an ordinary atlas. Of course, not all shippers will use these cheap providers, but there are times when exporters are short of cash or just greedy and resort to these operators.

The International Maritime Organization has tried to improve matters by getting international agreement on key issues. However, dealing with numerous governments is slow and, even when agreement is reached, implementation is by no means certain. Some governments simply lack the money to monitor their shippers, and some lack the will to do so, especially if the shipping services provide revenue for the nation.

Economists used to see the economic world in relatively static terms. Theirs was a world of supply and demand and flexible markets in which history did not matter. In their eyes entrepreneurs responded to market forces as changes were set upon them. The true picture is one where history matters. There are economies of time that shape the functioning of commerce. These economies include the timing on entering a market, and the subtlety between first-mover advantages versus the costs of being a pioneer, or alternatively, a late follower. But the most important are the legacies of historical investments on future productive activity. A nation with a historical legacy of capabilities in a growing area of commerce is well favoured.

By contrast, the opposite can entrap a nation on a downward spiral.

The West has only dominated the international economy for two and a half centuries. It is a very short time in the history of economic activity. We ignore the economies of time at our peril. There are forces in the economy that will help adaptation to change and the ability to stay competitive. These include globalization and our increased knowledge of change management, but we are still far from comfortable. The most problematic issue is the bounded rationality of the human mind and our cultural investments that reinforce the way we think.

Even the most flexible economic systems possess factors that restrict their future options. The very word 'investment' recognizes that what we invest in today will determine what activities we participate in tomorrow. Investment does not refer only to machines and capital. It refers to skills, relationships and ways of thinking. In this way, an economy's growth path is based on the knowledge and skills its members have developed in the past. This affects the way entrepreneurs operate. Only a brave or foolish entrepreneur would invest in an industry or market of which they have no knowledge or skills. Our future is determined by our past.

Despite these comments, the West need not fear the rise of the East. While there will be areas of competition, the rise of the East represents an age of excitement and opportunity. Wealthy foreign nations are necessary to provide markets for our industries. We need only remember that China and Gujarat both grew together and the growth of Malacca made this possible. We need hundreds of Malaccas around the world with which we can all grow.

NOTES

Waves of Prosperity

1. Landes, David S., *The Wealth and Poverty of Nations*, W. W. Norton, New York and London (1998), p.157.
2. Ibid., p.55.
3. Ibn Khaldun, *Muqaddimah,* ed. Rosenthal, Franz, Princeton (1967).
4. Ibid., II, pp.271–2.
5. Chang, Pin-tsun 'The evolution of Chinese thought on maritime foreign trade from the sixteenth to the eighteenth century', *International Journal of Maritime History*, Vol.1(1), June 1989, pp.51–64.

Chapter 1   The Riches of the East

1. Merson, John, *Roads to Xanadu: East and West in the Making of the Modern World*, Weidenfeld & Nicolson, London (1989), p.29.
2. Balazs, E., *Chinese Civilisation and Bureaucracy: Variations on a Theme*, Yale University Press. New Haven and London (1964), p.16.
3. Elvin, Mark, *The Pattern of the Chinese Past*, Eyre Methuen, London (1973), p.121.
4. Ibid., p.131.
5. Lin, Lee Chor, 'Textiles in Sino-South East Asian trade: Song, Yuan and Ming dynasties', in Scott and Gay, *South East Asia and China: Art Interaction and Commerce* (1995), pp.171–86.
6. Jones, E., Frost, L., White, C., Coming Full Circle: *An Economic History of the Pacific Rim*, Westview Press, Boulder, Colorado and Oxford (1993), p.25.

7. Shiba, Yoshinobu, (translated by Mark Elvin) *Commerce and Society in Sung China*, Michigan Abstracts of Chinese and Japanese Works on Chinese History, No.2 (1970), p.154.

8. Adshead, S. A. M., *China in World History*, 2nd ed., St Martin's Press, New York (1995), p.115.

9. Ibid., p.114.

10. Elvin, *Pattern of Chinese Past*, pp.174–5.

11. Quoted in Shiba, *Commerce and Society*, p.212.

12. Ibid., p.185.

13. Ibid., p.207.

14. Ibid., p.171.

15. Adshead, *China in World History*, p.117.

16. Balazs, *Chinese Civilisation*, p.10.

17. Ibid., pp.17–18.

18. Murphey, Rhoads, *The Treaty Ports and China's Modernization: What Went Wrong?*, Michigan Papers in Chinese Studies No.7, University of Michigan Centre for Chinese Studies (1970), p.17n.

19. Ibid., p.13.

20. Levathes, Louise, *When China Ruled the Seas: The Treasure Fleet of the Dragon Throne* 1405–33, Simon & Schuster, New York (1994), p.43.

21. Needham, Joseph, *Science and Civilisation in China*, Vol. 4, Part III and Vol.3, Sections 21 and 22, Cambridge University Press (1971), pp.601, 612.

22. Dupoizat, M. F., 'The ceramic cargo of a Song dynasty junk found in the Philippines and its significance in the China–South East Asian trade', in Scott and Gay (1995), pp.205–24.

23. Needham, Joseph, 'Poverties and triumphs of the Chinese scientific tradition', in Crombie, A.C. (ed.), *Scientific Change: Historical Studies in the Intellectual, Social and Technical Conditions for Scientific Discovery and Technical Invention from Antiquity to the Present*, Heinemann, London (1963), pp.131–2.

24. Gang Deng, *Chinese Maritime Activities and Socioeconomic Development c.2100 BC–1900 AD*, Greenwood Press, Connecticut (1997).

25. Ibid., p.46.

26. Quoted in Levathes, *When China Ruled the Seas*, p.41.

27. Ibid., p.41.

28. Merson, *Roads to Xanadu*, p.61.

29. Levathes, *When China Ruled the Seas*, pp.41–3.
30. Needham, *Science and Civilisation in China*, p.476.
31. Levathes, *When China Ruled the Seas*, p.43.
32. Medley, Margaret, *The Chinese Potter: A Practical History of Chinese Ceramics* 3rd ed., Phaidon Press, Oxford (1989), p.170.
33. Gang Deng, 'An evaluation of the role of Admiral Zheng He's voyages in Chinese maritime history', *International Journal of Maritime History*, Vol. 7, No. 2 (1995), p.175.
34. Gang Deng, *Chinese Maritime Activities*, p.86.
35. Quoted in Shiba, *Commerce and Society*, p.32.
36. Ibid., p.33.
37. Gungwu, Wang, 'Merchants without empire: the Hokkien sojourning communities', in Tracy, James, *The Rise of Merchant Empires: Long Distance Trade in the Early Modern World 1350–1750*, Cambridge University Press (1990), pp.400–422.
38. Gang Deng, *Chinese Maritime Activities*, p.113.
39. Beamish, J., 'The significance of yuan blue and white exported to South East Asia', in Scott and Gay, *South East Asia and China*, pp.225–51.
40. Père d'Entrecolle, quoted in Sullivan, Michael, *The Arts of China*, Thames & Hudson, London (1973), p.225.
41. Medley, Margaret, *Chinese Potter*, p.171.
42. Rossabi, Morris, 'The reign of Khubilai Khan', in Franke and Twitchett (eds.), *The Cambridge History of China* (1994), pp.414–89.
43. Gang Deng, 'Admiral Zheng He's voyages'.
44. Chang, Pin-tsun, 'The evolution of Chinese thought on maritime trade from the sixteenth to eighteenth century', *International Journal of Maritime History*, 1,1 June 1989, pp.51–64.
45. Needham, *Science and Civilisation*, p.509.
46. Levathes, *When China Ruled the Seas*, pp.177–9.
47. Chang, 'Evolution of Chinese thought', p.54; Meilink-Roelofsz, M. A. P., *Asian Trade and European Influence in the Indonesian Archipelego between 1500 and about 1630*, Martinus Nighoff, The Hague (1962), p.74.
48. Levathes, *When China Ruled the Seas*, p.177.
49. Merson, *Roads to Xanadu*, pp.75–7.
50. Gang Deng, *Chinese Maritime Activities*, p.93.

51. Ishii, Yoneo (ed.), *The Junk Trade from Southeast Asia: Translations from the Tosen Fusetsu-gaki*, 1674–1723, Institute of Southeast Asian Studies, Singapore (1998).

52. Sar Desai, D. R., *South East Asia: Past and Present*, Vikas Publishing House, New Delhi (1981).

53. Quoted in Wade, Geoff, 'Melaka in Ming Dynasty texts', *Journal of the Malaysian Branch of the Royal Asiatic Society* 70(1) (1997), pp.31–69.

54. Ma Huan, 'Ying-yai sheng-lan', translated by J.V.G. Mills, 'The overall survey of the ocean's shores', Hakluyt Society, Cambridge University Press (1970), p.113. 55. Meilink-Roelofsz, *Asian Trade*, p.74.

56. Pires, Tome, *Suma Oriental*, Vol.II, Hakluyt Society, London (1944), p.286.

Chapter 2   Textiles and Spices

1. Barbosa, Duarte, *The Book of Duarte Barbosa*, Hakluyt Society, London (1918), Vol.1, p.108.

2. Chaube, J., *History of the Gujarat Kingdom 1458–1537*, Munshiram Manoharlal Publishers, New Delhi (1975).

3. Mookerji, Radha Kumud, *Indian Shipping: A History of the Seaborne Trade and Maritime Activity of the Indians from the Earliest Times*, Kitab Mahal, Allahabad (1962).

4. Quoted in Chaube, *History of the Gujarat Kingdom*, p.107.

5. Quoted in Gopal, Surendra, *Commerce and Crafts in Gujarat: 16th and 17th Centuries*, People's Publishing House, New Delhi (1975), p.186.

6. Barbosa, *Book of Duarte Barbosa*, p.142.

7. Gopal, *Commerce and Crafts*, p.188.

8. Das Gupta, A., *Indian Merchants and the Decline of Surat c. 1700–1750*, Franz Steiner, Wiesbaden (1979), p.2.

9. Steensgaard, N., 'The growth and composition of the long distance trade of England and the Dutch Republic before 1750', in Tracy (ed.), *The Rise of Merchant Empires: Long Distance Trade in the Early Modern World 1350–1750*, Cambridge University Press (1990), pp.102–52; Habib, Ifran, 'Merchant communities in pre-colonial India', in Tracy, *Rise of Merchant Empires*, pp.371–99.

10. Gopal, *Commerce and Crafts*, p.121.

11. Arasaratnam, Sinnappah, *Maritime India in the Seventeenth Century*, Oxford University Press, Delhi (1994), pp.13–14.

12. Pearson, M. N., *Merchants and Rulers in Gujarat: The Response to the Portuguese in the 16th Century*, University of California Press, Berkeley (1976), p.11.

13. Pires, Toma, *Suma Oriental*, Vol. II, Hakluyt Society, London (1944), p.270.

14. Gopal, *Commerce and Crafts*, p.3.

15. Pires, *Suma Oriental*, Vol. I, p.4.2

16. Lewis, Archibald, 'Maritime skills in the Indian Ocean 1368–1500', *Journal of the Economic and Social History of the Orient*, Vol XVI (1973), pp.238–64.

17. Pires, Vol. I, p.45.

18. Ravichander, A., 'Coastal society of Gujarat in the sixteenth century', *Studia*, Lisbon (1989), pp.161–80.

19. Barbosa, *Book of Duarte Barbosa*, p.19.

20. Quoted in Pearson, *Merchants and Rulers in Gujarat*, pp.108–9.

21. Gopal, *Commerce and Crafts*, p.122.

22. Ibid., pp.124–5.

23. Pelsaert, Francisco, *Jahangir's India: The Remonstrantie of Francisco Pelsaert*, translated by W. H. Moreland and P. Geyl, Jayyed Press, Delhi (1972), p.60.

24. Richards, John F., *The Mughal Empire*, Cambridge University Press (1993), p.58.

25. Naqvi, H. K., *Urban Cities and Industries in Upper India 1556–1803*, Asia Publishing House, London (1968).

26. Ibid., p.136.

27. Richards, *Mughal Empire*, p.62.

28. Das Gupta, A., *Merchants of Maritime India 1500–1800*, Variorum, Aldershot (1994), I, p.422.

29. Richards, *Mughal Empire*, pp.60–1.

30. Quoted in Pearson, *Merchants and Rulers of Gujarat*, p.91.

31. Alpers, Edward, 'Gujarat and the trade of East Africa c.1500–1800', *The International Journal of African Historical Studies* 9 (1976), pp.22–44.

32. Arasaratnam, *Maritime India in the Seventeenth Century*, p.267; Das Gupta, *Merchants of Maritime India*, I, p.421.

33. Tavernier, J. B., *Travels in India*, II 43–4, translated by Ball, V., revised by

Cooke, W., London 1925, quoted in Habib, Ifran, 'Merchant communities in pre-colonial India', p.384.

34. Pires, *Suma Oriental*, Vol. I, p.41.

35. Burnell, A. C. (ed.), *The Voyage of John Huygen van Linschoten to the East Indies*, The Hakluyt Society, LXXX, London (1885), Vol. I, p.60.

36. Das Gupta, *Merchants of Maritime India*, Vol. I, p.419.

37. Gokhale, B. G., *Surat in the Seventeenth Century*, Scandinavian Institute of Asian Studies Monograph series no.28, Curzon Press (1979); Arasaratnam, *Maritime India in the Seventeenth Century*, op. cit., p.175.

38. Ravichandar, 'Coastal society of Gujarat', p.170; Alpers, op. cit., p.28.

39. Chaudhuri, K. N., *Trade and Civilisation in the Indian Ocean: An Economic History from the Rise of Islam to 1750*, Cambridge University Press (1985), p.211.

40. Meilink-Roelofsz, M. A.P., *Asian Trade and European Influence in the Indonesian Archipelago between 1500 and about 1630*, Martinus Nighoff, The Hague (1962), pp.63–4; Ravichandar, 'Coastal society of Gujarat', p.167; Pearson, M. N., *Coastal Western India: Studies from the Portuguese Records*, Concept Publishing, New Delhi (1981), p.138.

41. Quoted in Pearson, *Coastal Western India*, p.136.

42. Dale, Stephen Frederic, *Indian Merchants and Eurasian Trade 1600–1750*, Cambridge University Press (1994), p.74.

43. Ravichander, 'Coastal society of Gujarat', p.168.

44. Gopal, *Commerce and Crafts*, pp.199–203.

45. Alpers, 'Gujarat and the Trade of East Africa', p.31.

46. Das Gupta, *Merchants of Maritime India*, Vol. III, p.13.

47. Das Gupta, *Indian Merchants and the Decline of Surat* and *Merchants of Maritime India*.

48. Manguin, P. Y., 'Late medieval Asian shipbuilding in the Indian Ocean', *Moyen Orient et Océan Indien*, 2, no.2 (1986), pp.13–15.

49. Gang Deng, *Maritime Sector Institutions and Sea Power of Premodern China*, Greenwood Press, Connecticut (1999), p.164.

50. Manguin, P.Y., 'The vanishing jong: insular Southeast Asian fleets in trade and war (fifteenth to seventeenth centuries)', in Reid, Anthony (ed.), *Southeast Asia in the Early Modern Era: Trade, Power and Belief*, Cornell University Press, Ithaca and London (1993), p.203.

Chapter 3   God, Gold and Glory

1. Lopez, Robert S., *The Commercial Revolution of the Middle Ages, 950–1350*, Prentice Hall, New York (1971), pp.60–62.
2. Hunt, Edwin S. and Murray, J., *A History of Business in Medieval Europe 1200–1500*, Cambridge University Press (1999), pp.69–70.
3. Ibid.
4. Lopez, *Commercial Revolution*, p.76.
5. North, D. C. and Thomas, R. P., *The Rise of the Western World*, Cambridge University Press (1973), p.56.
6. Mauro, Frederic, 'Merchant Communities 1350–1750', in Tracy, James (ed.), *The Rise of Merchant Empires*, Cambridge University Press (1990), pp.255–86.
7. Quoted in Mollat du Jourdin, M., *Europe and the Sea*, Blackwell, Oxford (1993), p.117.
8. North and Thomas, *Rise of the Western World*, p.56.
9. Pearson, M. N., 'Merchants and states', in Tracy, James (ed.), *The Political Economy of Merchant Empires*, Cambridge University Press (1991), pp.41–116.
10. For development of early European technology see Mokyr, Joel, *The Lever of Riches: Technological Creativity and Economic Progress*, Oxford University Press (1990).
11. Menard, Russel R., 'Transport costs and long range trade 1300–1800: was there a European transport revolution in the early modern era?', in Tracy, *Political Economy of Merchant Empires*, p.239.
12. For the definitive work on the development of medieval European shipping see Unger, Richard, *The Ship in the Medieval Economy 600–1600*, Croom Helm, London (1980).
13. Unger, Richard, 'Ships of the Late Middle Ages', in Hattendorf, John B. (ed.), *Maritime History: Vol. I, The Age of Discovery*, Krieger Publishing Company, Florida (1996), pp.35–50.
14. Menard, 'Transport costs', pp.228–75.
15. Unger, *The Ship in the Medieval Economy*, p.277.
16. Friel, Ian, 'The carrack: the advent of the full rigged ship', in Gardiner, R. and Greenhill, B. (eds.), *Cogs, Caravels and Galleons*, Brassey, London (1994), p.86.

17. Bill, Jan, 'Ship Construction, Tools and Techniques', in Gardiner and Greenhill (eds.), *Cogs, Caravels and Galleons*, pp.151–9; Unger, *The Ship in the Medieval Economy*, op. cit., p.226.

18. Unger, *The Ship in the Medieval Economy*, op. cit., p.277.

19. Kennedy, Paul, *The Rise and Fall of British Naval Mastery*, Penguin, Harmondsworth (1976), p.16.

20. Verlinden, Charles, 'Italian influence in Iberian colonisation', *The Hispanic American Maritime Review*, Vol. XXXIII, May 1953, No. 2.

21. Russell, P., *Prince Henry 'The Navigator': A Life*, Yale University Press, New Haven (2000), pp.120–8.

22. Ibid., p.146.

23. Verlinden, Charles, 'Background and beginnings of Portuguese maritime expansion', in Hattendorf, *Maritime History*, pp.53–68.

24. Russell, P. E., *Portugal, Spain and the African Atlantic*, 1343–1490, Variorum, Aldershot (1995), p.11 XI; Boxer, C. R., *The Portuguese Seaborne Empire*, Hutchinson, London (1969), p.26.

25. Quoted in Russell, *Prince Henry 'The Navigator'*, p.110.

26. Ibid., pp.120–8.

27. Ibid., p.256.

28. Verlinden, Charles, 'The big leap under Dom Jao II: from the Atlantic to the Indian Ocean', in Hattendorf, *Maritime History*, pp.69–84.

29. McNeill, W. H., *The Rise of the West*, University of Chicago Press (1963).

30. Phillips, William D. and Phillips, Carla, 'Columbus and the European background: the first voyage', in Hattendorf, *Maritime History*, pp.149–80.

31. Ibid., p.155.

32. Fernandez-Armesto, F., 'The sea and chivalry in late medieval Spain', in Hattendorf, J. B. (ed.), *Maritime History: Vol. I, The Age of Discovery*, pp.123–135; Lundahl, Mats, 'Spain and the conquest of America', in Lundahl (ed.), *Themes in International Economics*, Ashgate Publishing, Aldershot (1998), pp.99–134.

33. Milton, G., *Nathaniel's Nutmeg*, Hodder & Stoughton, London (1999), p.25.

34. Duncan, T. Bentley, 'Navigation between Portugal and Asia in the sixteenth and seventeenth centuries', in Van Kley, E. J. and Pullapilly, C. K. (eds.), *Asia and the West*, Cross Roads (1986), p.6.

35. Zandvliet, K., *Mapping for Money: Maps, Plans, Topographical Paintings and*

their Role in Dutch Overseas Expansion during the 16th and 17th Centuries, Batavian Lion International, Amsterdam (1998), p.17.

36. de Jesus Teodoro Dos Martines Lopes, M., 'Seamen, soldiers and crew of the Carreira da India in the second half of the 18th century', in Mathews, K.S. (ed.), *Shipbuilding and Navigation in the Indian Ocean Region AD1400–1800,* Munshiram Manoharlal Publishers, New Delhi (1997), pp.132–9.

37. Duncan, 'Navigation between Portugal and Asia', p.23.

38. Magelhaes Godinho, V., 'The Portuguese and the "Carreira da India", 1497–1810', in Bruijn, Jaap R. and Gaastra, Femme S. (eds.), *Ships, Sailors and Spices: East India Companies and their Shipping in the 16th, 17th and 18th Centuries,* Neha, Amsterdam (1993), pp.1–48.

39. Hunt and Murray, *History of Business,* p.219.

40. Pearson, 'Merchants and states', p.78.

41. Boxer, Portuguese Seaborne Empire, p.30.

42. Sar Desai, D. R., South East Asia, Past and Present, Vikas Publishing House, New Delhi (1981), p.84.

43. Meilink-Roelofsz, M. A. P., *Asian Trade and European Influence in the Indonesian Archipelago between 1500 and about 1630,* Martinus Nighoff, The Hague (1962), p.125.

44. Pearson, M. N., *Merchants and Rulers in Gujarat: The Response of the Portuguese in the 16th Century,* University of California Press, Berkeley (1976), p.40.

45. Steensgaard, N., *Carracks, Caravans and Companies,* Copenhagen (1973) or *The Asian Trade Revolution of the Seventeenth Century: The East India Companies and the Decline of the Caravan Trade,* University of Chicago Press (1973).

46. Pearson, *Merchants and Rulers in Gujarat,* p.102.

47. Phillips, Carla Rahn, 'The growth and composition of trade in the Iberian empires 1450–1770', in Tracy, *The Rise of Merchant Empires,* op. cit., pp.34–101.

48. Boxer, *Portuguese Seaborne Empire,* p.221.

49. Pearson, 'Merchants and states', p.81.

50. Sayous, A. E., 'Partnerships in the trade between Spain and America and also in the Spanish colonies in the sixteenth century', *Journal of Economic and Business History I* (1928), pp.282–301.

51. Quoted in Lundahl, *Themes in International Economics,* p.108.

52. Ibid., p.107.
53. Quoted in Galbraith, J. Kenneth, *A History of Economics: The Past as the Present*, Penguin, Harmondsworth (1987), p.35.
54. Parry, J. H., *The Spanish Seaborne Empire*, Hutchinson, London (1966), p.169.
55. Haring, C. H., *Trade and Navigation between Spain and the Indies in the Time of the Hapsburgs*, Harvard University Press (1963) p.59.
56. Parry, *Spanish Seaborne Empire*, p.56–7.
57. Ibid., p.125.
58. Haring, C. H., *The Spanish Empire in America*, Harbinger Books, New York (1963), p.304.
59. Phillips, Carla Rahn, 'Growth and composition of trade', p.77–8.
60. Hoberman, Louis Schell, Mexico's *Merchant Elite, 1590–1660: Silver, State and Society*, Duke University Press (1991), p.130.
61. Sayous, 'Partnerships in the trade', p.283.
62. Ibid., p.296.
63. Pike, Ruth, *Aristocrats and Traders: Sevillian Society in the Sixteenth Century*, Ithaca, New York (1972), pp.106–7.
64. Ibid., pp.50–1.
65. Kamen, Henry (1983), *Spain 1469–1714: A Society of Conflict*, Longman (1983), p.104.
66. Quoted ibid., pp.104–5.
67. Parry, *Spanish Seaborne Empire*, p.125.
68. Kamen, *Spain*, p.114.
69. Elbl, Martin and Phillips, Carla Rahn, 'The caravel and the galleon', in Gardiner and Unger, *Cogs, Caravels and Galleons*; Clayton, Lawrence A., 'Ships and empire: the case of Spain', *The Mariner's Mirror*, Vol. 62, no. 3 (1976), p.239.
70. Parry, *Spanish Seaborne Empire*, p.134
71. Quoted in Elbl and Phillips, 'Caravel and galleon', p.107
72. Lundahl, *Themes in International Economics*, p.11.

Chapter 4   Northern Industrialists

1. Boyajian, J. C., *Portuguese Trade in Asia under the Hapsburgs: 1580–1640*, Johns Hopkins University Press, Baltimore (1993), pp.42, 65, 70.
2. Reid, Anthony, 'The unthreatening alternative: Chinese shipping to Southeast Asia 1567–1842', *Review of Indonesian and Malaysian Affairs* 27 (1993), p.15.
3. Parry, J. H., *The Spanish Seaborne Empire*, Hutchinson, London (1966), p.240.
4. Unger, Richard, *The Ship in the Medieval Economy 600–1650*, Croom Helm, London (1980), p.277.
5. Hope, Ronald, *A New History of British Shipping*, John Murray, London (1990), p.68.
6. Ryan, A. N., 'Bristol, the Atlantic and North America 1480–1509', in Hattendorf, John B. (ed.), *Maritime History: Vol. I, The Age of Discovery*, Krieger Publishing Company, Florida (1996), pp.241–55; Hope, *New History,* p.75.
7. Hope, *New History*, p.61.
8. Cummins, John, *Francis Drake: The Lives of a Hero*, Weidenfeld & Nicolson, London (1995), p.14.
9. Haring, C. H., *The Spanish Empire in America*, Harbinger Books, New York (1963), p.299.
10. Davis, Ralph, *The Rise of the English Shipping Industry in the Seventeenth and Eighteenth Centuries*, Macmillan, London (1962), p.4.
11. Hope, *New History*, pp.93–8.
12. Ibid., p.104
13. Keay, John, *The Honourable Company: A History of the English East India Company*, HarperCollins, London (1991), p.52.
14. Davis, Ralph, *A Commercial Revolution: English Overseas Trade in the Seventeenth and Eighteenth Centuries*, The Historical Association (1967), p.7.
15. Hope, New History, pp.144–50; Starkey, D., 'The economic and military significance of British privateering, 1702–83', *The Journal of Transport History*, Vol. 9, no.1 (1988), pp.50–9.
16. Cummins, *Francis Drake*, p.73; Milton, G., *Nathaniel's Nutmeg*, Hodder & Stoughton, London (1999), p.30.
17. Milton, *Nathaniel's Nutmeg*, p.35.
18. Ibid., p.52.

19. Andrews, Kenneth R.,'The Elizabethan seaman', *The Mariner's Mirror*, Vol. 68, no.3 (1982), pp.245–62.

20. Schama, S., *The Embarrassment of Riches: An Interpretation of Dutch Culture in the Golden Age*, Random House, New York (1987).

21. van Zanden, J. L., *The Rise and Decline of Holland's Economy: Merchant Capitalism and the Labour Market*, Manchester University Press (1993), p.39.

22. Israel, J. I., *Dutch Primacy in World Trade 1585–1740*, Clarendon Press, Oxford (1989), p.18.

23. de Vries, J. and van de Woude, A., *The First Modern Economy*, Cambridge University Press (1997), pp.356–8.

24. Ibid., p.667.

25. Israel, *Dutch Primacy in World Trade*, p.50.

26. Unger, Richard, *Dutch Shipping Before 1800*, Van Gorcum, Assen, The Netherlands (1978), p.35.

27. Mokyr, *Lever of Riches*, p.69.

28. Quoted in Unger, *Dutch Shipping Before 1800*, p.44.

29. de Vries and Van der Woude, *First Modern Economy*, p.694.

30. van Zanden, *Rise and Decline*, p.39.

31. Unger, *Dutch Shipping Before 1800*, p.6.

32. Bosscher, P., 'The Industrial Revolution in the northern Netherlands', Congress on the Conservation of Industrial Monuments, Bochum, 1978.

33. Unger, *Dutch Shipping Before 1800*, pp.7–8.

34. Israel, *Dutch Primacy in World Trade*, p.62.

35. Parker, G., 'Europe and the wider world 1500–1700: the military balance' in Tracy, J. (ed.), *The Political Economy of Merchant Empires: State Power and World Trade 1350–1750*, Cambridge University Press (1991), pp.161–95.

36. Parr, Charles McKew, *Jan van Linschoten: The Dutch Marco Polo*, Thomas Y. Crowell, New York (1964).

37. Zandvliet, K., *Mapping for Money: Maps, Plans, Topographical Paintings and their Role in Dutch Overseas Expansion during the 16th and 17th Centuries*, Batavian Lion International, Amsterdam (1998), p.40.

38. Boxer, C. R., *The Dutch Seaborne Empire 1600–1800*, Hutchinson, London (1965), p.22.

39. Israel, *Dutch Primacy in World Trade*, p.68.

40. Bruijn, Jaap R.,'Productivity, profitability, and costs of private and corporate

Dutch ship owning in the seventeenth and eighteenth centuries', in Tracy, J. (ed.), *The Rise of Merchant Empires: Long Distance Trade in the Early Modern World 1350–1750*, Cambridge University Press (1990), pp.174–94; Neal, L., 'The Dutch and English East India Companies compared: evidence from the stock and foreign exchange markets', in Tracy, *The Rise of Merchant Empires*, pp.195–223

41. Bruijn, Jaap R. and Gaastra, Femme S., *Ships, Sailors and Spices: East India Companies and their Shipping in the 16th, 17th and 18th Centuries*, Neha, Amsterdam (1993), p.189.

42. Steensgaard, N., *Carracks, Caravans and Companies*, Copenhagen (1973) or *The Asian Trade Revolution of the Seventeenth Century*, University of Chicago Press (1973), p.409.

43. Boxer, *Dutch Seaborne Empire*, p.206.

44. Israel, *Dutch Primacy in World Trade*, p.21; Bruijn, *Ships, Sailors and Spices*, p.184.

45. de Vries and Van der Woude, *First Modern Economy*, pp.398–401.

46. Israel, J. I., *Empires and Entrepots: The Dutch, the Spanish Monarchy and the Jews 1585–1713*, Hambledon Press, London (1990).

47. Emmer, P., *The Dutch in the Atlantic Economy, 1580–1880*, Variorum, Aldershot (1998), p.70.

48. Schama, op. cit., p.345; Israel, *Dutch Primacy in World Trade*, pp.76–8.

49. De Vries and Van der Woude, *First Modern Economy*, p149.

50. Ibid., p.147.

51. Schama, *Embarrassment of Riches*, pp.348–9.

Chapter 5   Crisis in Spain and a Dutch Golden Age

1. Portuguese reformer quoted in Scammel, G. V., *The World Encompassed*, Methuen (1981) p.290.

2. Harring, C. H., *The Spanish Empire in America*, Harbinger Books, New York (1963), p.313.

3. Kamen, Henry, *Spain 1469–1714: A Society of Conflict*, Longman, 1983, p.193; Parry, J. H., *The Spanish Seaborne Empire*, Hutchinson, London (1966), p.399; Boxer, C. R., *The Portuguese Seaborne Empire*, Hutchinson, London (1969) p.146.

4. Parry, *Spanish Seaborne Empire*, p.230; Boxer, *The Portuguese Seaborne Empire*, op. cit., p.117.

5. Cipolla, Carlo M., Guns, *Sails and Empires: Technological Innovation and the Early Phases of European Expansion 1400–1700*, Panthean Books, New York (1965), pp.86–7.

6. Father Vincenzo Maria quoted in Cipolla, *Guns, Sails and Empires*, pp.88–9.

7. Hoberman, Louis Schell, *Mexico's Merchant Elite, 1590–1660: Silver, State and Society*, Duke University Press, (1991), pp.14–5; Phillips, Carla Rahn, 'The growth and composition of trade in the Iberian empires 1450–1770', in Tracy, James, *The Rise of Merchant Empires: Long Distance Trade in the Early Modern World 1350–1750*, Cambridge University Press (1990), pp.86–8.

8. Harring, *Spanish Empire in America*, p.308.

9. Steensgaard, N., 'The growth and composition of the long distance trade of England and the Dutch Republic before 1750', in Tracy, *Rise of Merchant Empires*, p.118.

10. Israel, J. I., *Dutch Primacy in World Trade 1585–1740*, Clarendon Press, Oxford (1989).

11. Kamen, *Spain*, p.161.

12. Landes, David, *The Wealth and Poverty of Nations*, W. W. Norton, New York and London (1998), p.173.

13. Parry, *Spanish Seaborne Empire*; Landes, *The Wealth and Poverty of Nations*, p. 173.

14. Elliot, J. H., 'The Decline of Spain', in Cipolla, Carlo M. (ed.), *The Economic Decline of Empires*, Methuen, London (1970), pp.168–95.

15. Usher, A. P., 'Spanish ships and shipbuilding in the sixteenth and seventeenth centuries', in *Facts and Figures in Economic History for E. F. Gay*, Harvard University Press (1932), p.197.

16. Quoted in Clayton, 'Ships and empire: the case of Spain', *Mariner's Mirror*, Vol. 62, no.3, p.242.

17. Quoted in Usher, 'Spanish ships and shipbuilding' p.197.

18. Boxer, C. R., *The Dutch Seaborne Empire 1600–1800*, Hutchinson, London (1965), pp.155–7.

19. Ibid., pp.161–6.

20. Saul, John Ralston, *Voltaire's Bastards*, Penguin, Canada (1992), p.114.

21. Boyajian, J. C., *Portuguese Trade in Asia under the Habsburgs 1580 –1640*, Johns Hopkins University Press, Baltimore (1993), p.191.

22. Magelhaes Godinho, V., 'The Portuguese and the "Carriera da India", 1497–1810', in Bruijn, Jaap R. and Gaastra, Femme S., *Ships, Sailors and Spices: East India Companies and their Shipping in the 16th, 16th and 18th Centuries,* Neha, Amsterdam (1993), p.46.

23. Elliot, J. H., *The Count Duke of Olivares: The Statesman in an Age of Decline*, Yale University Press, New Haven, Mass. (1986), p.157.

24. Pearson, M. N., *Merchants and Rulers in Gujarat: The Response to the Portuguese in the 16th Century*, University of California Press, Berkeley (1976), pp.4–5.

25. Ibid., p.125.

26. Gokhale, B. G., *Surat in the Seventeenth Century*, in Scandinavian Institute of Asian Studies, Monograph series no. 28, Curzon Press (1979).

27. Arasaratnam, Sinnappah, *Maritime India in the Seventeenth Century*, Oxford University press, Delhi (1994), p. 194.

28. Unger, Richard, *Dutch Shipbuilding Before 1800: Ships and Guilds*, Van Gorcum, Assen-Amsterdam (1978).

29. Gokhale, *Surat*.

30. Gopal, Surenda, *Commerce and Crafts in Gujarat: 16th and 17th Centuries*, People's Publishing House, New Delhi (1975), p.111.

31. Das Gupta, A., *Merchants of Maritime India 1500–1800*, Variorum, Aldershot (1994), I, p.495.

32. Van Zanden, J. L., *The Rise and Decline of Holland's Economy: Merchant Capitalism and the Labour Market*, Manchester University Press (1993), pp.72–7.

33. Boyajian, *Portuguese Trade in Asia*, p.146.

34. Das Gupta, *Merchants of Maritime India*, op. cit., I, p.417.

35. Ibid., p.432.

36. Arasaratnam, *Maritime India in the Seventeenth Century* (1994), pp.197–8; Das Gupta, *Merchants of Maritime India*, II, p.40.

37. Gungwu, Wang, 'Merchants without empire: the Hokkien sojourning communities', in Tracy, *Rise of Merchant Empires*, p.409.

38. Ishii, Yoneo (ed.), *The Junk Trade from Southeast Asia: Translations from the Tosen Fusetsu-gaki*, 1674–1723, Institute of Southeast Asian Studies, Singapore (1988), p.220n; Reid, Anthony, 'The unthreatening alternative: Chinese

shipping to Southeast Asia 1567–1842', *Review of Indonesian and Malaysian Affairs* 27 (1993), p.28.

39. Reid, 'The unthreatening alternative', p.28.

Chapter 6   The Wealth of the Dutch

1. Quoted in Schama, S., *The Embarrassment of Riches: An Interpretation of Dutch Culture in the Golden Age*, Random House, New York (1987).

2. Israel, J. I., *Dutch Primacy in World Trade 1585–1740*, Clarendon Press, Oxford (1989), p.258.

3. Schama, *Embarrassment of Riches*, p.172.

4. Ibid., p.189.

5. Ibid., p.172.

6. Ibid., p.303.

7. Ibid., p.169.

8. Ibid., pp.165–84.

9. Ibid., p.346.

10. Sir William Patten, Surveyor of the British Navy, quoted in Pepys' Diary, see Ibid., p.234.

11. Quoted in Schama, *Embarrassment of Riches*, p.231.

12. Davis, Ralph, *The Rise of the English Shipping Industry in the Seventeenth and Eighteenth Centuries*, Macmillan, London (1962), pp.311–12; Wilson, Charles, *England's Apprenticeship 1603–1763*, Longman, London (1965), p.267.

13. Quoted in Wilson, *England's Apprenticeship*, p.165.

14. Davis, *Rise of the English Shipping Industry*, pp.12–13.

15. Wilson, *England's Apprenticeship*, p.184.

16. Davis, *Rise of the English Shipping Industry*, p.65.

17. Milton, G., *Nathaniel's Nutmeg*, Hodder & Stoughton, London (1999), p.252.

18. Marshall, P., 'Private British trade in the Indian Ocean before 1800', in Das Gupta, A. and Pearson, M. N. (eds.), *India and the Indian Ocean 1500–1800*, Oxford University Press (1987), p.279.

19. Steensgaard, N., 'The growth and composition of the long distance trade of England and the Dutch Republic before 1750', in Tracy, James, *The Rise*

of Merchant Empires: Long Distance Trade in the Early ModernWorld 1350–1750, Cambridge University Press (1990), p.113.

20. Chaudhuri, K. N., *The Trading World of Asia and the English East India Company 1660–1760*, Cambridge University Press (1978), pp.282–5.

21. Davis, *Rise of the English Shipping Industry*, p.388.

22. From *A New Discourse of Trade* (1693), quoted in Chaudhuri, *Trading World of Asia*, p.5.

23. Wilson, *England's Apprenticeship*, p.223.

24. Quoted in Mokyr, Joel, *The Lever of Riches: Technological Creativity and Economic Progress*, Oxford University Press (1990), p.240.

25. Davis, *The Rise of the English Shipping Industry*, op. cit., p.24.

26. Ibid., p.390.

27. Kennedy, Paul, *The Rise and Fall of British Naval Mastery*, Penguin, Harmondsworth, (1976), p.19.

28. Price, Jacob M., 'Transaction costs: a Note on merchant credit and the organization of private trade', in Tracy, J. (ed.), *The Political Economy of Merchant Empires: State Power and World Trade 1350–1750*, Cambridge University Press (1991), p.295; Walton, G. M., 'Obstacles to technical diffusion in ocean shipping, 1675–1775', in *Explorations in Economic History* 8 (1970), pp.123–40.

29. Davis, *Rise of the English Shipping Industry*, pp.300, 313–14.

30. North, D. C., 'Sources of productivity change in ocean shipping 1600–1850', *Journal of Political Economy* 76 (1968), pp.953–70.

31. French, C., 'Merchant shipping of the British Empire', in Gardiner, R. and Bosscher, P., *The Heyday of Sail: The Merchant Sailing Ship 1650–1830*, Brassey, London (1995), pp.10–33.

32. Menard, Russel R. (1991), 'Transport costs and long range trade 1300–1800: was there a European transport revolution in the early modern era?', in Tracy, *Political Economy of Merchant Empires*, pp.228–75.

33. Ibid., p.256; Austen, Ralph A., *African Economic History: Internal Development and External Dependency*, Heinemann, Portsmouth (1987), p.82.

34. Wilson, *England's Apprenticeship*, p.186.

35. Bosscher, P., Introduction to Gardiner and Bosscher, *Heyday of Sail*, pp7–9.

36. Lind, J., *A Treatise of the Scurvy. In Three Parts. Containing an Inquiry into the*

Nature, Causes and Cure of that Disease, Kincaid & Donaldson, Edinburgh (1753), p.viii.

37. de Vries, J. and van der Woude, A., *The First Modern Economy*, Cambridge University Press (1997), p.437.

38. Geyl, Pieter, *The Netherlands in the Seventeenth Century 1609–1648*, Vol.1, Ernest Benn, London, revised ed. (1961); Chaudhuri, K. N., *Trade and Civilisation in the Indian Ocean: An Economic History from the Rise of Islam to 1750*, Cambridge University Press (1985), p.87.

39. McPherson, Kenneth, *The Indian Ocean: A History of People and the Sea*, Oxford University Press, New Delhi (1993), p.204.

40. Quoted in Geyl, *The Netherlands in the Seventeenth Century*, Vol.2, p.348.

41. Boxer, C.R., *The Dutch Seaborne Empire 1600–1800*, Hutchinson, London (1965), pp.165–7.

42. Bruijn, Jaap R. and Gaastra, Femme S., *Ships, Sailors and Spices: East India Companies and their Shipping in the 16th, 17th and 18th Centuries*, Neha, Amsterdam (1993), p.196; Hoving, A. J., 'Seagoing ships of the Netherlands', in Gardiner, R. and Bosscher, P. (eds.), *The Heyday of Sail: The Merchant Sailing Ship 1650–1830*, Brassey, London (1995), pp.34–54.

43. Quoted in Boxer, C. R. 'The Dutch economic decline', in Cipolla, C., *The Economic Decline of Empires*, Methuen, London (1970), p.259.

44. Referred to in Boxer, *Dutch Seaborne Empire*, p.72.

45. Schama, *Embarrassment of Riches*, p.597.

46. Boxer, *Dutch Seaborne Empire*, pp.31, 47.

47. Wilson, *England's Apprenticeship*, p.10.

48. Unger, Richard, *Dutch Shipbuilding Before 1800*, Van Gorcum, Assen, the Netherlands (1978).

49. Boxer, *Dutch Seaborne Empire*, pp.105.

50. Hoving, 'Seagoing ships of the Netherlands', p.41.

51. Boxer, 'Dutch economic decline', p.260; Unger, *Dutch Shipbuilding Before 1800*, op. cit., p.9.

52. Boxer, 'Dutch economic decline', p.262.

53. Quoted ibid., p.238.

Chapter 7   Britannia Rules the Waves

1. Arasaratnam, Sinnappah, *Maritime India in the Seventeenth Century*, Oxford University Press (1994), p.88.

2. Das Gupta, A., *Merchants of Maritime India 1500–1800*, Variorum, Aldershot (1994), XII, p.111; Das Gupta, A., *Indian Merchants and the Decline of Surat c.1700–1750*, Franz Steiner, Wiesbaden (1979), pp.137–8.

3. Richards, John F., *The Mughal Empire*, Cambridge University Press (1993), p.288.

4. Das Gupta, *Merchants of Maritime India*, IX, pp.148–62.

5. Ibid., p.150.

6. Richards, op. cit., pp,278–9.

7. Das Gupta, *Merchants of Maritime India*, I, p.433.

8. Ibid., VI, p.195.

9. Marshall, P., 'Private British trade in the Indian Ocean before 1800', in Das Gupta, A. and Pearson, M. N., *India and the Indian Ocean 1500–1800*, Oxford University Press (1987), pp.276–300.

10. Das Gupta, Merchants of Maritime India, op. cit., X, p.222; Arasaratnam, Sinnappah, *Maritime Trade, Society and European Influence in Southern Asia 1600–1800*, Variorum, Aldershot (1995), XIV, pp.31, 36–7.

11. Arasaratnam, *Maritime Trade, Society and European Influence*, XIV, p.39.

12. Das Gupta, *Merchants of Maritime India*, VII, p.134.

13. Defoe, Daniel, *A Tour Through England and Wales* Vol. 2, J. M. Dent and Sons, London (1948), p.133

14. McKendrick, N., 'Commercialization and the economy', in McKendrick, N., Brewer, Kohn and Plumb, J. H., *The Birth of a Consumer Society: The Commercialization of Eighteenth Century England*, Europa, London (1982).

15. The following examples are taken from McKendrick, ibid., unless otherwise stated.

16. Lichtenberg, G. C., *Lichtenberg's Visits to England*, translated and edited by Mare, M. L. and Quarrel, W. H., Clarendon Press, Oxford (1938).

17. Strauss, R. (ed),' A Trip through the Town' (1735), quoted in McKendrick, 'Commercialization', p.60.

18. Wilson, C., *England's Apprenticeship 1603–1763*, Longman, London, (1965).

19. Mokyr, Joel, *The Lever of Riches: Technological Creativity and Economic Progress*, Oxford University Press (1990), p.377.

20. Kenwood, A. G. and Lougheed, A. L., *Technological Diffusion and Industrialisation Before 1914*, Croom Helm, London (1982), p.106.

21. Wedgwood, Josiah, *Letters*, ed. Farrer, Katherine, privately published (1903), Vol.2, pp.420–5, quoted in Klingender, Francis, *Art and the Industrial Revolution*, Evelyn, Adams & Mackay, Chatham (1968), p.112.

22. Wadsworth, Alfred P. and de Lacy Mann, Julia, *The Cotton Trade and Industrial Lancashire 1600–1780*, Manchester University Press (1931), p.503.

23. Klingender, *Art and the Industrial Civilisation*, pp.5–7.

24. Tylecote, Andrew, *The Long Wave in the World Economy: The Current Crisis in Historical Perspective*, Routledge, London (1992), p.42.

25. Mokyr, *Lever of Riches*, p.111.

26. Marx, Karl, *Selected Works*, Vol.II (1942), quoted in Klingender, *Art and the Industrial Civilisation*, p.167

27. Britton, John, *Autobiography* (1850), vol.I, pp.128–9.

28. Pollard, Sidney and Robertson, Paul, *The British Shipbuilding Industry 1870–1914*, Harvard University Press (1979), p.14.

29. Burton, Anthony, *The Rise and Fall of British Shipbuilding*, Constable, London (1994), p.65.

30. Greenhill, B., 'Steam before the screw', in Gardiner, R. and Greenhill, Basil, *The Advent of Steam: The Merchant Steamship before 1900*, Conway Maritime Press, London (1993), pp.11–27.

31. Lambert, A., 'The Ship Propeller Company and the promotion of screw propulsion 1836–1852', in Gardiner and Greenhill, op. cit., pp.136–45.

32. Ibid., p.145.

33. MacKenzie-Kennedy, C., *The Atlantic Blue Riband: Evolution of the Express Liner*, Ebor Press, York (1993), pp.6–9.

34. Greenhill, 'Steam before the screw', p.26.

35. Griffiths, D., 'Marine engineering development in the nineteenth century', in Gardiner and Greenhill, 'Advent of steam', p.106.

36. Davies, P. N., 'British shipping and world trade', in Yui, T. and Nakagawa, K. (eds.), *Business History of Shipping: Strategy and Structure, Proceedings of the Fuji Conference*, University of Tokyo (1985), pp.39–85.

37. Howarth, D. and Howarth, S., *The Story of P&O*, Weidenfeld & Nicolson, London (1986), p.73.

38. Hope, Ronald, *A New History of British Shipping*, John Murray, London (1990), p.341.

39. Smith, Adam, *An Inquiry into the Nature and Causes of the Wealth of Nations*, Book IV, J. M. Dent & Sons, London, (1921), p.73.

40. Keay, John, *The Honourable Company: A History of the English East India Company*, HarperCollins (1991), pp.451–2.

41. Harley, C. Knick (1988), 'Ocean freight rates and productivity 1740–1930: the primacy of mechanical invention confirmed', *Journal of Economic History* 48(4), pp.851–76.

42. Smith, Crosbie, 'Britain's shipbuilders: the years of progress 1840–1914', *Transport History* (1980), Vol. 11, pp.258–72.

43. Pollard and Robertson, *British Shipbuilding Industry*, p.62.

44. Ibid., p.46.

45. Ibid., pp.92–3; MacKenzie-Kennedy, *Atlantic Blue Riband*, p.42.

46. MacKenzie-Kennedy, *Atlantic Blue Riband*, p.10.

47. Ibid., p.183.

48. Chandler, Alfred D., *Scale and Scope: The Dynamics of Industrial Capitalism*, Belknap Press, Harvard (1990), p.265.

49. Lewis, Arthur W., *The Evolution of the International Economic Order*, Princeton University Press, N. J., (1978), p.7.

50. Duncan, T. and Foggarty, J., *Australia and Argentina on Parallel Paths*, Melbourne University Press (1984).

51. Green, E., 'Very private enterprise: ownership and finance in British shipping, 1825–1940', in Yui and Nakagawa, op. cit., pp.219–48; Hope, op. cit., p.316.

52. Sturmey, S. G., *British Shipbuilding and World Competition*, Athone Press, London (1962), p.395.

53. Hope, New History, p.318; Middlemiss, Norman L., *Travels of the Tramps: Twenty Tramp Fleets*, Shield Publication, Newcastle (1989), Vol. 1, p.10; Sturmey, *British Shipbuilding*, p.395.

54. Hope, *New History*, p.338.

55. Kennedy, Paul, *The Rise and Fall of the Great Powers*, Unwin & Hyman (1988), p.152.

Chapter 8   Changes in the West

1. Krooss, Herman E. and Gilbert, Charles, *American Business History*, Prentice Hall, Englewood Cliffs, New Jersey, (1972).

2. McCusker, John J., 'The rise of the shipping industry in colonial America', in Kilmarx, R. A., *American's Maritime Legacy: A History of the US Merchant Marine and Shipbuilding Industry since Colonial Times*, Westview, Boulder, Colorado (1979), pp.1–26.

3. Bates, W. W., *American Marine: The Shipping Question in History and Politics*, Houghton Mifflin, Boston and New York (1892), p.95.

4. Doerflinger, T. H., 'Commercial specialization in Philadelphia's merchant community, 1750–1791', *The Business History Review* (1983), 57(1), pp.20–49.

5. Brognan, H., *Longman History of the United States of America*, Longman, New York (1985), p.122.

6. Myers, Gustavus, *History of the Great American Fortunes*, The Modern Library, New York (1907), pp.95–8.

7. Bauer, Jack K., 'The golden age', in Kilmarx, *America's Maritime Legacy*, pp.27–64.

8. Cochran, T. C., *200 Years of American Business*, Basic Books, New York (1977), p.26.

9. Licht, W., *Industrializing America: The Nineteenth Century*, Johns Hopkins University Press, Baltimore and London (1995), p.117.

10. Poulson, B., 'Economic history and economic development: an American perspective', in Weiss, T. and Schaefer, D., *American Economic Development in Historical Perspective*, Stanford University Press (1994), pp.70–83.

11. In 1910–14 dollars. Weiss, T., 'Economic growth before 1860: revised conjectures', in Weiss and Schaefer, *American Economic Development*, pp.11–27.

12. Geisst, Charles R., *Wall Street: A History*, Oxford University Press, New York (1997).

13. Chandler, A., 'Patterns of American railroad finance, 1830–50', *The Business History Review*, (1954), 28(3), pp.248–63.

14. Bates, *American Marine*, p.146.

Chapter 9   Changes in the East

1. Teng, Ssu Yu and Fairbank, John K., *China's Response to the West*, Harvard University Press, Cambridge, Mass. (1954), p.19.
2. Adshead, S. A. M., *China in World History*, 2nd ed., St Martin's Press, New York (1995), p.296.
3. Braudel, F., *Civilisation and Capitalism*, Collins, London (1984), Vol.1, p.151.
4. Jones, E., Frost, L. and White, C., *Coming Full Circle: An Economic History of the Pacific Rim*, Westview Press, Boulder, Colorado and Oxford (1993), p.28.
5. Elvin, Mark, *The Pattern of the Chinese Past*, Eyre Methuen, London (1973), pp.284–7.
6. Ibid., p.258.
7. Murphey, Rhoads, *The Treaty Ports and China's Modernization: What Went Wrong?*, Michigan Papers in Chinese Studies No.7, University of Michigan Centre of Chinese Studies (1970), p.8.
8. Adshead, *China in World History*, p.319.
9. Crossen, C., *The Rich and How They Got That Way*, Nicholas Brealey Publishing, London and Naperville (2000), pp.171–94.
10. Jones, E. L., 'The real question about China: Why was the Song economic achievement not repeated?', *Australian Economic History Review* XXX (1990), Pattern of Chinese Past, pp.7–8; Elvin, op. cit., p.204.
11. Jones, 'The real question about China', p.11.
12. Teng and Fairbank, *China's Reponse to the West*, p.17.
13. Elvin, *Pattern of Chinese Past*, pp.225–34.
14. Lenz, W., 'Voyages of Admiral Zheng He before Columbus', in Mathews, K. S. (ed.), *Shipbuilding and Navigation in the Indian Ocean Region AD1400–1800*, Munshiram Manoharlal Publishers, New Delhi (1997), p.152.
15. Wong, Chu-Ming, 'Commentary', in Crombie, A. C., *Scientific Change: Historical Studies in the Intellectual, Social and Technical Conditions for Scientific Discovery and Technical Invention from Antiquity to the Present*, Heinemann, London (1963), pp.166–7.
16. Balazs, E., *Chinese Civilisation and Bureaucracy: Variations on a Theme*, Yale University Press, New Haven and London (1964), p.32.
17. Jones, Frost and White, *Coming Full Circle*, p.3; Landes, David S., *The Unbound*

Prometheus: Technological Change and Industrial Development in Western Europe from 1750 to the Present, Cambridge University Press (1969).

18. Elvin, *Pattern of China Past*, p.277.
19. Ibid., p.277.
20. Medley, Margaret, *The Chinese Potter: A Practical History of Chinese Ceramics*, 3rd ed., Phaidon Press, Oxford (198), p.265.
21. Atterbury, Paul (ed.), *The History of Porcelain*, Orbis Publishing, London. (1982), p.127.
22. Needham, Joseph, 'Poverties and triumphs of the Chinese scientific tradition', in Crombie, *Scientific Change*, p.139.
23. Hao, Yen Ping, *The Comprador in Nineteenth Century China: Bridge between East and West*, Harvard University Press, Cambridge, Mass. (1970), p.7.
24. Adshead, *China in World History*, p.246.
25. Murphey, *Treaty Ports*, p.13; Elvin, *Pattern of Chinese Past*, p.292.
26. Mokyr, Joel, *The Lever of Riches: Technological Creativity and Economic Progress*, Oxford University Press (1990), p234.
27. Jones, Frost and White, *Coming Full Circle*, p.29.
28. Jones, 'The real question', p.18.
29. Morse, H. B., *The Guilds of China*, Longmans, Green, London (1909), p.27.
30. Elvin, *Pattern of China Past*, p.314.
31. Reid, Anthony, 'The unthreatening alternative: Chinese shipping to Southeast Asia 1567–1842', *Review of Indonesian and Malaysian Affairs*, 27 (1993).
32. Davis, Ralph, *The Rise of the English Shipping Industry in the Seventeenth and Eighteenth Centuries*, Macmillan, London (1962), pp.298–9.
33. Das Gupta, A., *Merchants of Maritime India 1500–1800*, Variorum, Aldershot (1994), p.155.
34. Reid, 'The unthreatening alternative,' p.28.
35. Wong, Lin Ken, 'The trade of Singapore 1819–69', *Journal of the Malaysian Branch of the Royal Asiatic Society*, Vol. 33, Part 4, December 1960, p.123.
36. Kennedy, P., *The Rise and Fall of the Great Powers*, Unwin & Hyman, London, (1988).
37. Downs, J., 'American merchants and the China opium trade, 1800–1840', *The Business History Review* (1968), 42(4), pp.418–42.
38. Swisher, Earl, 'Chinese intellectuals and the Western impact, 1838–1900', *Comparative Studies in Society and History* (1958), 1(1), pp.26–37.

39. Teng and Fairbank, *China's Repsonse*, pp.266–9.

40. Forrest, D., *Tea for the British*, Chatto & Windus, London (1973).

41. Merson, John, *Roads to Xanadu: East and West in the Making of the Modern World*, Weidenfeld & Nicolson, London (1989), p.156.

42. Quoted in Teng and Fairbank, *China's Response*, p.76.

43. Ibid., pp.86–7.

44. Attempts to adopt modern shipbuilding are described in Chen, Gideon, *The Pioneer Promoters of Modern Industrial Technique in China: Three Studies*, Paragon Book Reprint Corporation, New York. (1968)

45. Quoted in Chen, ibid., p.30.

46. Ibid., p.19.

47. Ibid., p.32.

48. Ibid., p.46.

49. Ibid., p.15.

50. Ibid., p.15.

51. Ibid., p.40.

52. From Tso Wen-hsiang-kung Tsou-kao, quoted in Teng and Fairbank, *China's Response*, pp.82–3.

53. Liu, K.C., 'Steamship enterprise in nineteenth century China', *Journal of Asian Studies* 18 (1959).

54. Cheng, Sheng-shih Wei-yen, quoted in Liu, ibid., p.444.

55. Hao, *The Comprador*, pp.98–9, 120–4.

56. Ibid., pp.4, 147.

57. Murphey, *Treaty Ports*, p.53.

58. Teng and Fairbank, *China's Response*, p.90.

59. Forrest, *Tea for the British*.

Chapter 10   The Land of the Rising Sun

1. Roberts, J. G., *Black Ships and Rising Sun: The Opening of Japan to the West*, Julian Messner, New York (1971).

2. Ibid., p.10.

3. Ibid., p.28.

4. Allen, G. C., *A Short Economic History of Japan*, 4th ed., Macmillan, London (1981), p.23.

5. Westney, D. Eleanor, *Imitation and Innovation: The Transfer of Western Organisation Patterns to Meiji Japan*, Harvard University Press, Cambridge, Mass. (1987).

6. Miwa, R.,'Maritime policy in Japan: 1868–1937', in Yui, T. and Nakagawa, K. (eds.), *Business History of Shipping: Strategy and Structure*, Proceedings of the Fuji Conference, University of Tokyo (1985), pp.132–52.

7. Burks, Ardath W., 'Tokugawa Japan: post feudal society and change', in Burks, Ardath W. (ed.), *The Modernizers: Overseas Students, Foreign Employees and Meiji Japan*, Westview Press, Boulder, Col., (1985), pp.9–32.

8. Amioka, S.,'Changes in Educational Ideals and Objectives (From Selected Documents, Tokugawa era to the Meiji Period)', in Burks, *The Modernizers*, pp.323–57; Hirschmeier, Johannes and Yui, Tsunehiko, *The Development of Japanese Business 1600–1980*, 2nd ed., George Allen & Unwin, London (1981), pp.11–13.

9. Hirschmeier and Yui, *Development of Japanese Business*, p.47.

10. Allen, *Short Economic History of Japan*, p.24; and Fukasaku, Yukiko, *Technology and Industrial Development in Pre-war Japan: Mitsubishi Nagasaki Shipyard 1884–1934*, Routledge, London (1992).

11. Fukasaku, *Technology and Industrial Development*, p.17; and Masao, Watanabe, 'Science across the Pacific:American–Japanese scientific and cultural contacts in the late nineteenth century', in Burks, *The Modernizers*, pp.369–92.

12. Allen, *Short Economic History*, p.26.

13. Quoted in Murphey, Rhoads, *The Treaty Ports and China's Modernization: What Went Wrong?*, Michigan Papers in Chinese Studies No.7, University of Michigan Centre of Chinese Studies (1970), p.30.

14. Yoshio, Sakata (1985) 'The beginning of modernization in Japan', in Burks, *The Modernizers*, pp.69–84; Amioka, 'Changes in educational ideals', p.328.

15. Madoka, Kanai,'Fukui: domain of a Tokugawa collateral daimyo: its tradition and transition', in Burks, *The Modernizers*, pp.33–68.

16. Yoshio, 'Beginning of modernization in Japan', p.74.

17. Madoka, 'Fukui', p.64.

18. Burks, Ardath W., 'Japan's outreach: the Ryugakusei', in Burks, *The Modernizers*, pp.145–60.

19. Minoru, Ishizuki, 'Overseas study by Japanese in the early Meiji period', in Burks, *The Modernizers*, pp.161–86.

20. Masao, W., 'Science across the Pacific', in Burks, *The Modernizers*, p.370.

21. Quoted in Hirschmeier and Yui, *Development of Japanese Business*, p.107.

22. Fukasaku, Technology, p.28.

23. Allen, *Short Economic History*, p.29.

24. Yoshio, 'The Beginning of modernization', p.79.

25. Jones, Hazel, 'The Griffis thesis and Meiji policy toward hired foreigners', in Burks, *The Modernizers*, pp.219–53.

26. Brown, S. D., 'Okubu Toshimichi: his political and economic policies in early Meiji Japan', *Journal of Asian Studies* (1961–62), 21(2), pp.183–97.

27. Stinchcombe quoted in Westney, D. Eleanor, *Imitations and Innovations: The Transfer of Western Organisation Patterns to Meiji Japan*, Harvard University Press, Cambridge, Mass. (1987), p.16.

28. Westney, *Imitations and Innovations*, p.10.

29. Fukasaku, *Technology*, p.25.

30. Ibid., p.20.

31. Allen, *Short Economic History*, p.40.

32. Fukasaku, *Technology*, p.21.

33. Ibid., pp.20–1.

34. Hirschmeier and Yui, *Development of Japanese Business*, p.96.

35. Ibid., p.98.

36. Ibid., p.126.

37. Ibid., p.142.

38. Ibid., p.122.

39. Ibid., p.11.

40. Fukasaku, *Technology*, pp.17–22.

41. Chida, Tomohei and Davies, Peter N., *The Japanese Shipping and Shipbuilding Industries: A History of their Modern Growth*, Athlone Press, London (1990), p.5.

42. Miwa, 'Maritime policy in Japan: 1868–1937', in Yui and Nakagawa, *Business Histroy of Shipping*, p.124.

43. Fukasaku, *Technology*, p.21.

44. Chida and Davies, *Japanese Shipping and Shipbuilding*, p.6.

45. Yui and Nakagawa *Business History*, p.xiv; Miwa, 'Maritime Policy in Japan: 1868–1937', pp.125–6.

46. Quoted in Hirschmeier and Yui, *Development of Japanese Business*, p.139.

47. Chida and Davies, *Japanese Shipping*, p.6.

48. Ibid., p.8.

49. Ibid., p.89.

50. Nakagawa, K.,'Japanese shipping in the nineteenth and twentieth centuries: strategy and organisation', in Yui and Nakagawa, *Business History*, pp,1–33.

51. Ibid., p.4.

52. Chida and Davies, *Japanese Shipping*, p.10.

53. Yui and Nakagawa, *Business History*, 1985 p.xvii.

54. Chida and Davies, *Japanese Shipping*, p.9.

55. Miwa, 'Maritime Policy in Japan: 1868–1937', p.132.

56. Chida and Davies, *Japanese Shipping*, p.17.

57. Miwa, 'Maritime Policy in Japan: 1868–1937', p.130.

58. Yui and Nakagawa, *Business History*, p.xvii; Miwa,'Maritime Policy in Japan: 1868–1937', p.133.

59. Hirschmeier and Yui, *Development of Japanese Business*, p.6;Tatsuki, M.,'Comment', in Yui and Nakagawa, *Business History*, pp.307–8; Chida and Davies, op, cit., p.11.

60. Hirschmeier and Yui, *Development of Japanese Business*, p.191.

61. Yui and Nakagawa, *Business History*, p.16.

62. Ibid., p.6.

63. Fukasaku, *Technology*, p.23.

64. Yui and Nakagawa, *Business History*, p.xviii.

65. Nakagawa, 'Japanese shipping', p.314.

Chapter 11   The Corporate Age

1. Ray, Edward John, 'Changing patterns of protectionism: the fall in tariffs and the rise in non-tariff barriers', in Frieden, Jeffrey A. and Lake, David A., *International Political Economy: Perspectives on Global Power and Wealth*, 4th ed., Routledge, London (1991), p.343.

2. Krooss, H. E. and Gilbert, C., *American Business History*, Prentice Hall, New Jersey (1972), p.147.

3. Licht, Walter, *Industrializing America: The Nineteenth Century*, Johns Hopkins University Press, Baltimore and London (1995).

4. Kroos and Gilbert, *American Business History*, pp.155–8.

5. Ibid., pp.176–80; Chandler, Alfred D., *Scale and Scope: The Dynamics of Industrial Capitalism*, Belknap Press, Harvard (1990), p.25.

6. Krooss and Gilbert, *American Business History*, p.184.

7. Licht, *Industrializing America*, p.158.

8. Geisst, C. R., *Deals of the Century*, John Wiley & Sons, New Jersey (2004).

9. Galambos, L., 'The Triumph of Oligopoly', in Weiss, T. and Schaefer, D. (eds.), *American Economic Development in Historical Perspective*, Stanford University Press (1994), pp.241–53.

10. Chandler, *Scale and Scope*, p.8.

11. Ibid., p.9.

12. Taylor, F. W., *The Principles of Scientific Management*, W. W. Norton, New York (1967); Wrege, C. D. and Perroni, A. G.,'Taylor's pig tale: a historical analysis of Frederick W. Taylor's pig iron experiments', *The Academy of Management Journal* (1974), 17(1), pp.6–27.

13. Quoted in Misa, Thomas J., *A Nation of Steel: The Making of Modern America 1865–1925*, Johns Hopkins University Press, Baltimore. (1995), p.166.

14. Krooss and Gilbert, *American Business History*, p.158.

15. Chandler, *Scale and Scope*, p.82.

16. Misa, *Nation of Steel*, pp.200–1.

17. Licht, *Industrializing America*, p.183.

18. Weisberger, Bernard A., *Many People, One Nation*, Houghton Mifflin, Boston (1987), p.217.

19. Chandler, *Scale and Scope*, p.52.

20. Laux, James M., *In First Gear: The French Automobile Industry to 1914*, Liverpool University Press (1976), p.79.

21. Chandler, A., *Giant Enterprise: Ford, General Motors, and the Automobile Industry: Sources and Readings*, Harcourt, Brace & World (1964).

22. Bloomfield, G., *World Automotive Industry*, David and Charles (1978), pp.26–7.

23. Bauer, Jack K., *A Maritime History of the United States: The Role of America's Seas and Waterways*, University of South Carolina Press (1988), p.286.

24. Ibid., p.242.

25. Ibid., p.289.

26. Safford, J. J., 'The United States merchant marine in foreign trade, 1800–1939', in Yui, T. and Nakagawa, K. (eds.), *Business History of Shipping:*

Strategy and Structure, Proceedings of the Fuji Conference, University of Tokyo (1985), pp.91–118.

27. Allin, Lawrence C.,'The Civil War and the period of decline, 1861–1913', in Kilmarx, R. A. (ed.), *America's Maritime Legacy: A History of the US Merchant Marine and Shipbuilding Industry since Colonial Times*, Westview Press, Boulder, Colorado (1979), pp.65–110.

28. Ibid., p.72.

29. Safford, 'The United States merchant marine in foreign trade', p.100.

30. Ibid.

31. Quoted in Thiesen, William H., 'Building an "American Clyde": The development of iron shipbuilding on the Delaware River', paper presented at the Pennsylvania Historical Association Annual Meeting, Philadelphia (1997), p.19.

32. Baker, William A.,'Commercial shipping and shipbuilding in the Delaware Valley', paper presented to the Society of Naval Architects and Marine Engineers (1976), pp.1–23.

33. Heinrich, Thomas R., *Ships for the Seven Seas: Philadelphia Shipbuilding in the Age of Industrial Capitalism*, Johns Hopkins University Press, Baltimore (1997).

34. Misa, *Nation of Steel*, pp.96–7; Bauer, *A Maritime History of the United States*, p.290; Heinrich, *Ships for the Seven Seas*, p.105.

35. Heinrich, *Ships for the Seven Seas*, p.103; Misa, *Nation of Steel*, p.98.

36. Heinrich, *Ships for the Seven Seas*, p.107.

37. Navin, Thomas and Sears, Marion, 'A study in merger formation of the International Mercantile Marine', *Business History Review* (1954), Vol. 28, no.4, pp.291–328.

38. de la Pedraja, Rene, *The Rise and Decline of US Merchant Shipping in the Twentieth Century*, Twayne's Evolution of American Business Series no.8, Twayne Publishers, New York (1992), pp.8–9.

39. Clark, J. and Clark, M., 'The International Mercantile Marine Company: A financial analysis', *American Neptune* (1957),Vol. 57, no.2, pp.137–54.

40. Yui and Nakagawa, *Business History of Shipping*, p.xx.

41. Safford, Jeffrey J., 'World War I maritime policy and the national security: 1914–1919', in Kilmarx, *America's Maritime Legacy*, pp.111–48.

42. Bauer, *A Maritime History of the United States*, ibid., p.299.

43. Bauer p.298.

44. Heinrich, *Ships for the Seven Seas*, p.94.

45. Ibid., p.165.

46. Bauer, *A Maritime History of the United States*, p.301.

47. de la Pedraja, *Rise and Decline of US Merchant Shipping*, p.113.

48. Nakagawa, K.,'Japanese shipping in the nineteenth and twentieth centuries: strategy and organisation', in Yui and Nakagawa, *Business History of Shipping*, p.3.

49. Miwa, Ryoichi,'Government and the Japanese shipping industry, 1945–64', *Journal of Transport History*, March 1985, p.144.

50. Sturmey, S. G., *British Shipping and World Competition*, Athlone Press, London (1962), p.392.

Chapter 12   Coal, Oil and a Faster Rate of Change

1. Kennedy, Paul, *The Rise and Fall of the Great Powers*, Unwin & Hyman, London (1988), p.224.

2. Sampson, A., *Company Man: The Rise and Fall of Corporate Life*, Random House, London (1995).

3. Weiner, H. J., *English Culture and the Decline of the Industrial Spirit 1850–1980*, Cambridge University Press (1981).

4. Quoted in ibid., p.149.

5. Lazonick, William, *Business Organisation and the Myth of the Market Economy*, Cambridge University Press (1991).

6. Bloomfield, G., *World Automotive Industry*, David & Charles, Newton Abbott (1978), p.1.

7. Noble, D., *America by Design*, Oxford University Press, New York (1977); Freeman, C.,'Formal scientific and technical institutions in national systems of innovation' in Lundvall, Bengt-Ake (ed.), *National Systems of Innovation: Towards a Theory of Innovation and Interactive Learning*, Pinter Press (1992), pp.169–87.

8. Pollard, Sidney and Robertson, Paul, *The British Shipping Industry 1870–1914*, Harvard University Press, Cambridge, Mass. (1979), p.144.

9. Von Tunzelmann, G. N.,'Technical progress during the Industrial Revolution', in Floud, R.C. and McCloskey, D. N., *The Economic History of Britain since*

1700, Vol. 1, 1700–1860, Cambridge University Press (1981).

10. Pollard and Robertson, *British Shipping Industry*, p.148.

11. Burton, Anthony, *The Rise and Fall of British Shipbuilding*, Constable, London (1994), p.222.

12. Quoted in Weiner, *English Culture*, p.143.

13. Quoted in Burton, *Rise and Fall*, p.236

14. Harley, C. K. and McCloskey, D. N., 'Foreign trade: competition and the expanding international economy', in Floud, R. C. and McCloskey, D. N. (eds.), *The Economic History of Britain since 1700, Vol. 2, 1860 to the 1970s*, Cambridge University Press (1981), pp.50–69.

15. Based on Hilgerdt, F., Industrialization and Foreign Trade, League of Nations Table, in Dicken, Peter, *Global Shift: Industrial Change in a Turbulent World*, Harper & Row, London (1986), p.14.

16. Harley and McCloskey, 'Foreign Trade', p.69.

17. Chandler, Alfred D., *Scale and Scope: The Dynamics of Industrial Capitalism*, Belknap Press, Harvard (1990), pp.275–9.

18. Sandberg, L.G.,'The entrepreneur and technological change', in Floud and McClosky, *Economic History of Britain*, Vol. 2, pp.99–120.

19. Alford, B. W. E., 'New industries for old? British industry between the wars', in Floud and McClosky, *Economic History of Britain*, Vol. 2, p.330.

20. Chandler, *Scale and Scope*, p.335.

21. Quoted in Chandler, *Scale and Scope*, p.333.

22. Lorenz, Edward,'Organisational inertia and competitive decline: the British cotton, shipbuilding and car industries, 1945–1975', *Industrial and Corporate Change* (1994), Vol.3, no.1

23. Quoted in Weiner, *English Culture*, p.142.

24. Ibid.

25. Tomlinson, Jim,'The failure of the Anglo-American Council of Productivity', *Business History*, Vol. 33 (1991), no.1, pp.82–92.

26. Lorenz, 'Organisational inertia', p.338.

27. Cairncross, Alec, 'The Postwar Years 1945–77', in Floud and McClosky, *Economic History of Britain*, Vol. 2, pp.370–415.

28. Sturmey, S. G., *British Shipping and World Competition*, Athlone Press, London (1962), p.4.

29. Davies, P. N., 'British shipping and world trade', in Yui, T. and Nakagawa,

K. (eds.), *Business History of Shipping: Strategy and Structure*, Proceedings of the Fuji Conference, University of Tokyo (1985), pp.80–1.

30. Quoted in Howarth, D. and Howarth, S., *The Story of P&O*, Weidenfeld & Nicolson (1986), p.171.

31. Davies, 'British Shipping and World Trade', p.80; Sturmey, *British Shipping and World Competition*, pp.61, 70–3.

32. Hope, Ronald, *A New History of British Shipping*, John Murray, London (1990), pp.368, 399.

33. Middlemiss, Norman, *Travels of the Tramps: Twenty Tramp Fleets*, Shield Publications, Newcastle (1989), Vol.1, p.11.

34. Ibid., pp.109–13.

35. Sturmey, *British Shipping*.

36. Ibid., p.96.

37. Ibid., p.396.

38. Fletcher, Max, 'From coal to oil in British shipping', *The Journal of Transport History*, Vol. III, no. 1 (1975), p.6.

39. Ibid., p.10.

40. Robertson, Alex J., 'Backward British businessmen and the motor ship, 1918–39: the critique reviewed', *The Journal of Transport History*, Vol. 9, no.2 (1988), p.193.

41. Fletcher, 'From coal to oil', p.5.

42. Robertson, 'Backward British businessmen', p.196.

43. Ibid.

44. Sturmey, *British Shipping*, p.352.

45. Sugiyama, K. (1985), 'Shipbuilding finance of the shasen shipping firms: 1920s–1930s', in Yui and Nakagawa (eds.), pp.255–72.

46. Yui and Nakagawa, *Business History of Shipping*, p.xxii.

47. Nakagawa, K., 'Japanese Shipping in the Nineteenth and Twentieth Centuries: Strategy and Organisation', in Yui and Nakagawa p.14.

48. Sturmey, *British Shipping*, p.109.

49. Hope, *New History of British Shipping*, p.318.

50. Davies, 'British Shipping and World Trade', p.60.

51. Sturmey, *British Shipping*, p.396.

52. Ibid., p.78.

53. Ibid., p.94.

54. Ibid., p.262.

55. Hope, *New History*, p.369.

56. Sturmey, *British Shipping*, p.76.

57. Hope, *New History*, p.416.

58. Sturmey, *British Shipping*, p.61.

59. Ibid., pp.106–7.

60. Strange, J.,'Oil Tankers, Chemical Carriers and Gas Carriers', in Gardiner, R. and Greenhill, Basil (eds.), *The Shipping Revolution: The Modern Merchant Ship*, Conway Maritime Press, London (1992), p.66.

61. Sturmey, *British Shipping*, p.400.

62. Quoted in Hope, *New History*, p.399.

Chapter 13   Pacific Tsunami

1. Nelson, Richard R. and Wright, Gavin, 'The rise and fall of American technological leadership: the postwar era in historical perspective', *Journal of Economic Literature* (1992), Vol. XXX, pp.1931–64.

2. Dennison, Edward and Puillier, Jean-Pierre, *Why Growth Rates Differ*, Brookings Institution, Washington D.C. (1967) referred to in ibid.

3. Galbraith, J. K., *The New Industrial State*, 2nd ed., Andre Deutsch, London (1967), p.58.

4. Snowman, D. *America Since 1920*, Heinemann, London (1980) p.137.

5. Ibid., p.141.

6. Dertouzos, Michael L., Lester, Richard K., Solow, Robert M. and the MIT Commission on Industrial Productivity, *Made in America: Regaining the Productive Edge*, Massachusetts Institute of Technology Press, Cambridge, Mass.(1989), p.24.

7. Bauer, Jack K., *A Maritime History of the United States: The Role of America's Seas and Waterways*, University of South Carolina Press (1988), pp.309–11.

8. de la Pedraja, Rene, *A Historical Dictionary of the US Merchant Marine and Shipping Industry*, Greenwood Press, Connecticut (1994), p.150.

9. de la Pedraja, Rene, *The Rise and Decline of US Merchant Shipping in the Twentieth Century*, Twayne's Evolution of American Business Series, no. 8, Twayne Publishers, New York (1992), p.218.

10. Safford, J. J., 'The United States merchant marine in foreign trade, 1800–1939', in Yui, T. and Nakagawa, K. (eds.), *Business History of Shipping: Strategy and Structure*, Proceedings of the Fuji Conference, University of Tokyo (1985), pp.91–118.

11. de la Pedraja, *A Historical Dictionary*, p.151.

12. Toyoda, E., *Toyoda Fifty Years in Motion: An Autobiography of the Chairman*, Kodansha International (1985), p.49.

13. Ibid., p.49

14. Ibid., p.53.

15. Ibid., p.57.

16. Ibid., pp.58–9.

17. Aoki, Masahiko, 'Towards an economic model of the Japanese firm', *Journal of Economic Litterature* (1990), Vol. XXVIII, pp.1–27.

18. Hayes, Robert H. and Abernathy, William J., 'Managing our way to economic decline', *Harvard Business Review* 58 (1980), pp.67–77.

19. Allen, G. C., *A Short Economic History of Japan*, 4th ed., Macmillan, London (1981), p.206

20. Ibid., p.227.

21. Zimbalist, A., Sherman H. J. and Brown, S., *Comparing Economic Systems*, 2nd ed., Harcourt Brace Jovanovich International edition (1989), p.54.

22. Ohkawa, K. and Kohama, H., *Lectures on Developing Economies: Japan's Experience and its Relevance*, University of Tokyo Press (1989).

23. Hirschmeier, Johannes and Yui, Tsunehiko, *The Development of Japanese Business 1600–1980*, 2nd ed., George Allen & Unwin, London (1981), p.315.

24. Amsden, Alice H. and Singh, Ajit, 'The optimal degree of competition and dynamic efficiency in Japan and Korea', *European Economic Review* 38 (1994), pp.941–51.

25. Johnson, C., *MITI and the Japanese Miracle*, Stanford University Press (1982), p.240.

26. Freeman, C., 'Japan: a new national system of innovation', in Dosi, G., Freeman, C., Nelson, R., Silverberg, G. and Soete, L. (eds.) *Technical Change and Economic Theory*, Pinter Press, London (1988), p.333.

27. Quoted in Ohkawa, and Kohama, *Lectures on Developing Economies*, p.286.

28. Freeman, 'Japan', p.337; Aoki, 'Towards an economic model'.

29. Hayes and Abernathy, 'Managing our way', p.74.

30. Dertouzos et al., *Made in America*, p.21.

31. Hayes and Abernathy, Managing our way', p.68.

32. Dertouzos et al., *Made in America*, p.46.

33. Ibid., p.51.

34. Chida, Tomohei and Davies, Peter N., *The Japanese Shipping and Shipbuilding Industries: A History of their Modern Growth*, Athlone Press, London (1990), p.113.

35. Dertouzos et al., *Made in America*, p.94

36. Lazonick, William, *Business Organisation and the Myth of the Market Economy*, Cambridge University Press (1991), p.38.

37. Aoki, 'Towards an economic model'.

38. Quoted in Allen, *Short Economic History of Japan*, p.234.

39. Miwa, R., 'Maritime Policy in Japan: 1868–1937', in Yui and Nakagawa (eds.), *Business History of Shipping*, pp.123–52.

40. de la Pedraja, *Rise and Decline of US Merchant Shipping*, op. cit., p.100.

41. Ibid., p.163.

42. Ibid., p.172.

43. Ibid., p.176.

44. Chida and Davies, *Japanese Shipping and Shipbuilding Industries*, p.101.

45. de la Pedraja, *Rise and Decline of US Merchant Shipping*, p.159.

46. Ibid., p.162.

47. de la Pedraja, *A Historical Dictionary*, pp.324–8.

48. Bauer, *A Maritime History*, p.323.

49. Whitehurst, Clinton H., *The US Merchant Marine: In Search of an Enduring Maritime Policy*, United States Naval Institute, Annapolis, Md (1983), p.146.

50. Mansfield, Edwin, 'Industrial innovation in Japan and the United States', Science 241, Vol.1 (1988), pp.1769–74.

51. Chida and Davies, *Japanese Shipping*, p.152.

52. Quoted in de la Pedraja, *Rise and Decline of US Merchant Shipping* p.178.

53. Chida and Davies, *Japanese Shipping*, p.145.

54. Bauer, *A Maritime History*, p.321.

55. de la Pedraja, *Rise and Decline of US Merchant Shipping*, p.283.

56. Whitehurst, *US Merchant Marine*, p.42.

57. Ibid., p.105.

58. de la Pedraja, *Rise and Decline of US Merchant Shipping Century*, p.219.

59. Ibid.

60. Whitehurst, *US Merchant Marine*, p.105.

Chapter 14 A Rapidly Changing World

1. Castelli, Emilio, 'Power shifts and economic development: when will China overtake the USA?', *Journal of Peace Research* Issue 40 (2003), pp.661–75.

2. 'China ahead in foreign direct investment', OECD *Observer*, Issue 237 (2003), p.56.

3. Collins, David, *Organizational Change: Sociological Perspectives*, Routledge, London (1998).

4. Kotter, John P., 'Leading change: why transformation efforts fail', *Harvard Business Review*, March–April 1995, pp.59–67.

5. Grove, Andrew, *Only the Paranoid Survive*, Currency, New York (1999), p.91.

6. Hope, Ronald, *A New History of British Shipping*, John Murray, London (1990), p.458.

BIBLIOGRAPHY

BRITAIN

Alford, B. W. E., 'New industries for old? British industry between the wars', in Floud, R. C. and McCloskey, D. N. (eds.), *The Economic History of Britain since 1770*, Vol.2, Cambridge University Press (1981), pp.308–31.

Anderson, G. M., 'The economic organisation of the East India trade', *Journal of Economic Behaviour and Organization* (1983), Vol.4, pp.221–38.

Andrews, Kenneth R., 'The Elizabethan seaman', *Mariner's Mirror* (1982), Vol.68, No.3, pp.245–62.

Burton, Anthony, *The Rise and Fall of British Shipbuilding*, Constable, London (1994).

Cairncross, Alec, 'The Postwar Years, 1945–77', in Floud, R. C. and McCloskey, D. N. (eds.), *The Economic History of Britain since 1770*, Cambridge University Press (1981), Vol.2, pp.370–415.

Central Office of Information, *British Industry Today: Shipping*, London (1974).

Chaudhuri, K. N., 'The English East India Company's shipping (c.1660– 1760)', in Bruijn, Jaap R. and Gasstra, Femme S. (eds.), *Ships, Sailors and Spices*, Neha, Amsterdam (1993), pp.49–80.

Corbett, E. C., 'The screw propeller and merchant shipping, 1840–1865', in Gardiner, B. and Greenhill, B. (eds.), *The Advent of Steam: The Merchant Steamship Before 1900*, Conway Maritime Press, London (1993), pp.83–105.

Cummins, John, *Francis Drake: The Lives of a Hero*, Weidenfeld & Nicolson, London (1995).

Davies, P. N., 'British shipping and world trade', in Yui, T. and Nakagawa, K. (eds.),

Business History of Shipping: Strategy and Structure, Proceedings of the Fuji Conference, University of Tokyo (1985), pp.39–85.

Davis, Ralph, *A Commercial Revolution: English Overseas Trade in the Seventeenth and Eighteenth Centuries*, The Historical Association, London (1967).

Davis, Ralph, *The Rise of the English Shipping Industry in the Seventeenth and Eighteenth Centuries*, Macmillan, London (1962).

Duncan, T. and Foggarty, J., *Australia and Argentina on Parallel Paths*, Melbourne University Press (1984).

Fletcher, Max E., 'From Coal to Oil in British Shipping', *The Journal of Transport History* (1975), Vol.3, No.1.

Floud, R. C. and McCloskey, D. N., *The Economic History of Britain Since 1770: Vol.1, 1700–1860*, Cambridge University Press (1981).

Floud, R. C. and McCloskey, D. N., *The Economic History of Britain Since 1770: Vol.2, 1860 to the 1970s*, Cambridge University Press (1981).

Gardiner, R. and Greenhill, B. (eds.), *Sails Last Century: The Merchant Sailing Ship, 1830–1930*, Conway Maritime Press, London (1993).

Green, E., 'Very private enterprise: ownership and finance in British shipping, 1825–1940', in Yui, T. and Nakagawa, K. (eds.), *Business History of Shipping: Strategy and Structure*, Proceedings of the Fuji Conference, University of Tokyo (1985), pp.219–48.

Greenhill, B., 'Introduction', in Gardiner, R. and Greenhill, B., *The Advent of Steam: The Merchant Steamship Before 1900*, Conway Maritime Press, London (1993), pp.7–10.

Greenhill, B., 'Steam before the screw', in Gardiner, R. and Greenhill, B., *The Advent of Steam: The Merchant Steamship Before 1900*, Conway Maritime Press, London (1993), pp.11–27.

Harley, C. K., 'Aspects of the economics of shipping, 1850–1913', in Lewis, R. Fischer and Panting, G. E. (eds.), *Change and Adaptation in Maritime History: The North Atlantic Fleets in the Nineteenth Century*, St Johns, Newfoundland (1985).

Harley, C. K., 'Ocean freight rates and productivity, 1740–1930: the primacy of mechanical invention confirmed', *Journal of Economic History* 48(4) (1988), pp. 851–76.

Harley, C. K. and McCloskey, D. N., 'Foreign trade: competition and the expanding international economy', in Floud, R. C. and McCloskey, D. N. (eds.), *The*

Economic History of Britain Since 1770: Vol.2, 1860 to the 1970s, Cambridge University Press (1981), pp.50–69.

HMSO, *Decline in the UK Registered Merchant Fleet*, London (1987).

Hope, Ronald, *A New History of British Shipping*, John Murray, London (1990).

Howarth, D. and Howarth, S., *The Story of P&O*, Weidenfeld & Nicolson, London (1986).

Keay, John, *The Honourable Company: A History of the English East India Company*, HarperCollins, London (1991).

Kennedy, Paul, *The Rise and Fall of British Naval Mastery*, Penguin, London (1976).

Klingender, Francis, *Art and the Industrial Revolution*, Evelyn, Adams & Mackay, Chatham (1968).

Knowles, L. C. A., *Economic Development of the Overseas Empire*, Vol.1, 2nd edn, George Routledge & Sons, London (1928).

Lambert, A., 'The Ship Propeller Company and the promotion of screw propulsion, 1836–1852', in Gardiner, R. and Greenhill, B., *The Advent of Steam: The Merchant Steamship Before 1900*, Conway Maritime Press, London (1993), pp.136–45.

Lloyd, T. O., *The British Empire, 1558–1983*, Oxford University Press (1984).

Lorenz, Edward, 'Organisational inertia and competitive decline: the British cotton, shipbuilding and car industries, 1945–1975', *Industrial and Corporate Change*, Vol.3, no.1 (1994).

McCloskey, D. N., 'The Industrial Revolution, 1780–1860', in Floud, R. C. and McCloskey, D. N. (eds.), *The Economic History of Britain since 1770*, Vol.1, Cambridge University Press (1981), pp.103–27.

McCracken, Grant, *Culture and Consumption*, Indiana University Press, Bloomington and Indianapolis (1988).

MacGregor, David R., 'The wooden sailing ship: over 300 tons', in Gardiner, R. and Greenhill, B. (eds.), *Sail's Last Century*, Conway Maritime Press, London (1993), pp.20–41.

McKendrick, N., 'Commercialisation and the Economy', in McKendrick, N., Brewer, K. and Plumb, J. H., *The Birth of a Consumer Society*, Europa, London (1982), pp.9–194.

McKendrick, N., Brewer, K. and Plumb, J. H., *The Birth of a Consumer Society: The Commercialization of Eighteenth Century England*, Europa, London (1982).

MacKenzie-Kennedy, C., *The Atlantic Blue Riband: Evolution of the Express Liner*, Ebor Press, York (1993).

Marshall, P., 'Private British trade in the Indian Ocean before 1800', in Das Gupta, A. and Pearson, M. N. (eds.), *India and the Indian Ocean 1500–1800*, Oxford University Press (1987), pp.276–300.

Middlemiss, Norman L., *Travels of the Tramps: Twenty Tramp Fleets*, Vol.1, Shield Publication, Newcastle (1989).

Middleton, Sir Henry, *The Voyage of Sir Henry Middleton to the Moluccas, 1604–1606*, Hakluyt Society, London (1943).

Milton, G., *Nathaniel's Nutmeg*, Hodder & Stoughton, London (1999).

North, D. C., 'Sources of productivity change in ocean shipping, 1600–1850', *Journal of Political Economy* 76 (1968), pp.953–70.

Plumb, J. H., 'Commercialisation and society', in McKendrick et al., *The Birth of a Consumer Society*, Europa, London (1982), pp.265–334.

Pollard, Sidney and Robertson, Paul, *The British Shipbuilding Industry, 1870–1914*, Harvard University Press (1979).

Robertson, Alex J., 'Backward British businessmen and the motor ship, 1918–39: the critique reviewed', *The Journal of Transport History*, Vol.9, no.2 (1988).

Roger, N. A. M., *The Safeguard of the Sea: A Naval History of Britain*, Vol.1, HarperCollins, London (1997).

Rolt, L. T. C., *Isambard Kingdom Brunel*, 6th edn, Longman, London (1970).

Root, J. W., *Trade Relations of the British Empire*, J. W. Root, Liverpool (1903).

Rose, M. E., 'Social change and the Industrial Revolution', in Floud, R. C., and McCloskey, D. N. (eds.), *The Economic History of Britain since 1770*, Vol.1, Cambridge University Press (1981), pp.253–75.

Ryan, A. N., 'Bristol, the Atlantic and North America, 1480–1509', in Hattendorf, John B. (ed.), *Maritime History: Vol. 1, The Age of Discovery*, Krieger Publishing Company, Florida (1996), pp.241–55.

Sandberg, L. G., 'The entrepreneur and technological change', in Floud, R. C. and McCloskey, D. N. (eds.), *The Economic History of Britain since 1770*, Vol.2, Cambridge University Press (1981), pp.99–120.

Sandberg, L. G., *Lancashire in Decline: A Study in Entrepreneurship, Technology, and International Trade*, Ohio State University Press, Columbus (1974).

Scammel, G., 'European seamanship in the great age of discovery', *Mariner's Mirror*, Vol.68, No.4 (1982).

Smith, Adam, *An Inquiry into the Nature and Causes of the Wealth and Poverty of Nations*, J.M. Dent & Sons, London (1921).

Smith, Crosbie, 'Britain's shipbuilders: the years of progress, 1840–1914', *Transport History*, Vol.11 (1980), pp.258–72.

Smith, Crosbie, 'Britain's shipbuilders: part 2, the years of depression, 1919–1939', *Transport History*, Vol.12 (1981), pp. 93–116.

Starkey, D., 'The economic and military significance of British privateering, 1702–83', *The Journal of Transport History*, Vol.9, no.1 (1988), pp.50–59.

Starkey, D., 'The industrial development of steam', in Gardiner, R. and Greenhill, B. (eds.), *The Advent of Steam: The Merchant Steamship before 1900*, Conway Maritime Press, London (1993), pp.127–35.

Steven, Margaret, *Trade, Tactics and Territory*, Melbourne University Press (1983).

Strange, J., 'Oil tankers, chemical carriers and gas carriers', in Gardiner, R. and Greenhill, B. (eds.), *The Shipping Revolution: The Modern Merchant Ship*, Conway Maritime Press, London (1992), pp.63–83.

Sturmey, S. G., *British Shipping and World Competition*, Athlone Press, London (1962).

Thomas, R. P., 'Overseas trade and empire, 1700–1860', in Floud, R. C. and McCloskey, D. N. (eds.), *The Economic History of Britain since 1770*, Vol.1, Cambridge University Press (1981), pp.87–102.

Tomlinson, Jim, 'The failure of the Anglo-American Council of Productivity', *Business History*, Vol.33, no.1 (1991), pp.82–92.

Von Tunzelmann, G. N., 'Technical progress during the Industrial Revolution', in Floud, R. C. and McCloskey, D. N. (eds.), *The Economic History of Britain since 1770*, Vol.1, Cambridge University Press (1981), pp.143–63.

Wadsworth, Alfred P. and de Lacy Mann, Julia, *The Cotton Trade and Industrial Lancashire, 1600–1780*. Manchester University Press (1931).

Weiner, H. J., *English Culture and the Decline of the Industrial Spirit, 1850–1980*, Cambridge University Press (1981).

Williams, L. J., *Britain and the World Economy, 1919–1970*. Fontana-Collins, London (1971).

Wilson, Charles, *England's Apprenticeship, 1603–1763*, Longman, London (1965).

401

CHINA

Adshead, S. A. M., *China in World History*, 2nd edn, St Martin's Press, New York (1995).

Atterbury, Paul (ed.), *The History of Porcelain*, Obis Publishing, London (1982).

Balazs, E., *Chinese Civilisation and Bureaucracy: Variations on a Theme*, Yale University Press, New Haven and London (1964).

Beamish, J., 'The significance of yuan blue and white exported to South East Asia', in Scott, Rosemary and Gay, John (eds.), *South East Asia and China: Art Interaction and Commerce* (1995), pp.225–51. 4.

Braudel, F., *Civilisation and Capitalism*, Vol.1, Collins, London (1984).

Chang, Pin-tsun, 'The evolution of Chinese thought on maritime trade from the sixteenth to eighteenth century', *International Journal of Maritime History*, 1,1 June 1989, pp.51–64.

Chen, Gideon, *The Pioneer Promoters of Modern Industrial Technique in China: Three Studies*, Paragon Book Reprint Corporation, New York (1968).

Cheong, W. E., *Mandarins and Merchants: Jardine Matheson and Co., A China Agency of the Early Nineteenth Century*, Scandinavian Institute of Asian Studies: Monograph Series No.26., Curzon Press (1979).

Chuimei, Ho, 'Intercultural influence between China and South East Asia as seen in historical ceramics', in Scott, Rosemary and Gay, John (eds.), *South East Asia and China: Art Interaction and Commerce* (1995), pp.118–40.

Crammer-Byng, J. L. (ed.), *An Embassy to China: Lord MacCartney's Journal, 1793–4*, Longman, London (1962).

Dupoizat, M. F., 'The ceramic cargo of a Song dynasty junk found in the Philippines and its significance in the China–South East Asian trade', in Scott, Rosemary and Gay, John (eds.), *South East Asia and China: Art Interaction and Commerce* (1995), pp.205–24.

Endicott-West, Elizabeth, 'The Yuan government and society', in Franke, H. and Twitchett, D. (eds.), *The Cambridge History of China* (1994), pp.587–615.

Elvin, Mark, *The Pattern of the Chinese Past*, Eyre Methuen, London (1973).

Franke, H., 'The Chin dynasty', in Franke, H. and Twitchett, D. (eds.), *The Cambridge History of China* (1994), pp.215–320.

Franke, H. and Twitchett, D. (eds.), *The Cambridge History of China: Vol. 6, Alien Regimes and Border States*, Cambridge University Press (1994), pp. 907–1368.

BIBLIOGRAPHY

Gang Deng, *Chinese Maritime Activities and Socio-economic Development c.2100 BC –1900 AD*, Greenwood Press, Conn. (1997).

Gang Deng, 'An evolution of the role of Admiral Zheng He's voyages in Chinese maritime history', *International Journal of Maritime History*, Vol.7 No.2 (1995).

Gang Deng, *Maritime Sector Institutions and Sea Power of Premodern China*, Greenwood Press, Conn. (1999).

Godden, Geoffrey A., *Oriental Export Market Porcelain and Its Influence on European Wares*, Granada Publishing, London (1979).

Gungwu, Wang, 'Merchants without empire: the Hokkien sojourning communities', in Tracy, James (ed.), *The Rise of Merchant Empires: Long Distance Trade in the Early Modern World, 1350–1750*, Cambridge University Press (1990), pp.400–422.

Hao, Yen Ping, *The Comprador in Nineteenth-Century China: Bridge between East and West*, Harvard University Press, Cambridge, Mass. (1970).

Hillier, Bevis, *Pottery and Porcelain, 1700–1914*, Weidenfeld & Nicolson, London (1968).

Hodder, Rupert, *Merchant Princes of the East*, Wiley, Chichester (1996).

Humble, Richard, *Marco Polo*, Weidenfeld & Nicolson, London (1975).

Ishii, Yoneo (ed.), *The Junk Trade from Southeast Asia: Translations from the Tosen Fusetsu-gaki, 1674–1723*, Institute of Southeast Asian Studies, Singapore (1998).

Jones, E. L., 'The real question about China: why was the Song economic achievement not repeated?' *Australian Economic History Review* Vol.30 (1990).

Jones, E., Frost, L. and White, C., *Coming Full Circle: An Economic History of the Pacific Rim*. Westview Press, Boulder, Col., and Oxford (1993).

Latourette, K. S., *The Chinese: Their History and Culture*, 3rd edn, Macmillan, New York (1960).

Lenz, W., 'Voyages of Admiral Zheng He before Columbus', in Mathews, K. S. (ed.), *Shipbuilding and Navigation in the Indian Ocean Region AD1400–1800*, Munshiram Manoharlal Publishers, New Delhi (1997), pp.147–54.

Levathes, Louise, *When China Ruled the Seas: The Treasure Fleet of the Dragon Throne, 1405–33*, Simon & Schuster, New York (1994).

Lin, Lee Chor, 'Textiles in Sino-South East Asian Trade: Song, Yuan and Ming dynasties', in Scott, Rosemary and Gay, John (eds.), *South East Asia and China: Art Interaction and Commerce* (1995), pp.171–86.

Liu, K. C., 'Steamship enterprise in nineteenth-century China', *Journal of Asian Studies* 18 (1959).

Lo, C. P., *Hong Kong*, Belhaven Press, London (1992).

Medley, Margaret, *The Chinese Potter: A Practical History of Chinese Ceramics*, 3rd edn, Phaidon Press, Oxford (1989).

Merson, John, *Roads to Xanadu: East and West in the Making of the Modern World*, Weidenfeld & Nicolson, London (1989).

Morse, H. B., *The Guilds of China*, Longman, Green, London (1909).

Murphey, Rhoads, *The Treaty Ports and China's Modernization: What Went Wrong?*, Michigan Papers in Chinese Studies, No.7, University of Michigan Centre for Chinese Studies (1970).

Needham, Joseph, 'Poverties and triumphs of the Chinese scientific tradition', in Crombie (ed.), *Scientific Change: Historical Studies in the Intellectual, Social and Technical Conditions for Scientific Discovery and Technical Invention from Antiquity to the Present*, Heinemann, London (1963), pp. 117–53.

Needham, Joseph, *Science and Civilisation in China*, Vol.4, Part III and Vol.3, Sections 21 and 22, Cambridge (1971).

Ping Ti Ho, 'Economic and institutional factors in the decline of the Chinese empire', in Cipolla, Carlo M. (ed.), *The Economic Decline of Empires*, Methuen, London (1970), pp.264–77.

Polo, Marco, *The Travels*, Penguin, London (1958).

Reid, Anthony, 'The unthreatening alternative: Chinese shipping to Southeast Asia, 1567–1842', *Review of Indonesian and Malaysian Affairs* 27 (1993), pp.13–32.

Rossabi, Morris, 'The reign of Khubilai Khan', in Franke, H. and Twitchett, D. (eds.), *The Cambridge History of China* (1994), pp.414–89.

Scott, Rosemary and Gay, John (eds.), *South East Asia and China: Art Interaction and Commerce*, Percival David Foundation of Chinese Art, No.17 (1995).

Seagrave, Sterling, *Lords of the Rim: The Invisible Empire of the Overseas Chinese*, G. P. Putnam's Sons, New York (1995).

Shiba, Yoshinobu, *Commerce and Society in Sung China*, trans. Mark Elvin, Michigan Abstracts of Chinese and Japanese Works on Chinese History, No.2 (1970).

Silcock, Arnold, *An Introduction to Chinese Art and History*, 3rd edn, Faber and Faber, London (1947).

Speiser, Werner, *China: Art of the World – A Series of Regional Histories of the Visual Arts*, Methuen, London (1960).

Spence, Jonathan, *The Gate of Heavenly Peace: The Chinese and their Revolution, 1895–1980*, Faber and Faber, London (1982).

Sullivan, Michael, *The Arts of China*, Thames & Hudson, London (1973).

Teng, Ssu Yu and Fairbank, John K., *China's Response to the West*, Harvard University Press, Cambridge, Mass. (1954).

Viraphol, Sarasin, *Tribute and Profit: Sino-Siamese Trade, 1652–1853*, Council on East Asian Studies, Harvard University, Cambridge, Mass. (1977).

Watson, Andrew, *Transport in Transition: The Evolution of Traditional Shipping in China*, Michigan Abstracts of Chinese and Japanese Works on Chinese History, University of Michigan (1972).

Wong, Chu-Ming, 'Commentary', in Crombie (ed.), *Scientific Change: Historical Studies in the Intellectual, Social and Technical Conditions for Scientific Discovery and Technical Invention from Antiquity to the Present*, Heinemann, London (1963), pp.166–7.

Wong, Lin Ken, 'The Trade of Singapore, 1819–69', *Journal of the Malaysian Branch of the Royal Asiatic Society*, Vol.33, Part 4, December 1960.

EUROPE

Arruda, Jose Jobson de Andrade, (1991), 'Colonies as mercantile investments: the Luso Brazilian empire, 1500–1808', in Tracy, James (ed.), *The Political Economy of Merchant Empires: State Power and World Trade, 1350–1750*, Cambridge University Press (1991),

Austen, Ralph A., *African Economic History: Internal Development and External Dependency*, Heinemann, Portsmouth (1987).

de Barros, J., 'Pioneers of Portuguese navigation in the Indian Ocean', in Mathews, K. S. (ed.), *Shipbuilding and Navigation in the Indian Ocean Region, AD1400–1800*, Minshiram Manoharlal Publishers, New Delhi (1997), pp.165–71.

Bill, Jan, 'Ship construction, tools and techniques', in Gardiner, R. and Greenhill, B. (eds.), Cogs, *Caravels and Galleons: The Sailing Ship, 1000–1650*, Brassey, London (1994), pp.151–9.

Bosscher, P., 'Introduction', in Gardiner, R. and Bosscher, P. (eds.), *The Heyday of Sail*, Brassey, London (1995), pp.7–9.

Bosscher, P., 'Shipping economics and trade', in Gardiner, R. and Bosscher, P. (eds.), *The Heyday of Sail*, Brassey, London (1995), pp.133–51.

Boxer, C. R., 'The Dutch economic decline', in Cipolla, Carlo (ed.), *The Economic Decline of Empires*, Methuen, London (1970), pp.235–63.

Boxer, C. R., *The Dutch Seaborne Empire, 1600–1800*, Hutchinson, London (1965).

Boxer, C. R., *Portuguese Conquest and Commerce in Southern Asia, 1500–1700*, Variorum, Aldershot (1985).

Boxer, C. R., *The Portuguese Seaborne Empire*, Hutchinson, London (1969).

Boxer, C. R., 'War and trade in the Indian Ocean and the South China Sea, 1600–1650', *Mariner's Mirror*, Vol.71, No.4 (1985), pp.417–36.

Boyajian, J. C., *Portuguese Trade in Asia under the Hapsburgs, 1580–1640*, Johns Hopkins University Press, Baltimore (1993).

Brady, Thomas A., 'The rise of merchant empires, 1400–1700: a European counterpoint', in Tracy, James, *The Political Economy of Merchant Empires: State Power and World Trade, 1350–1750*, Cambridge University Press (1991), pp.117–60.

Bruijn, Jaap R., 'Productivity, profitability, and costs of private and corporate Dutch ship owning in the seventeenth and eighteenth centuries', in Tracy, James, *The Rise of Merchant Empires: Long Distance Trade in the Early Modern World, 1350–1750*, Cambridge University Press (1990), pp.174–94.

Bruijn, Jaap R. and Gaastra, Femme S. (eds.), *Ships, Sailors and Spices: East India Companies and their Shipping in the 16th, 17th and 18th Centuries*, Neha, Amsterdam (1993).

Cipolla, Carlo M. (ed.), *The Economic Decline of Empires*, Methuen, London (1970).

Cipolla, Carlo M., *Guns, Sails and Empires: Technological Innovation and the Early Phases of European Expansion, 1400–1700*, Pantheon Books, New York. (1965).

Clayton, Lawrence A., 'Ships and empire: the case of Spain', *Mariner's Mirror*, Vol.62, No.3 (1976), pp.235–48.

De Jonge, C. H., *Delft Ceramics*, Pall Mall Press, London (1970).

Descola, J., *The Conquistadors*, Allen & Unwin, London (1957).

De Vries, J., *The Economy of Europe in an Age of Crisis, 1600–1750*, Cambridge University Press (1976).

De Vries, J. and van de Woude, A., *The First Modern Economy*, Cambridge University Press (1997).

Duncan, T. Bentley, 'Navigation between Portugal and Asia in the sixteenth and seventeenth centuries', in Van Kley, E. J. and Pullapilly, C. K. (eds.), *Asia and the West: Encounters and Exchanges from the Age of Explorations: Essays in Honor of Donald F. Lach*, Cross Roads, Notre Dame, Ill. (1986), pp.3–25.

Elbl, Martin and Phillips, Carla Rahn, 'The caravel and the galleon', in Gardiner, R. and Greenhill, B. (eds.), *Cogs, Caravels and Galleons: The Economic Decline of Empires*, Methuen, London (1994), pp.91–114.

Elliot, J. H., *The Count Duke of Olivares: The Statesman in an Age of Decline*, Yale University Press (1986).

Elliot, J. H., 'The decline of Spain', in Cipolla, *The Economic Decline of Empires*, Methuen, London (1970), pp.168–95.

Emmer, P., *The Dutch in the Atlantic Economy, 1580–1880*, Variorum, Aldershot (1998).

French, C., 'Merchant shipping of the British empire', in Gardiner, R. and Bosscher, P. (eds.), *The Heyday of Sail: The Merchant Sailing Ship, 1650–1830*, Brassey, London (1995), pp.10–33.

Friel, Ian, 'The carrack: the advent of the full rigged ship', in Gardiner, R. and Greenhill, B. (eds.), *Cogs, Caravels and Galleons: The Sailing Ship, 1000 –1650*, Brassey, London (1994), pp.77–90.

Gardiner, R. and Bosscher, P. (eds.), *The Heyday of Sail: The Merchant Sailing Ship, 1650–1830*, Brassey, London (1995).

Gardiner, R. and Greenhill, B. (eds.), *Cogs, Caravels and Galleons: The Sailing Ship, 1000–1650*, Brassey, London (1994).

Geyl, Pieter, *The Netherlands in the Seventeenth Century, 1609–1648*, Vols.1 and 2, rev. edn, Ernest Benn, London, (1961).

Gies, Francis and Joseph, *Cathedral, Forge and Waterwheel: Technology and Innovation in the Middle Ages*, HarperCollins, New York (1994).

Goodman, David, *Spanish Naval Power, 1589–1665: Reconstruction and Defeat*, Cambridge University Press (1997).

Haring, C. H., *The Spanish Empire in America*, Harbinger Books, New York (1963).

Haring, C. H., *Trade and Navigation between Spain and the Indies in the Time of the Hapsburgs*, Harvard University Press (1964).

Hattendorf, John B., *Maritime History: Vol. 1, The Age of Discovery*, Krieger Publishing Company, Florida (1996).

Hoberman, Louis Schell, *Mexico's Merchant Elite, 1590–1660: Silver, State and Society*, Duke University Press (1991).

Hoving, A. J., 'Seagoing ships of the Netherlands', in Gardiner, R. and Bosscher, P. (eds.), *The Heyday of Sail: The Merchant Sailing Ship, 1650–1830*, Brassey, London (1995), pp.34–54.

Hunt, Edwin S. and Murray, J., *A History of Business in Medieval Europe, 1200–1500*, Cambridge University Press (1999).

Israel, J. I., *Dutch Primacy in World Trade, 1585–1740*, Clarendon Press, Oxford (1989).

Israel, J. I., *Empires and Entrepôts: The Dutch, the Spanish Monarchy and the Jews 1585–1713*, Hambledon Press, London (1990).

Jago, Charles, 'The crisis of the aristocracy in seventeenth century Castile', *Past and Present* 84 (1979), pp.60–90.

Kamen, Henry, *Spain, 1469–1714: A Society of Conflict*, Longman House. (1983).

Kennedy, Paul, *The Rise and Fall of the Great Powers*, Unwin & Hyman, London (1988).

Landes, David S., *The Unbound Prometheus: Technological Change and Industrial Development in Western Europe from 1750 to the Present*, Cambridge University Press (1969).

Landes, David, *The Wealth and Poverty of Nations*, W. W. Norton, New York and London (1998).

Lane, F., *Venice: A Maritime Republic*, Johns Hopkins University Press, Baltimore (1973).

Lee, S. J., *Aspects of European History, 1494–1789*, 2nd edn, Methuen, London (1984).

Lewis, Arthur W., *The Evolution of the International Economic Order*, Princeton University Press, NJ (1978).

Lobato, M., 'Maritime trade from India to Mozambique: A study of Indo-Portuguese enterprise (16th to 17th centuries)', in Mathews, K. S. (ed.), *Shipbuilding and Navigation in the Indian Ocean Region, AD1400–1800*, Munshiram Manoharlal Publishers, New Delhi (1997), pp.113–131.

Lopez, Robert S., *The Commercial Revolution of the Middle Ages, 950–1350*, Prentice Hall, New York (1971).

Lundahl, Mats, 'Spain and the conquest of America', in Lundahl, Mats (ed.), *Themes in International Economic*, Ashgate, Aldershot (1998), pp.99–134.

McNeill, W. H., *The Rise of the West*, University of Chicago Press (1963).

Magelhaes Godinho, V., 'The Portuguese and the "Carreira da India", 1497–1810', in Bruijn, Jaap R. and Gaastra, Femme S. (eds.), *Ships, Sailors and Spices*, Neha, Amsterdam (1993), pp.1–48.

Mathews, K. S. (ed.), *Shipbuilding and Navigation in the Indian Ocean Region, AD 1400–1800*, Munshiram Manoharlal Publishers, New Delhi (1997).

Mauro, Frederic, 'Merchant communities, 1350–1750', in Tracy, James (ed.), *The Rise of Merchant Empires: Long Distance Trade in the Early Modern World*, 1350–1750, Cambridge University Press (1990), pp.255–86.

Menard, Russel R., 'Transport costs and long range trade 1300–1800: was there a European transport revolution in the early modern era?', in Tracy, James (ed.), 1991, *The Political Economy of Merchant Empires: State Power and World Trade, 1350–1750*, Cambridge University Press (1991), pp.228–75.

Mollat du Jourdin, M., *Europe and the Sea*, Blackwell, Cambridge (1993).

Neal, L., 'The Dutch and English East India Companies compared: evidence from the stock and foreign exchange markets', in Tracy, James (ed.), *The Rise of Merchant Empires: Long Distance Trade in the Early Modern World, 1350–1750*, Cambridge University Press (1990), pp.195–223.

North, D. C. and Thomas, R. P., *The Rise of the Western World*, Cambridge University Press (1973).

North, M., *Art and Commerce in the Dutch Golden Age*, Yale University Press (1997).

Parr, Charles McKew, *Jan van Linschoten: The Dutch Marco Polo*, Thomas Y. Crowell Company, New York (1964).

Parry, J. H, *The Spanish Seaborne Empire*, Hutchinson, London (1966).

Pearson, M. N., 'Merchants and states', in Tracy, James (ed.), *The Political Economy of Merchant Empires: State Power and World Trade, 1350–1750*, Cambridge University Press (1991), pp.41–116.

Phillips, Carla Rahn, 'The growth and composition of trade in the Iberian empires, 1450–1770', in Tracy, James (ed.), 1990 *The Rise of Merchant Empires: Long Distance Trade in the Early Modern World, 1350–1750*, Cambridge University Press (1990), pp.34–101.

Phillips, William D. and Phillips, Carla (1996), 'Columbus and the European background: the first voyage', in Hattendorf, John B. (ed.), *Maritime History: Vol. 1, The Age of Discovery*, Krieger Publishing Company, Florida (1996), pp.149–80.

Phillips, William D. and Phillips, Carla, 'The later voyages of Columbus', in Hattendorf, John B. (ed.), *Maritime History: Vol. 1., The Age of Discovery*, Krieger Publishing Company, Florida (1996), pp.181–214.

Pike, Ruth, *Aristocrats and Traders: Sevillian Society in the Sixteenth Century*, Ithaca, New York (1972).

Pires, Tome, *Suma Oriental*, Hakluyt Society, London (1994).

Price, Jacob M., 'Transaction costs: a note on merchant credit and the organization of private trade', in Tracy, James (ed.), *The Political Economy of Merchant Empires: State Power and World Trade, 1350–1750*, Cambridge University Press (1991), pp.276–97.

Roberts, J. M., *The Triumph of the West*, BBC Books, London (1985).

Rodrigues, Francisco, 'The book of Francisco Rodrigues: rutter of a voyage in the Red Sea, nautical rules, almanac and maps, written and drawn in the East before 1515', in Pires, Tome, *Suma Oriental*, Hakluyt Society, London (1994).

van Royen, P. C., 'Seamen and the merchant service, 1650–1830', in Gardiner, R. and Bosscher, P. (eds.), *The Heyday of Sail*, Brassey, London (1995), pp.152–59.

Russell, P. E., Portugal, *Spain and the African Atlantic, 1343–1490*, Variorum, Aldershot (1995).

Russell, Peter, *Prince Henry 'The Navigator': A Life*, Yale University Press (2000).

Sayous, A. E., 'Partnerships in the trade between Spain and America and also in the Spanish colonies in the sixteenth century', *Journal of Economic and Business History*, I (1928), pp.282–301.

Schama, Simon, *The Embarrassment of Riches: An Interpretation of Dutch Culture in the Golden Age*, Random House, New York (1987).

Sharp, Andrew, *The Voyages of Abel Janszoon Tasman*, Oxford University Press (1968).

Steensgaard, N., 'The growth and composition of the long distance trade of England and the Dutch Republic before 1750', in Tracy, James (ed.), *The Rise of Merchant Empires: Long Distance Trade in the Early Modern World 1350–1750*, Cambridge University Press (1990), pp.102–52.

Subrahmanyam, Sanjay and Thomas, Luis Felipe F.R. (1991), 'Evolution of empire: The Portuguese in the Indian Ocean during the sixteenth century', in Tracy, James (ed.), *The Political Economy of Merchant Empires: State Power and World Trade, 1350–1750*, Cambridge University Press (1991), pp.298–331.

Thunberg, Carl Peter, *Travels in Europe, Africa and Asia: Performed Between the Years 1770 and 1779*, 4 Vols, London (1795).

Tracy, James (ed.), *The Political Economy of Merchant Empires: State Power and World Trade, 1350–1750*, Cambridge University Press (1991).

Tracy, James (ed.), *The Rise of Merchant Empires: Long Distance Trade in the Early Modern World, 1350–1750*, Cambridge University Press (1990).

Unger, Richard, *Dutch Shipbuilding Before 1800*, Van Gorcum, Assen, The Netherlands (1978).

Unger, Richard, 'The fluit: specialist cargo vessel, 1500–1650', in Gardiner, R and Greenhill, B. (eds.), *Cogs, Caravels and Galleons: The Sailing Ship 1000–1650*, Brassey, London (1994), pp.115–30.

Unger, Richard, *The Ship in the Medieval Economy, 600–1600*, Croom Helm, London (1980).

Unger, Richard, 'Ships of the late Middle Ages', in Hattendorf, John B. (ed.), *Maritime History: Vol. 1, The Age of Discovery*, Krieger Publishing Company, Florida (1996), pp.35–50.

Unger, Richard, 'Theoretical and practical origins of methods of navigation', in Hattendorf, John B. (ed.), *Maritime History: Vol. 1, The Age of Discovery*, Krieger Publishing Company, Florida (1996), pp.21–34.

Usher, A. P., 'Spanish ships and shipbuilding in the sixteenth and seventeenth centuries', in *Facts and Figures in Economic History for E. F. Gay*, Harvard University Press (1932).

Verlinden, Charles, 'Background and beginnings of Portuguese maritime expansion', in Hattendorf, John B. (ed.), *Maritime History: Vol. 1, The Age of Discovery*, Krieger Publishing Company, Florida (1996), pp.53–68.

Verlinden, Charles, 'The big leap under Dom Jao II: from the Atlantic to the Indian Ocean', in Hattendorf, John B. (ed.), *Maritime History: Vol. 1, The Age of Discovery*, Krieger Publishing Company, Florida (1996), pp.69–84.

Verlinden, Charles, 'Italian influence in Iberian colonisation', *The Hispanic American Maritime Review*, Vol.33, May 1953, No.2.

Verlinden, Charles, 'Portuguese discoveries and international cartography', in Hattendorf. John B. (ed.), *Maritime History: Vol. 1, The Age of Discovery*, Krieger Publishing Company, Florida (1996), pp.99–110.

Vicens Vives, Jaime, 'The decline of Spain in the seventeenth century', in Cipolla, Carlo (ed.), *The Economic Decline of Empires*, Methuen, London (1970), pp.121–67.

Walton, G. M., 'Obstacles to technical diffusion in ocean shipping, 1675–1775', in *Explorations in Economic History* 8 (1970), pp.123–40.

White, L. Jr., 'What accelerated technological progress in the Western Middle Ages', in Crombie, A. C., *Scientific Change: Studies in the Intellectual, Social and Technical Conditions for Scientific Discovery and Technical Invention from Antiquity to the Present*, Heinemann, London (1963), pp.272–91.

van Zanden, J. L., *The Rise and Decline of Holland's Economy: Merchant Capitalism and the Labour Market*, Manchester University Press (1993).

Zandvliet, K., *Mapping for Money: Maps, Plans, Topographical Paintings and their Role in Dutch Overseas Expansion during the 16th and 17th Centuries*, Batavian Lion International, Amsterdam (1998).

GUJARAT AND THE INDIAN OCEAN

Alpers, Edward, 'Gujarat and the trade of East Africa, c.1500–1800', *The International Journal of African Historical Studies* 9 (1976), pp.22–44.

Arasaratnam, S., *Maritime India in the Seventeenth Century*, Oxford University Press, Delhi (1994).

Arasaratnam, S., *Maritime, Trade, Society and European Influence in Southern Asia, 1600–1800*, Variorum, Aldershot (1995).

Barbosa, Duarte, *The Book of Duarte Barbosa*, 2 Vols, Hakluyt Society, London (1921).

Burnell, A. C. (ed.), *The Voyage of John Huygen van Linschoten to the East Indies*, Hakluyt Society, LXXX, London (1885).

Chaudhuri, K. N., *Trade and Civilisation in the Indian Ocean: An Economic History from the Rise of Islam to 1750*, Cambridge University Press (1985).

Chaudhuri, K. N., *The Trading World of Asia and the English East India Company, 1660–1760*, Cambridge University Press (1978).

Dale, Stephen Frederic, *Indian Merchants and Eurasian Trade, 1600–1750*, Cambridge University Press (1994).

Das Gupta, A., *Indian Merchants and the Decline of Surat, c.1700–1750*, Franz Steiner, Weisbaden (1979). Das Gupta, A., Merchants of Maritime India, 1500–1800, Variorum, Aldershot (1994).

Digby, Simon, 'The maritime trade of India', in *Cambridge Economic History of India*, Cambridge University Press (1982), pp.125–59.

Gokhale, B. G., *Surat in the Seventeenth Century*, Scandinavian Institute of Asian Studies, Monograph series, No.28, Curzon Press (1979).

Gopal, Surendra, *Commerce and Crafts in Gujarat: 16th and 17th Centuries.* People's Publishing House, New Delhi (1975).

Habib, Ifran, 'Merchant communities in pre-colonial India', in Tracy, James (ed.), *The Rise of Merchant Empires: Long Distance Trade in the Early Modern World 1350–1750,* Cambridge University Press (1990), pp.371–99.

Hasan, A.Y. and Hill, D. R., *Islamic Technology,* Cambridge University Press (1986).

Hourani, Albert, *A History of the Arab Peoples,* Faber and Faber, London (1991).

Janaki, V. A., 'The textile industry and trade of western India with particular reference to Gujarat in the seventeenth century', *Journal of The Maharaja Sayajirao University of Baroda,* Vol.35–6, No.1 (1986–7), pp.5–26.

Johnstone, T. M. and Muir, J., 'Portuguese influences on shipbuilding in the Persian Gulf', *Mariner's Mirror,* Vol.48 (1962).

Lewis, Archibald, 'Maritime skills in the Indian Ocean, 1368–1500', *Journal of the Economic and Social History of the Orient,* Vol.16 (1973), pp.238–64.

Linschoten, J. H., *The Voyage of John Van Linschoten to the East Indies,* 2 Vols, London (1995).

McPherson, Kenneth, *The Indian Ocean: A History of People and the Sea,* Oxford University Press, New Delhi (1993).

Manguin, P. Y., 'Late medieval Asian shipbuilding in the Indian Ocean', *Moyen Orient et Océan Indien,* 2, (1986), pp.13–15.

Manguin, P.Y., 'The vanishing jong: insular Southeast Asian fleets in trade and war (fifteenth to seventeenth centuries)', in Reid, Anthony (ed.), *Southeast Asia in the Early Modern Era: Trade, Power and Belief,* Cornell University Press, Ithaca and London (1993).

Meilink-Roelofsz, M. A. P., *Asian Trade and European Influence in the Indonesian Archipelago between 1500 and about 1630,* Martinus Nighoff, The Hague (1962).

Mookerji, R. K., *Indian Shipping: A History of the Seaborne Trade and Maritime Activity of the Indians from the Earliest Times,* Kitab Mahal Private Ltd. Allahabad (1962).

Moosvi, Shireen, *The Economy of Mughul India, c.1595: A Statistical Study,* Oxford University Press, Delhi (1987).

Moreland, W. H., *India at the Death of Akbar: An Economic Study,* Atma Ram & Sons, Delhi (1962).

Moreland, W. H., 'Ships of the Arabian Sea about AD 1500', *Journal of the Royal Asiatic Society,* London (1939).

413

Naqvi, H. K., *Urban Cities and Industries in Upper India, 1556–1803*, Asia Publishing House, London (1968).

Ovington, J., *A Voyage to Surat in the Year 1689*, ed. Rawlinson, H. C., London (1929).

Pearson, M. N., *Coastal Western India: Studies from the Portuguese Records*, Concept Publishing, New Delhi (1981).

Pearson, M. N., *Merchants and Rulers in Gujarat; The Response to the Portuguese in the 16th Century*, University of California Press, Berkeley (1976).

Pearson, M. N., 'Merchants and states', in Tracy, James (ed.), *The Political Economy of Merchant Empires: State Power and World Trade, 1350–1750*, Cambridge University Press (1991), pp.41–116.

Pelsaert, Francisco, *Jahangir's India: The Remonstrantie of Francisco Pelsaert*, trans. Moreland, W. H. and Geyl, P., Jayyed Press, Delhi (1972).

Pines, S., 'What was original in Arabic science?' in Crombie (ed.), *Scientific Change: Historical Studies in the Intellectual, Social and Technical Conditions for Scientific Discovery and Technical Invention from Antiquity to the present*, Heinemann, London (1963), pp.181–205.

Qaisar, A. J., *The Indian Response to European Technology and Culture, AD 1498–1707*, Oxford University Press, Delhi (1982).

Qaisar, A. J., 'Shipbuilding in the Mughul empire during the seventeenth century', *Indian Economic and Social History Review* 5,2 June 1968.

Ravichander, A., 'Coastal society of Gujarat in the sixteenth century', Studia, Lisbon (1989), pp.161–80.

Richards, John F., *The Mughal Empire*, Cambridge University Press (1993).

Roe, Sir Thomas, *The Embassy of Sir Thomas Roe to India, 1615–19*, Oxford University Press (1926).

Sar Desai, D. R., *South East Asia: Past and Present*, Vikas Publishing House, New Delhi (1981).

Sentance, D., 'Ships and their significance in the re-appraising of Indian Ocean history', *The History of Commercial Exchange and Maritime Transport*, Section 3, International Conference on Indian Ocean Studies, I, Perth (1979).

Steensgaard, N., *Carracks, Caravans and Companies*, Copenhagen (1973). (Also published as *The Asian Trade Revolution of the Seventeenth Century: The East India Companies and the Decline of the Caravan Trade*, University of Chicago Press (1973).)

Subrahmanyam, Sanjay, Luis, Felipe and Thomas, F. R., 'Evolution of empire: the Portuguese in the Indian Ocean during the seventeenth century', in Tracy, James (ed.), *The Political Economy of Merchant Empires: State Power and World Trade, 1350–1750*, Cambridge University Press (1991), pp.298–331.

JAPAN

Allen, G. C., *A Short Economic History of Japan*, 4th edn, Macmillan, London (1981).

Amioka, Shiro, 'Changes in educational ideals and objectives: from selected documents, Tokugawa era to the Meiji period', in Burks, Ardath W. (ed.), *The Modernizers: Overseas Students, Foreign Employees and Meiji Japan*, Westview, Boulder, Col. (1985), pp.323–57.

Amsden, Alice H. and Singh, Ajit, 'The optimal degree of competition and dynamic efficiency in Japan and Korea', *European Economic Review* 38 (1994), pp. 941–51.

Aoki, Masahiko, 'Towards an economic model of the Japanese firm', *Journal of Economic Literature*, Vol.28 (1990), pp.1–27.

Burks, Ardath W., 'Japan's outreach: the ryugakusei', in Burks, Ardath W. (ed.), *The Modernizers: Overseas Students, Foreign Employees and Meiji Japan*, Westview, Boulder, Col. (1985), pp.145–60.

Burks, Ardath W., 'The legacy: products and by-products of cultural exchange', in Burks, Ardath W. (ed.), *The Modernizers: Overseas Students, Foreign Employees and Meiji Japan*, Westview, Boulder, Col. (1985), pp.359–68.

Burks, Ardath W. (ed), *The Modernizers: Overseas Students, Foreign Employees and Meiji Japan*, Westview, Boulder, Col. (1985).

Burks, Ardath W., 'The role of education in modernisation', in Burks, Ardath W. (ed.), *The Modernizers: Overseas Students, Foreign Employees and Meiji Japan*, Westview, Boulder, Col. (1985), pp.254–64.

Burks, Ardath W., 'Tokugawa Japan: post feudal society and change', in Burks, Ardath W. (ed.), *The Modernizers: Overseas Students, Foreign Employees and Meiji Japan*, Westview, Boulder, Col. (1985), pp.9–32.

Chida, Tomohei and Davies, Peter N., *The Japanese Shipping and Shipbuilding Industries: A History of their Modern Growth*, Athlone Press, London (1990).

Conlan, R., 'Japan: a dynamo fueled by human energy', extract from *Time/Life Library of Nations* (1985).

Freeman, C., 'Japan: a new national system of innovation', in Dosi, G., Freeman, C., Nelson, R., Silverberg, G. and Soete, L. (eds.), *Technical Change and Economic Theory*, Pinter Press, London (1988).

Fukasaku, Yukiko, *Technology and Industrial Development in Pre-war Japan: Mitsubishi Nagasaki Shipyard, 1884–1934*, Routledge, London (1992).

Hirschmeier, Johannes and Yui, Tsunehiko, *The Development of Japanese Business, 1600–1980*, 2nd edn, George Allen & Unwin, London (1981).

Johnson, C., *MITI and the Japanese Miracle*, Stanford University Press (1982).

Jones, Hazel, 'The Griffis thesis and Meiji policy toward hired foreigners', in Burks, Ardath W. (ed.), *The Modernizers: Overseas Students, Foreign Employees and Meiji Japan*, Westview, Boulder, Col. (1985), pp.219–53.

Madoka, Kanai, 'Fukui: domain of a Tokugawa collateral daimyo: its tradition and transition', in Burks, Ardath W. (ed.), *The Modernizers: Overseas Students, Foreign Employees and Meiji Japan*, Westview, Boulder, Colorado (1985), pp. 33–68.

Masao, Watanabe, 'Science across the Pacific: American–Japanese scientific and cultural contacts in the late nineteenth century', in Burks, Ardath W. (ed.), *The Modernizers: Overseas Students, Foreign Employees and Meiji Japan*, Westview, Boulder, Col. (1985), pp.369–92.

Minoru, Ishizuki, 'Overseas study by Japanese in the early Meiji period', in Burks, Ardath W. (ed.), *The Modernizers: Overseas Students, Foreign Employees and Meiji Japan*, Westview, Boulder, Col. (1985), pp.161–86.

Miwa, R., 'Government and the Japanese shipping industry, 1945–64', *Journal of Transport History*, March, 1988.

Miwa, R., 'Maritime policy in Japan: 1868–1937', in Yui. T. and Nakagawa, K. (eds.), *Business History of Shipping: Strategy and Structure*, Proceedings of the Fuji Conference, University of Tokyo (1985), pp.123–52.

Nakagawa, K., 'Japanese shipping in the nineteenth and twentieth centuries: strategy and organisation', in Yui, T. and Nakagawa, K. (eds.), *Business History of Shipping: Strategy and Structure*, Proceedings of the Fuji Conference, University of Tokyo (1985), pp.1–33.

Ohkawa, K. and Kohama, H., *Lectures on Developing Economies: Japan's Experience and its relevance*. University of Tokyo Press (1989).

Sugiyama, K., 'Shipbuilding finance of the Shasen shipping firms, 1920s–1930s', in Yui, T. and Nakagawa, K. (eds.), *Business History of Shipping: Strategy and Structure*, Proceedings of the Fuji Conference, University of Tokyo (1985), pp.255–72.

Tatsuki, M., 'Comment', in Yui, T. and Nakagawa, K. (eds.), Business History of Shipping: Strategy and Structure, Proceedings of the Fuji *Conference, University of Tokyo (1985),* pp.306–9.

Westney, D. Eleanor, *Imitation and Innovation: The Transfer of Western Organisation Patterns to Meiji Japan*, Harvard University Press (1987).

Wray, W. D., 'NYK and the commercial diplomacy of the Far Eastern freight conference, 1896–1956', in Yui, T. and Nakagawa, K. (eds.), *Business History of Shipping: Strategy and Structure*, Proceedings of the Fuji Conference, University of Tokyo (1985), pp.255–72.

Yoshio, Sakata, 'The beginning of modernization in Japan', in Burks, Ardath W. (ed.), *The Modernizers: Overseas Students, Foreign Employees and Meiji Japan*, Westview, Boulder, Col. (1985), pp. 69–84.

Yui, T. and Nagagawa, K. (eds.), *Business History of Shipping: Strategy and Structure*, Proceedings of the Fuji Conference, University of Tokyo (1985).

Zimbalist, A., Sherman, H. J. and Brown, S., *Comparing Economic Systems*, 2nd edn, Harcourt Brace Jovanovich International edition (1989).

UNITED STATES

Abramovitz, Moses, 'Catching up, forging ahead and falling behind', *Journal of Economic History*, June 1986 46(2), pp.386–406.

Allin, Lawrence C., 'The civil war and the period of decline 1861–1913', in Kilmarx, R. A. (ed.), *America's Maritime Legacy: A History of the US Merchant Marine and Shipbuilding Industry since Colonial Times*, Westview, Boulder, Col. (1979), pp.65–110.

Baker, William A., 'Commercial shipping and shipbuilding in the Delaware Valley', paper presented to the Society of Naval Architects and Marine Engineers (1976).

Barsness, Richard W., 'Maritime activity and port development in the United States since 1900: a survey', *The Journal of Transport History*, Vol.2, No.3 (1974), pp.167–84.

Bates, W. W., *American Marine: The Shipping Question in History and Politics*, Houghton Mifflin, Boston and New York (1892).

Bauer, Jack K., 'The golden age', in Kilmarx, R. A. (ed.), *America's Maritime Legacy: A History of the US Merchant Marine and Shipbuilding Industry since Colonial Times*, Westview, Boulder, Col. (1979), pp.27–64.

Bauer, Jack K., *A Maritime History of the United States: The Role of America's Seas and Waterways*, University of South Carolina Press (1988).

Chandler, Alfred D., *Scale and Scope: The Dynamics of Industrial Capitalism*, Belknap Press, Harvard, Cambridge, Mass. (1990).

Chandler, Alfred D., *Strategy and Structure: Chapters in the History of Industrial Restructuring*, Harvard University Press, Cambridge, Mass. (1962).

Chapelle, Howard I., *The History of American Sailing Ships*, W. W. Norton, New York (1935).

Clark, A. H., *The Clipper Ship Era*, 7C's Press, Riverside, Conn. (1910).

Clark, J. and Clark, M., 'The International Mercantile Marine Company: a financial analysis', *American Neptune* (1957), Vol.57, no.2, pp.137–54.

Dertouzos, Michael L., Lester, Richard K., Solow, Robert M. and the MIT Commission on Industrial Productivity, *Made in America: Regaining the Productive Edge*, Massachusetts Institute of Technology Press, Cambridge, Mass. (1989).

Galambos, L., 'The triumph of oligopoly', in Weiss, T. and Schaefer, D. (eds.), *American Economic Development in Historical Perspective*, Stanford University Press (1994), pp.241–53.

Gallman, J. M., 'Entrepreneurial experiences in the civil war: evidence from Philadelphia', in Weiss, T. and Schaefer, D. (eds.), *American Economic Development in Historical Perspective*, Stanford University Press (1994), pp.205–22.

Gardiner, R. and Greenhill, B., *The Advent of Steam: The Merchant Steamship before 1900*, Conway Maritime Press, London (1993).

Gardiner, R. and Greenhill, B., *The Shipping Revolution: The Modern Merchant Ship*, Conway Maritime Press, London (1992).

Geisst, Charles R., *Wall Street: A History*, Oxford University Press, New York (1997).

Hayes, Robert H. and Abernathy, William J., 'Managing our way to economic decline', *Harvard Business Review* 58 (1980), pp. 67–77.

Heinrich, Thomas R., *Ships for the Seven Seas: Philadelphia Shipbuilding in the Age of Industrial Capitalism*, Johns Hopkins University Press, Baltimore (1997).

Hirshfield, Deborah A., 'From Hog Islanders to liberty ships: the American Government and merchant ship construction in two world wars', *American Neptune* 54, Spring 1994, pp.85–98.

Isaksen, Mark, 'Shipbuilding on the Delaware River: a brief history of the industry and eight important shipyards', (unpublished) (1993).

Kay, C. J., 'Changing patterns of protectionism: the fall in tariffs and the rise in non-tariff barriers', in Freiden, J. A. and Lake, D. A. (eds.), *International Political Economy: Perspectives on Global Power and Wealth*, St Martin's Press, New York (1991), pp.338–52.

Kawahito, K., 'Japanese steel in the American market: conflict and causes', *The World Economy*, Vol.4, no.3 (1981), pp.229–50.

Kemble, John H. and Kendall, Lan C., 'The years between the wars, 1919–1939', in Kilmarx, R. A. (ed.), *America's Maritime Legacy: A History of the US Merchant Marine and Shipbuilding Industry since Colonial Times*, Westview, Boulder, Col. (1979), pp.149–74.

Kilmarx, R. A. (ed.), *America's Maritime Legacy: A History of the US Merchant Marine and Shipbuilding Industry since Colonial Times*, Westview, Boulder, Col. (1979).

Krooss, Herman E. and Gilbert, Charles, *American Business History*, Prentice Hall, Englewood Cliffs, NJ (1972).

Licht, Walter, *Industrializing America: The Nineteenth Century*, Johns Hopkins University Press, Baltimore and London (1995).

McCusker, John J., 'The rise of the shipping industry in colonial America', in Kilmarx. R. A. (ed.), *America's Maritime Legacy: A History of the US Merchant Marine and Shipbuilding Industry since Colonial Times*, Westview, Boulder, Col. (1979), pp.1–26.

Mansfield, Edwin, 'Industrial innovation in Japan and the United States', *Science* 241, Vol.1 (1988), pp.1769–74.

Misa, Thomas J., *A Nation of Steel: The Making of Modern America, 1865–1925*, Johns Hopkins University Press, Baltimore (1995).

Myers, Gustavus, *History of the Great American Fortunes*, The Modern Library, New York (1907).

Navin, Thomas and Sears, Marion, 'A study in merger formation of the International Mercantile Marine', *Business History Review*, Vol.28, no.4 (1954), pp.291–328.

Nelson, R., 'Institutions supporting technical change in the United States', in Dosi, G., Freeman, C., Nelson, R., Silverberg, G. and Soete, L. (eds.), *Technical Change and Economic Theory*, Pinter Press, London (1988), pp.312–29.

Nelson, Richard and Wright, Gavin, 'The rise and fall of American technological leadership: the postwar era in historical perspective', *Journal of Economic Literature*, Vol.30 (1992), pp.1931–64.

North, D. C. and Thomas, R. P., *The Growth of the American Economy to 1860*, Harper Torchbooks, New York (1968).

Patterson, J. E., *The Vanderbilts*, Harry N. Abrams Inc., New York (1989).

de la Pedraja, Rene, *A Historical Dictionary of the US Merchant Marine and Shipping Industry*, Greenwood Press, Conn. (1994).

de la Pedraja, Rene, *The Rise and Decline of US Merchant Shipping in the Twentieth Century*, Twayne's Evolution of American Business Series, No.8, Twayne Publishers, New York (1992).

Poulson, B., 'Economic history and economic development: an American perspective', in Weiss, T. and Schaefer, D. (eds.), *American Economic Development in Historical Perspective*, Stanford University Press (1994), pp.70–83.

Ray, Edward John, 'Changing patterns of protectionism: the fall in tariffs and the rise in non-tariff barriers', in Freiden, J. A. and Lake, D. A. (eds.), *International Political Economy: Perspectives on Global Power and Wealth*, St Martin's Press, New York (1991).

Reid, Robert, 'The growth and structure of multinationals in the banana export trade', in Casson, Mark (ed.), *The Growth of International Business*, George Allen & Unwin, London (1983).

Reynolds, Clark G., 'American maritime power since World War II', in Kilmarx, R. A. (ed.), *America's Maritime Legacy: A History of the US Merchant Marine and Shipbuilding Industry Since Colonial Times*, Westview, Boulder, Col. (1979), pp.215–54.

Safford, J. J., 'The United States merchant marine in foreign trade, 1800–1939', in Yui, T. and Nakagawa, K. (eds.), *Business History of Shipping: Strategy and Structure*, Proceedings of the Fuji Conference, University of Tokyo (1985), pp.91–118.

Safford, J. J., 'World War I maritime policy and the national security, 1914–1919', in Kilmarx, R. A. (ed.), *America's Maritime Legacy: A History of the US Merchant Marine and Shipbuilding Industry since Colonial Times*, Westview, Boulder, Col. (1979), pp.111–48.

Starkey, David J., 'Schooner development in Britain', in Gardiner, R. and Greenhill, B. (eds.), *Sail's Last Century*, Conway Maritime Press, London (1993), pp.133–47.

Still, W. N., Watts, G. P. and Rogers, B., 'Steam navigation in the United States', in Gardiner, R. and Greenhill, B. (eds.), *The Advent of Steam: The Merchant Steamship before 1900*, Conway Maritime Press, London (1993), pp. 44–82.

Thiesen, William H., 'Building an "American Clyde": the development of iron shipbuilding on the Delaware River', paper presented at the Pennsylvania Historical Association Annual Meeting, Philadelphia (1997).

Weisberger., Bernard A., *Many People, One Nation*, Houghton Mifflin, Boston (1987).

Weiss, T., 'Economic growth before 1860: revised conjectures', in Weiss, T. and Schaefer, D. (eds.), *American Economic Development in Historical Perspective*, Stanford University Press (1994), pp.11–27.

Weiss, T. and Schaefer, D. (eds.), *American Economic Development in Historical Perspective*, Stanford University Press (1994).

Whitehurst, Clinton H., *The US Merchant Marine: In Search of an Enduring Maritime Policy*, United States Naval Institute, Annapolis, Md. (1983).

INDEX

A Brief History of Slavery
Jeremy Black

Available to buy in ebook and paperback

A new global history of slavery from ancient origins through the horrors of the Atlantic trade to the present day

In this panoramic history, Jeremy Black tells how slavery was first developed in the ancient world, and reaches all the way to the present day and the contemporary crimes of trafficking and bonded labour. He shows how slavery has taken many forms throughout history and across the world – from the uprising of Spartacus, the plantations of the Indies, and the murderous forced labour of the gulags and concentration camps.

Slavery helped consolidate transoceanic empires and mould new-world societies such as America and Brazil. In the Atlantic trade, Black also looks at the controversial area of how complicit the African peoples were in the trade. He then charts the long fight for abolition in the nineteenth century, including both the campaigners as well as the lost voices of the slaves themselves who spoke of their misery.

Mr China
Tim Clissold

Available to buy in ebook and paperback

The incredible story of a Wall Street banker who went to China with $400,000,000 and learned the hard way how (not) to do business there.

In the early nineties, China finally opened for business and Wall Street wanted in on the act. When the investment bankers arrived from New York with their Harvard MBAs, pinstripes and tasselled loafers, ready to negotiate with the Old Cadres, the stage was set for collision.

This is the true story of a tough Wall Street banker who came to China looking for glory. He teamed up with an ex-Red Guard and a Mandarin-speaking Englishman. Together, they raised over $400,000,000 and bought up factories all over China. Only as they watched those millions slide towards the abyss did they start to understand that China really doesn't play by anyone else's rules.

How Rich Countries Got Rich . . . and Why Poor Countries Stay Poor
Erik S. Reinart

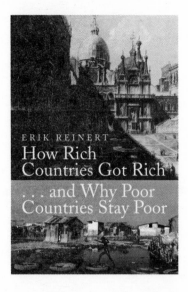

Available to buy in paperback

In Erik S. Reinert's narrative history of modern economic development from the Italian Renaissance to the present day, he shows how rich countries developed through a combination of government intervention, protectionism and strategic investment. He suggests that this set of policies in various combinations has driven successful development in nations throughout the world. Yet despite its demonstrable success, orthodox development economists have largely ignored this approach and insisted instead on the importance of free trade.

Reinert presents a strongly revisionist history of economics and shows how the discipline has long been torn between the continental Renaissance tradition on one hand and the free market theories of English and later American economics on the other. *How Rich Countries Got Rich* buries the economic orthodoxy once and for all and shows why free trade is not the best answer for our hopes of worldwide prosperity.

'It lands powerful punches' *Sunday Telegraph*